THE CURRENT STATE OF INTERLANGUAGE

THE CURRENT STATE OF INTERLANGUAGE

STUDIES IN HONOR OF WILLIAM E. RUTHERFORD

Edited by

LYNN EUBANK
University of North Texas

LARRY SELINKER
Birkbeck College, University of London

MICHAEL SHARWOOD SMITH
University of Utrecht

JOHN BENJAMINS PUBLISHING COMPANY
AMSTERDAM/PHILADELPHIA

The paper used in this publication meets the minimum requirements of American National Standard for Information Sciences — Permanence of Paper for Printed Library Materials, ANSI Z39.48-1984.

Library of Congress Cataloging-in-Publication Data

The current state of interlanguage : studies in honor of William E. Rutherford / edited by Lynn Eubank, Larry Selinker, Michael Sharwood Smith.
    p.   cm.
    Includes bibliographical references and index.
1. Interlanguage (Language learning) 2. Second language acquisition. I. Eubank, Lynn. II. Selinker, Larry, 1937- III. Sharwood Smith, Michael. 1942- . IV. Rutherford, William E.
P118.2.C867   1995
418--dc20   95-41315
ISBN 90 272 2152 9 (Eur.) / 1-55619-506-0 (US) (alk. paper)   CIP

© Copyright 1995 - John Benjamins B.V.
No part of this book may be reproduced in any form, by print, photoprint, microfilm, or any other means, without written permission from the publisher.

John Benjamins Publishing Co. • P.O.Box 75577 • 1070 AN Amsterdam • The Netherlands
John Benjamins North America • P.O.Box 27519 • Philadelphia PA 19118-0519 • USA

Table of Contents

The current state of interlanguage: Introduction Lynn Eubank, *University of North Texas* Larry Selinker, *Birkbeck College, University of London* Michael Sharwood Smith, *University of Utrecht*	1
Prominence in applied linguistics: Bill Rutherford Peter Jordens, *Vrije Universiteit Amsterdam*	11
I-interlanguage and typology: The case of topic-prominence Virginia Yip, Chinese *University of Hongkong* Stephen Matthews, *University of Hongkong*	17
Universals, SLA, and language pedagogy: 1984 revisited Susan Gass, *Michigan State University*	31
Learnability, pre-emption, domain-specificity, and the instructional value of "Master Mind" David Birdsong, *University of Texas at Austin*	43
Why we need grammar: Confessions of a cognitive generalist Ellen Bialystok, *York University*	55
Chasing after linguistic theory: How minimal should we be? Lydia White, *McGill University*	63
The irrelevance of verbal feedback to language learning Susanne E. Carroll, *University of Potsdam*	73
Indirect negative evidence, inductive inferencing, and second language acquisition India C. Plough	89

TABLE OF CONTENTS

The negative effects of 'positive' evidence on L2 phonology 107
    Martha Young-Scholten, *University of Durham*

German plurals in adult second language development: Evidence 123
for a dual-mechanism model of inflection
    Harald Clahsen, *University of Essex*

Universal Grammar in L2 acquisition: Some thoughts on Schachter's 139
Incompleteness Hypothesis
    Sascha Felix, *University of Passau*

Acquiring linking rules and argument structures in a second language: 153
The unaccusative/unergative distinction
    Antonella Sorace, *University of Edinburgh*

Data, evidence and rules 177
    Maria Beck, *University of North Texas*
    Bonnie D. Schwartz, *University of Durham*
    Lynn Eubank, *University of North Texas*

Markedness aspects of case-marking in L1 French/L2 English 197
interlanguage
    Helmut Zobl, *Carleton University*

Language transfer: What do we really mean? 205
    Gita Martohardjono, *Queens College, City University of New York*
    Suzanne Flynn, *Massachusetts Institute of Technology*

Age before beauty: Johnson and Newport revisited 219
    Eric Kellerman, *University of Nijmegen*

Style-shifting in oral interlanguage: Quantification and definition 233
    Jean-Marc Dewaele, *Birkbeck College, University of London*

Observations of language use in Spanish immersion classroom 241
interactions
    Susana Blanco-Iglesias, *University of Minnesota*.
    Juaquina Broner, *University of Minnesota*
    Elaine Tarone, *University of Minnesota*

TABLE OF CONTENTS

Some neurolinguistic evidence regarding variation in interlanguage use: The status of the 'switch mechanism' Marjorie Perlman Lorch, *Birkbeck College, University of London*	255
Beyond 2000: A measure of productive lexicon in a second language Batia Laufer, *University of Haifa*	265
A first crosslinguistic look at paths: The difference between end-legs and medial ones Háj Ross, *University of North Texas*	273
Index	287

The current state of interlanguage
Introduction

The formal study of that independent system of knowledge developed by second-language (L2) learners–interlanguage–had its beginnings nearly a quarter of a century ago. By now it has been a little over ten years since we had the first attempt to produce a state-of-the-art volume in the area of interlanguage studies: This was the well-known series of studies in honor of Professor S. Pit Corder of the University of Edinburgh (Davies et. al 1984). We wanted to continue that tradition with studies in honor of Professor William E. Rutherford, and to that end we called for a series of shorter contributions that address issues associated with interlanguage. Having shorter contributions created a number of possibilities, among them, a focus on single issues as well as an increase in the number of contributions, thereby making space available for newer as well as more seasoned researchers. The result is the present volume.

As some of the studies in this volume demonstrate, Bill Rutherford has had a wide ranging career from being interested in the most theoretical questions (e.g., Rutherford 1982, 1983, 1988) to their impact upon the difficult daily task of language teaching (e.g., Rutherford 1987). One sees in fact a strong trend, with interesting collaborations, from English as a Second Language (e.g., Rutherford 1968, 1975/1977) to pedagogical grammar (e.g., Rutherford and Sharwood Smith 1987) to second language acquisition (SLA; e.g., Schachter and Rutherford 1979). We thus see two constant threads–viz., wide interests and attention to language and linguistics (especially the *L* in SLA). In this body of work one can also see, in a sense, a natural synthesis in what is nearing publication: the awaited Rutherford (forthcoming). This latter work started out as a small workbook but is now a large and rich text showing structures of English from diverse theoretical perspectives, relating these to both native language (L1) acquisition and L2 acquisition. Importantly for all of us, Bill has been aiming for a long time to discover ways of getting linguists and acquisitionists to talk to each other. This approach prompted his 1982 conference (the first of its kind), from which came the much quoted John Benjamins volume: Rutherford (1984). But to tell only of Bill's interests in SLA is to miss perhaps the most fascinating part: Those who have visited Bill outside of the 'office'–those, in other words, who have seen his early keyboard collection, observed first-hand his commitment to *Musica Pacifica* (of which he is a founder) and heard him perform with like-minded devotees–these people also know that Bill is an academic in the very best of the Renaissance tradition.

In this book, we begin with some papers that directly relate to Bill's work and then move to several others that relate to issues he has considered in the field. Peter Jordens, for example, relates to Bill's discussion of the influence of L1-typological features on semantic properties of interlanguages. He is concerned with the acquisitional route that learners from a topic-prominence language, L1-Mandarin, take in gaining L2-English syntax. He observes in Bill's developmental data from L1-Mandarin learners of English both that there appear to be two general types of constructions involved and that there is a curious gap in the types of constructions. He then proposes an interesting way in which the two parallel constructions may well be intertwined in development, which explains the curious gap in the data, as well. Jordens' paper is complemented by that of Virginia Yip and Stephen Matthews, who re-examine and re-interpret the problems that Chinese-speaking learners of English apparently encounter when attempting to sort out the topic-prominence of their native language from the subject-prominence of English. Jordens argues that the developmental sequence observed among these learners may involve not just the problem of subject vs. topic prominence, but also an interaction with the English presentative construction. By contrast, Yip and Matthews propose an understanding of such problems that is based specifically in Universal Grammar (UG). In fact, these two contributions are equally important because, while they highlight different aspects of the essentially similar problems, both propose solutions that, together, ultimately serve to provide a more complete picture of the processes involved.

In her contribution, Susan Gass also examines language typology. However, Gass argues that the typological perspective that she and Josh Ard pioneered may well provide a better explanation of L2 acquisition than the UG-based perspective. To do so, Gass re-examines data from several well-known 'UG areas', namely, *pro*-drop, verb raising, and reflexive binding. In each of these, Gass makes the case that universals based in the way that speakers interact have a greater chance of being noticed by L2 learners than the more abstract universals of UG. In effect, universals that are visible in superficial relations, that is, typological universals, will have a stronger impact on L2 acquisition than universals that are not related in this way. This paper is fascinating because Gass is among the very few in the literature to compare different linguistic theories (here UG and typological universals) on the same interlanguage data.

David Birdsong moves to Bill's interest in the intersection of theory and teaching, arguing for the value of a particular game to the teaching of SLA. Because of the cognitive reality of domain-specificity and its importance to L2 acquisition, Birdsong is able to present a pedagogical tool, "MasterMind", that he argues is very useful in helping students of SLA to understand such theory-dependent terms such as *learnability, pre-emption*, and *domain specificity*. Also, this tool appears to provide a valuable and effective means by which we can communicate the findings of our trade to newcomers.

Ellen Bialystok comments on Bill's early understanding of the importance of theorizing about the implications of the cognitive representation of two (or more) languages. She discusses the problems inherent in 'generalist' explanations of language acquisition and shows how such problems may well affect the interpretation of individual studies in SLA. Her contribution shows how it is possible to evaluate particular studies in terms drawn from general observations about explanation.

Lydia White's essay dovetails with Bill's work detailing how linguistic theory can benefit from interlanguage analysis in a UG framework and that the influence should not be one way, that second language acquisition should inform linguistic theory, as much as the reverse. In her paper, White considers the problems caused by changes in prevailing linguistic theory. She argues that, while constant changes in theory may well be uncomfortable, there are numerous advantages, too, not the least of which are that changes in theory signal health and development and that such changes shed light on areas that were difficult to understand in the past, L2 ultimate attainment, in this case.

One factor central to another of Bill's interests, learnability, involves what is called poverty of the stimulus. This is handled in an interesting conjunction with a fundamental problem raised by Susanne Carroll: What drives change in interlanguage systems? She investigates the common concern of negative evidence by arguing that a learner's capacity to interpret verbal feedback that appears as negative evidence must be evaluated in terms of such maxims as cooperation vs. relevance. Bringing in concerns of relevance into L2 acquisition for our inspection is an important contribution in itself. Carroll specifically illustrates ways in which the interpretation of negative verbal feedback may very well obey the cooperative principle, but violate the relevance principle. This contribution is important because it provides a unique view of the way that learners evaluate the potential usability of verbal feedback. Just as importantly, for learners and teachers alike, this may very well undermine the usefulness of such feedback.

Another paper that discusses negative evidence is that of India Plough. She presents the results of experimental research on the potential usefulness of indirect negative data by L2 learners. The importance of this paper is that it is one of the first explicit attempts to examine this aspect of the data of exposure. One valuable contribution of this work is the explicit attempt to define these illusive concepts in terms of general cognitive concepts and then to attack the problem of validation in terms of what sorts of evidence are relevant to these concepts. This is a serious contribution to research methodology in SLA and thus to theoretical concerns. She also adds to the concern that in our field we have a serious lack of longitudinal studies. If more evidence be needed, it has been clear for a long time that without such studies many of our most intractable problems will remain so.

Concern for evidence also motivates Martha Young-Scholten's review of research on an underrepresented area in L2 research, namely, the acquisition of interlanguage phonology. She points out that many past studies are problematic in that there is a lack of understanding of the influence of input to learners. She handles the question of ultimate attainment and transfer and their relation to the fossilization issue of, in her words: "Why ... the observed lack of eventual complete attainment–or even near attainment?" The idea that exposure to some input data might not be what a learner is ready for returns us to central earlier interlanguage concerns, what Corder (1981) referred to as the internal syllabus of the learner.

Concerns of fossilization can also be looked at in terms of a lack of complete attainment. In this regard, Harald Clahsen presents data in an area of interlanguage study that has also been neglected in recent work: morphology. This work on plural and compound formation shows concern for individual differences, an early interlanguage issue that is still unresolved. His results add further evidence to one view of the interlanguage perspective, namely, that the grammatical systems learners create comprise the same fundamentals present in native speaker grammars, even though the two may be different in particular form. Clahsen has found that L2 learners of German have two qualitatively different kinds of pluralization: irregular forms and what he calls "default" plurals which become overregularized and which are not used in compounds.

Concerning himself with the important theme of careful commentary on a colleague's work, Sascha Felix reexamines Jacquelyn Schachter's *Incompleteness Hypothesis* and relates this to the modularity issue: Which cognitive modules govern which type of acquisition. He usefully starts with several basic facts that all SLA researchers would apparently agree with: Most basic is that L1 and L2 acquisition are not totally identical; next is that fossilized variation occurs with adults; then that some L2s are more difficult than others; and, finally, that native language transfer exists–all highly contentious issues in the past. He then argues from these facts that there are conceptual, theoretical and linguistic reasons why Schachter's central conclusion that adult L2 learners have is no access to UG cannot hold in its present form. Schachter's response should be interesting, especially as more data is gathered to deal with accessibility problems.

Looking in depth at one linguistic phenomenon, Antonella Sorace reviews recent research on the L2 acquisition of the unaccusative-unergative distinction inherent in the intransitive verbs of, for example, Italian. She argues that what one observes in interlanguage development in this regard is best explained in terms of linking rules that connect lexical-semantic representations to argument structure. Sorace's findings are of importance because she pioneers a way of viewing L2 learners' difficulties with this area in theoretically well-defined ways.

Moving concerns of research methodology directly onto questions of linguistic theory and evidence, Maria Beck, Bonnie Schwartz and Lynn Eubank begin their combined, three-part contribution by distinguishing among different types of input *data* that may or may not be useful to learners as *evidence* for the activation of parametric principles in the building of interlanguage grammars. They argue that a precise understanding of grammar building needs to take place in terms of linguistic theory. Further, it is their conclusion that certain types of linguistic data in the input to learners may well be unusable for the building of interlanguage grammars. Their paper provides food for thought for pedagogical implications of data presentation and grammatical instruction, for much of what they conclude goes against much current practice. Whether all target language-like behavior is the result of interlanguage grammars or not should be carefully considered by a range of disciplines.

Continuing concern for linguistic properties of interlanguage grammars, Helmut Zobl argues that certain relationships between interlanguage use of specific syntactic patterns and the use of lexical vs. pronominal subjects may well find explanation in the theory of case-marking. In particular, Zobl points out that the relationship between pronominalization and, for example, subject-auxiliary inversion follows automatically if one assumes a view in which the pronominals are in fact clitics attached to the auxiliary. This paper is important because it shows once again how it is possible to understand superficially unrelated matters (here roughly, pronominalization and word order) within a unified theory.

Moving to another of Bill's concerns, that of transfer, Suzanne Flynn and Gita Martohardjono present data from two experimental studies, both indicating that a view of L2 knowledge that is based on pattern transfer cannot be maintained. They conclude that whatever theory of SLA does evolve must take into account L2 learners' capacity to transcend both the nature of input and the knowledge provided to them by their native language. Interestingly, parts of their findings indicate once again that, in the acquisition of some structures at least, learners appear to ignore what is possible in the native language.

In his reframing of the fossilization question as whether adults can ever acquire native-like competence in an L2, Eric Kellerman re-examines a plethora of central issues–age, transfer, typology, amount of exposure to both language data and formal grammar, the fact that some structures appear easier than others–in a reexamination of perhaps the most well-known of the studies of an L2 critical period, those of Johnson and Newport. Kellerman shows that, despite numerous accolades in the literature, a number of aspects of the Johnson and Newport studies are particularly problematic. He argues, for example, that concentration on a 'yes/no' answer to grammaticality judgments has serious methodological faults in regard to how one establishes the state of interlanguage knowledge at a particular point in time. Johnson and Newport's response should be interesting.

Context is also important in interlanguage learning, so one needs to move to questions of style, register, domain, and the like. In this regard, Jean-Marc Dewaele provides an explicit means by which one can distinguish between different speech styles. Specifically, he finds that variation in word-class proportion at the token level shows a strong relationship to the genre of interlanguage talk and writing. In looking for governing factors for application of wide-spread principles in the building of interlanguage grammars, Dewaele is the first to specifically consider empirically various personality factors in a precise way.

Continuing with concerns of style, style-shifting and context in interlanguage, Susana Blanco-Iglesias, Joaquina Broner and Elaine Tarone build on earlier work which strongly shows that immersion classrooms should be regarded as special types of communities where increasing diaglossia occurs. In terms of research methodology, they argue for notetaking as a central tool in some situations and, in terms of this, usefully discuss validation problems. They show changes over time in classroom language use in Spanish immersion classrooms through grade five. They also show that differential switches to the children's native language (English) relate to their need to use a previously unreported style which they term: vernacular kid-speak. This may be used for the pragmatic reason that these children do not have that style in their interlanguage.

Continuing with the topic of switching in language and interlanguage, Marjorie Perlman Lorch brings to bear neurolinguistic evidence and argumentation. We would all agree that having some idea of the neural substrate underlying cognitive and linguistic mechanisms would be helpful in terms of constraining theory, and would clearly strengthen them. Lorch takes a strong context-dependent view and subscribes to the importance of context dependent cues in the establishment of contextualized fossilized forms. Relating to the constantly discussed modularity issue, she claims the neurological evidence only supports the view that in order to produce interlanguage talk which is contextually sensitive, cognitive systems outside any conceived language modules must come into play.

Measuring style differences, Batia Laufer summarizes results from a number of her studies on methods of estimating the size of the interlanguage lexicon. She proposes a new metric, a computerized measure which she calls "Beyond 2000". Reviewing previous studies, she suggests that this new tool provides a measure that is simpler than those used heretofore and, importantly, that is at least as accurate as other measures.

Finally, Háj Ross presents a special honor to Bill with his contribution on paths, "those macro-constituents which specify the route through spaces of various sorts which is traversed by the Theme of a sentence". In his paper, Ross provides examples and definitions of the various parts ("legs") of paths as well as cross-linguistic evidence for their structure. Ross also points out that some languages employ adpositional means to express certain legs while other languages express them verbally. It is here that Ross speculates to invoke another of Bill's concerns, namely, *markedness*: If, as it appears, the verbal expression of certain legs is less marked than the adpositional expression, then L2 acquisition from marked L1 (e.g., English) to an unmarked L2 (e.g., Korean) should be easier than from an unmarked L1 to a marked L2.

What have we learned from these works about state-of-the-art of interlanguage since 1984? What are the issues that we are concentrating on now and which ones have apparently been resolved? We feel that it is necessary to contemplate at regular intervals where we have been as a field and where we might be going. For a discipline as young as SLA, it is especially true that one should have a vehicle to keep track of issues over the decades. If we do not do this, we find that people keep reinventing the wheel. (We will not give examples here since they are too embarrassing at times.) We thus begin by reviewing where we were ten years ago at the time of the Festschrift for Pit Corder. We said then:

> At the end of the seminar, before hearing the oral version of this summary, we polled the participants for their views of critical issues in IL studies. They were not told in advance of this survey, as we did not wish to bias their listening to the discussion. The raw survey data were coded by those participants who were able to attend the "Workshop on data analysis" held for two days after the seminar. We refer now to those items (arranged alphabetically) that kept coming up again and again:
> - Agreement on what IL is
> - Context: use and acquisition (including input)
> - General theory of language acquisition
> - Language transfer
> - Pedagogical implications
> - Research methodology
> - Variation
>
> For historical reasons, it might be interesting to note some other issues that were mentioned: age, cognitive constraints, communicative success, comparison between language learning and other kinds of learning, competence/performance, fossilization, grammatical framework for IL, IL and other disciplines, initial IL hypothesis, interrelationships of IL subsystems, metalinguistic knowledge and use, relationships between non-native and native linguistic systems, relationship of perception and production, role of fixed expressions, schemata as a basis for IL, sequencing and stages, simplifies languages, strategies, universal grammar, and universals and implicational clusterings. It would be most interesting, we felt, to compare these lists with ones gathered five or ten years from now. (Selinker 1984:342)

Looking at the state of our art in 1995, we do not claim that the studies included here are representative of the field as a whole. Indeed, caution is important as we know, for example, that the matter of the initial IL hypothesis–under the title of the 'initial state' of the interlanguage system–is under consideration today. With that caveat, we now present what we think we have found as a basis of this exercise. First, note that here we are able to present more detail than we did in 1984. Second, and not unrelated, unlike in 1984, we feel that in 1995 we have a growing consensus on a number of issues that were at one point highly controversial. This is important for us and we should be celebrating; among these issues are the following:

- The application of neither Universal Grammar nor of language transfer processes to form interlanguage grammars are all or nothing affairs; they are each somewhat accessible. Each then has a cognitive reality and the research question is of the what, where, when and how variety. We still do not have a general theory of how UG and language transfer intersect with each other and with other processes to create interlanguage grammars.

- First and second language acquisition are not totally identical. Thus, the old L1=L2 question is solved in the negative, but again we are at the point of researching the detail of exactly how and when and where, they are same or different.

- Fossilization of interlanguage grammars is a very real process and acts variably. Again, we have the same sorts of questions whose answers demand careful empirical work, in this case longitudinal studies, which by definition are very hard to do. There still seem to be few theoretical principles, if any, to cover this all-pervasive phenomenon.

- Some L2s are more difficult than others, but also some structures in the same L2 are more difficult than others. This acts variably as well. Again, we have no clear theoretical story here.

Thus, among major current issues, we find:

- The place of Universal Grammar in forming interlanguage grammars;
- The place of language transfer in forming interlanguage grammars;
- The intersection of these in forming interlanguage grammars;
- The empirical detail of fossilization;
- The detail of the effects of variation of all sorts; and

- The detail of difficulty of some structures and some languages over others.

There were, of course, many other important issues handled in these papers, far too many to list except in a note.[1] Nonetheless, we firmly believe that the historical dimension is central: We have tried, with a volume in honor of Bill Rutherford, to continue the splendid tradition begun with the volume in honor of Pit Corder in 1984, comparing issues then and now, and hopefully, with a challenge to the future, we are leaving a touchstone for the next state-of-the-art update, a decade from now.

Fall, 1995

| Lynn Eubank | Larry Selinker | Michael Sharwood Smith |
| Denton | London | Utrecht |

Acknowledgments

We would like to thank those who have helped us complete the book. In the call for papers we specifically requested colleagues to help us develop the field by stating, "We would especially like to hear some new voices and hope that graduate students will also be encouraged by you to propose contributions." In several instances, our request has been honored with presentations by new colleagues, recently completed PhDs, and even some current students. We thank all of the authors for presenting their best work in honor of Bill–and all of the reviewers of these papers for their necessarily anonymous labor. At Birkbeck College, Beatrice Baumgartner-Cohen read and commented on all of the final manuscripts. Kees Vaes from John Benjamins has, as usual, been a force for high quality work in linguistics.

Notes

1. Some of the other major issues we see here, in alphabetical order: acquisitional routes; age and critical period; cognitive representation of two (or more) languages; completeness/ incompleteness; context; domain-specificity; style; positive/negative evidence; intersection of linguistic levels; learnability; modularity; neurolinguistic substrate; personality factors; practical implications/applications; research methodology; strategies; typological influences; ultimate attainment in L2.

References

Corder, S. P. 1981. *Error Analysis and Interlanguage*. Oxford University Press.
Davies, A., C. Criper & T. Howatt. 1984. *Interlanguage*. Edinburgh: Edinburgh University Press

Rutherford, W. R. 1968. *Modern English: A textbook for foreign students*. Harcourt, Brace & World.

Rutherford, W. R. 1975/1977. *Modern English*. Revised and expanded edition. Harcourt Brace Jovanovich.

Rutherford, W. R. 1982. "Markedness in Second Language Acquisition". *Language Learning* 32.85-108.

Rutherford, W. R. 1983. "Language Typology and Language Transfer". *Language Transfer in Language Learning* ed. by S. Gass & L. Selinker, 358-370. Ann Arbor: University of Michigan Press.

Rutherford, W. R. 1984. Language Universals and SLA. *Typological Studies in Language* ed. by T. Givon, Vol. 5. Amsterdam: John Benjamins.

Rutherford, W. R. 1987. "The Meaning of Grammatical Consciousness-Raising". *Pedagogical Grammar of English* ed. by Y. Kachru. Special issue of *World Englishes* 6(3).

Rutherford, W. R. 1988. "Grammatical Theory and L2 Acquisition: A brief overview". *Linguistic Theory in Second Language Acquisition* ed. by S. Flynn & W. O'Neil, 1-25. Dordrecht: Reidel.

Rutherford, W. R. Forthcoming. *Workbook in the Structure of English: Linguistic principles and language acquisition*.

Rutherford, W. R. & M. Sharwood Smith, eds. 1987. *Grammar and Second Language Teaching: A book of readings*. New York: Newbury House.

Schachter, J. & W. R. Rutherford. 1979. "Discourse Function and Language Transfer". *Second Language Learning: Contrastive analysis, error analysis, and related aspects* ed. by B. Robinett & J. Schachter. Ann Arbor: University of Michigan Press.

Selinker, L. 1984. "The Current State of IL Studies: An attempted critical survey". *Interlanguage* ed. by A. Davies, C. Criper & T. Howatt. Edinburgh University Press.

Prominence in applied linguistics
Bill Rutherford

Peter Jordens
Vrije Universiteit Amsterdam

During his professional career Bill Rutherford has become an internationally highly regarded and well respected scholar. His personal charm and warmth have given him many friends, professionally and privately. His ideas have turned out to be of great importance for the field of applied linguistics. More specifically, Bill Rutherford has been able to demonstrate the relevance of linguistics for the explanation of developmental processes in second-language (L2) learners.

One of the areas where Rutherford's thinking has had a major impact on the field is the area of crosslinguistic influence in second language acquisition, in particular the influence of typological features of the native language (NL) on systematic properties of interlanguages. For several reasons, Rutherford's studies on the acquisition of English by Mandarin spekers and speakers of Japanese and Korean have always kept me intrigued. One reason is that Rutherford has convincingly demonstrated that a particular set of interlanguage data should be looked at from a perspective that was by then absolutely new for those studying L2 acquisition. The other reason is that Rutherford's study on the influence of underlying NL-typology on interlanguage structure still has a few observations that call for further investigation. One such observation relates to the acquisitional route of Mandarin speakers of English who start out assuming that in L2-English, as in Mandarin, topic prominence is a major typological property. In "Language Typology and Language Transfer" (1983), Rutherford identifies several stages that these learners go through before they reach the relevant stage at which they have discovered that English, unlike Mandarin, is a subject-prominent language.

Examples from the six stages that Rutherford found relevant are in (1).

(1) a. Take good physical care of themselves is very important
    b. A lot of people, they know how to take good physical care by themselves
    c. There are a small amount of people get married in their teenage
    d. There are many elements to maintain a successful marriage

e. There are many problems that can make marriage unsuccessful
f. More people do physical exercises now than before

Rutherford carefully adds that one should realize that there is "heavy overlap" between these stages. This does not preclude, however, that each of these six construction types corresponds "very roughly to a different proficiency level" (363).

Looking at these six types of sentence in terms of developmental stages, I have always wondered about the relation between sentences such as (1a), (1b) and (1f), on the one hand, and (1c), (1d) and (1e), on the other. With respect to (1a), (1b) and (1f), it seems clear to me that these types of sentence are part of a developmental process starting out with a topic-prominent structure underlying (1a) and ending with a subject-prominent structure underlying (1f), while (1b) is ambivalent with respect to both topic- and subject-prominence. A representation of this analysis which is similar to the one in Rutherford (1986:363-364) is given in (1a'), (1b') and (1f').

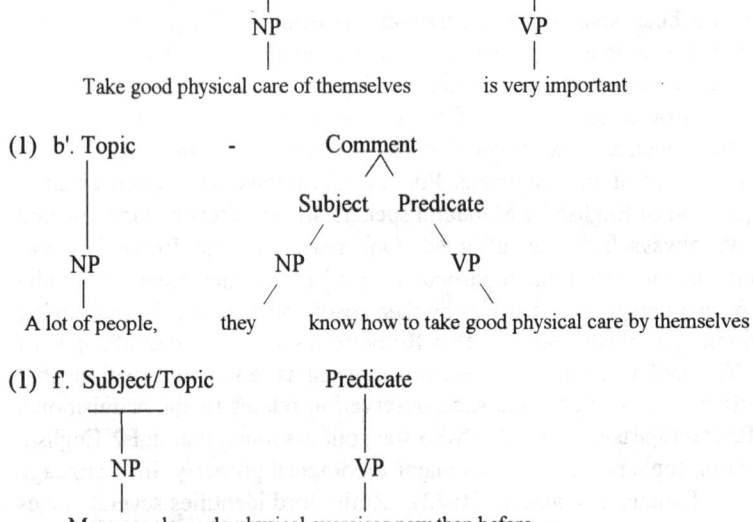

On the other hand, (1c), (1d) and (1e) seem to be part of a developmental process, too. (1c) is a so-called "serial-verb construction" in which the topic is introduced by existential *there*. Both (1d) and (1e) are correct with respect to the target, although (1e) is more elaborate in the sense that the embedded sentence is finite with a relative pronoun functioning as the subject of the relative clause. A representation of this analysis, based on Rutherford (1986: 364), is given in (1c'), (1d') and (1e').

(1) c'. [Topic marker + Topic]_Subject - [Comment]_Predicate

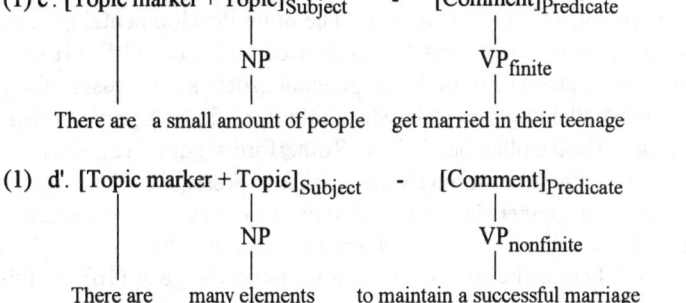

There are a small amount of people get married in their teenage

(1) d'. [Topic marker + Topic]_Subject - [Comment]_Predicate

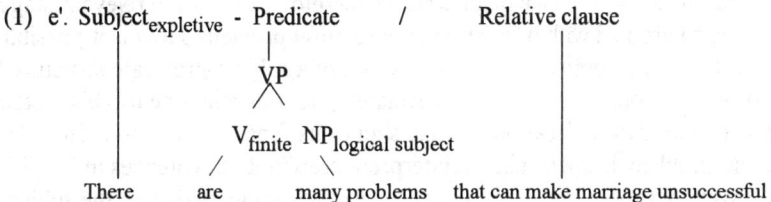

There are many elements to maintain a successful marriage

(1) e'. Subject_expletive - Predicate / Relative clause

VP

V_finite NP_logical subject

There are many problems that can make marriage unsuccessful

As pointed out, the examples in (1a) through (1f) are representative of the stages of interlanguage development of Mandarin speakers of L2-English. The examples are utterances that learners actually produced.

In order to understand L2 development, interlanguage research has shown that it is often as relevant to look at possible sentences that systematically do not occur. Hence, in his Note 7 Rutherford points out that sentences such as (2) below "[are] simply not produced by native Mandarin speakers" (369).

(2) *There are a small amount of people they got married in their teenage

Why should this be the case? Rutherford assumes that "interlanguage development has here reached the point where topic and subject are no longer separate entities" (369). Furthermore, he refers to Thompson (personal communication.) in pointing out that "presentative serial verb sentences in Mandarin never show a subject in the second clause" (369). This explanation, however, still leaves me with a question. If it is indeed the case that for these L2 learners' topic and subject are no longer separate categories, why is it that they do not produce (1f) simultaneously with (1c)? In other words, is there any particular reason for the use of *presentative sentences* at this very stage?

Since (1a), (1b) and (1f), on the one hand, and (1c), (1d) and (1e), on the other, are different types of sentences, one should consider the possibility that what

Rutherford believes to be one developmental route in fact comprises two developmental processes that pass off in parallel. One of these processes may concern the acquisition of the L2 subject-predicate typology starting from the NL-induced topic-comment typology, as in (1a), (1b), (1f). The other developmental process deals with the acquisition of L2-presentative sentences, as in (1c), (1d), (1e).

If this is true, an analysis of both developmental orders as processes taking place more or less in parallel might explain why Rutherford finds "heavy overlap" between the six stages. On the other hand, if, as Rutherford argues, (1c), (1d) and (1e) are indeed representative of a development that is prerequisite to (1f), the question is why Mandarin speakers have to learn to produce presentative sentences before they are in the position to acquire subject-predicate typology.

What is relevant here is the state of the learner's knowledge at (1b). At this stage, learners are able to produce sentences with a topic that is followed by a subject-predicate structure. One might assume, therefore, that at the relevant stage the learner is confronted with one particular structural problem: How is it possible for one NP to function both as a topic and as part of a subject-predicate structure?

The learner could move to (1f) immediately, but this might be too big a step because in (1f) the subject lacks any formal sign of its function as a topic. In order to solve this problem, learners might reinterpret presentative sentences in English in such a way that *there are* functions as the explicit topic marker of the subject NP and a (relative) clause as the predicate (see the analysis in (1c')). Such an analysis leads to serial-verb sentences as in (1c).

If it is true that presentative sentences are interpreted as subjects that are explicitly marked as topics, it is possible to account for two observations. Such an interpretation first explains why presentatives occur exactly at this point in the developmental process, and it secondly explains why these sentences do not have a resumptive pronominal subject as in the missing (2). It is precisely because learners may interpret a presentative sentence as a subject constituent that is explicitly marked as topic by *there is/are* that the learning problem of how to have an NP function both as subject and topic is solved.

Further elaboration on the basis of (1c) leads to (1d). Whereas (1c) is incorrect with respect to the target, (1d) is correct. However, I would argue that it is only correct as far as its superficial form is concerned. I assume that *there are* is still the explicit topic marker of the subject (*many elements*) while the infinitival structure functions as the predicate.

In (1e) the incorrect analysis of presentative sentences is given up. The use of a clause (*that can make marriage unsuccessful*) instead of an infinitival complement forces the learner to abandon the monoclausal $Topic_{Subject}$-$Comment_{Predicate}$ structure. As a consequence, the NP-analysis of the [There are +Topic]$_{Subject}$ structure is given up in favor of a clausal analysis with a subject-predicate structure. In such a clause structure *there* functions, target-like, as the expletive grammatical subject, while the former NP becomes the nominal predicate.

At this point, the situation the learner sees himself confronted with can be evaluated in two ways. First, he might conclude that he has failed to reach his aim to produce subjects that are explicitly marked as topics. Hence, for him the only alternative left is to give up the whole idea of simultaneously expressing topic prominence and subject prominence. If he does so, he is ready to use (1f) in which *More people* solely functions as the subject. On the other hand, however, I assume that a reanalysis of *there* not as a topic marker, but as an expletive, functions not just as a dead end of the developmental process. For learners who used to mark nominal entities explicitly as topics, reinterpretation of a former topic marker *there* as an expletive is evidence that a pronominal constituent can be both topic and subject. Having acquired this, the learner is also ready to use a nominal element, as in (1f), as both subject and topic without an explicit topic marker.

Summarizing, in the L2-English of native speakers of Mandarin, the acquisition of utterances with a regular subject-predicate structure, as in (1a), (1b) and (1f), and the acquisition of presentative sentences, as in (1c), (1d) and (1e), could be interpreted as two developmental processes taking place more or less in parallel. Upon closer examination, however, there is reason to believe that the acquisition of presentatives has a particular function in the acquisition of subject prominence in L2-English. A description of the developmental process of the acquisition of the subject function in the L2 English of Mandarin speakers is given in (3).

(3) stage 1: NP topic + NP subject (as in 1b')
  stage 2: [*There is/are*$_{\text{topic marker}}$ + NP]$_{\text{NP subject}}$ (as in 1c',1d')
  stage 3: *There*$_{\text{expletive subject/topic}}$ (as in 1e')
  stage 4: NP$_{\text{subject/topic}}$ (as in 1f')

Initially, presentative sentences are used as structures to replace the use of a topic and a subject constituent (stage 1) by one subject constituent that is explicitly marked as topic by the topic marker *there is* (stage 2). Further reanalysis of *there* as an expletive leads to another restructuring of the learner's grammar. Now the learner knows that it is possible to attribute topic and subject function to one and the same (pronominal) element (stage 3). Finally, the learner discovers that nominal elements can also function as both subject and topic (stage 4), which is precisely the kind of typological knowledge learners of subject-prominent languages need. This analysis accounts for two observations. First, it explains why presentative sentences, as in (1c), (1d) and (1e), are acquired before learners use nominal NPs as part of subject-predicate structure, as in (1f). Second, it explains the observation of Rutherford: The English presentative serial-verb sentences of

Mandarin speakers, as in (1c), never show both a topic and a subject NP, as in (1b).

References

Rutherford, W. E. 1983. "Language Typology and Language Transfer". *Language Transfer in Language Learning* ed. by S. Gass & L. Selinker, 358-370. Rowley, MA: Newbury House.

I-interlanguage and typology
The case of topic-prominence

Virginia Yip
Chinese University of Hongkong

Stephen Matthews
University of Hongkong

Introduction

The notion of topic-prominence (Li and Thompson 1976, 1981) was introduced into second-language acquisition (SLA) research by Schachter and Rutherford (1979) and Rutherford (1983), who argued that the discourse organization of topic-prominent languages could undergo transfer. Using production data from Chinese and Japanese learners, they identified several interlanguage features reflecting topic-prominent discourse organization, including the pseudo-passive such as (1-2) below, and the overgeneration of existential constructions as in (3-4) below, which were exclusively found in Chinese learners' writing.

(1) These ways can classify two types.

(2) Irrational emotions are bad but rational emotions must use for judging.

(3) There is a tire hanging from the roof served as their playground.

(4) There were many new patriots in my country gathered together and established a new country.

In an early application of typological insights to interlanguage (IL) analysis, Schachter and Rutherford (1979:8) analyzed these as "a direct reflection of the surface syntax of Chinese and Japanese and topic-comment form," manifesting "the carryover into the target language of native language function-form characteristics." These and other features of Chinese-English interlanguage are further analyzed in Yip (1989, 1995). In this paper, we focus on the pseudo-passive as in (1-2) and an additional type as in (5-6) below, which we shall term the 'periphrastic topic construction'.

(5) For Japanese speakers, they may think more positively about this claim [than English speakers].

(6) For those who violate our policy, CSC will stop them using our facilities. [announcement on computer network]

Topic-prominent features in interlanguage have been pursued empirically in a number of subsequent works. Huebner (1983) described transfer of a number of topic-prominent properties in a Hmong speaker's English interlanguage. Zobl (1986) discussed the logical problems arising in the acquisition of a subject-prominent L2 by speakers of topic-prominent languages. Fuller and Gundel (1987) described topic-prominent features in the English interlanguage of speakers of both topic-prominent and non-topic-prominent languages, arguing that these features characterize a universal stage in IL development. Recently, studies have reversed the focus to consider the development from subject-prominent to topic-prominent grammar. Jin (1994) found that subject-prominent features underwent transfer in the acquisition of Chinese by English speakers, contrary to Fuller and Gundel's (1987) findings. These studies use insights from Li and Thompson's typology to illuminate aspects of interlanguage development.

Like Li and Thompson's (1976) typological proposals themselves, the application of topic-prominence to interlanguage has not been uncontroversial. Tomlin (1994) raises an important issue about the logic of these studies:

> ... typological generalizations, which represent empirical observations about sets of languages, have been used to provide explanations of some second language acquisition behavior... To the extent that such efforts really import typological generalizations in SLA directly, their logic is flawed, because the individual language learner has no access to such generalizations. To the extent that such efforts represent a shorthand means of expressing more individual-specific cognitive or linguistic principles, then appropriate clarification is needed to articulate what those individual-specific general linguistic principles must be. (p. 152)

In Chomsky's (1986) terms, the problem which Tomlin raises is that typological generalizations are stated at the level of E-language, whereas the transitional competence of the learner takes the form of internalized knowledge (I-language).[1] Assuming the view of interlanguages as natural languages (Adjemian 1976) and the Chomskyan view that observable language structures are epiphenomena of underlying knowledge, it follows that interlanguage should be analyzed in I-language terms, with the focus on the learner's competence. *I-interlanguage* in this sense consists of knowledge located in the mind of individual L2 speakers; its grammar does not reside in discourse, texts, social interaction or real-time language use. Thus, to identify typological features such as topic-prominence in interlanguage can only be a descriptive enterprise. If these features are to be ascribed to interlanguage competence, principled analyses of these features at the level of I-language are called for. That is, the content of the typological generalization should be spelt out in terms of I-language principles in order for it to have explanatory value in interlanguage research.

In this paper, we shall argue that the logic to which Tomlin refers above is not flawed so much as incomplete, with missing steps in the argument in need of elaboration. To impute a typological generalization to learners is to assume that they have access to whatever knowledge underlies the typological characteristics in question. This assumption may be methodologically justified to the extent that the relevant grammatical properties are not fully understood at the I-language level. Typological concepts can indeed help to reveal properties of interlanguage, but in order to be explanatory, they must be expressed in terms which can be attributed to the learner's competence.[2] This is a special case of the relationship between E-language research (such as typology) and I-language research (such as work conducted within the principles and parameters framework), where it has been argued that the two approaches are complementary, with typological research often providing the explananda for I-language theory (Hawkins 1985).

In the case of topic-prominence, the move from a descriptive typology to an I-language framework involves a number of steps, including the establishment of topic as a syntactic position (as opposed to a discourse-functional notion; see below), and elaboration of the relationship between subjects and topics. The notion of vacuous topicalization is an important element here.

Topic as a syntactic position

The hypothesis that discourse patterns of a topic-prominent L1 can influence L2 syntax seems to imply a view of topicalization as a discourse function. Givón's (1979) notion of *syntacticization*—"in which discourse and/or pragmatic relations are gradually reanalyzed as grammatical or syntactic relations through the emergence of grammatical machinery" (cited in Rutherford 1983:363)—is misleading in the context of IL development to the extent that it implies that topic-prominent features of Chinese imply a lack of syntactic structure, existing only as discourse-pragmatic notions. Similarly, Jin (1994) assumes *pragmaticization* to take place in the development of topic-prominent features in the Chinese interlanguage of English learners, implying that to acquire Chinese is to acquire a set of pragmatic rules rather than a different syntax. Progress in Chinese linguistics has made it clear that Chinese grammar, including the topic-prominent features, has formal properties which can be stated in rigorous syntactic terms. For example, the omission of subjects and objects is constrained by syntactic as well as pragmatic factors (Huang 1984, 1989), and word order, far from being free, is subject to strict structural constraints (Li 1990).

Relationship between subject and topic

It is now widely acknowledged that subject and topic represent distinct syntactic positions in Chinese (see Shi 1989). However, in a very large number of sentences the initial NP could be analyzed as subject, topic or both. In (7), *Laoshi* could be subject as in (7a) below, or a topic as in (7b) ("As for the teacher, she's gone").

(7)　Laoshi zou le.
　　　teacher leave PRT
　　　'The teacher's gone.'

(7a)　[NP Laoshi] [VP zou le]

(7b)　[TOP Laoshi] [S ∅ zou le]

The relationship between subject and topic in such cases may be clarified by formalizing an idea that is implicit in Li and Thompson (1976) and other treatments of topic-prominent languages. This is the idea that if no other element is topicalized in a main clause, a subject may be topicalized in a 'vacuous' sense invisible on the surface, as indicated in (8) below.[3]

(8)

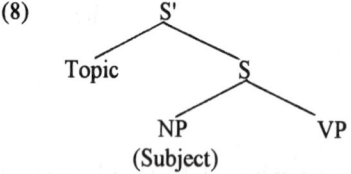

The clearest motivation for this analysis comes from languages such as Japanese and Korean, where the subject of a main clause is generally marked with the topic marker (Japanese *wa*, Korean *un/nun*) instead of the subject/nominative case marker (Japanese *ga*, Korean *i/ka*) in a main clause with no other topic. Although Chinese has no specifically grammaticalized topic particle such as those in Japanese and Korean, a particle may be inserted after a topicalized subject, often followed by an intonation break, as in (9).

(9)　Ni ne, you-mei-you　kong ne?
　　　you PRT have-not-have free　PRT
　　　'How about you, are you free?'

This is also a common position for the particles *àh*, *lā* and *nē/lē* in Cantonese, and it has been argued that such subjects have undergone topicalization (Matthews and Yip 1994:341).[4]

Chinese-English interlanguage and topic-prominence

To bridge the gap between typological insights and interlanguage competence, Yip (1989, 1995) appeals to principles and specific analyses developed within generative grammar. The resulting derivations and representations can be attributed to I-interlanguage competence without assuming the learner's access to typological generalizations. Below we outline how two IL topic structures may be characterized in I-language terms.

The pseudo-passive

The strengths and limitations of typologically inspired interlanguage analysis may be seen in the case of the pseudo-passive as illustrated in (1) and (2) above. The analysis suggested for these structures in Schachter and Rutherford (1979; henceforth SR) is as shown in (10) and (11), respectively.

(10) [These ways] [∅ can classify two types]
     TOPIC   COMMENT

(11) Irrational emotions are bad but [rational emotions] [∅ must use for judging].
                                      TOPIC   COMMENT

According to this analysis, the clause-initial NP is interpreted as "a topic, unrelated grammatically to the following verb, whose actual subject and often object are simply not required by the native language's discourse conventions" (SR:8). We shall argue that the analysis is essentially correct, in identifying the NP *rational emotions* as a topic rather than a subject of a passive clause.[5] At the same time, it raises some problems:

> (i) whether the topic is "unrelated grammatically to the following verb". We shall argue that this is true for a subset of cases, as represented by (10), but not for the type represented by (11) which involves topicalization of the object.

> (ii) the analysis implies the presence of a null subject, shown in the representations above as ∅. In E-language terms, all that need be said is that Chinese is a null subject language, which justifies the postulation of a null subject in the analysis. In I-language terms, this point must be articulated further to specify what type of null subjects is involved and what principles or parameters permit their presence.[6]

While these questions are tangential to the analysis of the structure as a case of topicalization, they must be answered if the typologically-inspired analysis is to be attributed to learners' I-interlanguage. Rutherford (1983:365) noted that "the matter of formal representation of these interlanguage data is...certainly open to further discussion". The investigation of topicalization structures, triggered to a large extent by the work of Li and Thompson (1976), has resulted in a distinction between base-generated topic structures and those derived by movement, with Chinese allowing both types (Huang 1984). Base-generated topic structures include those such as (12) below, where the topic does not represent a subcategorized complement of the predicate.

(12) Beijing hen duo ren qi jixingche.
Beijing very many people ride bicycle
'In Beijing, many people ride bicycles.'

The topic *Beijing* does not represent a subcategorized complement of the verb *qi* 'ride' and must be generated in situ. Topicalization structures derived by movement are those containing a gap in a subcategorized position corresponding to the topic, as in (13).

(13) Beijing wo meiyou qu-guo.
Beijing I have-not go-EXP
'I have not been to Beijing.'

The topic *Beijing* here represents the object of the verb *qu* 'go', and has undergone movement from the object position, as shown by co-indexation between the NP and its trace in (13a).

(13a) Beijing$_i$ wo meiyou qu-guo t_i

Applying this distinction to Chinese speakers' interlanguage, we see both types of topic structure. In (14) below, the topic *these ways* is not syntactically related to the verb, just as SR proposed, although it is semantically related by way of a part-whole relation (i.e. there are two types of ways).

(14) These ways can classify two types.

The same may be seen in the case of the Chinese counterpart in (15).

(15) Zhexie fangfa keyi fen liang zhong.
these way can classify two type
'These methods can be classified into two types.'

In a case such as (16) below, where the topic represents an argument of the verb, Yip (1995, Ch.4) argues instead for a movement analysis of the topicalization as in (16a).

(16) New cars must keep inside.

(16a) [New cars]$_i$ ∅ must keep t_i inside.

The second problem raised by the SR analysis concerns the nature of the null subject. The SR description of the null subject as "not required by the language's discourse conventions" implies that dropping the subject is discourse-related. However, the missing subjects are not identified by a discourse topic; indeed, the sentences already have an overt topic, as argued above. The pseudo-passives are generic statements in which the missing subject is interpreted as referring to *one* or *people* in general. Yip (1995) identifies the null subject as pro_{arb}, a null subject with arbitrary reference. The S-structure is then as in (17) below.

(17) [New cars]$_i$ pro_{arb} must keep t_i inside.

This analysis formalizes SR's insight in a way compatible with current syntactic theory, thereby making the analysis more plausible as a putative I-language construct. Rather than invalidating the typologically based (E-language) analysis, this reanalysis in fact validates it by spelling out what it means in the more precise and rigorous framework of syntactic theory. Note also that the development of a typology of empty categories postdates Schachter and Rutherford's work. The notion of pro_{arb} in particular derives from Suñer (1983) and Jaeggli (1986).

Periphrastic topic constructions

Another interlanguage structure which appears to instantiate topic-prominence is represented in examples (18-22) below, produced by Hongkong university students whose L1 is Cantonese.

(18) For most people, they would learn their mother tongue only, but nowadays schools in many countries start to teach language other than the local language.

(19) For Yule, he associates human language with animal communication. But for Saussure, he adopts a scientific approach to the problem.

(20) For Japanese speakers, they may think more positively about this claim [than English speakers].

(21) For first language, every child develops it almost at the same time.

(22) For L1 learners, their goal is target language competence.

Like the pseudo-passive construction, these examples invite a division into topic and comment as in (23).

(23) TOPIC   COMMENT
    [For NP$_i$] [... pronoun$_i$ ...]

Note that most of the examples are contrastive: Yule's view is contrasted with Saussure's in (19), Japanese speakers with English speakers in (20). This is a typical function of topicalization, in Chinese as in other languages. The topic serves as the subject of the clause (18-20), the object (21) or the possessor (22), with a pronoun coreferential with the topic in each case.

Like many IL constructions, this is highly systematic both within and across learners. It often appears regularly in a single learner's writing, as in (24) below, where the construction occurs three times in consecutive sentences.

(24) *For* every normal child, *he* will learn his first language when he is only a few years old. Therefore, *for* the first language acquisition, *it* can be occurred when the learner has been without a language so far and acquires one. *For* second language acquisition, *it* can be defined as the language that people learn for communication besides their mother tongue.

A sample of 27 essays by first-year Hongkong university students suggests that the construction is also prevalent across learners. The essay topic "Discuss the similarities and differences between first and second language acquisition" calls for comparison and contrast, giving ample opportunities for topicalization. Of the 27 essays, 16 show the construction with *for*; one essay contains as many as 11 exemplars.[7]

The form of the construction cannot be straightforwardly attributed to transfer, although some possible sources in Chinese grammar deserve consideration. Left-dislocation with a resumptive pronoun is possible with animate subjects as in (25), but this option is restricted as an overt pronoun cannot readily be used with an inanimate antecedent as in (26).[8]

(25) Zhangsan, ta mei-you lai.
      Zhangsan, he not-have come
      'Zhangsan, he hasn't come.'

(26) ?*Di   yi ge juzi,   ta bijiao jiandan.
      number one LP sentence, it more simple
      'The first sentence, it is more simple.'

Moreover, there is no counterpart to *for* here. Another Chinese construction has the preposition *dui* parallel to *for* in the IL construction, as shown in (27) below.

(27) Dui Zhangsan lai shuo, zhei bu chezi tai gui.
      for Zhangsan come say this CL car   too expensive
      'For Zhangsan, this car is too expensive.'

This is not a likely source since the IL examples lack any counterpart to *lai shuo*, and *dui* in (27) is meaningful (assigning the role of experiencer to *Zhangsan*, as in the English translation) while *for* in the IL examples in (18-22) is semantically empty. A closer counterpart is *zhi yu* 'as for', an expression used in written Chinese to mark contrast. This is shown in (28) below.

(28) Zhi yu zhe ge wenti, mingtian zai shuo.
    as-for this CL problem tomorrow again speak
    'As for this problem, we'll discuss it again tomorrow.''

zhi yu would not be appropriate in many cases where the *for* construction appears, such as (29), where there is no element of contrast.

(29) For both first and second language acquisition, learners do imitate at the beginning of the process of learning a particular language.

While such structures may provide a precedent for the interlanguage construction, the formal means of marking the topic are based on English grammar, resembling the paraphrases often used to translate Chinese and Japanese topic structures as in (30-31).

(30) Pijiu ne, Qingdao zui hao.
    beer PRT Tsingtao most good
    'As for beer, Tsingtao is the best.'

(31) Sakana-wa tai-ga ii.
    fish-TOP snapper-SUBJ good
    'As for fish, snapper is good.'

Given the function of contrastive topicalization from Chinese and the preposition from English, the periphrastic topic construction might be said to represent an interlanguage structure of the type described in SR (p. 10): "a new variety of transfer, namely from L1 function to L2 form." But what does this imply in terms of syntactic structure?

As in the case of the pseudo-passive, it is important to distinguish argument topics, which have a grammatical relation to the predicate, from adjunct topics, which do not. Where the topic bears a grammatical relation to the predicate, as in (32) below, the *for* construction is anomalous and the repeated subject redundant.

(32) For Japanese speakers, *they* may think more positively about this claim.

Where the topic phrase is an adjunct, as in (33), the structure itself is grammatical (although the choice of the preposition *for* is not quite appropriate).

(33) For L1 acquisition, success is not influenced by personality, motivation or attitudes.

The breakdown of topics according to grammatical function in our sample is shown in Table 1. In the sample of 27 essays, 30 cases involve argument topics (22 topicalized subjects, with a few object and possessor NPs) while 34 are adjuncts, hence more or less grammatical as in the case of (32). The distinction between adjunct and argument topics can be seen clearly in (34), where the first clause justifiably adds *for* with an adjunct NP and the second does so redundantly with

Table 1: Grammatical function of topic NPs in 27 essays

	Argument		Adjunct
Subject	Object	Possessor	
22	3	5	34

Table 2: Argument and adjunct topics introduced by for

Learner	Argument	Adjunct	Total
1	5	6	11
2	3	5	8
3	2	5	7
4	5	1	6
5	3	3	6
6	3	2	5
7	3	1	4
8	0	4	4
9	1	1	2
10	1	1	2
11	2	0	2
12	0	2	2
13	0	2	2
14	1	0	1
15	1	0	1
16	0	1	1

a subject NP.

(34) *For first language acquisition*, the acquiring process is unconscious...while *for L2 learners, they* also imitate and follow the pronunciation of their target language.

Such learners fail to make a distinction between argument and adjunct topics, introducing both with *for*.[9] That this is a general pattern is confirmed by Table 2, which shows that out of 16 essays where the construction occurs, 9 use both argument and adjunct types. The treatment of topics as in (34) suggests that the learners have internalized the constraint that English does not allow an NP without a grammatical relation to the predicate to appear as a topic, as in Chinese and Japanese (29-30). Thus we do not find errors like (35) below.

(35)*First language acquisition, the acquiring process is unconscious...

Sentences like (35) are ruled out because the topic NP lacks both Case and a theta role (see Japanese *wa* as discussed above). The preposition *for* in the interlanguage examples fulfils this case-marking function. When the same structure is applied to an argument topic, the pronoun serves to spell out the subject or object coreferential with the topic NP, in accordance with the requirement that all subjects and objects be overt in English. In the case of topicalized subjects, this amounts to spelling out the vacuous topicalization structure (36a) as (36b).

(36) a. Chinese: [$_{TOP}$ NP$_i$] *pro*$_i$ VP
    b. Interlanguage: [$_{PP}$ for NP$_i$] Pronoun$_i$ VP

The topic is thus represented syntactically as a PP adjoined to S, as indicated in (37) below.

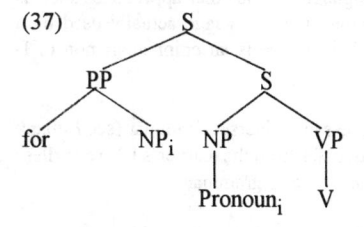

(37)

```
              S
            /   \
          PP     S
         /  \   / \
       for  NP_i NP  VP
                |   |
             Pronoun_i V
```

In E-language terms, the periphrastic topic construction might be described as a further case of transfer from L1 discourse function to L2 form. In I-language terms, it realizes this function by supplying a preposition as a Case marker for the topic NP. Just as we argued for the pseudo-passive, the analysis elaborates on the E-language description rather than replacing it, thereby bridging the gap between description and competence noted by Tomlin (1994).

Conclusion

We have discussed the properties of two constructions in Chinese learners' English interlanguage, pseudo-passives and periphrastic topic structures, which instantiate the typological characteristics of topic-prominence. The pseudo-passives include base-generated types and those derived by movement, with the null subject *pro*$_{arb}$. For the periphrastic topic construction, learners do not distinguish between argument and adjunct topics, using the preposition *for* as a Case marker for both types. These interlanguage structures illustrate how an E-language analysis can be formulated in I-language terms, consistent with the assumptions of the interlanguage hypothesis. In order for typological insights such as topic-prominence to be incorporated into theories of interlanguage, they need to be articulated in terms of I-language principles. To make explicit the grammar of I-interlanguage in this sense is a challenge to SLA researchers.

Acknowledgment

This research was partially supported by a grant from the Hongkong Research Grants Council (project HKU/238/92H).

Notes

1. The terms 'I-language' and 'E-language' were introduced by Chomsky (1986) to counter the ambiguity of the term 'language'. Grammar as studies in the Chomskyan framework addresses the internalized competence of an individual speaker (I-language), while other approaches such as typology and discourse analysis focus on the description of the language actually used by a community of speakers (E-language). For Chomsky, E-language is an epiphenomenon of I-language, which is the ultimate focus of inquiry.

2. Note that this is logically independent of the issue of access to Universal Grammar (see Eubank 1991). I-language properties can be assumed to undergo transfer from the learner's L1, regardless of whether UG in its initial form informs the construction of the IL grammar.

3. The account is similar to that commonly assumed for Wh-movement. A subject Wh-phrase as in (i) below undergoes vacuous Wh-movement from subject position to the [Spec,CP] position, while an object Wh-phrase as in (ii) may be seen to have moved on the surface.

    (i) Who$_i$ t_i is coming to dinner?

    (ii) Who$_i$ are we inviting t_i to dinner?

    Part of the motivation for the vacuous movement analysis in (i) is that the same process of movement is involved in each case, and the Wh-phrase lands in the same position, namely, the specifier of CP. Wh-questions thus have a unified structural representation.

4. One question that arises here is whether topicalization takes place by default in the absence of another topic. If so, this analysis would also account for properties of subjects which would be expected to hold of topics, such as the definiteness constraint on subjects in Chinese. The definiteness constraint applies naturally and universally to topics, which are necessarily definite; a subject which is topicalized, even vacuously, is thus subject to the same condition (see Yip 1995 for definiteness and existential constructions in Chinese-English interlanguage).

5. There are other logically possible analyses, such as an ergative or middle derivation, in which the NP would be the subject. These possibilities are discussed and rejected in Yip (1989, 1995).

6. It is also necessary to specify which syntactic contexts the learner allows a null subject to appear in. Yip (1995, Ch. 3) argues that learners who allow pro_{arb} do not necessarily allow referential *pro*. That is, many learners who use pseudo-passives do not use null subjects referring to a specific referent as in **[pro] is missing*.

7. Naturally, absence of the construction from a particular essay does not entail that the learner's grammar does not allow it. Judgment tasks would be needed to show this.

8. As shown in (i) below, the object pronoun is possible with inanimate reference.

(i) Di　　yi　ge　juzi,　ni　yao　xiugai ta.
   number one CL sentence you need correct it
   'The first sentence needs correcting.'

9. Grammatical adjunct topics may serve as the basis for overgeneralization of the construction from adjunct topics, where a preposition is required, to argument topics, where it is not. This situation raises issues of learnability (e.g., how the learner would recover from the overgeneral grammar) which are beyond the scope of this paper.

References

Adjemian, C. 1976. "On the Nature of Interlanguage Systems". *Language Learning* 26.297-320.
Chomsky, N. 1986. *Knowledge of Language: Its nature, origin, and use*. New York: Praeger.
Eubank, L. ed. 1991. *Point Counterpoint: Universal Grammar in the second language acquisition*. Amsterdam: John Benjamins.
Fuller, J.& J. Gundel. 1987. "Topic-Prominence in Interlanguage". *Language Learning* 37.1-18.
Givón, T. 1979. "From Discourse to Syntax: Grammar as a processing strategy". *Syntax and Semantics* 12 ed. by T. Givón, 81-112. New York: Academic Press.
Hawkins, J. 1985. "Complementary Methods in Universal Grammar: A reply to Coopmans". *Language* 61.569-587.
Huang, J. C-T. 1984. "On the Distribution and Reference of Empty Pronouns". *Linguistic Inquiry* 15.531-574.
Huang, J. C-T. 1989. "Pro-drop in Chinese: A generalized control theory". *The Null Subject Parameter* ed. by O. Jaeggli & K. Safir, 185-214. Dordrecht: Kluwer Academic.
Huebner, T. 1983. *A Longitudinal Analysis of the Acquisition of English*. Ann Arbor: Karoma Publishers.
Jaeggli, O. 1986. "Arbitrary Plural Pronominals". *Natural Language and Linguistic Theory* 4.43-76.
Jin, H-G. 1994. "Topic Prominence and Subject-Prominence in L2 Acquisition: Evidence of English-to-Chinese typological transfer". *Language Learning* 44.101-22.
Li, C. & S. Thompson. 1976. "Subject and Topic: A new typology of language". *Subject and Topic* ed. by C. Li, 457-489. New York: Academic Press.
Li, C. & S. Thompson. 1981. *Mandarin Chinese: A functional reference grammar*. Berkeley and Los Angeles: University of California Press.
Li, Y-H. A. 1990. *Word Order and Constituency in Mandarin Chinese*. Dordrecht: Kluwer.
Matthews, S. & V. Yip. 1994. *Cantonese: A comprehensive grammar*. London: Routledge.

Rutherford, W. 1983. "Language Typology and Language Transfer". *Language Transfer in Language Learning* ed. by S. Gass & L. Selinker, 358-370. Rowley: Newbury House.

Schachter, J. & W. Rutherford. 1979. "Discourse Function and Language Transfer". *Working Papers in Bilingualism* 19.1-12.

Shi, D. 1989. "Topic Chain as a Syntactic Category in Chinese". *Journal of Chinese Linguistics* 17.223-262.

Suñer, M. 1985. "Pro-arb". *Linguistic Inquiry* 14.188-191.

Tomlin, R. 1994. "Functional Grammars, Pedagogical Grammars, and Communicative Language Teaching". *Perspectives on Pedagogical Grammar* ed. by T. Odlin, 140-178. Cambridge: Cambridge University Press.

Yip, V. 1989. *Aspects of Chinese/English Interlanguage: Syntax, semantics and learnability*. Unpublished Ph.D. dissertation, University of Southern California.

Yip, V. 1995. *Interlanguage and Learnability: From Chinese to English*. Amsterdam: John Benjamins.

Zobl, H. 1986. "A Functional Approach to the Attainability of Typological Targets in L2 Acquisition". *Second Language Research* 2.16-32.

Universals, SLA, and language pedagogy
1984 revisited

Susan Gass
Michigan State University

An understanding of the phenomenon of how a second (i.e., non-primary) language is learned entails being able to (at least probabilistically) predict when something will occur and when it will not. In 1984 Gass and Ard proposed a model for predicting the potential relationship between language universals and second language acquisition. In that model, which was primarily concerned with typological universals, it was predicted that universals that are based on ways in which humans interact with and/or perceive the world around them are most likely to affect acquisition. For example, universals that have a physical basis, such as many phonological universals, have a strong likelihood of constraining second language acquisition. This type of influence is contrasted with universals that are themselves abstractions (i.e., based on abstract principles of language)[1] which are predicted not to influence the acquisition of a second language to the same extent. This is so since it is more difficult for learners to notice connections among structures that are not superficially related (i.e., that are abstractions) than it is to notice surface relatedness (see Gass 1988; Schmidt 1990, 1992; Tomlin and Villa 1994).

In the past decade the field of second language acquisition has changed in a number of ways. Particularly relevant is the fact that there has been a change in emphasis in the types of universals that have been the focus of second language studies and hence that have been predicted to impact the acquisition of a second language. The purpose of this squib is twofold: to update the earlier 1984 model and to relate this work to issues of language pedagogy.

Most recent research dealing with language universals and second language acquisition is conducted within the framework of Universal Grammar (UG) (see, e.g., Eubank 1991; White 1989; White forthcoming a). Universal Grammar is comprised of a set of principles and parameters, the latter of which represent the ways in which languages can vary cross-linguistically. From the perspective of acquisition, UG is hypothesized to be innate, a fact that for children allows rapid and accurate acquisition of linguistic knowledge that is much richer than what is provided in the input. With regard to second language acquisition, the question is more complex, not only because there is first language information that is additionally available to learners, but also because the end result of acquisition is not native-like competence, as it is in first language acquisition. Thus, the debate centers around the extent to which second language learners have access to the innate system that is presumably available to children (see Bley-Vroman 1989; Schachter 1988).

The literature of the past decade has yielded contradictory results concerning the question of access to UG. Some studies suggest that second language learners do not behave according to the precepts of UG parameters (e.g., Bennett 1994; Broselow and Finer 1991; Finer 1991; Finer and Broselow 1986; Flynn 1987, 1988; Hirakawa 1990; Thomas 1989, 1991, 1993; Uziel 1993; White 1989, 1990/1991); other studies suggest the opposite (e.g., Clahsen 1988; Clahsen and Muysken 1986, 1989; Schachter 1988; Bley-Vroman 1989; Felix and Weigl 1991). In this part of the squib I will relate the 1984 model of Gass and Ard to current work on UG-based second language acquisition.

The claim in that earlier paper is complex, but simply put, it is argued that universals that have their basis in cognitive/perceptual/physical facts of language will have a major influence on second language acquisition. In other words, when the underlying rationale for the universal itself is one that has to do with the way that the world is or the way that humans interact with their environment/each other or with the way that the human vocal tract is shaped, the greater the likelihood that these universals will be operative in second language acquisition. To support this view, data were presented from the acquisition of relative clauses and from tense/aspect.

From the perspective of second language acquisition, one of the most interesting areas is that of parameters. Parameters represent a clustering of grammatical properties that vary from language to language. In other words, languages will vary as to the value of the clusters present in that language. For example, given three grammatical structures, it is possible that one language will have the presence of all three whereas another will have the absence of all three. If this is the case, a learner (child or adult) only has to notice the presence or absence of one such structure; the acquisition of all structures should theoretically result. I will argue that the clustering of grammatical properties will constrain acquisition in just those cases where there is structural and/or functional relatedness; where there is not, acquisition is not affected. In other words, we can expect learners' grammars to be in conformity with universal clusterings of properties in the former case, but not in the latter.

To apply the Gass and Ard model to UG is to some extent not a 'fair' task since the underlying assumption in the earlier model is that the effect of universals will in some sense be determined by the way learners perceive the world: Surface facts of language are of crucial concern. So in some sense, the 1984 approach argues against the position that learners come to the task with abstract knowledge. But, a theory of language based on UG is one based on knowledge of abstractions. White (forthcoming a) claims that "parameters account for clusters of properties, which superficially seem to be unrelated" (p. 5, ms.).[2] Taken at face value, this requires that superficially (and obviously) related properties are not part of a single parameter. However, Berent (1990, 1994) has argued that the Accessibility Hierarchy (originally proposed by Keenan and Comrie, 1977 within a typological universal framework) should be reconfigured within a Principles and Parameters framework as a parameter with different languages selecting different values. If this argument is a correct one, the lack of superficial relatedness as an aspect of parameters is no longer valid.

In what follows, I will present three cases which may be taken to test the Gass and Ard model: (1) *pro*-drop, (2) Verb Raising and (3) Reflexive binding.

Pro-Drop

One of the earliest areas of investigation within this framework was the '*pro*-drop parameter'. This parameter was intended to account for the following clusterings in languages: (1) the omission of subject pronouns, (2) the inversion of subjects and verbs in declarative sentences, and (3) *that*-trace effects–that is, the extraction of a subject (leaving a trace) out of a clause that contains a complementizer. A language will either have all of these properties or none of them. As the examples in Table 1 below show, languages like Italian and Spanish are [+*pro*-drop] and have all of the associated properties, whereas English and French are [-*pro*-drop], having none of them.

When looking at how second language learners acquire these structures, there does not appear to be strong evidence in support of these clusterings. White (1985) and Lakshmanan (1986) present data from Spanish and French learners of English (White) and Spanish, Japanese and Arabic learners of English (Lakshmanan) on precisely these three structures. White found that the learners did not recognize these three structures as related. While there was a difference between the Spanish and the French speakers on the first type of sentences (i.e., those with and without overt subject pronouns), there was no difference between the two groups on the other two sentences. Thus, these learners did not appear to see these three properties as a unified parameter. Lakshmanan's results were similar. Her groups of learners responded similarly to the first two sentence types, but dif-

Table 1: Properties of the pro-drop parameter (Italian and English)

Italian	English
Subject pronouns	
Va al cinema sta sera	She is going to the movies this evening
goes to the movies this evening	*is going to the movies this evening
Subject verb inversion	
E arrivata Laura	Laura has arrived.
is arrived Laura	*has arrived Laura
that-trace	
Chi hai detto che e venuto?	Whom did you say came?
who you have said that is come?	*Whom did you say that has come?

ferently with regard to the third, again suggesting that these properties were not perceived by these learners as unified under the umbrella of a single parameter.

There is evidence, however, that is more compelling with regard to the clustering of properties. Hilles (1986) assumes different properties of the *pro*-drop parameter in her investigation of the acquisition of English by a native speaker of Spanish, named Jorge: (1) obligatory pronoun use; (2) use of non-referential *it*, as in weather terms (e.g., *it's raining, it's pouring*) and use of non-referential *there*, as in *There is rain in the forecast*; and (3) the use of uninflected modals. Hilles showed that these three features are related in the speech of her subject. Specifically, there was an inverse relationship between Jorge's lack of referential subject use and the appearance of modal verbs. As Jorge began to use subject pronouns in English, he also began to use modals as noninflected forms. She hypothesized that the triggering factor for the switch from [+*pro*-drop] to [-*pro*-drop] was the use of nonreferential subjects. This was an indication that this learner had truly understood the mandatory nature of subjects in English.[3]

The questionable results (particularly with regard to adult learners) is predicted given the lack of structural/functional relatedness of these three structures. However, the question does not end here. Of the three structures that White used, one could argue that subject-verb inversion and subject omission are more closely related to each other than either is to *that*-trace sentences, and that as a result there is a greater likelihood that learners will be aware that these two form a 'pair' of sorts, whereas there is no connection between either of these and *that*-trace constructions. In the first two cases, the relatedness has to do with the freedom of subjects (whether or not they are overt and the extent to which their position in the sentence is free) in languages like Italian or Spanish. This is so due to the rich morphological system that allows easy recoverability of subjects. It seems reasonable to assume that learners recognize the relatedness of these two structures which both have to do with the use and/or position of subject pronouns. In fact, when one looks at White's results on each of the three structures, one sees that the responses (grammaticality judgments) are more similar between the two structures (subject omission and subject verb placement) than either is to the *that*-trace sentences. Her results are repeated in Table 2 below, first for Spanish speakers and second for French speakers. Each row represents a different sentence.[4]

As can be seen, for both French and Spanish subjects, the responses appear to be much more similar for the two grammatical structures that have some overt similarity (subject verb inversion and subject omission), whereas there is little that is similar in the results between *that*-trace sentences and either of the others. In fact, White suggests that the lack of relatedness may be due not to a lack of access to UG, but to an inadequate account of the parameter itself. I would argue that the results suggest that learners are able to perceive the structural similarity in some cases, but not in others and it is the surface similarity that allows them to connect the structures. Learners do not appear to have access to underlying abstractions.

Table 2: Percentages responding correct on aspects of pro-drop

Spanish-speaking learners (n=54)

missing subjects	subject-verb inversion	*that*-trace
37	33	91
39	33	70
35	7	67
48	2	80
41	33	98
57		87

French-speaking learners (n=19)

missing subjects	subject-verb inversion	*that*-trace
21	42	90
37	37	63
5	16	74
10	5	74
16	21	84
21		84

Verb Raising

The second grammatical structure I examine is what is called 'verb-raising'. This parameter accounts for the clustering of the following properties in language (a) negatives, (b) questions, and (c) adverb placement. Because of this clustering, it also accounts for differences in languages like English and French (see White 1990/1991 and 1991 for a discussion of the theoretical position underlying the verb-movement parameter). Table 3 shows relevant examples from French and English that are encompassed in this parameter.

In work looking at the acquisition of two of these properties (questions and adverbs), White found little evidence of their relatedness. She proposes a number of possibilities, among them: (a) parameters of UG do not operate in L2 acquisition[5]; (b) instruction interfered; (c) learners assume that verb-raising is optional; (d) the theoretical description of the parameter is inaccurate; and (e) verb-raising and questions are not related at an abstract level. Within the framework of Gass and Ard, the unrelatedness of questions and adverbs is not surprising since there is nothing in the input nor in the superficial structures of these properties that learners could use to relate them. While there is not comparable data from the acquisition of questions and negatives, it would be predicted that there is a greater likelihood of these two properties being perceived as related in English given the use of *do* in English in both of these structures in English.

Table 3: Verb-raising parameter (French and English)

French	English
Questions	
Voulez-vous aller á Paris?	*Want you to go to Paris?
want you to go to Paris	Do you want to go to Paris?
"Do you want to go to Paris?"	
Negatives	
Elle ne veut pas aller á Paris.	*She not wants to go to Paris.
She (part.) wants not to go to Paris.	She doesn't want to go to Paris.
"She doesn't want to go to Paris"	
Adverbs	
La femme embrasse toujours l'homme.	The woman always kisses the man.
The woman kisses always the man.	*The woman kisses always the man.
"The woman always kisses the man"	
*La femme toujours embrasse l'homme	

Reflexive Binding

The final UG parameter that I will deal with is perhaps the most problematic for the Gass and Ard framework–reflexive binding. There are differences in languages of the world as to whether the antecedent of a reflexive must be within the same clause as a reflexive (known as local binding), as shown in (1a-b) below.

(1) a. Josh washed himself.
     b. Ethan knew that Seth washed himself.

In (1a) the solution is easy since there is only one possible antecedent. However, in (1b) the only possible antecedent in English is *Seth*. In languages like Japanese, the antecedent can be either within (here, the subject of the second clause) or outside of the clause (here, the subject of the main clause), so that the Japanese translation equivalent of (1b) is ambiguous, with either *Ethan* or *Seth* as possible antecedents. Ambiguity in English is seen in the sentence in (2) below.

(2) Aaron asked Roger about himself.

The requirement in English is that the reflexive be in the same clause, but antecedents can be either subjects or objects. In Japanese, the requirement is such that only subjects can be antecedents.[6] The same clause requirement does not hold. White (forthcoming b), in characterizing current theory, notes that these properties cluster in a single parameter. That is, there is a connection between 'long-distance' binding (i.e., languages in which the reflexive pronoun can refer to something in or out of its clause) and the impossibility of binding to object.

White (forthcoming b, 1994) reports on a study which tested the relationship between these two properties. In other words, does knowledge of one entail knowledge of the other. Her subjects were Japanese and Francophone learners of English. The link between long-distance binding and non-object binding was not supported. This clearly presents a problem for a view of language learning that claims that there are innate properties of language and that these properties are available to all second language learners. It also presents a problem for the Gass and Ard model since we are dealing with the same grammatical structure,[7] so that the link should be more transparent. Within the latter framework, one could argue that while linking certain grammatical facts 'should' be obvious to learners, the ultimate test is the learner him/herself and these learners did not make the appropriate connection.[8] This is, of course, a weak argument since, even if it were accepted as reasonable, there is no way empirically to verify it or to disprove it. However, the difficulty of noticing the similarity of these structures may in part stem from the nature of the grammatical structure in question. In general, unlike with most aspects of grammatical acquisition, when dealing with reflexives, the issue is one of interpretation, not grammaticality. In other words, when we speak of the ambiguity of sentences such as (1b), there may be little possibility for a learner to determine the correct antecedent in English. In fact, one of the treatment groups in White's study was given explicit grammatical instruction that included the fact that non-subjects can be antecedents, but that did not include the fact that long-distance binding is not possible in English. This group did show some improvement from pre-test to post-test on their knowledge of binding to objects. These results, while not strong, do lend support to both the Gass and Ard position of superficial similarity and the UG position involving more abstract knowledge of language. Because reflexives fall somewhere in the middle of the abstract/superficial continuum and because they deal less directly with issues of grammaticality (grammatical input does not provide information on how one should interpret reflexives) and more with interpretation, it is particularly difficult to isolate the factors involved in acquisition.

The research reported thus far has for the most part been conducted with learners in a classroom situation, and in fact, has been used to demonstrate the kind of input necessary to generate grammars that are compatible with grammars licensed by UG. Because the theoretical basis of this research is often being tested along with the implications for learning, it has often been difficult to determine the extent to which learners are or are not adhering to the constraints of UG. Nonetheless, the implications for classroom learning and, more specifically, for the ways in which input can be manipulated to bring about more efficient learning are striking.

In fact, classrooms are where input can be organized and packaged to make the most efficient use of learners' energy and time (see also Gass 1991, forthcoming). This being the case, it is easy to see that research into universals is of utmost importance since, once we understand where learners naturally make connections, we can structure input to take advantage of learners' natural capacities. In other words, if instruction on one grammatical structure entails the learning of another, then we can provide instruction on one with the expectation that no (or minimal) instruction on the other will still result in knowledge of the other (see Gass 1982; Eckman, Bell and Nelson 1988). Or, alternatively, classroom time can be spent on providing instruction on showing relationships rather than dealing with separate structures.

What I have argued in this squib is that learning and hence classroom practice will be fruitful in just those areas where learners are able to notice the relationships among structures. Importantly, the ability to notice is based on surface phenomena and not on linguistic abstractions.

Notes

1. I am grateful to one of the reviewers of this paper for pointing out the relevance of a discussion in Atkinson (1992:200-201) regarding the distinction between learning and triggering. Drawing on Fodor (1978, 1981), Atkinson argues that "learning is an externally occasioned change in epistemic state *where there is an appropriate relation of content* between the learner's representation of the externally occasioning event(s) and the consequent change in epistemic state." He contrasts this with *triggering*, which he refers to as having a "defining characteristic ... an *arbitrary* relationship of content between the representation of the external event(s) (if they have content at all) and the change in epistemic state." Within the context of UG and typological universals, the former link disparate constructions (see discussion below), whereas the latter are concrete and relate constructions that are structurally similar (however defined).

2. How one defines superficial unrelatedness is, of course, an open question. One might get some insight from Atkinson (1992) in his discussion of content relatedness. Differentiating between learning and triggering (see note 1), he notes that learning must result in a change in epistemic state on the basis of some external event and more importantly that there be an "appropriate relation of content" (p. 201). Where there is no relation of content, there is triggering. While this specifies that there be a relation of content, it only pushes the problem one step further backwards, since there is no precise definition of what it means to have content relatedness.

3. As an anonymous reviewer pointed out, a major difficulty with Hilles' study is that there is no control structure that is unrelated to the parametric structures under consideration. We have no way of knowing that the relationship between/among structures is due to the parameter as opposed to the learning of individual structures. "One would expect that as any learner advances, he/she would improve in the number of pronominal subjects as well as pleonastic pronouns and auxiliaries" (personal communication, anonymous reviewer).

4. As is apparent, within each category, there is at times quite a difference among the sentences. The reader is urged to consult the original article for the fuller set of data, since dealing with this issue goes beyond the scope of the present discussion.

5. As White (1990/1991) notes, the difficulty with this explanation lies in the fact that it is generally accepted that children do have access to UG and that her data were collected from children in grades 5 and 6 (typically 11 and 12 year olds).

6. I omit from discussion the complicating factor in Japanese of the fact that there are two reflexive pronouns, one morphologically simple and the other morphologically complex.

7. See note 2 for a discussion of the difficulty of this concept.

8. There were two learners, one Francophone and one Japanese (out of a total of 19 Francophones and one Japanese) who did make the appropriate link.

References

Atkinson, M. 1992. *Children's Syntax: An introduction to principles and parameters theory*. Oxford: Basil Blackwell.
Bennett, S. 1994. "Interpretation of English Reflexives by Adolescent Speakers of Serbo-Croatian". *Second Language Research* 10.125-156.
Berent, J. 1990. "Relative Clause Learnability: Second language and deaf learner data". Paper at the 24th Convention of Teachers of English to Speakers of Other Languages. San Francisco, CA. March.
Berent, J. 1994. "The Subset Principle in Second-Language Acquisition". *Research Methodology in Second-Language Acquisition* ed. by E. Tarone, S. Gass & A. Cohen, 17-39. Hillsdale, NJ: Lawrence Erlbaum Associates.
Bley-Vroman, R. 1989. "What is the Logical Problem of Foreign Language Learning?" *Linguistic Perspectives on Second Language Acquisition* ed. by S. Gass & J. Schachter, 41-68. Cambridge: Cambridge University Press.
Broselow, E. & D. Finer. 1991. "Parameter Setting in Second Language Phonology and Syntax". *Second Language Research* 7.35-59.
Clahsen, H. 1988. "Parameterized Grammatical Theory and Language Acquisition: A study of acquisition of verb placement and inflection by children and adults". *Linguistic Theory in Second Language Acquisition* ed. by S. Flynn & W. O'Neil, 47-75. Dordrecht: Kluwer Academic Publishers.
Clahsen, H. & P. Muysken. 1986. "The Accessibility of Universal Grammar to Adult and Child Learners". *Second Language Research* 2.93-119.
Clahsen, H. & P. Muysken. 1989. "The UG Paradox in L2 Acquisition". *Second Language Research* 5.1-29.
Broselow, E. & D. Finer. 1991. "Parameter Setting in Second Language Phonology and Syntax". *Second Language Research* 7.35-59.
Eckman, F., L. Bell & D. Nelson. 1988. "On the Generalization of Relative Clause Instruction in the Acquisition of English as a Second Language". *Applied Linguistics* 9.1-20.
Eubank, L., ed. 1991. *Point Counterpoint: Universal Grammar in the second language*. Amsterdam: John Benjamins.
Felix, S. & W. Weigl. 1991. "Universal Grammar in the Classroom: The effects of formal instruction on second language acquisition". *Second Language Research* 7.162-180.
Finer, D. 1991. "Binding Parameters in Second Language Acquisition." *Point Counterpoint: Universal Grammar in the second language* ed. by L. Eubank, 351-374. Amsterdam: John Benjamins.
Finer, D. & E. Broselow. 1986. "Second Language Acquisition of Reflexive Binding". *Proceedings of the Northeastern Linguistics Society* 16.154-168.
Flynn, S. 1987. *A Parameter-Setting Model of L2 Acquisition*. Dordrecht: Reidel Publishing Company.

Flynn, S. 1988. "Nature of Development in L2 Acquisition and Implications for Theories of Language Acquisition in General". *Linguistic Theory in Second Language Acquisition* ed. by S. Flynn & W. O'Neil, 76-89. Dordrecht: Kluwer Academic Publishers.

Fodor, J. A. 1978. "Computation and Reduction". *Perception and Cognition: Minnesota studies in the philosophy of science*, Vol. 9 ed. by W. C. Savage,229-260. Minneapolis: University of Minnesota Press.

Fodor, J. A. 1981. "The present status of the innateness controversy". *Representations* ed. by J. A. Fodor, 257-316. Hassocks: Harvester.

Gass, S. 1982. "From theory to Practice". *On TESOL '81* ed. by M. Hines & W. Rutherford, 129-139. Washington, D.C.: TESOL.

Gass, S. 1988. "Integrating Research Areas: A framework for second language studies". *Applied Linguistics* 9.198-217.

Gass, S. 1991. "Grammar Instruction, Selective Attention and Learner Processes". *Claus Faerch: In memoriam* ed. by M. Swain, E. Kellerman, L. Selinker & P. Phillipson, 134-141. Clevedon: Multilingual Matters.

Gass, S. Forthcoming. "Learning and Teaching: The necessary intersection". To appear in *Second Language Acquisition Theory and Pedagogy* ed. by F. Eckman, D. Highland, P. Lee, J. Mileham, R. Rutkowski Weber. Hillsdale, N.J.: Lawrence Erlbaum Associates.

Gass, S. & J. Ard. 1984. "L2 Acquisition and the Ontology of Language Universals". *Second Language Acquisition and Language Universals* ed. by W. Rutherford, 33-68. Amsterdam: John Benjamins.

Hirakawa, M. 1990. "A Study of the L2 Acquisition of English Reflexives". *Second Language Research* 6.60-85.

Hilles, S. 1986. "Interlanguage and the *pro* drop parameter". *Second Language Research* 2.33-52.

Keenan, E. & B. Comrie. 1977. "Noun Phrase Accessibility and Universal Grammar". *Linguistic Inquiry* 8.63-99.

Lakshmanan, U. 1986. "The Role of Parametric Variation in Adult Second Language Acquisition: A study of the 'pro-drop' parameter". *Papers in Applied Linguistics-Michigan* 2.97-118.

Lakshmanan, U. & K. Teranishi. 1994. "Preferences versus Grammaticality Judgments: Some methodological issues concerning the governing category parameter in second-language acquisition". *Research Methodology in Second-Language Acquisition* ed. by E. Tarone, S. Gass & A. Cohen, 185-206. Hillsdale, N.J.: Lawrence Erlbaum Associates.

Schachter, J. 1988. "Second Language Acquisition and its Relationship to Universal Grammar". *Applied Linguistics* 9.219-235.

Schmidt, R. 1990. "The Role of Consciousness in Second Language Learning". *Applied Linguistics* 11.127-158.

Schmidt, R. 1992. "Awareness and Second Language Acquisition". *Annual Review of Applied Linguistics* 13.206-226.

Thomas, M. 1989. "The Interpretation of English Reflexive Pronouns by Non-native Speakers". *Studies in Second Language Acquisition* 11.281-303.

Thomas, M. 1991. "Universal Grammar and the Interpretation of Reflexives in a Second Language". *Language* 67.211-239.

Thomas, M. 1993. *Universal Grammar and Knowledge of Reflexives in a Second Language*. Amsterdam: John Benjamins.

Tomlin, R. & V. Villa. 1994. "Attention in Cognitive Science and SLA". *Studies in Second Language Acquisition* 16.183-203.

Uziel, S. 1993. "Resetting Universal Grammar Parameters: Evidence from second language acquisition of subjacency and the empty category principle". *Second Language Research* 9.49-83.

White, L. 1985. "The 'Pro-drop' Parameter in Adult Second Language Acquisition. *Language Learning* 35.47-62.

White, L. 1989. *Universal Grammar and Second Language Acquisition*. Amsterdam: John Benjamins.

White, L. 1990/1991. "The Verb-Movement Parameter in Second Language Acquisition". *Language Acquisition* 1.337-360.

White, L. 1991. "Adverb Placement in Second Language Acquisition: Some effects of positive and negative evidence in the classroom". *Second Language Research* 7.131-161.

White, L. 1994. "Input and Second Language Acquisition: Can UG be manipulated?" Paper at the Second Language Research Forum. Montreal, Canada. October.

White, L. Forthcoming a. "Universal Grammar and Second Language Acquisition: Current trends and new directions". To appear in *Handbook of Language Acquisition* ed. by W. Ritchie & T. Bhatia. New York: Academic Press.

White, L. Forthcoming b. "Input, Triggers and Second Language Acquisition: Can binding be taught?" To appear in *Second Language Acquisition Theory and Pedagogy* ed. by F. Eckman, D. Highland, P. Lee, J. Mileham, R. Rutkowski Weber. Hillsdale, N.J.: Lawrence Erlbaum Associates.

Learnability, pre-emption, domain-specificity, and the instructional value of "Master Mind"

David Birdsong
University of Texas at Austin

Introduction

Bill Rutherford is to be honored not only for his research in linguistics and second-language acquisition (SLA) theory, but as a teacher as well. One only has to look at the extensive, cutting-edge selections on a Rutherford graduate course syllabus to know that Rutherford is a challenging teacher and is up-to-date on current research. Typical of his focus on teaching is 1994 paper at the conference of the *American Association for Applied Linguistics*, "Teaching linguistics and the acquisition research literature" and his textbook in progress, *Workbook in the Structure of English*. Rutherford also operates at the intersection of SLA theory and teaching, emphasizing the role of formal grammar knowledge and language acquisition. Thus such articles as "Functions of grammar in a language teaching syllabus" and the co-edited volume (Rutherford & Sharwood Smith 1989) entitled *Grammar and Second Language Teaching*.

In the area of SLA theory proper, Rutherford has tackled issues ranging from consciousness-raising to Universal Grammar (see in fact Rutherford and Sharwood Smith's (1987) discussion of the possibility that access to Universal Grammar could be facilitated by consciousness-raising). More recent papers look at the issues of learnability and pre-emption (e.g., Rutherford 1989) and learnability and modularity (e.g., Rutherford forthcoming). In the present paper, I would like to address these current topics in SLA theory and, at the same time, pay tribute to Rutherford the teacher and scholar. My way of doing this is by offering to our field a contribution in the area of teaching SLA theory.

In my own teaching, I have found that the issues Rutherford raises in his writings on SLA theory can be brought into sharp focus through the medium of a board game called "Master Mind".[1] Two of the key issues exemplified by the game are domain-specificity (to what extent the declarative and procedural knowledge brought to the game is 'special'), and the pre-emption component of learnability (how broad hypotheses are narrowed, how narrow hypotheses are broadened, how incorrect hypotheses–especially those involving free variation–are rejected). All told, I have found that some two dozen linguistic and cognitive topics relative to SLA theory can be illustrated with "Master Mind".

In the next section of this paper, I outline the rules of "Master Mind", and walk through several moves of a typical game. I then concentrate on the instructional values of the game, as I describe the relationship of its features to topics in SLA theory, especially those discussed by Rutherford.

A "Master Mind" tutorial

The object of "Master Mind" is to identify the exact sequence of variously-colored pegs that one player (the 'encoder') has laid out in holes shielded from view. The opponent (the 'decoder') tries in successive approximations to match the hidden sequence on the basis of strategic guesswork and feedback from the encoder. The feedback is by nature only partially informative, making the task of the decoder a matter of repeated hypothesis-testing. The object is to 'break the code' in a minimum of moves or tests of hypotheses.

The game board prior to play looks something like this:

```
            (A)
    0    0    0    0    0
```

		(B)			(C)
O	O	O	O	O	O O O O O
O	O	O	O	O	O O O O O
O	O	O	O	O	O O O O O
O	O	O	O	O	O O O O O
O	O	O	O	O	O O O O O
O	O	O	O	O	O O O O O
O	O	O	O	O	O O O O O
O	O	O	O	O	O O O O O
O	O	O	O	O	O O O O O
O	O	O	O	O	O O O O O
O	O	O	O	O	O O O O O
O	O	O	O	O	O O O O O

The game board has three major fields, which I have labeled A, B, and C. The shadowed circles in field A represent the holes where the encoder puts down the colored Code Pegs that constitute the hidden code. The line beneath the field is meant to suggest the opaque shield that is used to keep the encoder's pegs from the view of the decoder. Field B is comprised of the dozen rows of holes where the decoder sets down strings of pegs which are successive approximations of the hidden code. Alongside each of these rows, in field C, are small holes for Feedback Pegs.

Here is an example of how the game proceeds. The encoder lays down a series of 5 Code Pegs (some versions of the game are limited to 4 Code Pegs) behind the opaque screen. The Code Pegs come in 8 colors: blue, green, red, black, white, brown, yellow, and orange (some versions have fewer colors). Let's say the sequence laid down by the encoder is the following:

(A)
BROWN   RED   GREEN   BROWN   BROWN

The decoder then sets down a series of Code Pegs, for example:

(Move 1)   RED   ORANGE   GREEN   BLUE   YELLOW   o o o o o

On this move, the decoder has correctly guessed that the encoder has a green peg in the middle hole. The decoder has also guessed correctly that one of the pegs in the hidden code is red; however, the decoder's red peg is not in the proper corresponding hole. Now that the decoder has put down his guess, the encoder supplies feedback with the tiny Feedback Pegs that are placed alongside the encoder's attempt. A black Feedback Peg indicates that a hidden Code Peg and its location were correctly guessed, while a white Feedback Peg informs the decoder that he has correctly guessed the color of a hidden Code Peg, but not its location. Crucially, the placement of the black and white Feedback Pegs is arbitrary; they are placed in any of the five holes alongside a move. Thus no information can be given as to *just which* guesses were correct. Thus, the board after one turn with feedback now looks like this:

(Move 1)   RED   ORANGE   GREEN   BLUE   YELLOW   b w o o o

Note again that the Feedback Pegs are not placed in corresponding holes; from the feedback the decoder knows only that one of his guesses is the right color in the right hole, and one guess is the right color and the wrong hole. At this point, the decoder has a choice among several strategies. He may, for example, wish to have information about other possible colors of Code Pegs, in which case he would put down an assortment of Code Pegs that differs maximally from those in the first move. On the other hand, the decoder might wish to have information the status of ORANGE, in which case he may put down 5 orange Code Pegs. Obviously, the feedback on this move would be no white pegs and no black pegs, since in the hidden code there are no orange Code Pegs. This would be useful information, as ORANGE could be eliminated from the repertoire of potential pegs in play, thus narrowing the range of choices. If the decoder wishes information about GREEN, he might lay down 5 green Code Pegs; the encoder's feedback would be a single black feedback peg. From this the decoder would infer, correctly, that the green Code Peg in the first move was the right color in the proper hole. Let us assume that this is the decoder's second move. The board would now look like this:

(Move 2) GREEN GREEN GREEN GREEN GREEN b o o o o

Now the decoder might want to try to resolve the question of which peg in Move 1 was the right color in the wrong hole. One way of doing this would be to rearrange all but the green peg from the first move. For example:

(Move 3) ORANGE BLUE GREEN YELLOW RED b w o o o

The feedback to this move would be a single black peg (confirming the right color-right hole status of GREEN) and a single white peg, since none of the four colors manipulated ended up in the proper corresponding hole.

After such a turn of events the decoder might consider altering his strategy. For example, he may choose arbitrarily the color blue and see what happens if he puts down all blue Code Pegs. In response to this move, the encoder would put down no Feedback Pegs, and blue could be eliminated from the possible choices. Imagine, however, that the decoder sets down all red pegs. This move, with feedback, would look like this:

(Move 4) RED RED RED RED RED b o o o o

The decoder now knows that RED is one of the other pegs in the hidden code. Imagine that on the next move the decoder wants to try to find out exactly in which hole RED resides; he knows from Move 1 that RED is not in the leftmost hole, and from Move 2 he knows that it is not in the middle hole. At the same time, he wants feedback on the other colors he has yet to try: brown, black, or white. Move 5 might then be the following:

(Move 5) BLACK BROWN GREEN RED WHITE b w w o o

Again, the black Feedback Peg merely re-confirms that GREEN is in the right hole. The two white Feedback Pegs give useful, but ambiguous information. One of them tells the decoder that RED is in the wrong hole; by inference he can now assume that RED must go in either the second hole or the last hole. The other white Feedback Peg tells the decoder that one of the pegs BLACK, BROWN, and WHITE is the correct color, but is in the wrong hole. Recall from previous plays that, of the 5 colors that were tested (red, green, blue, yellow, orange, green), only two colors were confirmed; hence the strategy of getting feedback on the three complementary colors in the repertoire (black, brown, white). Surprisingly, the feedback given on this turn informs that only one of these three colors is represented in the code. This leads to the inference of a significant feature of the hidden code on this turn: There are three Code Pegs of the same color.

THE INSTRUCTIONAL VALUE OF "MASTER MIND"

At this juncture a skilled player would recognize that the game is almost over: At most a couple of turns would be required to determine which of the colors brown, black, or white is represented trebly in the code; in the process, the decoder could manipulate the RED peg to see whether it belongs in the second hole or in the last hole. The endgame might go as follows:

(Move 6) WHITE   WHITE   GREEN   WHITE   RED   b w o o

The feedback confirms that GREEN is the right color, right hole, while RED is the right color, wrong hole. WHITE is eliminated from the repertoire of possible Color Pegs.

(Move 7) BLACK   RED   GREEN   BLACK   BLACK   b b o o o

The two black Feedback Pegs inform that GREEN and RED are the right colors in the right holes. BLACK is eliminated from the repertoire of possible Code Pegs. The remaining holes must all be filled with brown Code Pegs.

(Move 8) BROWN   RED   GREEN   BROWN   BROWN   b b b b b

The five black Feedback Pegs signal the end of the game: All colors have been correctly identified and are in the correct holes. The decoder removes the shield that has been concealing his code. Scoring is based on the number of moves; the fewer the better. This turn took eight moves to resolve (about average).

Note that every move and its accompanying feedback remain on the board throughout the game, thus affording the decoder full access to previous attempts and feedback. Note too that the order of progress of the moves is from the decoder's end toward the hidden code; thus, the board looks like this at the end of the game.

	BROWN	RED	GREEN	BROWN	BROWN	
(Move 9, etc.)						
(Move 8)	BROWN	RED	GREEN	BROWN	BROWN	b b b b b
(Move 7)	BLACK	RED	GREEN	BLACK	BLACK	b b o o o
(Move 6)	WHITE	WHITE	GREEN	WHITE	RED	b w o o o
(Move 5)	BLACK	BROWN	GREEN	RED	WHITE	b w w o o
(Move 4)	RED	RED	RED	RED	RED	b o o o o
(Move 3)	ORANGE	BLUE	GREEN	YELLOW	RED	b w o o o
(Move 2)	GREEN	GREEN	GREEN	GREEN	GREEN	b o o o o
(Move 1)	RED	ORANGE	GREEN	BLUE	YELLOW	b w o o o

"Master Mind" and SLA theory

As is often the case when one is teaching abstract content, the trick is to make the matter relevant and immediate. The abstract must somehow be rendered concrete.

"Master Mind" is a superlative vehicle for this purpose. Though not designed as an analogue to second language (L2) acquisition, "Master Mind" nevertheless represents a heuristic for grasping procedural and epistemological variables discussed by Rutherford and other SLA theorists.

Learnability Theory

As a simple illustration of the utility of "Master Mind", consider the Subset Principle. A keystone premise of native-language (L1) learnability (see, for example, the papers in MacWhinney 1987) is that children initially posit a narrow grammar–a subset of the adult grammar–and progressively broaden it to conform to the adult grammar. Rutherford (forthcoming and elsewhere), following studies such as White (1989), has asked whether SLA similarly observes the Subset Principle, or whether, instead, SLA proceeds by progressive narrowing of an overly-inclusive 'superset' grammar. Indeed, given positive evidence only, the issue is whether grammars are learnable at all if the direction of assimilation of the learner grammar to the target grammar is from broad to narrow. In the game of "Master Mind", the hidden code can be compared to a licit string in the L2 grammar.[2] The decoder's hypotheses about the form of that string are constantly changing in response to feedback and as a function of the decoder's imagination. Players of the game uniformly report that sometimes they entertain only a narrow set of possibilities, while at other times the range of possibilities seems endless. (Note that, as a macro-level feature of the game, play proceeds by narrowing the number of possible strings to conform ultimately to the unique string laid out by the encoder.)

At this point, several other issues start coming into focus. What kind of feedback is required to successfully narrow a superset grammar? "Master Mind" gives both positive and negative feedback; are both necessary? The feedback given in "Master Mind" is incomplete, indirect; in what ways does this resemble feedback given in language learning? How well do players of "Master Mind"–and learners of L2–utilize negative evidence? What are the typical attributes of the decoder's initial hypotheses about the form of the grammar? Are they in some sense 'marked'?

Let us start with the markedness question. Novice players with only a game or two under their belts report an 'Aha' experience with respect to markedness. Almost all note an initial assumption that the hidden code will be a mixture of five colors. Repetition of colors seems as unnatural as double-object passives and as implausible as center-embedding. Students even attest to an intuition for relative markedness (see, e.g., Eckman 1985): The more repeated colors, the more marked. In addition, students note a strong tendency to shy away from certain colors (usually brown, black, and white) in their initial hypotheses (see Move 1, above). A string containing one of these colors is considered marked. The most marked string of all is one that is comprised of multiple pegs of an unlikely color, such as brown. So strong is the sense of markedness that players employing impeccable inductive logic will nonetheless balk at an inference such as that exemplified in Move 5, above, that is, the accurate conclusion that there are three pegs of the same color in the hidden code. Their disbelief often translates into persevering with a misguided hypothesis, thus delaying the resolution of the game. (On perseverant behavior based on assumptions of 'reasonableness' see Birdsong 1989, Ch. 5). Once it is revealed that there are indeed three pegs of one color, and that the color is brown, decoders are often openly resentful that such an unnatural sequence was encoded. At this point they may be reminded of the ample literature on intuitions for markedness, as well as the difficulties in learning marked structures (see, e.g., Kellerman 1983; Mazurkewich & White 1984). The lesson they learn is a vivid one indeed.

Pre-emption

At the heart of the "Master Mind" game is the nature of feedback, and the decoder's use of it. Just as Rutherford draws the field's attention to the issue of pre-emption (Rutherford 1989; forthcoming), the game's most salient procedural feature is pre-emption of faulty hypotheses. And, just as in language acquisition (L1 and L2), the feedback in "Master Mind" is not always optimally informative, and it is not always used felicitously. Despite these hindrances, the puzzle can be solved in a finite number of moves. Students report grappling intellectually with the realization that pre-emption of hypotheses takes place even though the feedback is apparently inadequate and even though they make errors in reasoning based on this limited feedback. They then move on to consider the acquisition of a given feature of the L1 or L2: Does it happen in a linear and algorithmic fashion or are there discontinuities, false starts and setbacks, U-shaped behaviors?

Until the final, winning move, the decoder is faced with several varieties of uncertainty. For example, on Move 5 it is not known whether RED occupies the second hole or the last hole. Note that this uncertainty is to be distinguished from free variation: It is not a question of RED occupying either hole, but uniquely one or the other. In L2 acquisition, learners often persevere with inappropriate free-variation type hypotheses (Birdsong 1989; Rutherford 1989; Schachter 1986); that is, a faulty assumption of multiple-form-to-single-meaning correspondences. In contrast, players of "Master Mind" learn quickly that free-variation hypotheses cannot be entertained (cf. the Uniqueness Principle and its avatars in L1 acquisition); rather, they must act aggressively to determine a unique correspondence of peg color-to-hole. This apparent divergence of SLA and "Master Mind" is itself instructive. In addition, students typically make an association with negative evidence, which is required for disconfirmation of misguided hypotheses of free variation: What is the role of negative evidence in "Master Mind"?

Players of "Master Mind" observe that negative evidence is abundant, that it comes in several forms, and that it is necessary for progress toward solving the puzzle. On any given move, numerous parallels and contrasts with SLA and L1 acquisition can be made. For example, a white Feedback Peg gives both positive and negative evidence (right color, wrong hole), but both types of evidence are indeterminate, and expertise is required in order to make them useful (see Birdsong 1989). Black Feedback Pegs are, at first blush, positive evidence. However, since they provide no information about which Code Peg is the correct color in the proper hole, they constitute probabilistic evidence that is at once positive and negative (a single black Feedback Peg indicates that there is a 20% probability that a correctly colored peg is in the right hole, and an 80% probability that it is in the wrong hole). Finally, the absence of Feedback Pegs, white or black, constitutes negative evidence. Though it is 'implicit' negative evidence (no Feedback Pegs are present, but relevant negative evidence is nevertheless supplied), the absence of Feedback Pegs is extremely useful feedback, as it allows the decoder to pre-empt all the hypotheses tested on that move.

Pre-emption of incorrect hypotheses presents a certain paradox for players of "Master Mind". It is the essential process in solving the puzzle, but players (especially novices) often respond with disappointment when negative evidence is given. In particular, the absence of Feedback Pegs on a given move is met with groans of frustration, since what players want is evidence that they are on the right track, not on the wrong track. Such a confirmatory bias is amply documented in the general problem solving literature (e.g., Wason 1968; see Long 1983, for discussion in the SLA context). Novice players of "Master Mind" often fail to recognize the informational value of negative evidence (see discussion of this general tendency in Whitfield 1951). Thus, from the perspective of expertise, one notes that advanced players of "Master Mind"–rather like advanced L2 learners–welcome negative evidence and put it to use, while beginners often ignore or deny it, and instead persevere with misguided hypotheses.

Domain-specificity

It is commonly argued that L1 acquisition is 'special': It involves an epistemological component specific to language (knowledge of UG) and a procedural component or learning principles that are specially suited to language acquisition. There is considerably less agreement on the 'specialness' of SLA. Indeed, in one way or another much of the debate in SLA theory for the past decade has focused on to what degree SLA resembles the special case of L1 learning. Rutherford (forthcoming) is an up-to-date summary of the relevant issues.

Obviously, playing "Master Mind" will not in itself contribute to the resolution of the debate. Still, it is useful for highlighting the issues. Above I noted players' strong intuitions for the markedness of certain colors and the markedness of repeated colors. One of the first questions that arises from this observation is whether our sense of markedness develops with experience, or is innate. From this point of departure other provocative questions arise. Is players' knowledge of color markedness and repeated symbols markedness specific to the domains of colors and symbols, or is it derivative from a generalized sense of markedness (which would presumably be applicable, *mutatis mutandis*, not only to contexts such as colors and repeated symbols, but to phonology, syntax, lexis, etc. as well)? Given that players have intuitions for peripheral colors and the unnaturalness of repeated colors, is it reasonable to believe that they are invoked only in the context of "Master Mind"?

Similar heuristic exercises may be carried out for questions of domain-specific learnability. What is the interplay of deductive and inductive knowledge? If one's starting point is a subset of the end point, does such conservatism apply only in the domain of (first) language learning? When learnability is a matter of induction, does it proceed by narrowing hypotheses, broadening them, or by a combination of the two? In what domains is learning (or puzzle solving) typified by moving from broad to narrow hypotheses?

Solving for the "Master Mind" code, like language learning, takes place on the basis of impoverished evidence. In my experience, students are eager to compare and contrast the two 'logical problems', and to reflect on the possibility that there are other domains where knowledge seems to exceed input. They then ponder the means by which epistemological gaps are bridged in each case. Discussion moves to questions of contexts in which deductive knowledge is required, and to qualitative differences between deductive and inductive knowledge (e.g., whether, compared to deductive knowledge, the knowledge given by induction is inferior, incomplete, unreliable, etc.).

Conclusion

With respect to topics in learnability, pre-emption, and domain-specificity, the preceding illustrations of "Master Mind"'s instructional utility are merely a beginning. Imagine, for example, the Pandora's Box of parallels and contrasts that is opened when the encoder leaves one or more holes unfilled! Also, there are many more areas of SLA theory that can be addressed through "Master Mind". In examining the possibility that SLA is mediated by general problem solving, for example, one can point to set effects, incubation effects, transfer of training, trainability of strategies, strategy shifts, cognitive flexibility, development of expertise and automaticity, heuristics and biases, finite information processing capacity, and so on.

As contributions to SLA theory and teaching go, my offering of the "Master Mind" game is trivial compared to what Bill Rutherford has brought to our field. But, since there is a significant coincidence of Bill's interests and what the game illustrates, I hope the gesture will at least be viewed as fitting–a meeting of Master Minds.

Notes

1. "Master Mind" is registered under the company labels Invicta (UK) and Pressman (US). In the following description, the terms I use for the game pieces, players, and procedures do not always coincide with those used in the game's instructional literature; this is done merely to make the game easier to understand. For the same reason, I do not replicate exactly the game board.

2. Note that the hidden code may also be compared to an abstract rule in grammar. And, since on a given turn it is the *only* rule in the grammar, it could be considered the grammar itself.

References

Birdsong, D. 1989. *Metalinguistic Performance and Interlinguistic Competence*. Berlin and New York: Springer-Verlag.
Birdsong, D. 1994. "Decision Making in SLA". *Studies in Second Language Acquisition* 16.169-182.
Eckman, F. 1985. "Some Theoretical and Pedagogical Implications of the Markedness Differential Hypothesis". *Studies in Second Language Acquisition* 7.289-307.
Kellerman, E. 1985. "If at First You Do Succeed ..." *Input in Second Language Acquisition* ed. by S. Gass & C. Madden, 345-353) Rowley, MA: Newbury House.
Long, M. H. 1983. "Does Second Language Instruction Make a Difference? A review of research". *TESOL Quarterly* 17.359-382.
MacWhinney, B., ed. 1987. *Mechanisms of Language Acquisition*. Hillsdale, NJ: Lawrence Erlbaum.
Mazurkewich, I. & L. White. 1984. "The Acquisition of the Dative Alternation: Unlearning overgeneralizations". *Cognition* 16.261-283.
Rutherford, W. 1986. "Grammatical Theory and L2 Acquisition: A brief overview". *Second Language Research* 2.1-15.

Rutherford, W. 1989. "Preemption and the Learning of L2 Grammars". *Studies in Second Language Acquisition* 11.441-457.
Rutherford, W. Forthcoming. "SLA: Universal Grammar and learnability". To appear in *Implicit and Explicit Learning of Languages* ed. by N. Ellis. New York: Academic Press.
Rutherford, W. E., & M. Sharwood Smith. 1987. "Consciousness-Raising and Universal Grammar". *Applied Linguistics* 6.274-282.
Rutherford, W. E. & M. Sharwood Smith, eds. 1989. *Grammar and Second Language Teaching: A book of readings*. New York: Newbury House.
Schachter, J. 1986. "Three Approaches to the Study of Input". *Language Learning* 36.211-225.
Wason, P. 1968. "'On the Failure to Eliminate Hypotheses...'–A Second Look". *Thinking and Reasoning* ed. by P. Wason & J. N. Johnson-Laird, 165-174. London: Penguin.
White, L. 1989. "The Adjacency Condition on Case Assignment: Do learners observe the subset principle?" *Linguistic Perspectives on Second Language Acquisition* ed. by S. Gass & J. Schachter, 134-158. Cambridge: Cambridge University Press.
Whitfield, J. W. 1951. "An Experiment in Problem Solving". *Quarterly Journal of Experimental Psychology* 3.184-197.

Why we need grammar
Confessions of a cognitive generalist

Ellen Bialystok
York University

After the great behaviorist machine had bulldozed its way through an unimaginably (and unimaginatively) large number of organismic responses, relegating them all to the heap of S-R explanation, it turned its insatiable appetite towards a peculiarly species-specific behavior: language. This, too, was to be churned through the machinery that identified free operants, discovered effective reinforcers and felicitous schedules, and shaped familiar behaviors. Indeed, the project was carried out (without a single experiment ever being conducted) and duly reported in the now infamous book by B.F. Skinner (1957) titled *Verbal Behavior*. But he didn't quite get away with it. A good portion of the credit usually (and correctly) goes to Chomsky (1959) for his apparently single-handed feat of slaying the proverbial dragon by a single blow of his whistle, but one would like to believe that anyone who had spent even five minutes trying to understand how children learned language would have seen the utter folly in Skinner's enterprise, at least in this matter.

It is the nature of generalist explanations to overstep the conservative boundaries laid down by generations of polite academics who have divided up knowledge into sacred territories and more or less refrained from crossing borders. Indeed, this is what makes them potentially powerful and exciting alternatives to the more piecemeal, or inbred solutions. If such a theory could be found, the reward would be enormous. In spite of unmoving scepticism from their colleagues, for example, there is a group of physicists who are steadfast in their pursuit of the great "unified theory", the one that will explain all natural forces of the universe in terms of a few powerful generalities. If they succeed, the "new physics" will be far different from our traditional conceptions.

There is, at the same time, a prevailing risk, comprised of two related steps, that is endemic to generalist explanations. The first part of the problem is that a theory that is intended to cover a widely diverse range of phenomena must necessarily be pitched at a level of generality so high that it ultimately fails to make any interesting claims. The theory ends up being like Woody Allen's précis of *War and Peace*: "Its about Russia". There is no doubt that continual extrapolation from diverse data sets can distill a few commonly essential points, but these do not necessarily contribute productively to our understanding of basic mechanism or process. Indeed, the spectacular explosion (or, more strictly, implosion) of behaviorism came at a time when the theory was no longer leading to new insights, but was lost in the rarefied atmosphere of its general laws.

The second, and related, part is that a generalist does not pay sufficient attention to the accumulated wisdom of the specialists. As one steps higher into the realm of generalities, one ignores the minutia on the ground. Individual disciplines operate under a set of assumptions and tenets that are unique to that domain, and the minuscule step-by-step progress that is the true nature of scientific discovery proceeds by systematically working through the interpretations and implications of these assumptions. Much of these domain-specific foundations are contained in the terminology, or more pejoratively, the jargon, used by the specialists. These definitions, arcane as they may seem, need to be respected if the concepts are lifted from the specific field and placed on general view. Skinner did not do this when he put language acquisition on the table, and the error was fatal.

Some of these tensions are at work in the field of second language (L2) acquisition. In this case, the problem domain itself is complex because it is a hybrid–a convergence of a number of disciplines onto a common problem. In addition to the conflicts between generalist and specialist explanations, there is the competition among disciplines themselves for the territory. The result is that the field is populated by groups bearing hyphenated allegiances: sociolinguists, applied linguists, psycholinguists, educational linguists, and so on. Although it is clear that each relies in its own way on the parent field of linguistics, it is not at all clear, and certainly not consistent, what role linguistics plays in each research program.

In the heady early days of research into L2 acquisition, there was a need to incorporate the wisdom and insight of each contributing field. There was little question of constructing a generalist explanation because there were not even enough pieces to clearly define the problem in need of solution. These pieces had to be supplied from researchers working independently, whose theories and methods imported the perspectives from their diverse home disciplines. From psycholinguistics, we needed to know how linguistic information was perceived and processed; from developmental psychology we needed to know how children learned their native language (NL); from language pedagogy we needed to know how language could be taught as curriculum; from sociolinguistics we needed to know how language was used in interaction and in context. Much attention was paid to applied linguistics, where researchers engaged in paradigmatic studies of the sort, *How do speakers of X learn the Y of Z?*, where X is a native language, Y is some structure, and Z is a second language. These perspectives provided exciting and critical foundations upon which the study of L2 acquisition came to be built. The only voices that were not audible through this time were the linguists. The field has evolved immensely since that time, and researchers have embarked on the more lofty mission of speaking across disciplines to the soul of the issue (for related discussion, see Beretta 1991). It is these more broadly-based theories, ones that take account of knowledge from across sources, that hold the promise for propelling the next great leap in our understanding of L2 acquisition. And yet, the historical development of the field has placed it firmly in the grip of the two-sided risk entailed by the search for general theories: overly-broad generalizations, and insufficient attention to the concepts and distinctions from a central field, namely, linguistics. The first, overgeneralization, produces models that end up not saying anything. The second, linguistic insensitivity, produces incorrect interpretations of research findings.

There is a statistical dimension to these two risks. Research is interpreted by deciding if an empirical outcome reflects a true event or is an aberration. In the latter case, the null hypothesis, which is a statement that nothing special has happened to produce the data, must be adopted. The researcher makes the decision about whether to accept or reject the null hypothesis by considering a number of information sources, most notably the probability result of statistical analysis, or p value. Although this probability shifts gradually through a complete range of possible values, once a decision is made regarding the veracity of a research outcome, that decision is categorical. In other words, a research outcome based on a probability value of .01 is not more true than one based on an outcome of .05, or, for that matter, .20 if the researcher chooses to interpret that result as valid. This process leads to a probabilistic risk of error. If the researcher decides that the experimental result is a true description of an event and rejects the null hypothesis, but in fact, peering into the real world would reveal that the researcher is wrong, then the conclusion constitutes a Type I error. This is the mistake of believing there is an effect when none exists. If, on the other hand, an overly-conservative researcher refrains from accepting the interpretation of an effect and instead accepts the null hypothesis, but the real state of affairs is that the effect is true, then the error is Type II. This is the mistake of not recognizing that an effect actually exists.

The probability of these errors is decreased as the researcher incorporates more information into the decision about accepting or rejecting the null hypothesis. In studies of L2 acquisition, one of these critical sources is detailed information about the language under investigation. Failing to include sufficient linguistic constraints can lead to an incorrect judgment about the null hypothesis. For example, it may be that a study shows an empirical effect, but it holds for only the type of linguistic structure included in the experiment. In this case, the researcher would believe there is an general effect when there is not (i.e., linguistic insensitivity→Type I error). Conversely, failing to include sufficient linguistic constraints may cause an investigator to miss an effect that would be true if the linguistic data were analyzed more precisely (i.e., overgeneralization→Type II error). By grouping together linguistic samples that, for linguistic reasons, should be kept apart, a researcher may not see an important pattern.

A similar problem was noted in psycholinguistic research more than two decades ago. Clark (1973) pointed out that in psycholinguistic studies of language processing, researchers virtually never considered the nature of the language used in the research as a statistical factor. Rather, they assumed that any bit of language was equally representative of language as a whole, and that effects could be generalized from any sample of language (the words used in an experiment, the structures examined on a language task, the concepts explored or manipulated). He introduced a means of analyzing the generalizability of results on the basis of the language used in a psycholinguistic experiment. With his more stringent test, many well-accepted conclusions of psycholinguistic research fell to the ruins of Type I error, unreplicated and now invalid.

An example from L2 acquisition in which an incomplete linguistic analysis may have led to a Type I error is illustrated in a study by Johnson and Newport (1989). They were investigating the question of whether or not there is a maturational decline in the ability to learn a second language, and they based their evidence on the English proficiency of Chinese- and Korean-speaking learners of English. Their results are widely accepted as confirming their claims regarding both the existence and nature of such a maturational limitation. Closer examination of their data, however, shows that the evidence does not simply and directly support their conclusion. The required effect is not equally conveyed by all syntactic features and is examined in only two specific NL and L2 language pairs. The age-related effects were most apparent for structures in which the Nl and L2 were maximally different. This limitation is more clear in the replication by Johnson (1992) using a written version of the task; only 3 of the 12 structures tested indicated age effects, and all three are points of strong linguistic contrast. Ignoring linguistic structure, it appears as though there is a critical period at around 7 years old. However, considering the interaction between age and linguistic structure (which is reported, but not analyzed) leads to an entirely different conclusion (Bialystok 1994; Bialystok & Hakuta 1994). By not paying attention to important linguistic structures in a cross-linguistic comparison, researchers may believe that a general effect has been found when the effect may be restricted to certain linguistic forms and therefore take a different kind of explanation.

It is more difficult to find examples in which a research hypothesis has been stated too generally and therefore missed finding a hidden effect, that is, a Type II error. The reason is simple and pragmatic: Studies which fail to support the experimental hypothesis rarely get published. Nonetheless, the risk of missing important effects because of inadequate attention to linguistic structure is an equally serious hazard for a general theory and undoubtedly occurs regularly. A version of this problem was pointed out long ago by Schachter (1974) in her critique of error analysis. She showed that when this analysis was applied only after the data had been obtained from L2 learners (i.e., looking for mistakes rather than predicting errors), important 'hot spots' went unnoticed. She was able to show that Chinese and Japanese students had given the illusion of mastering English relative clauses because they systematically avoided using them. Thus an analysis of the data would indicate no effect (compared to native speakers) in an examination of errors. She demonstrated, however, how a more detailed error analysis would have easily predicted difficulty. That difficulty showed up as frequencies. She advised researchers that linguistic analysis needed to be done, and furthermore, needed to be done prior to any data collection.

An approach to studying L2 acquisition that remains faithful to the wisdom of linguistic analysis is needed to discover the underlying generalities without committing the sin of (over-)generalization. One example of an issue in L2 acquisition that has so far failed to reveal a consensus opinion, but that might benefit from more detailed linguistic analysis, is the problem of the cognitive representation of two languages. How do bilingual children build the mental representations for two languages that they are learning? Are these representations constructed individually for each language (see Genesee 1989) or are they installed into a common structure (see Cook 1992)? Although both positions have been defended, the solution may more properly be found by considering individual linguistic categories (Bialystok 1994). Language, that is, may require a more complex representation, only some of which is shared across languages. If so, it would be important to describe that representation because it has consequences for many problems in language learning, language representation, and language processing. That is, the representation is the basis of a general description of language and its role in cognition. The discovery of that representation, however, requires a detailed examination of the linguistic structure in individual research studies. Ironically, our access to the general depends on our reliance on the specific.

The importance of this kind of theorizing was seen early by Rutherford (1984). Since then, L2 acquisition research has been moving in exactly this direction through the contributions of such researchers as Flynn (e.g., Flynn and O'Neil 1988) and White (1989). These are important developments, but there is another side to the problem as well. As we hyphenated linguists become more familiar with and careful about the basic concepts studied by linguists, the concepts that have been borrowed from other fields must similarly be scrutinized for their accuracy. Territory works both ways. Terms such as mental representation, attention, processing, consciousness and strategy are but a few of the ideas linguists adopt with little regard for their conceptual and empirical origins. In this regard, the contribution of Sharwood Smith (1994) is particularly important, as he has probed some of the central concepts in L2 acquisition by examining their origins and use in cognitive science. A truly interdisciplinary field needs to find a way to use all its resources, including the conceptual ones, accurately and productively.

There is an important lesson in all of this for those who investigate linguistic, or language-related processing. What we have to consider is that the special structure of language is not a trivial or superficial task variable but in fact a profound factor that determines the nature of cognitive processing. Learning language is never exactly like learning everything else, no matter how much general cognitive apparatus is shared. Communicating through language is never exactly the same as communicating non-verbally, no matter how much semantic content can be conveyed. Reading written language is never exactly the same as recognizing other visual patterns, no matter how much pattern detection is at the base of it. And understanding spoken language is probably unlike every other cognitive activity humans engage in. Unless we acknowledge these as special skills, distinguished at least as much by their uniqueness as by their generality, we cannot hope to understand how any of these processes develop and function in humans. Our spirit inclines us towards general theories, ones that make use of the theoretical bits and pieces that are already used for other problems, sometimes in other domains. Parsimony, efficiency, and Occam all preach the virtues of simplicity. But we need to attend to the limitations and conditions of general theories. We need to avoid the scenario, *pace* Skinner, in which special properties of a domain are overlooked as the domain is unceremoniously squeezed into a broad pattern. It is probably syntax that most significantly makes language unlike other domains, even other communicative ones. My prediction is that when a compelling theory of L2 acquisition is finally written, it will take as its assumption a highly segmented and dissected view of language that grows out of its syntax. Our debt is to the linguists who remind us of that structure and struggle to describe it.

References

Beretta, A. 1991. "Theory Constructions in SLA: Complementarity and opposition". *Studies in Second Language Acquisition* 13.493-511.

Bialystok, E. 1994. "Representation and Ways of Knowing: Three issues in second language acquisition", *Implicit and Explicit Factors in Second Language Learning: Interdisciplinary perspectives* ed. by N. Ellis, 549-569. London: Academic Press.

Bialystok, E. & K. Hakuta. 1994. *In Other Words: The science and psychology of second language acquisition*. New York: Basic Books.

Chomsky, N. 1959. "Review of B.F. Skinner's *Verbal Behavior*". *Language* 35. 26-129.
Clark, H. H. 1973. "The Language-as-Fixed-Effect Fallacy: A critique of language statistics in psychological research". *Journal of Verbal Learning and Verbal Behavior* 12.335-359.
Cook, V. 1992. "Evidence for Multi-Competence". *Language Learning* 42.557-591.
Flynn, S. & W. O'Neil, eds. 1988. *Linguistic Theory in Second Language Acquisition*. Dordrecht: Kluwer.
Genesee, F. 1989. "Early Bilingual Development: One language or two?" *Journal of Child Language* 16.161-179.
Johnson, J. S. 1992. "Critical Period Effects in Second Language Acquisition: The effects of written versus auditory materials on the assessment of grammatical competence. *Language Learning* 42.217-248.
Johnson, J. S. & E. L. Newport. 1989. "Critical Periods Effects in Second Language Learning: The influence of maturational state on the acquisition of English as a second language". *Cognitive Psychology* 21.60-99.
Rutherford, W. E., ed. 1984. *Language Universals and Second Language Acquisition*. Amsterdam: John Benjamins.
Schachter, J. 1974. "An Error in Error Analysis". *Language Learning* 24. 205-214.
Sharwood Smith, M. 1994. *Second Language Learning: Theoretical foundations*. London: Longmans.
Skinner, B. F. 1957. *Verbal Behavior*. New York: Appleton-Century-Crofts.
White, L. 1989. *Universal Grammar and Second Language Acquisition*. Amsterdam: John Benjamins.

Chasing after linguistic theory
How minimal should we be?

Lydia White
McGill University

Second language (L2) acquisition researchers working within the framework of current linguistic theory accept that one cannot begin to arrive at a theory of language acquisition without having a theory of what it is that is acquired (Gregg 1989; Schwartz 1986; White 1989). Proposals within current linguistic theory as to the nature of grammar are adopted and tested, in an attempt to ascertain the nature of interlanguage competence, and to verify whether interlanguages are natural languages, subject to the constraints imposed by Universal Grammar (UG).

Close connections between linguistic theory and L2 acquisition research have not always been seen to be necessary. Generative grammar in the 1960s and 1970s placed great emphasis on transformational rules rather than linguistic principles and concentrated on language-specific issues more than universal ones. Although linguistic theory did have some influence on L2 acquisition research at the time, there was comparatively little general recognition in the field of the usefulness of or need for a close relationship between the linguistic theory and theories of L2 acquisition (for overview, see Lightbown and White 1987). Over the last ten years, however, there has been a fruitful interaction between these areas, as well as a recognition of the importance of this interaction even by those who do not accept the tenets of current generative grammar. Some researchers have argued that the interaction should by a two-way one; not only should linguistic theory inform L2 acquisition theory, but L2 data should be used to test linguistic theory (Gass 1992; Rutherford 1993).

The enriched relationship between linguistic theory and L2 acquisition research can largely be attributed to a shift that took place within generative grammar in the late 1970s and early 1980s, namely the introduction of the Principles and Parameters framework (Chomsky 1981a, 1981b). This framework accommodated variation between languages by introducing the concept of parameters; in addition, proposals for universal principles became much more highly developed than they were in earlier versions of generative grammar. The emphasis on parameters allowed researchers to look at L2 issues where variation between languages is crucial, such as language transfer, as well as investigating whether or not parameters can be (re)set in L2 acquisition (e.g., Flynn 1987; White 1985). As far as principles are concerned, much research in the last ten years has focussed on the general question of whether UG remains available in non-primary acquistion, and whether interlanguages are natural languages, constrained by principles of UG (e.g., Bley-Vroman 1990; Schachter 1989; White 1988).

However, these close ties between linguistic theory and L2 acquisition theory are not without problems for the L2 researcher. Linguistic theory is not static; rather, it is constantly being developed and revised, often in fairly major ways. Linguistic theory is currently going through another shift, this time towards what has become known as the 'Minimalist' program (Chomsky 1991, 1993, 1994). On the face of it, the change to Minimalism seems quite radical: D-structure and S-structure have been dropped from the model, leaving only logical form (LF) and phonetic form (PF); the role and functioning of parameters have been recast, variation now being associated almost exclusively with functional elements and the lexicon; 'economy' principles have been introduced. In related developments proposed by Kayne (1994), it is argued that all languages share the same underlying word order, namely SVO, and that no rightward movement is possible.

Such developments raise problems for the L2 researcher; changes in the theory affect our assumptions about the nature of interlanguage, as well as the predictions that one might want to make and test for L2 acquisition. For example, in the Minimalist approach, the assumption is that constraints operate at the level of LF, where they are universal and common to all languages; this has implications for L2 acquisition research which tried to look at the operation of principles by comparing languages with and without operation of constraints assumed to apply at S-structure (e.g., Schachter 1989). This change in the theory means that it will be hard or impossible to find cases where languages differ as to operation of principles of UG; consequently, it will be harder to rule out the L1 as the only source of knowledge of UG principles in L2 acquisition. Similarly, the move to confine variation to properties of functional categories rather than to old-style parameters will require us to question certain concepts which have been taken for granted. For example, the status of the null subject parameter or parameterized bounding nodes for Subjacency is unclear in the new framework. Both of these parameters have been investigated in L2 acquisition, especially with a view to determining whether L1 parameter settings are adopted by L2 learners and whether they can be reset to L2 values (e.g., White 1985, 1988). Word order parameters in L2 acquisition have been investigated by Flynn (e.g., 1987); however, if all languages are essentially SVO, the role of parameters in shaping word order has to be rethought. Such issues must now be approached in the context of parameters relating to functional categories (e.g., Eubank 1992; White 1992).

Some L2 researchers dismiss research that looks at UG in L2 acquisition precisely because linguistic theory is constantly changing. However, this is not a reasonable reaction. Healthy theories are not static; changes in a theory are often a sign of growth and development. While it is true that it can be difficult to keep up with changes, one should not reject a framework just because it is undergoing rapid development. There are many advantages to working within a framework that is not static; in particular, new developments in linguistic theory stimulate productive research in other areas and allow us to extend our understanding of what might be going on in L2 acquisition. Furthermore, although the theory changes, the data or phenomena to be accounted for often remain the same; there is, on the whole, agreement about what properties of language are likely to be universal and what sentence types are ungrammatical, even though the theories that account for their universality or ungrammaticality vary. Thus, one does not necessarily have to abandon one's L2 research every time there is a change in linguistic theory.

On the other hand, there is a need to keep up with changes in the theory as much as possible, since these changes provide new avenues of exploration for L2 acquisition theory. For example, the Minimalist Program argues that grammars are driven by principles of economy; this raises the question of whether L2 grammars are also 'economical'. Furthermore, a particular theory makes predictions and offers explanations which will not necessarily fall out from some earlier theory, so that there will be a need to adjust one's hypotheses and the means to test these hypotheses.

Shifts and developments in theories raise the practical problem of what to do with data which has been gathered to test the predictions of some theory which has been superseded by a more recent one. A major problem here is that the tests researchers devise to test one theory may fail to include material which is crucial to test the new or revised theory. Thus, one has to be cautious about applying new theories to old data, as there will often only be a partial fit. On the other hand, if one has gathered data to test some theory, and has found that the theory cannot account for the data or that the data do not support the theory, it may be that new theoretical developments will allow for a reinterpretation of the data, as well as offering further hypotheses for investigation.

An example may serve to illustrate the problems and advantages of keeping up with changes in theory.[1] A number of researchers have looked at the L2 acquisition of reflexive binding, assuming the Governing Category Parameter of Wexler & Manzini (1987). As is well known, there are cross-linguistic differences in the behavior of reflexive pronouns. Languages differ as to whether they require a reflexive to have an antecedent which is close (or 'local' in a technically defined sense) or whether they allow long-distance ('nonlocal') binding of reflexives. In languages like English, only local binding is permitted, whereas in languages like Japanese, the antecedent of a reflexive can be local or nonlocal. In languages like Russian, a local antecedent is required in finite clauses, but nonlocal is permitted in nonfinite clauses. Thus, considering sentences like those in (1), and looking at whether *Jane* can serve as antecedent of the reflexive, in English binding is only possible in (1a). In Russian, binding is also permitted in (1b) but not in (1c). In Japanese, binding is permitted in all cases.

(1) a. Jane$_i$ introduced herself$_i$ (English, Russian, Japanese)
    b. Jane$_i$ told Susan to introduce herself$_i$ (*English, Russian, Japanese)
    c. Jane$_i$ said that Susan introduced herself$_i$ (*English, *Russian, Japanese)

Wexler and Manzini (1987) account for these differences in terms of a five-valued Governing Category Parameter (GCP), which specifies the locality domains within which anaphors, such as reflexives, must be bound. An independent parameter, the Proper Antecedent Parameter (PAP), determines whether reflexives are bound only by subjects or by subjects and non-subjects. A number of studies have investigated what values of the GCP are adopted by L2 learners (Finer 1991; Finer and Broselow 1986; Hirakawa 1990; Thomas 1991). Results suggest that some L2 learners adopt parameter values that do not hold in either the L1 or L2. For example, Finer and Broselow (1986), Finer (1991) and Hirakawa (1990) report that Japanese and Korean learners of English are significantly more likely to allow long-distance binding in sentences like (1b) than in sentences like (1c). The finite/nonfinite distinction does not distinguish binding possibilities in the L1 or the L2; in fact, it appears that these learners may be adopting the Russian value of the GCP.

Assuming that L2 acquisition involves an interaction of UG, the existing grammar and the input, it would be understandable for learners to adopt L1 settings, based on their L1 grammar, or to adopt L2 values, based on the L2 input interacting with UG. However, the GCP account cannot explain why learners should adopt some other value of a parameter. Why should L2 learners change their governing category? What input might trigger this?

A solution is offered by more recent analyses of binding which assume that there are two types of anaphors: morphologically complex phrasal anaphors (XPs), consisting of a pronoun and a morpheme meaning *self*, such as *himself, herself* in English, and morphologically simple head anaphors (X°), which do not have such internal structure, like *zibun (self)* in Japanese (Cole, Hermon and Sung 1990; Pica 1987; Progovac 1992, 1993). Each anaphor type has a cluster of properties associated with it, as shown in (2).

(2) a. XP anaphors: morphologically complex, allow subject and non-subject antecedents, require local binding, e.g., *himself, herself.*
b. X° anaphors: morphologically simple, require a subject antecedent, allow long-distance binding, e.g., *zibun*.

These analyses assume that governing categories are not parameterized. Instead, differences in binding domains are a consequence of properties of XPs versus heads. In addition, long-distance binding and the possibility of subject-only antecedents are linked, rather than falling out from two independent parameters, as on the Wexler and Manzini account.

One version of the XP/X° analysis of binding is proposed by Progovac (1992, 1993). She argues that anaphors must be bound in the domain of a relativized subject: Head anaphors must be bound in the domain of the nearest available head having person/number features, namely AGR; XPs must be bound in the domain of the nearest XP subject. This analysis accounts for binding facts as follows: XP anaphors will always require local binding because the nearest XP subject will be in the Spec of the clause that the reflexive is in. X° anaphors, on the other hand, only need to be in the domain of an AGR. If AGR is not realized in the clause containing the reflexive, the reflexive can have an antecedent outside its clause. Thus, long-distance binding is permitted out of nonfinite clauses in languages like Russian because these clauses lack morphological AGR and the reflexive is an X°. In languages with no morphological AGR, such as Japanese, long-distance binding is possible across any clause boundary. In this analysis, differences in nonlocal binding possibilities across languages are explained by differences in properties of functional heads (in this case, AGR) and lexical properties (namely, the morphological status of the reflexive), in the spirit of Minimalism (Progovac 1993).

As pointed out by Progovac & Connell (1991), these intersecting possibilities provide an explanation for the behaviour of the L2 learners reported in the above studies. Consider the Japanese learners of English who accept nonlocal binding *only* out of nonfinite clauses. If these learners misanalyse English as having a head anaphor (like the L1) but correctly recognize that English has morphologically realized AGR in finite clauses (on the basis of the relative richness of agreement in English compared to Japanese), this explains why they allow long-distance binding only out of nonfinite clauses, that is, clauses lacking AGR.

Both the GCP account and the relativized subject account of reflexive binding offer a description of what L2 learners are doing: Japanese learners of English appear to attribute Russian binding possibilities to the L2. Only Progovac's account, however, offers an explanation. The L2 input may be interpreted in different ways by L2 learners, depending on how AGR is realized in the L1 grammar. If AGR in the L2 is relatively rich or impoverished with respect to AGR in the L1, it will be perceived as such, with certain consequences for the interlanguage grammar.

So far, we have seen that the more recent theory has greater explanatory power than the earlier one. In this case, it is not too difficult to take existing data and use the new theory to account for it; that is, the already existing results which suggest that Japanese learners of English allow long-distance binding out of nonfinite clauses are amenable to interpretation within the newer theory. However, this theory also makes predictions which are different from the earlier one. Consider cases where reflexives can be bound to objects, as in (3).

(3) The nurse asked the patient about himself

For Wexler and Manzini (1987), binding to objects is a property independent of the GCP, and is accounted for by an independent parameter, the PAP. However, long-distance reflexives are always subject oriented. The more recent theories of reflexive binding link the property of subject orientation with that of long-distance binding. If these properties are indeed linked, L2 learners who treat reflexive anaphors as $X°$ (hence allowing nonlocal binding in the L2) ought at the same time *not* to allow binding to objects. To test such a claim, one would have to ensure that interpretations of sentences like (3) were tested; in other words, experiments would have to be designed to test this issue. Recent experimental studies on the acquisition of L2 reflexives specifically investigate connections between long-distance binding and subject orientation in the interlanguage grammar (Thomas 1995; White 1994, forthcoming a); in these studies, changes in the theory of reflexive binding have led to changes in the hypotheses being tested, as well as changes in the sentence types that must be manipulated in the experiments.

Another property that is crucially linked to local binding is the morphological complexity of the anaphor (a lexical property). If L2 learners assume long-distance binding, they ought to fail to realize the morphological complexity of English anaphors. Earlier work on L2 reflexives does not look at this question, so this remains to be tested. Here, again, changes in the theory demand changes in the questions that are asked about the nature of interlanguage; this in turn necessitates changes in the hypotheses to be investigated and in the kind of testing that is conducted.

While it is clear that one can sometimes interpret old data in the light of new theories, it is also clear that adjustments have to be made in the area of L2 acquisition theories and hypotheses when a linguistic theory is discarded or outgrown. Researchers are often faced with a decision as to when to change theories; a particular dilemma arises over what to do with data that has been gathered in the framework of a theory which has subsequently undergone revision. On the whole, data gathered to test hypotheses derived on the basis of one theory cannot provide a suitable test of some other theory. They should, therefore, be considered primarily in terms of the theory they were originally designed to test.

The field of L2 acquisition is an interdisciplinary one. This means that theories in a number of different areas, such as cognitive science, psychology and linguistics, are of potential relevance. Researchers who are seriously interested in the nature of interlanguage competence cannot avoid trying to keep up with developments in theory. Nor should they keep up with these developments only at second or third hand. It may seem, then, that we are setting ourselves the impossible task of having to keep up with theories in numerous different domains. In fact, this is not necessarily the case. If a modular approach is adopted, whereby different aspects of L2 acquisition are not expected to be handled by one global theory but rather by a number of different theories, it should remain possible to keep up with theoretical developments in those fields that are most relevant to one's focus in L2 acquisition.

In conclusion, researchers in L2 acquisition need to keep abreast of theoretical developments in linguistic theory, as well as with relevant theories in other domains. The nature of our discipline is such that we cannot turn our backs on what is going on in related fields. In other words, we must be Minimal (that is, keep up with current theory, whatever it may happen to be), not minimal (avoiding theory altogether).

Notes

1. This example is also discussed in White (forthcoming b), in a somewhat different context.

References

Bley-Vroman, R. 1990. "The Logical Problem of Foreign Language Learning". *Linguistic Analysis* 20.3-49.
Borer, H. 1984. *Parametric Syntax*. Dordrecht: Foris.
Chomsky, N. 1981a. *Lectures on Government and Binding*. Dordrecht: Foris.
Chomsky, N. 1981b. "Principles and Parameters in Syntactic Theory". *Explanation in Linguistics: The logical problem of language acquisition* ed. by N. Hornstein & D. Lightfoot, 32-75. London: Longman.
Chomsky, N. 1991. "Some Notes on Economy of Derivation and Representation". *Principles and Parameters in Comparative Grammar* ed. by R. Freidin, 417-454. Cambridge, MA: MIT Press.
Chomsky, N. 1993. "A Minimalist Program for Linguistic Theory". *The View from Building 20: Essays in linguistics in honor of Sylvain Bromberger* ed. by K. Hale & S. J. Keyser, 1-52. Cambridge, MA: MIT Press.

Chomsky, N. 1994. "Bare phrase structure". *MIT Occasional Papers in Linguistics* 5.
Cole, P., G. Hermon & L.-M. Sung. 1990. Principles and Parameters of Long-Distance Reflexives". *Linguistic Inquiry* 21.1-22.
Eubank, L. 1992. "Verb Movement, Agreement, and Tense in L2 Acquisition". *The Acquisition of Verb Placement: Functional categories and V2 phenomena in language acquisition* ed. by J. Meisel, 225-244. Dordrecht: Kluwer.
Finer, D. 1991. "Binding Parameters in Second Language Acquisition". *Point Counterpoint: Universal Grammar in the second language* ed. by L. Eubank, 351-374. Amsterdam: John Benjamins.
Finer, D. & E. Broselow. 1986. "Second Language Acquisition of Reflexive-Binding". *Proceedings of NELS* 16.154-168. University of Massachusetts at Amherst: Graduate Linguistics Students Association.
Flynn, S. 1987. *A Parameter-Setting Model of L2 Acquisition*. Dordrecht: Reidel.
Gass, S. 1992. "The Need to Win Fields and Influence Disciplines". Paper at the Second Language Research Forum, Michigan State University, April 1992.
Gregg, K. 1989. "Second Language Acquisition Theory: The case for a generative perspective". *Linguistic Perspectives on Second Language Acquisition* ed. by S. Gass & J. Schachter, 15-40. Cambridge: Cambridge University Press.
Hirakawa, M. 1990. "A Study of the L2 Acquisition of English Reflexives". *Second Language Research* 6.60-85.
Kayne, R. 1994. *The Antisymmetry of Syntax*. Cambridge, MA: MIT Press.
Lightbown, P. M. & L. White. 1987. "The Influence of Linguistic Theories on Language Acquisition Research: Description and explanation". *Language Learning* 37. 483-510.
Pica, P. 1987. "On the Nature of the Reflexivation Cycle". *Proceedings of NELS* 17. 483-499. University of Massachusetts at Amherst: Graduate Linguistics Students Association.
Progovac, L. 1992. "Relativized SUBJECT: Long-distance reflexives without movement". *Linguistic Inquiry* 23.671-680.
Progovac, L. 1993. "Long-Distance Reflexives: Movement-to-Infl vs. relativized subject". *Linguistic Inquiry* 24.755-772.
Progovac, L. & P. Connell. 1991. "Long-Distance Reflexives, Agr-Subjects, and Acquisition". Paper at the Formal Linguistics Society of Mid-America, Ann Arbor.
Rutherford, W. 1993. "Linguistics and SLA: The two-way street phenomenon". *Confluence: Linguistics, L2 acquisition and speech pathology* ed. by F. Eckman, 3-14. Amsterdam: John Benjamins.
Schachter, J. 1989. "Testing a Proposed Universal." *Linguistic Perspectives on Second Language Acquisition* ed. by S. Gass & J. Schachter, 73-88. Cambridge: Cambridge University Press.
Schwartz, B. 1986. "The Epistemological Status of Second Language Acquisition". *Second Language Research* 2.120-159.
Thomas, M. 1991. "Universal Grammar and the Interpretation of Reflexives in a Second Language". *Language* 67.211-239.

Thomas, M. 1995. "Acquisition of the Japanese Reflexive *zibun* and Movement of Anaphors in Logical Form". *Second Language Research* 11.
Wexler, K. & R. Manzini. 1987. Parameters and Learnability in Binding Theory". *Parameter Setting* ed. by T. Roeper & E. Williams, 41-76. Dordrecht: Reidel.
White, L. 1985. "The Pro-Drop Parameter in Adult Second Language Acquisition". *Language Learning* 35.47-62.
White, L. 1988. "Island Effects in Second Language Acquisition". *Linguistic Theory in Second Language Acquisition* ed. by S. Flynn & W. O'Neil, 144-172. Dordrecht: Kluwer.
White, L. 1989. *Universal Grammar and Second Language Acquisition*. Amsterdam: John Benjamins.
White, L. 1992. "Long and Short Verb Movement in Second Language Acquisition". *Canadian Journal of Linguistics* 37.273-286.
White, L. 1994. "Can UG be Manipulated in Second Language Acquisition?" Plenary address at the Second Language Research Forum, Montreal, Oct. 1994.
White, L. Forthcoming a. "Input, Triggers and Second Language Acquisition: Can binding be taught?" To appear in *Second Language Acquisition Theory and Pedagogy* ed. by F. Eckman, D. Highland, P. Lee, J. Mileman & R. Rutkowski. Hillsdale, NJ: Lawrence Erlbaum.
White, L. Forthcoming b. "Universal Grammar and Second Language Acquisition: Current trends and new directions". To appear in *Handbook of Language Acquisition* ed. by W. Ritchie & T. Bhatia. New York: Academic Press.

The irrelevance of verbal feedback to language learning

Susanne E. Carroll
University of Potsdam

Introduction

This paper is about feedback, correction and other forms of 'negative' verbal input to language acquisition. It is, to my knowledge, the first attempt to point out some of the specific problems underlying the *interpretation* of explicit and/or implicit verbal feedback. Although essential to any theory of language acquisition which relies on the provision of feedback and correction to solve the *Poverty of the Stimulus* and the *What drives change?* problems, I will make no attempt here, because of space limitations, to develop a formal model of how verbal feedback is interpreted. I will simply presuppose that Relevance Theory (Sperber and Wilson 1986) can handle it. I will also suggest, without making the case here, that the very complexity of the interpretation processes raises serious difficulties for the proposal that the provision of verbal feedback (either explicit or implicit) could constitute a *central* solution to these explanatory problems.[1] To the extent that it cannot, then other types of accounts (for example, involving recourse to knowledge of linguistic universals) become more plausible.

Motivating feedback in a theory of language learning

The Poverty of the Stimulus

When constructing a theory of language learning for either first (L1) or second (L2) language acquisition, researchers face two basic problems of explanation. One is the so-called *Poverty of the Stimulus*: Linguistic stimuli alone, that is, forms and meanings arising from the analysis and interpretation of speech heard in communicative interactions, do not appear to be an adequate basis for the learning of the complex and subtle properties of language. One cannot explain how people know what they (tacitly) know or "cognise" of a language (Chomsky 1980:73) by adopting the commonsense view that they learn what they hear. This is because what they hear does not directly reflect what they ultimately come to know.

There are basically five ways in which the input arising from normal conversational interactions (so-called 'positive input') is inadequate. The first is the *Sampling Problem*; the learner at any moment in time is dealing with only an incomplete sample of the language and his linguistic knowledge goes far beyond the properties of his samples. A second inadequacy is the *Ambiguity Problem*: The primary linguistic data may be analysable in any number of ways. A third inadequacy is the *Uniformity Problem*. If the learner is only sampling the language, and his sample depends completely on features of the situation (the addressee, the context, the topic, etc.), then it is reasonable to assume that one learner's sample of, for example, English may look different from another learner's sample. The question then arises: How do we explain the fact that despite observable differences in the linguistic input, learners end up knowing the same things about their language? By 'the same things' I mean abstract grammatical properties, for example, categories like Comp or Inflection, or relations like Subjacency or the constraints on reflexives and possible antecedents. A fourth inadequacy is the *Robustness Problem*. It must be the case that learners are not led astray by odd, unique or infrequent properties of a given sample of language. Learners must be impervious to 'noise' which might potentially mislead them. But just how does the learner distinguish good input from bad? The fifth inadequacy is the *Incompleteness Problem*: the complete absence of certain kinds of useful information in the input. If the information just isn't encoded in either observable semantic properties of the situation or in acoustic-phonetic features of speech, how does the learner learn it?[2] Inductive approaches claim that the learner induces them. However, after almost 40 years of inductive puzzles raised by Chomsky in a variety of writings (Chomsky 1975, 1980, 1986, 1988 *inter alia*), there is still no general inductive theory of language acquisition which will explain how the abstract categories and constraints of grammar could be induced from linguistic stimuli.

One of the reasons why is that a general inductive learning theory must have a way to guarantee that the learner's experiences and natural language stimuli will be just the "right" ones. It must guarantee that the learner's generalizations will be restricted to those which are appropriate and correct, and that errors can be disconfirmed by phenomena which are frequent and robust in ordinary speech. In other words, a general learning theory must also incorporate a component which deals directly with the learner's interactions with the environment, but goes beyond the properties of the primary linguistic data as defined above (henceforth Type 1 input). Explicit and implicit forms of verbal feedback, correction and other forms of so-called *negative input* (henceforth Type 2 input), that is, information about what strings, forms, rules, or constraints are not part of the grammar, are, by hypothesis, just such a component. I will refer throughout to Type 1 and Type 2 input in order to have a theory-neutral terminology, and to avoid confusing explicit and implicit verbal forms of feedback with other conceivable types.[3] Type 2 input is supposed to provide a means of overcoming the inadequacies of Type 1 input by giving the learner additional sorts of information which could then, in principle at least, be used to make correct inferences about the language-to-be-learned.

What drives change?

A second fundamental explanatory problem in the development of a general language acquisition theory is: What drives change? Why does a learner learn anything at all? Setting aside macro-level accounts in terms of motivation and accomodation to focus on psycholinguistic processes, every model of language acquisition presupposes that the learner can perceive and internalize differences between Type 1 input and her own output. In simple terms, the learner can 'monitor' her own production, compare it to some internalized representation of the Type 1 input, and 'hear' when she has made a mistake. This perception initiates reanalysis and restructuring of the to-that-point internalized grammar. Learning is thus error-driven.

In some models of acquisition, for instance, connectionist models (Rumelhart and McClelland 1986, 1987; Sokolik and Smith 1992) and models based on Universal Grammar (UG) à la Berwick (1985), restructuring occurs *only* when errors are perceived.[4] In other models (Karmiloff-Smith 1992), restructuring can also be initiated by internal nonperceptual factors. In all cases, there is a second fundamental distinction to be made among models according to which 'errors' are detected only with respect to Type 1 input, and those where 'errors' can be detected on the basis of either explicit verbal correction or feedback (e.g., *That's wrong; You should say rather 'X'*; etc.), or implicit verbal forms of feedback such as repetitions of the learner's utterance, clarification questions, communication breakdowns, and so forth. UG and connectionist models are alike in restricting learning to Type 1 input. Folk theories of learning, explicit models of language instruction, and certain 'interactionist' models of language learning (Bohannon and Stanowicz 1988; Demetras, Post and Snow 1986; Hirsh-Pasek, Treiman and Schneiderman 1984; Pica 1987; Snow and Hoefnagel-Hohle 1982; Varonis and Gass 1985; Wagner-Gough and Hatch 1975) all allow Type 2 input to play a role in initiating restructuring. We restrict our attention in what follows to how this might in principle happen.

How could Type 2 input initiate restructuring?

Assigning Type 2 input a role in language acquisition forces on us certain assumptions. One crucial assumption is about the basic architecture of cognition: Information can flow from the conceptual system to the grammar in a nonmodular fashion since Type 2 input does not constitute a distinction in the form of an utterance (as does the distinction between, say, declaratives and interrogatives) nor even a semantic distinction (as does the difference between, e.g., statements and requests) but a pragmatic distinction. The Corrector is expressing his attitudes about the form of something that has been said in a given context. Feedback of the Type 2 sort is quintessentially metalinguistic in nature (Birdsong 1989); in order for the learner to understand the Corrector to be correcting, she must construe the Corrector's utterance to be a metalinguistic commentary, or construe the Corrector's behaviour as pointing to a metalinguistic commentary. This construal will take place in that part of the functional architecture dedicated to inferencing, thinking and the construction of mental models of the on-going discourse. Since we assume that this component of the mind is outside of any language module (Fodor 1983; Schwartz 1986, 1987, 1993), to play any role in the restructuring of the learner's grammar, information arising from the construal would have to flow from the inferencing component to the grammar. Linguistic cognition would have to be interactive and nonmodular. If it isn't, there can be no place for Type 2 input in a general theory of language learning. If Type 2 input cannot explain away the *Poverty of the Stimulus* and the *What drives change?* problems, the potential for developing such a general theory of language acquisition (one without recourse to innate universals of mind) is greatly reduced.

A second important assumption is that the learner can in fact make the right construal. The basic thesis of this paper is that explicit and implicit forms of verbal feedback are largely Irrelevant to the ongoing communicative event in which they may occur. By the use of the capital letter 'I' here, I mean that they violate Grice's (1975) Maxim of Relevance, in (1) below.

(1) Relevance: The speaker makes her contribution relevant to the purpose of the talk at that point in the exchange.

Because it is Irrelevant to the ongoing purpose of the talk at that point, Type 2 input represents a rupture in the discourse which can only be resolved if the learner is capable of attributing some alternate purpose to it. I will attempt to demonstrate that this resolution is itself a complex matter with no guarantee that the correct induction will be drawn. This is because the feedback interpretation requires that the learner apply a first-order interpretation to the Corrector's utterance—and then reject that interpretation. She must then assign a second-order interpretation to the Corrector's utterance, in so doing attributing a particular informative intention to the Corrector (i.e., that he is correcting). Making this interpretation presupposes, however, that the learner can re-represent language itself as an object of thought. The ability to think about language, to represent it conceptually, develops with age and does not manifest itself until approximately age 6.[5] Its development may be connected to literacy (Gombert 1992:178). There is some suggestion therefore that metalinguistic re-representation is not a universal phenomenon. If the very capacity to represent speech as an object of thought were to prove to be related to literacy, this would seriously undermine general theories of language acquisition which rely on it. First and second language acquisition do not depend on literacy.

The interpretation of feedback

To count as feedback an utterance must be interpreted

Pinker (1989:10-14) observes that for Type 2 input to play any role in language learning at least three things must be true of it: It must be available in the learner's environment; it must be usable; and it must be used. I will limit myself to some observations of what makes Type 2 input usable.

I take the *usability* of Type 2 input to mean that it must be *interpretable*. In other words, the learner must be able to parse the stimulus (both phonologically and syntactically) and assign it an interpretation. It is not necessarily true that the learner must already know a lot of a given language to interpret explicit or implicit verbal feedback. In other words, the learner's parse of the feedback-containing stimulus might be incomplete or inaccurate. It is true, however, that the more limited the learner's knowledge of a given language, the more limited the information that can be conveyed *to him in that language*. The less information that can be conveyed directly in the L1 or L2, the more Type 2 input must be interpreted through inductive inferencing based on a perceptually-based interpretation of the environment, through recall of previously stored information, or (in the case of L2 learners) through communication in the L1 (see (4) below for illustration). My point is that *to the extent that the learner cannot decode and interpret the stimulus itself, then it becomes difficult to claim that it is the feedback which is causally related to changes in the learner's grammar*. It follows that Type 2 input provided in a given language will play only a limited role during the earliest stages of acquisition when the learner's ability to parse and interpret utterances in that language will be the most limited. It will exclude Type 2 input as a *central* mechanism in certain learning situations; in the earliest stages of L1 acquisition where there can be no recourse to a 'shared' medium of communication between Corrector and learner (since the infant is simultaneously learning both L1 forms and semantic/pragmatic systems expressed via the L1), and in L2 acquisition contexts where recourse to the L1 is severely limited, as in pidgin contact situations.

The Irrelevance of linguistic feedback

(2) Scenario 1: a German grocery store. An American (male) approaches a German (male), who is carrying several bottles of wine.

American: Ah! Wo haben Sie das Wein gefunden?
 where have you the-N wine found
 "Where have you found the wine?"

German: DEN!
 the-ACC

American: ...Danke, danke
 "Thank you, thank you"

End of interaction.[6]

What makes feedback interpretable? It is a basic assumption of the analysis of speech in discourse (Bach and Harnish 1982; Grice 1975; Searle 1969, 1979, 1983; Sperber and Wilson 1989, among others) that discourse is conventional and arises from communicative intentions on the part of the participants. In the unmarked case, interlocutors agree to move a conversation towards some mutually-defined goal. They cooperate and contribute by making each contribution Relevant to the conversation. To take a simple example, when one asks another person a question, as in (2) above, the person addressed is expected to cooperate by providing an answer if he can. Clearly the American in (2), wanting some wine in the grocery store, could expect that his interlocutor, who is holding bottles of wine in his arms, would know where to find the wine section. If he knows this, by Grice's (1975) Principle of Cooperation, he ought to reply by giving the location. But he doesn't do this. At the same time, he does not flagrantly violate the Principle of Cooperation; he doesn't look away, refuse to say anything, or shout *Yankee, go home!*. He gives a verbal response, which the learner acknowledges by thanking him. One would only thank an interlocutor for information that one thought was helpful, but it is perfectly clear that the Respondant's response is not a response to the question asked. *It is a metalinguistic comment which is clearly Irrelevant to the objectives of the on-going conversation.* The construal of verbal feedback must be based on something like (3).

(3) How to construe feedback from an utterance:
 a. The Corrector does not violate the Cooperativeness Principle and is not perceived by the Learner to have violated it.
 b. The Corrector's contribution is Irrelevant to the on-going discourse.

c. The Learner assumes that the Corrector has a Corrective Informative Intention, that is, that he wants to say something about the form of the Learner's previous utterance.

However, I want to make a stronger claim: Not only is the Corrector's utterance Irrelevant, it *must* be Irrelevant to the on-going discourse in order to be construed as metalinguistic correction. Consider in this regard a second example where an interpretive problem arises precisely because the Learner construes the Corrector's contribution to the discourse as Relevant. This example, along with those in the rest of this paper, come from a now quite large corpus of spontaneously given examples of Type 2 input that I have been collecting since 1989.[7] In each example, the learner is an adult, learning the L2 largely in an untutored fashion, in surroundings where the L2 is the medium of common communication. Feedback comes from native speakers of the Learner's L2.

(4) Scenario 2: (A = Native Speaker, B = Learner)

A: Ich überlege seit drei Stunde was ich anziehen werde.
I think-over for 3 hours what I put-on will
"I've been thinking for 3 hours about what I will put on"

B: ...ich verstehe nicht
I understand not
"I don't understand"

A: Was verstehst du nicht?
what understand you not?
"What don't you understand?"

B: ummmmmm ich...der Substantiv
I the noun
"ummmmmm I ... the noun"

A: Es gibt kein Substantiv
it-PL give no noun
"There is no noun"

B: Well then I don't understand the verb

A: réfléchis
"think"

B: *(thinking hard)*
ummmmmmm...ich...ich...
"ummmmmm ... I ... I ..."

(unable to formulate a statement in German; switches to French too)

    je ne comprends pas
    I CL understand not
    "I don't understand"
A: RÉFLÉCHIS!
B: *(thinking harder)*
    I can't guess, what is it?
A: RÉFLÉCHIS!
B: oh! ça veut dire 'réfléchir' *(bursts out laughing)*
    that want say think-INF
    "oh! That means 'to think'"

    J'ai   pensé   que tu   aies voulu que je devine le sens.
    I have thought that you have wanted that I guess   the meaning
    "I thought that you wanted me to guess the meaning"

    Certain details are necessary to understand what is going on here. First of all, it is important to note that Speakers A and B use both French and English on a regular basis to communicate. Secondly, both switch in and out of these two languages, so there would be nothing unusual about A's switch from German to French although B had previously been using English. Speaker B has said explicitly that he does not understand the verb in Speaker A's original utterance. Speaker A chooses to provide him with a translation equivalent; in other words, his utterance could be construed as an abbreviated version of the proposition *the verb means 'think about'*. But Speaker A is even more helpful. He provides the translation in the first person singular corresponding to his original utterance, in a form which just happens to be homophonous with the imperative second person singular. This means that the form of his response is ambiguous between several interpretations. This discourse thus nicely illustrates the *Ambiguity Problem* discussed above.

    Speaker B chooses to interpret the utterance *réfléchis* as a command, that is, as a non-metalinguistic instruction, even though this involves his making the assumption that Speaker A is being less than direct. I would like to suggest that the impetus to interpret stimuli in a non-metalinguistic way is so strong that it could lead Speaker B to assume that Speaker A is "bending" the Cooperativeness Principle and wants to play a little game. *One thus moves to a metalinguistic construal only when none other is possible.* Since a non-metalinguistic construal is available here, the learner simply fails to understand the utterance as Type 2 input.

    Because of the *Ambiguity Problem*, there is no guarantee that the Speaker's informative intention (the Corrective Informative Intention) with respect to language form will be manifest to the Hearer/Learner. It follows therefore that the usefulness of Type 2 input depends first and foremost on the learner and his inferencing capacities, rather than on the Corrector and his communicative intentions. A Corrector may at any time attempt to provide feedback, but only the Learner's construal can make an utterance a successful provision of feedback.

On what basis would Speaker B finally come to reject his initial assumption about Speaker A's informative intention in the above example? How does he come to make the right assumptions? There are a number of additional assumptions which he must make to get there. The first obviously is Grice's Cooperative Principle; the Corrector must be seen as attempting to communicate something. Since the Corrector repeats the same utterance *réfléchis* even after Speaker B has said that he cannot guess the meaning of *überlege*, either Speaker B assumes that Speaker A is being uncooperative or he searches for another intended meaning. The second option is adopted. Speaker B can now conclude that the utterance *réfléchis*, on a non-metalinguistic interpretation, is Irrelevant to the on-going discourse. In the face of violations to Grice's maxims, Hearers are expected to make any additional assumptions needed to come up with a Relevant interpretation (Sperber and Wilson 1988:35).

Next we need what we might call the Felicity Conditions for the provision of Type 2 input. Speaker B must assume that Speaker A possesses metalinguistic knowledge to pass on. Attempts to provide Type 2 input will fail if the learner assumes that the Corrector does not know what he is talking about, or is in no position to provide linguistic feedback, for example, if both are L2 learners at the same stage of acquisition. An additional dimension here is that there is a shared code which can serve as an appropriate medium for the transmission of information about the non-shared code. Speaker B must assume that Speaker A assumes that he (B) can work back from an interpretation of a French form to the meaning of the German verb. One possible construal of the above dialogue, given these assumptions, is that *réfléchis* is a translation-equivalent of *überlege*.

Several points are worth noting here. First, the inferencing process is 'global' in that it has access to all conceptual information in memory. It is, therefore, relatively unspecialized, not restricted to perception of Type 1 input, and clearly falls outside of postulated language modules. This raises the explanatory problem of *Uniformity* discussed above. Second, relevant information is new information, which, when combined with old information, gives rise to further new information (Sperber and Wilson 1988:48). To correctly interpret the feedback, therefore, the Hearer must select the appropriate new information to add to current assumptions. Nothing in what the Corrector says can guarantee that the correct new information will be identified, as example (5) below shows. The third point results from the first two: Inferencing is non-demonstrative (Sperber and Wilson 1988: 65); it's an iffy sort of thing at best. Finally, explicit feedback depends on the perceptions of the Corrector, but she will often be in a difficult position to determine if her intended Correction constitutes new information for the learner. Example (5) illustrates this point as well.

The Relevance of feedback depends on its informativeness

(5) *(A = the L2 learner, B = the native speaker)*

A: Willst du mir die Tasche bringen?
   want you to-me the bag bring
   "Do you want to bring me my bag?"

B: Wirst du/
   will you
   "Will you"

A: Wirst du/
   (self-correction based on previous error-feedback interactions involving the use of 'werden' and 'wollen')

B: Du hast 'willst du' gesagt
   you have 'willst du' said
   "You said 'willst du'"

A: Wirst du mir ... die Tasche bringen?
   will you to-me...the bag bring
   "Will you bring me my bag?"

B: Bringst du meine Tasche?
   bring you my bag
   "Will you bring me my bag?"

A: Okay! bringst du meine Tasche!

B: Welche?
   which
   Which one?

A: Die ist unten die...die...Wie sagt man 'sink'?
   it is beneath the...the...how say one 'sink'
   "It's beneath the...the...how do you say 'sink'?"

B: Waschbecken
   sink

A: *(hears 'Waschbecke')*
   Die ist unten die *Waschbecke*
   ART is beneath the *waschbecke*

B: unter dem Waschbecken
under the+DAT sink
"under the sink"

A: *(hears 'unten dem Waschbecke')*
unten dem *Waschbecke*
beneath the+DAT *waschbecke*

B: *(exasperated)*
UNTER DEM WASCHBECKEN!

A: *(equally exasperated)*
well if you'd stop eating the ends of your words!

To initiate knowledge restructuring in the learner, feedback must be *informative*. It is not sufficient that the learner assign an interpretation to the Type 2 input stimulus. It must tell the learner something that she does not already know. A stimulus which does not add to her stock of knowledge is not informative; it is merely redundant. Redundant information is Irrelevant information. The first correction by B dealing with the correct choice of verb to express futurity did not provide the learner with any new information about the German verbal system since she had made this mistake before and been corrected on it several times. She was able to self-correct. While the Corrector may intend the utterance as a Type 2 input, and the learner will discern the Corrector's information intention (because one doesn't answer a question by repeating it), its information content as *feedback* is zero. The utterance fails as *feedback*.

It seems to me that the informativeness of Type 2 input for a learner is often overestimated in discussions of the development of a general language learning theory. In other words, it is assumed that all attempts at feedback by the Corrector contribute new information to the learner. But this is clearly false, as (5) shows. *Indeed, the more knowledgable the learner is, the more likely it is to be false.* Once a learner has acquired a grammatical distinction and can reproduce it at least some of the time, Type 2 input about it will merely provide the learner with evidence that she has made a performance mistake.[8]

The second correction that B provides focuses on the correctness of choosing the future tense. Speaker A acknowledges that she has made an error by repeating the proffered correction. The third bit of Type 2 input is the important one here. During the earliest stages of learning, Speaker A had considerable difficulty representing accurately the phonological shape of certain sounds, in particular the shape of unstressed syllables. Because she has not heard the distinction between her pronunciation and that of B's, she does not grasp that it is the focus of the correction. Rather she attends to and alters her formulation of the case-marked determiner, substituting one form (*dem*) for another (*die*). It is only because B presents the correction a second time with considerable insistence that A directs her attention to other aspects of her utterance.

The blame-assignment problem

Example (5) illustrates well what Pinker (1989:12) has called the "blame-assignment" problem. The provision of Type 2 input indicates an error, but it doesn't say what the error is. Consequently, the learner must analyse or guess where he has probably made a mistake in the sentence and what level of planning or execution (speech act, lexical choice, morphosyntax, linear order, articulation) is implicated. When feedback will be most useful to the learner, namely in the early stages of language learning, is precisely the time when the learner's ability to compare a faulty utterance (even to a model in Type 1 input) will be heavily restricted due to limitations on the learner's ability to attend to and process input.[9] As here.

The Corrective Informative Intention and tacit forms of feedback

The provision of explicit Type 2 input lies in the hands (or mouth) of the Corrector. In other words, she must perceive that there is a need to provide feedback and be willing to do so. Explicit Type 2 input of the sort illustrated here thus differs from implicit or indirect forms of feedback such as repetitions of an erroneous utterance or clarification questions since there the Corrector has no intention to correct.[10] But if the Corrector has no intention to correct, then there will normally be no Corrective Informative Intention to attribute to the Corrector. *If the Learner cannot attribute a Corrective Informative Intention to the Corrector, there is no reason to assume that in normal discourse, he will construe repetitions or clarification requests as forms of linguistic feedback.* It follows that although indirect and tacit forms of negative evidence may be more frequent in native speaker/non-native speaker discourses than overt forms, they are less likely to be construed as feedback.

Conclusions

The study of the interpretation of Type 2 input (explicit and implicit forms of verbal feedback) is critical to a resolution of debates about which types of properties a language learning theory must have. Indeed, it is essential to determining whether it is possible to develop a general (non-UG-based) theory. Some models of language learning presuppose that Type 2 input is available, usable and informative. Others exclude it altogether on the assumption that linguistic cognition is modular (excluding in principle a role for metalinguistic information in the restructuring of grammatical knowledge), or that Type 2 input is in fact not available, usable or used.

In this paper, I have focused attention on what makes linguistic feedback usable. The interpretation of Type 2 input requires first of all a metalinguistic capacity since the correct construal of the Corrective Intention requires treating language itself as an object of thought. Type 2 input would thus appear to be excluded in certain language learning situations because the Learner has limited or no metalinguistic capacity (early L1 acquisition, possibly L2 acquisition in illiterates). Interpretation also requires an ability to parse and interpret the stimuli, which also precludes a central role for Type 2 input in early L1 acquisition and in those cases of L2 acquisition where there is no recourse to a common code (pidgin contact situations).

I have shown (through an analysis of a corpus of spontaneously provided forms of Type 2 input to adult L2 learners) that the interpretation of linguistic feedback requires interpreting an utterance as obeying the Principle of Cooperation but violating Relevance. Hearers, however, will make this move only when no other interpretation is possible--the move to a metalinguistic interpretation is therefore a move of 'last' and not first resort. I have also shown that assigning an utterance a feedback interpretation involves attributing a Corrective Informative Intention to the Corrector. Since repetitions, failures to comprehend and other commonly-cited forms of indirect feedback do not require making such an attribution, the correct interpretation for such utterance-types is less likely. The more inferencing the Learner must make on the basis of (non-verbal) perceivable events or information in longterm memory, the less likely she is to identify the Corrective Intention. Contrary to common assertions in the interactionist literature, the 'best' Type 2 input is the most explicit--which has been identified in the L1 literature as the least likely to occur. Finally, it was observed that a given utterance can be doubly Irrelevant, namely, when the Corrector violates Relevance in order to provide feedback, but the information construed by the learner is not new. I conclude that for this reason the provision of Type 2 input may be comparatively useless in the advanced stages of acquisition when the Corrector is less able to discern errors from 'slips of the tongue' made by the Learner, and when Type 2 input is more likely to be redundant.

In short, considerations of an interpretive nature suggest that even if Type 2 input is 'in the air', its utility will be severely restricted in both the early and the most advanced stages of language acquisition, making it unlikely that it could play a central role in the development of a general theory of language acquisition.

Acknowledgments

I would like to thank an audience at the Universität Konstanz for questions and comments on a very early form of this paper, an anonymous reviewer for an important reference, and Lynn Eubank for helpful comments in improving the final version.

Notes

1. It is not my intention to demonstrate that feedback cannot be a mechanism of language learning, for such a demonstration would be impossible. The logic of my argument is that the interpretive processes required to make sense of feedback are neither simple, culturally universal, nor guaranteed, but this is not a demonstration that they *never* work. There is empirical evidence to show that feedback can work in very limited circumstances for certain kinds of linguistic phenomena in the case of adult L2 learners (Carroll, Roberge and Swain 1992; Carroll and Swain 1993a, 1993b).

2. Assuming here for the sake of the argument that properties of the learner's representational system does not force analysis in the right direction.

3. A reviewer with intimate knowledge of flatworm behavior has correctly reminded me of the need for terminological precision; I want to focus here on language-mediated forms of feedback and not on purely physiological forms such as electrical shocks and other forms of gratuitous cruelty practiced in behaviorist experiments.

4. I am assuming here that it is correct to talk about the back propatation mechanism of connectionist functional architecture in terms of perception.

5. Gombert (1992:10) makes an important distinction between metalinguistic and epilinguistic representations and behaviors. The latter, such as the ability to monitor one's speech and to self-correct or to make rhymes are unconscious and unavailable for reflection and reporting. Epilinguistic behaviors show up earlier than metalinguistic behaviors and indeed may be a necessary precursor to them.

6. I owe this example to the late, and deeply missed, Fernando Tarallo.

7. A reviewer claims with respect to explicit verbal feedback that "there is no evidence that such feedback exists", citing Brown and Hanlon (1970) and Hirsh-Pasek et al. (1984), both papers dealing with L1 acquisition. This is clearly one area where proponents of a general theory of language acquisition would be obliged to differentiate between L1 and L2 acquisition since adult L2 learners clearly do get both explicit and implicit forms of Type 2 input, as my corpus demonstrates. I stopped counting simple lexical provisions and phonetic corrections early on in gathering my corpus since the numbers of these forms that I was hearing were large and they all looked basically the same. Therefore, I am in no position to state exactly how many instances of Type 2 input I have witnessed since I began, but a conservative estimate would put the number in the hundreds.

8. Correcting a knowledgable learner's performance mistakes is about as socially acceptable as correcting the pronunciation of someone with a permanent speech defect.

9. The correction provided here did not lead to restructuring of the learner's grammar; she continued for a long time after to confuse *unter* and *unten*, and *Waschbecken* has led a tenuous existence in her mental lexicon.

10. Repetitions which reformulate an erroneous uterance are different in that they provide primary linguistic data which the learner can then compare to a just-uttered error. Such repetitions fall under the category of Type I input.

References

Bach, K. & R. M. Harnish. 1982. *Linguistic Communication and Speech Acts*. Cambridge, MA: MIT Press.
Berwick, R.C. 1985. *The Acquisition of Syntactic Knowledge*. Cambridge, MA: MIT Press.
Birdsong, D. 1989. *Metalinguistic Performance and Interlinguistic Competence*. Berlin: Springer.
Bohannon, J.N. & L. Stanowicz. 1988. "The Issue of Negative Evidence: Adult responses to children's language errors". *Developmental Psychology* 24.684-89
Carroll, S., Y. Roberge & M. Swain. 1992. "The Role of Feedback in Adult Second Language Acquisition: Error correction and morphological generalizations". *Applied Psycholinguistics* 13.173-198.
Carroll, S. & M. Swain. 1993a. "Explicit and Implicit Negative Feedback: An empirical study of the learning of linguistic generalizations". *Studies in Second Language Acquisition* 15.357-386.
Carroll, S. & M. Swain. 1993b. "More on Second Language Learning from Negative Feedback". Ms., University of Potsdam and the Ontario Institute for Studies in Education.
Chomsky, N. 1975. *Reflections on Language*. New York: Pantheon.
Chomsky, N. 1980. *Rules and Representations*. Oxford: Blackwell.
Chomsky, N. 1986. *Knowledge of Language: Its nature, origin and use*. New York: Praeger.
Chomsky, N. 1988. *Language and Problems of Knowledge*. Cambridge, MA: MIT Press.
Demetras, M.J., K. N. Post & C. E. Snow. 1986. "Feedback to First Language Learners: The role of repetitions and clarification questions". *Journal of Child Language* 13.275-92.
Fodor, J.A. 1983. *The Modularity of Mind*. Cambridge, MA: MIT Press.
Gombert, J.-E. 1992. *Metalinguistic Development*. Chicago: University of Chicago Press. (Originally as *Le Développment Métalinguistique*. Paris: Presses Universitaires de France, 1990).
Grice, H.P. 1975. "Logic and Conversation". *Syntax and Semantics*, Vol. 3, ed. by P. Cole & J. Morgan, 41-58. New York: Academic Press.

Hirsh-Pasek, K., R. Treiman & M. Schneiderman. 1984. "Brown and Hanlon Revisited: Mothers' sensitivity to ungrammatical forms". *Journal of Child Language* 11.81-88.
Karmiloff-Smith, A. 1992. *Beyond modularity*. Cambridge, MA: MIT Press.
Pica, T. 1987. "Second Language Acquisition, Social Interaction, and the Classroom". *Applied Linguistics* 8.3-21.
Pinker, S. 1989. *Learnability and Cognition: The acquisition of argument structure*. Cambridge, MA: MIT Press.
Rumelhart, D.E. & J. L. McClelland. 1986. "On Learning the Past Tenses of English Verbs". *Parallel Distributed Processing*, Vol. 2, ed. by D. E. Rumelhart & J. L. McClelland, 216-271. Cambridge, MA: Bradford Books/MIT Press.
Rumelhart, D.E. & J. L. McClelland. 1987. "Learning the Past Tenses of English Verbs: Implicit rules or parallel distributed processing". In B. MacWhinney (ed.), *Mechanisms of Language Acquisition* ed. by B. MacWhinney, 195-248. Hillsdale, N.J: Erlbaum.
Schwartz, B. D. 1986. "The Epistemological Status Second Language Acquisition". *Second Language Research* 2.120-59.
Schwartz, B. D. 1987. *The Modular Basis of Second Language Acquisition*. Ph.D. dissertation, University of Southern California.
Schwartz, B. D. 1993. "On Explicit and Negative Data Effecting and Affecting Competence and Linguistic Behavior". *Studies in Second Language Acquisition* 15.147-63.
Searle, J. R. 1969. *Speech Acts: An essay in the philosophy of language*. Cambridge: Cambridge University Press.
Searle, J. R. 1979. *Expression and Meaning: Studies in the theory of speech acts*. Cambridge: Cambridge University Press.
Searle, J. R. 1983. *Intentionality: An essay in the philosophy of mind*. Cambridge: Cambridge University Press.
Snow, C. & M. Hoefnagle-Hohle. 1982. "School Age Second Language Learners' Access to a Simplified Linguistic Input". *Language Learning* 32.411-30.
Sokolik, M. E. & M. E. Smith. 1992. "Assignment of Gender to French Nouns in Primary and Secondary Language: A connectionist model". *Second Language Research* 8.39-58.
Sperber, D. & D. Wilson. 1986. *Relevance: Communication and cognition*. Cambridge, MA: Harvard University Press.
Varonis, E. & S. Gass. 1985. "Native/Non-Native Conversations: A model for negotiation of meaning". *Applied Linguistics* 6.71-90.
Wagner-Gough, J. & E. Hatch. 1975. "The Importance of Input Data in Second Language Acquisition Studies". *Language Learning* 35.297-307.

Indirect negative evidence, inductive inferencing, and second language acquisition

India C. Plough

Introduction

In spite of Chomsky's (1981:8-9) suggestion that indirect negative evidence (INE) may be relevant to acquisition, its potential significance has been all but ignored in both first-language (L1) and second-language (L2) acquisition studies and has only recently become the focus of theoretical arguments (Lasnik 1989; Valian 1990; Saleemi 1990, 1992; Archibald 1993; Plough 1994). This situation may be due, at least in part, to the apparent elusiveness of the concept and to the difficulty of developing a research design to test for the use of INE. However, I would like to suggest that a reexamination of the original definition of INE is in order, especially since, given the continued empirical and theoretical difficulties over the roles of positive and negative evidence in L2 acquisition (see White 1991a, 1991b, 1992a; Trahey and White 1993; Schwartz and Gubala-Ryzak 1992; Schwartz 1993), the use of INE may prove to be a partial solution to the problem of learnability. In what follows, therefore, I present not only a reevaluation of the fundamental definition of INE, but also data from an empirical study pertaining to its use by L2 learners.

Defining indirect negative evidence

If we return to the original definition, we see that INE is an indirect means of letting the learner know that a feature is not possible because it is never present in the *expected* environment. As pointed out by Pinker (1989), INE is not, strictly speaking, a part of the learner's linguistic environment in the same way that explicit negative evidence is. In order to qualify as negative data, the implicit information, or absence of a structure, must be equated with ungrammaticality. This necessarily involves a learning strategy or procedure and must be treated as distinct from explicit negative data.

The use of INE crucially depends on the assumption that a domain of expectation exists. The absence of a feature must be noticed. Without a domain of expectation, what is not present is potentially infinite. The question then becomes what is it which provides this domain of expectation. For both L1 and L2 acquisition, Universal Grammar (UG) might be understood to define this domain. However, the debate continues in the L2 literature over whether or not principles of UG are directly accessible (Mazurkewich 1984; Schwartz 1993), partially accessible (White 1989; Sharwood Smith 1990), or not accessible at all (Clahsen and Muysken 1989; Bley-Vroman 1989; Schachter 1988). While my goal here is not to argue for or against the accessibility of UG, I would like to suggest that once the focus narrows to the role of INE in L2 acquisition, and specifically to the assumed domain of expectation, the prudent supposition would be that this domain is provided by the L1. There is initially no justification to invoke UG and thus assume the larger domain. The present research begins from this position.

In order to investigate the use of INE by L2 learners, I propose that this process is analogous to the use of inductive inferencing and that induction is the learning principle at the core of INE in a specifically-linguistic framework. That the operative principle in such a framework relies on induction has already been alluded to, but not elaborated on, by Saleemi (1990, 1992) in L1 acquisition and by Archibald (1993) in L2 acquisition. These researchers have referred to the use of INE at various times as a learning procedure, a learning strategy, and induction. However, while it has been implicitly accepted that the use of INE is analogous to induction, the possibility has yet to be substantiated.[1]

Drawing on Carton (1966, 1971), Bialystok (1978, 1979, 1990), O'Malley and Chamot (1990), and Oxford and Cohen (1992), I define inductive inferencing as a multi-stage comprehension process which results in a probably-true hypothesis (see also Kess 1992; Moore 1986; Trusted 1979). The stages of this process are shown in (1) below.

(1) Stage 1: Scanning what is known (either L1, L2, and/or world knowledge)
    Stage 2: Linking new material with what is known (it is at this stage where the absence of a structure may be noticed)
    Stage 3: Establishing probably true conclusions or generalizations based on the (mis)match between new material and what is already known.

This process may be involved in the acquisition of the syntax, morphology, phonology, pragmatics, or semantics of a language. In other words, rather than being reserved exclusively for the specifically-linguistic domain, this process is domain-general.[2] It is also important to note that each stage is dependent on the previous stage(s). In addition, the processes at each stage are dependent on multiple variables. For example, factors such as frequency of input, prior knowledge, and affective variables may play a role in determining if the input becomes "apperceived" (Gass 1988). Other factors may consist of the medium of presentation and a wide range of learner variables. At any point, the process of inductive inferencing may break down, perhaps as a result of such variables. Morever, a learner may be strong in one aspect of the process (e.g., scanning L2) and weak in another aspect (e.g., linking new material with known material).

A parallel can be drawn between the use of INE in a specifically-linguistic framework and the multi-stage inferencing process in (1). The operative principle of a specifically-linguistic acquisition system relies on an inferencing process. The domain of expectation can thus be assumed to be UG (or that which has already been acquired of the L1). This is analogous to the known material of stage 1 in the domain-general process shown in (1). New material (L1 input) and known material (UG) must be scanned and linked. If what is known or expected fails to be instantiated in the new material, a conclusion or generalization would be chosen which would exclude a certain structure in the grammar of the learner. Specifically-linguistic discussions of INE such as that of Chomsky (1981) rarely elaborate on how expected structures would not be found.[3] My view is that the relevant operative principle would necessarily involve a scanning and linking process.

It still remains to be shown, however, that this process is in fact a case of induction and not deduction. By definition (Kess 1992; Trusted 1979), deduction operates in accordance with accepted rules of logic. If the rules are correctly followed, the conclusion cannot be false if the premises are true, because the conclusion cannot contain more information than is found in the premises. In contrast, induction is based on minimal evidence and the logic that connects the evidence to the generalization is questionable. The generalization or conclusion necessarily includes more information than what is available in the premises, or the input in the case of language acquisition. Given the 'poverty-of-the-stimulus' argument and research findings suggesting that direct negative evidence is either minimally provided and/or is ignored by learners, it therefore follows that the generalizations 'formulated' by L2 learners may indeed not be based solely on deductive reasoning.[4]

I would now like to provide justification for the proposal that inductive inferencing plays a role in the acquisition of the contrasts in (2) through (9) by native speakers of English learning French (see White 1991a, 1991b, 1992a, 1992b).

(2) Jean boit son café rapidement.
(3) John drinks his coffee quickly.
(4) Lentement les jeunes filles finissent leur travail.
(5) Slowly the girls finish their work.
(6) Marie regarde souvent la TV.
(7) *Mary watches often TV.

(8) *Marie souvent regarde la TV.
(9) Mary often watches TV.

In the context of this specific linguistic example, I argue that the absence of expected material must be noticed in order for the L2 learner to reach the correct conclusion, and that the process of inductive inferencing is a means to that end. Both English and French allow Subject-Verb-Object-Adverb (SVOA) and Adverb-Subject-Verb-Object (ASVO) word orders as in (2) to (5); however, the two languages differ in that only French allows Subject-Verb-Adverb-Object (SVAO) word order as in (6), and only English allows Subject-Adverb-Verb-Object (SAVO) word order as in (9).[5] Importantly, if one assumes the lack of negative feedback, nothing in the French positive input informs English speaking learners of French that the SAVO order allowed in their native language is disallowed in the target language. Utilizing the inferencing process described above, the four possible courses of action shown in (i) to (iv) below can be hypothesized:

i. Assume that the learner uses L2 information to reach the generalization that only SVAO word order is possible. The only way to disconfirm this would be the presence of SAVO word order, which will not be forthcoming in the L2. Can we assume that the learner who only uses the correct SVAO word order has confirmed the generalization through noticing the absence of the incorrect SAVO word order? In order to conclude that the learner has not progressed beyond Stage 1 and has only scanned what is known in the L2, that is, has reached a generalization based only on positive input, it would be necessary to find a learner who has never used the incorrect SAVO word order in French. This is highly unlikely.

ii. Assume that the learner uses L1 information and only uses the incorrect SAVO word order. This learner has not advanced beyond Stage 1. That is, the learner has not related the new material (L2) with what is known in the L1 and is relying solely on the L1.

iii. Assume that the learner uses both L1 and L2 information to form the generalization that both SAVO and SVAO word orders are possible in French. This generalization cannot be confirmed and can only be disconfirmed when the learner notices the absence of the incorrect SAVO word order. We can assume that the learner who continues to use both SVAO and SAVO word orders has not noticed the absence of the SAVO word order in French.

iv. Assume the learner uses both L1 and L2 information, notices the absence of SAVO word order in the L2 and comes to the generalization that only the SVAO word order is possible. Importantly, given the implausibility of the IL of (i) above (i.e., the learner never uses the incorrect SAVO word order), this last learner would exhibit, for a period of time, the IL of (iii) above (i.e., using both SAVO and SVAO word orders) before progressing to the final stage. In order for the learner to 'switch' from the incorrect SAVO word order to the correct SVAO word order, the absence of SAVO word order in French must be noticed by the learner. While the absence of the structure may be noticed at Stage 2 (the linking stage), its absence must be noticed in order to progress to the appropriate generalization at Stage 3.

In the following, I present empirical data from L2 learners of French designed to test these hypotheses.

Method

Volunteers were obtained from four sections of intensive first-year French at Michigan State University. These sections are designed for students who have had French previously, but do not quite place into second-year French. All volunteers (45 learners) took three pretests. Two of these tests, a word-order correction task (WOC) and an acceptability judgment (AJ) task, were adapted from White (1991a, 1992b) and Trahey and White (1993) and were used to test students' knowledge of adverb placement in French. Test sentences contained adverbs of frequency or manner and lexical verbs in the present tense. The WOC task was in the form of a cartoon story. Students were asked to correct those sentences which were incorrect. The AJ task contained pairs of sentences, and students were asked to decide whether both sentences were correct, both sentences were incorrect, only one sentence was correct, or they did not know. The third test was Raven's Standard Progressive Matrices (SPM) (see Raven 1976), which is a nonverbal test and is considered a valid and reliable measure of inductive reasoning (Alderton and Larson 1990). It consists of five sets of 12 problems each which are presented in abstract figures and designs. Each problem consists of a 3X3 matrix with the lower right hand element blank. Given 8 options, students must choose the one which will complete the matrix by inferring the rule(s) of the columns and rows. The sets in the test become increasingly more complex and difficult. Students were allowed unlimited time to complete all tasks. The order in which tests were taken was alternated both within a testing session and for each student.

Volunteers were divided into two groups based on class section. Grouping in this way resulted in 15 learners (1 male, 14 female) in group 1 and 30 learners (3 male, 27 female) in group 2. Teachers were asked not to correct students with respect to adverbs in either group, nor were they to teach students the rule of adverb placement. For a two-week period (8 days) in group 1, which I will refer to as the noninferencing group, the teachers' regular lessons were altered so that, wherever possible, the exercises contained adverbs. In group 2, which I will refer to as the inferencing group, students received, in addition to the adverb exercises, verbal inductive inferencing exercises in both French and English. These consisted of exercises in analogies, series completions, and classifications (Sternberg 1988).[6] Table 1 provides a summary of variables by treatment group: age; previous years of French; SPM score; and adverb input score (defined below).[7]

Immediately following the two-week instructional period, both groups were posttested on the WOC and AJ tasks. Three weeks after the first posttest, students were posttested again to determine any 'long-term' effects of the teaching material. Two scores were computed for each learner on the WOC task and on the AJ task. An SAVO error score consisted of the number of acceptances of or changes to this ungrammatical order; an SVAO correct score consisted of the number of acceptances of or changes to this grammatical order.[8] A student's total SPM score is the number of problems solved correctly. The maximum score is 60. If an item was not answered or if two (or more) options were selected, that item was not counted as correct. The student's total score is composed of the subscores for each of the five sets of problems. The total score is then compared with the expected score composition for that score, where expected score compositions are based on independent SPM standardization (see Raven, Raven and Court 1991). The difference between the student's score on each set and the score normally expected for that total score is listed as a 'discrepancy'.

In an attempt to take into account student absences and the possible confounding variable of teaching style, a questionnaire was administered to the teachers after the two-week instructional period. I was working with four different teachers, and even though the teachers were working from the same syllabus (that is, all students received the same number of adverb exercises), I could not be assured that the exercises were being employed in the same way. In order to in-

Table 1: Learner variables (age, years of French, adverb input, SPM) by treatment group (inferencing, noninferencing)

variable	group	n	$\bar{x}$	med	SD	min	max
age	inferencing	30	18.53	18.0	1.04	17.0	22.0
	noninferencing	15	18.27	18.0	0.88	17.0	20.0
years of	inferencing	30	3.46	3.8	0.86	2.0	5.0
French	noninferencing	15	4.13	4.2	1.05	2.0	5.6
adverb	inferencing	30	84.17	90.0	12.87	37.0	92.0
input	noninferencing	15	69.6	75.0	15.24	17.0	75.0
SPM	inferencing	30	49.40	51.0	5.56	34.0	56.0
	noninferencing	15	49.27	51.0	5.05	38.0	57.0

clude this variable of teaching style in the multiple regression analysis, an attempt was therefore made to 'quantify' adverb input by having teachers tell how each of the lessons was taught. Each student was then assigned an adverb input score (see Table 1) based on the teachers' responses to the questionnaires. Scoring was based on perceived amount and attendance to input by individuals: Whole-class exercises were awarded 1 point per exercise; group-work exercises, 2 points; pair-work exercises, 3 points; and individual/homework exercises, 4 points. The reasoning behind this quantification was that the learner is presumably attending to the task and receiving input if an exercise is done individually while activities involving ever larger groupings may not foster as much individual attention. Following the instructional period, a questionnaire was also administered to the learners. The goal was to obtain a description of learners' perceptions of input and to ensure that no corrective feedback or explicit rules on adverb placement had been provided to students.[9]

The analysis of resulting data involved not only descriptive statistics reported below, but also repeated measure ANOVAs and multiple regressions. The ANOVAs were run to determine significant differences between and within groups across testing sessions. Multiple regressions were performed to determine significant predictors of test scores and changes in test scores.

Results

Descriptive statistics for the AJ task are shown in Table 2. The table indicates for each test (pretest, posttest1, posttest2) the number of correct answers (K=18) and the number of errors (K=18) by treatment group (inferencing, noninferencing). Descriptive statistics for the WOC task are provided in Table 3, which is organized like Table 2. I discuss the ANOVA results first and then turn to the results of the multiple regression analysis.

As noted above, repeated measures ANOVAs on correct scores and error scores for the AJ and WOC tasks for both groups were run to determine any significant differences between and within groups across testing sessions.[10] Where significant differences between mean scores were found, *post hoc* Scheffé procedures were used to determine the source of differences.

On the AJ task, the differences between the inferencing and non-inferencing groups are not significant on either the correct scores (F(1,82)=.33, p>.05) or the error scores (F(1,82)=2.48, p>.05). There are significant differences between testing sessions for both groups on the correct score (F(2,164)=32.32, p<.01) and on the error score (F(2,164)= 20.21, p<.01). Scheffé tests show that the changes in both scores from pre test to posttest 1 and from posttest 1 to posttest 2 are not significant. The interaction between group and testing session is not significant on correct score (F(2,164) = .19, p>.05) or error score (F(2,164) = .17, p>.05).

Table 2: Descriptive statistics for AJ task: test (pretest, post1, post2) and score (correct, error; K=18) by treatment group (inferencing, noninferencing)

test/score	group	n	$\bar{x}$	med	SD	min	max
pretest	inferencing	30	9.20	9.0	4.38	2.0	18.0
correct	noninferencing	15	9.27	10.0	2.84	4.0	14.0
pretest	inferencing	30	7.13	7.0	3.98	0.0	15.0
error	noninferencing	15	6.20	6.0	2.37	3.0	13.0
post1	inferencing	30	11.03	11.0	5.14	0.0	18.0
correct	noninferencing	15	11.33	14.0	4.43	5.0	18.0
post1	inferencing	30	5.9	6.0	4.54	0.0	17.0
error	noninferencing	15	4.93	4.0	3.28	0.0	10.0
post2	inferencing	29	12.45	14.0	4.79	2.0	18.0
correct	noninferencing	13	13.31	14.0	4.31	6.0	18.0
post2	inferencing	29	4.66	3.0	4.28	0.0	16.0
error	noninferencing	13	3.39	3.0	3.02	0.0	10.0

Table 3: Descriptive statistics for WOC task: test (pretest, post1, post2) and score (correct, error; K=16) by treatment group (inferencing, noninferencing)

test/score	group	n	$\bar{x}$	med	SD	min	max
pretest	inferencing	30	7.93	8.0	2.39	2.0	14.0
correct	noninferencing	15	7.47	8.0	2.85	3.0	13.0
pretest	inferencing	30	3.97	4.0	2.16	0.0	11.0
error	noninferencing	15	3.93	3.0	2.55	0.0	9.0
post1	inferencing	30	8.97	9.5	3.26	2.0	14.0
correct	noninferencing	15	7.93	9.0	2.55	4.0	11.0
post1	inferencing	30	3.20	2.0	2.99	0.0	13.0
error	noninferencing	15	3.53	3.0	2.53	0.0	8.0
post2	inferencing	29	9.69	10.0	3.71	1.0	16.0
correct	noninferencing	13	9.31	10.0	2.93	4.0	12.0
post2	inferencing	29	2.79	2.0	2.70	0.0	12.0
error	noninferencing	13	2.62	1.0	2.84	0.0	9.0

On the WOC task, the differences between the inferencing and non-inferencing groups are not significant on either the correct scores (F(1,82)=.61, p>.05) or the error scores (F(1,82)=.00, p>.05). There are significant differences between testing sessions for both groups on the correct score (F(2,164)=14.31, p< .01) and on the error score (F(2,164)= 9.66, p< .01). Scheffé tests show that the changes in both scores from pretest to posttest 1 and from posttest 1 to posttest 2 are not significant. The interaction between group and testing session is not significant on correct score (F(2,164)=.57, p>.05) or on error score (F(2,164)=.59, p>.05).

After checking for relevant assumptions, multiple regression analyses were performed to determine the significant predictors of change (signified by ∆) among each of the correct-score and error-score outputs shown in (10) below for the AJ task and in (11) for the WOC task.

(10) AJ correct score   AJ error score
   a. pretest   e. pretest
   b. ∆pre-post1   f. ∆pre-post1
   c. ∆post1-post2   g. ∆post1-post2
   d. ∆pre-post2   h. ∆pre-post2

(11) WOC correct score   WOC error score
   a. pretest   e. pretest
   b. ∆pre-post1   f. ∆pre-post1
   c. ∆post1-post2   g. ∆post1-post2
   d. ∆pre-post2   h. ∆pre-post2

The variables that were examined as potential predictors of change were age, years of French, gender, inferencing group/inferencing input[11], adverb input[12], and SPM score.

Each of the outputs shown in (10) and (11) was run with all of the variables, producing combined equations for each value.[13] The results of multiple regressions for the WOC task are summarized in Table 4, and the results for the AJ task are summarized in Table 5. All signicant predictors have been included; the variables account for 10 to 32% of the variance in change.

With respect to the variables under investigation, the summary of the WOC data in Table 4 shows that adverb input, when combined with previous years of French, approaches significance as a predictor of the change in the correct and error scores of the WOC task from posttest 1 to posttest 2 of both groups together. As the summary of AJ data in Table 5 shows, the SPM score alone is a significant predictor of the pretest correct score of both groups. When the SPM score is combined with gender, these variables are significant predictors of the pretest error score of the WOC task of both groups. When the SPM score is combined with age, these variables approach significance as predictors of the change in the correct score of the AJ task from the pretest to posttest 2 of both groups.

Table 4: Multiple regressions for all variables (age, years of French, male-female, SPM, adverb input, inferencing input) for the WOC task: test (pretest, post1, post2) and score (correct, error) by treatment group (inferencing, both).

score	group	pretest	post1-pretest	post2-post1	post2-pretest
correct	inferencing		fre↑△↓/age↑△↓	age↑△↓	
	both		fre↑△↑	fre↑△↓/age↑△↓ (fre+adv)↑△↑	
error	inferencing	mf	mf/fre↑-△	age↑+△/fre↑+△	**m+inf↑-△**
	both	**f+SPM↑↓**	mf/fre↑-△	age↑+△/fre↑+△ (fre+adv)↑-△	

Note: Figures that are the focus of investigation are shown in boldface. All figures give direction (↑,↓) of change (△). Changes in error scores are represented as either negative (-) or positive (+); a negative change from posttest 1 to posttest 2, for example, indicates fewer errors on posttest 2 than on posttest 1. Variables separated by a slash (/) are significant when considered separately, but not when considered together. Variables joined with plus (+) are significant only when taken together. Figures in parentheses indicate the Onmibus test along with one predictor are significant (p<.05), and the other approaches significance.

Table 5: Multiple regressions for all variables (age, years of French, male-female, SPM, adverb input, inferencing input) for the AJ task: test (pretest, post1, post2) and score (correct, error) by treatment group (inferencing, both).

score	group	pretest	post1-pretest	post2-post1	post2-pretest
correct	inferencing		age↑△↑	**infer↑△↑**	
	both	**SPM↑↑**	age↑△↑		**[age+SPM]** age↑△↑ SPM↑△↓
error	inferencing			**infer↑-△**	**infer↑-△**
	both	age↑↓			

Note: Figures that are the focus of investigation are shown in boldface. All figures give direction (↑,↓) of change (△) (see Table 4). Variables separated by a slash (/) are significant when considered separately, but not when considered together. Variables joined with plus (+) are significant only when taken together. Figures in parentheses indicate that the Onmibus test along with one predictor are significant (p<.05), and the other predictor approaches significance. Figures in brackets indicate that the Onmibus test along with one predictor approach significance, and the other predictor is significant.

Inferencing input alone is a significant predictor of the change in correct score of the AJ task from posttest 1 to posttest 2, as well as a predictor of the change in the error score of this task from the pretest to posttest 2 and from posttest 1 to posttest 2. Inferencing input and gender combined are significant predictors of change in the error score of the WOC task from the pretest to posttest 2.

Discussion

Inferencing vs. noninferencing

The first observation is that results of the repeated measures ANOVAs reveal no significant difference between the two groups on either correct scores or error scores of the AJ task and the WOC task. While both groups showed significant improvement from the pretest to posttest 2 in both their acceptance/usage of the correct (SVAO) word order and their rejection/ usage of the incorrect (SAVO) word order on both tasks, the interaction between group and testing session is not significant. In other words, there is no significant difference between the groups in how they changed over time.

However, results of the multiple regression analyses as shown in Tables 4 and 5 reveal that the variables contributing to the change of each group on each task are not necessarily the same. That is to say, just because there is no quantitative difference between the improvement exhibited by each group, one cannot necessarily conclude that this improvement is characteristically similar. As seen in the tables, different predictors were found at different times on different tasks. For example, older subjects, or perhaps those subjects with fewer years of French study, are predicted to show more improvement on the AJ correct score from the pretest to posttest 1; more years of French study predict improvement on the WOC task from the pretest to posttest 1; and, finally, inferencing input predicts improvement from posttest 1 to posttest 2 both on scores of the AJ task and on the overall change in error score on the WOC task. Perhaps the fluctuating influence of a variable depends on both the type of task and the relative presence of other variables. For example, it may be that the effect of inferencing input, only on the AJ task, varies with previous years of French study.

We have seen (see note 6) that the groups differ with respect to adverb input, previous years of French, and, of course, inferencing input. In spite of these differences, however, the groups performed similarly with respect to their quantitative change over time. In addition, the change of one group relative to the other cannot be adequately described in terms of their differences with respect to these variables. For example, while fewer years of French study, as reflected in the age variable, predict change on the AJ correct score, the inferencing group, which had fewer years of French study, did not show greater change than the noninferencing group.

That the groups did differ is one of the major shortcomings of the study. As a result of this shortcoming, explanations of the performance of one group relative to the other become extremely speculative. However, I would like to point out that it may still be informative to consider the performance of the inferencing group alone in terms of one of the variables which is the focus of this study, namely, inferencing input. Even though this input did not result in this group's performance differing significantly from the noninferencing group, it was a significant predictor of change in performance of the inferencing group on both scores of the AJ task and on the WOC error score.[14] If one assumes that the inferencing exercises utilized inductive reasoning, this finding lends support to the proposals that inductive reasoning is a learning strategy which can be developed, and that inductive reasoning can facilitate performance on certain linguistic tasks.

Standard Progressive Matrices (SPM)

The second observation is that inductive ability, as measured by the SPM score, is to some extent an indicator of L2 acquisitional ability. This score is a predictor of the pretest correct score on the AJ task and of the pretest error score on the WOC task. In addition, it may be reflected in the age predictor of the pretest error score of the AJ task, as there was a weak positive correlation between the SPM score and age. I would like to point out two possible implications of these findings. First, that the SPM score is a predictor on these particular tests suggests that a high SPM score indicates that the incorrect (SAVO) word order has been eliminated from the learner's grammar. Moreover, further analysis revealed that a high SPM score is not only a predictor of a lower error score on the WOC task, but also of those errors which consist of active changes to the incorrect (SAVO) word order rather than passive acceptance of this incorrect word order. This finding appears to support the proposal that there is a positive relationship between the use of inductive reasoning and knowledge of the ungrammaticality of a structure.

Furthermore, unlike the variable of previous years of French study, the SPM score crosses tasks as a predictor. I have suggested that the effect of certain variables depends, in part, on the demands of the task. This appears not to be the case with the SPM score, which is a clear predictor of the error score on the WOC task and of the correct score on the AJ task. This finding suggests that, relative to the other variables, inductive reasoning has a more global and 'steadfast' effect on L2 acquisition.

Conclusion

I believe that the two observations discussed above are of use: They highlight the need for methodological modifications, and they have specific implications for future research. First, that there was no significant difference between groups emphasizes the need for more longitudinal studies in L2 acquisition. A long-term study, with periodic testing, would perhaps reveal a cumulative effect of treatment in addition to allowing time for differences between treatment and control groups to emerge. Second, the fact that different predictors were found at different times on different tasks suggests that further investigation of task type is in order. While much recent work (Crookes and Gass 1993a, 1993b) has examined the effects of task type on performance, and in turn how that output affects acquisition, the findings of the present study suggest that more research is needed which investigates the relationship between the specific demands of the task and specific learner variables such as prior linguistic knowledge and inductive ability which respond to those demands. Finally, the fact that SPM was a significant predictor of certain pretest scores and that inferencing input was a significant predictor of the overall improvement on certain scores indicates that further investigation into the role of inductive reasoning in L2 acquisition is justified. The former finding supports, to some extent, proposals made by Carroll (1981) suggesting that inductive reasoning plays a role in foreign language aptitude. The latter finding supports, limitedly at least, proposals made by Neufeld (1978) and those working within a learning strategy paradigm which suggest that inductive inferencing is a strategy that can be partially developed or reinforced through instruction.

Manifested in the results of this study is the now trite fact of the interrelatedness of variables involved in L2 acquisition such as input, tasks, prior linguistic knowledge, grammatical structure, and teaching style. Just as one of these variables cannot be examined in isolation from the others, so too, the cognitive processes which both affect and are affected by these variables must be considered. I believe that the use of INE or inductive inferencing is one such cognitive process. While the results of the current study do not conclusively show that the use of INE facilitates the English-speaking L2 learner's recognition of SAVO as ungrammatical in French, they do suggest that the use of inductive inferencing plays a role in L2 acquisition. Future research in this area is needed to determine more precisely the nature of that role.

Acknowledgments

The research reported in this paper was undertaken as part of my doctoral dissertation and was supported in part by a Dissertation Fellowship from the College of Arts and Letters, Michigan State University. A version of this chapter was presented at the October, 1994 Second Language Research Forum, Montréal. I wish to thank Susan Gass, Carolyn Harford, Paul Mensell, and Dennis Preston for their guidance and many contributions. I am also grateful to Gary Cook for his statistical expertise. Special thanks to Lynn Eubank for his advice, support, and insightful suggestions. Any remaining flaws are of course my own.

Notes

1. A review of the learning strategy research supports the assumption that inductive inferencing as defined here may be considered a learning strategy/process. Elaboration of the present definition and a discussion of the similarities and differences between the present definition and previous conceptualizations of the process of inductive inferencing goes beyond the scope of this paper and can be found in Plough (1994).

2. See McCawley (1983) for the view that "general purpose learning faculties" (p. 180) may be involved in language acquisition.

3. See, however, Lasnik (1988) and Saleemi (1990, 1992) for suggestions on how children might notice the absence of null subjects in ambient exposure to English.

4. I do not intend to suggest that deductive reasoning be excluded from SLA processes. Rather, inductive reasoning should be included.

5. This characterization excludes the exceptional cases of adverb placement that appear in certain emphatic contexts (French) or in cases of so-called 'heavy' NP-shift (English). Pollock (1989) has proposed that the differences in word order shown in (6) to (9) may be explained in terms of the 'strength' of Agreement, differences which result in the differing verb raising characteristics of the two languages. The Principles and Parameters approach adopted by White (1991a, 1991b, 1992a, 1992b) and Trahey and White (1993) is not assumed in the present study.

6. While inductive ability may be unchanging, it has been suggested that it can be developed, refined, and displayed in activities that people value (Raven, Raven and Court 1991:G5). Sternberg (1988) is one of the strongest proponents of the possibility that individuals may improve their *performance* in activities that require inductive reasoning and has set out to develop exercises that will achieve this goal.

7. Multiple regression will determine if two variables are strongly related to each other; that is, the correlation must be .80 or greater. To uncover weak correlations, Pearson-r correlations were calculated for age, previous years of French, adverb input, inferencing input, and SPM score. Based on these correlations, several generalizations can be made. First, there is a small, but significant negative correlation between age and previous years of French ($r= -.356$, $p<.01$). In other words, younger subjects tended to have more years of French. Second, there is a small, but

significant negative correlation between inferencing input and previous years of French (r=-.318, p<.01). In other words, subjects in the inferencing group tended to have fewer years of French than subjects in the noninferencing group. Finally, there is a significant positive correlation between adverb input and inferencing input (r=.581, p<.001). That is, subjects in the inferencing group received higher adverb input scores (i.e., they performed more pair work) than subjects in the noninferencing group. For discussion of these findings, see Plough (1994).

8. The scoring procedures employed here differ from those employed by Trahey and White (1993), whose correct scores include acceptance of the incorrect word order. In the procedures employed here, a response of 'both right' or 'both wrong' is counted neither as erroneous nor as correct. Hence, while Trahey and White focus on the inclusion of the correct word order, the present study is equally interested in the exclusion of the incorrect word order.

9. While a much more reliable description of classroom activities would have been obtained by tape recording the classes, I was not granted permission to implement this procedure.

10. The data from three subjects were excluded from the ANOVA analysis because they were absent when posttest 2 was administered.

11. The interval data from inferencing input and the nominal data from inferencing group were found to be multicollinear; therefore, the inferencing input score was removed from the multiple regressions which considered subjects as a single group. In addition, the interval data on the inferencing input score, which incorporated students absences, was used in the regressions on the inferencing group. This variable was not included in the regressions of the pretest.

12. The adverb input variable was not included in the regressions of the pretests.

13. For each equation, an Omnibus test was performed to determine if the variability between predictors and outcome could be accounted for by chance alone. If the Omnibus test proved significant, then subsequent *t*-tests were performed on the predictors. Regressions which combined all subjects (as a single output) were run first. Regressions on the inferencing group alone were then run to determine any significant predictors within this group which were not revealed by placing the groups together. Regressions could not be performed on the noninferencing group alone because of the small size of the sample (n=15).

14. It could be argued that the variable of inferencing input is merely an indicator of student attendance. However, if this were the case, one would need to explain why adverb input, in which absences were also incorporated, was not a predictor of performance.

References

Alderton, D. & G. Larson. 1990. "Dimensionality of Raven's Advanced Progressive Matrices Items". *Educational and Psychological Measurement* 50.887-900.
Archibald, J. 1993. "Indirect Negative Evidence and Blame Assignment in L2 Parameter Setting". Paper presented at the 22nd University of Wisconsin at Milwaukee Linguistics Symposium. October, 1993.

Bialystok, E. 1978. "A Theoretical Model of Second Language Learning". *Language Learning* 28.69-83.
Bialystok, E. 1979. "The Role of Conscious Strategies in Second Language Proficiency". *Canadian Modern Language Review* 35.372-394.
Bialystok, E. 1990. *Communication Strategies*. Cambridge: Basil Blackwell.
Bley-Vroman, R. 1989. "What is the Logical Problem for Foreign Language Learning?" *Linguistic Perspectives on Second Language Acquisition* ed. by S. Gass & J. Schachter, 41-68. Cambrige: Cambridge University Press.
Carroll, J. B. 1981. "Twenty-five Years of Research on Foreign Language Aptitude". *Individual Differences and Universals in Language Learning Aptitude* ed. by K. C. Diller, 83-118. Rowley, MA: Newbury House.
Carton, A. 1966. *The 'Method of Inference' in Foreign Language Study*. New York: The Research Foundation of the City University of New York.
Carton, A. 1971. "Inferencing: A process in using and learning language". *The Psychology of Second Language Learning* ed. by P. Pimsleur & T. Quinn, 45-58. Cambridge: Cambridge University Press.
Chomsky, N. 1981. *Lectures on Government and Binding*. Dordrecht: Foris.
Clahsen, H. & P. Muysken. 1989. "The UG Paradox in L2 Acquisition". *Second Language Research* 5.1-29.
Crookes, G. & S. Gass, eds. 1993a. *Tasks and Language Learning: Integrating theory & practice*. Clevedon: Multilingual Matters.
Crookes, G. & S. Gass, eds. 1993b. *Tasks in a Pedagogical Context: Integrating theory & practice*. Clevedon: Multilingual Matters.
Gass, S. 1988. "Integrating Research Areas: A framework for second language studies". *Applied Linguistics* 9.198-217.
Kess, J. 1992. *Psycholinguistics: Psychology, linguistics, and the study of natural language*. Amsterdam: John Benjamins.
Lasnik, H. 1989. "On Certain Substitutes for Negative Evidence". *Learnability and Linguistic Theory* ed. by R. J. Matthews & W. Demopoulos, 89-105. Dordrecht: Kluwer.
Mazurkewich, I. 1984. "The Acquisition of the Dative Alternation by Second Language Learners and Linguistic Theory". *Language Learning* 34.91-109.
McCawley, J. 1983. "Towards Plausibility in Theories of Language Acquisition". *Communication and Cognition* 16.169-183.
Moore, T. 1986. "Reasoning and Inference in Logic and Language". *Reasoning and Discourse Processes* ed. by T. Myers, K. Brown & B. McGonigle, 51-66. London: Academic Press.
Neufeld, G. G. 1978. "A Theoretical Perspective on the Nature of Linguistic Aptitude". *International Review of Applied Linguistics* 16.15-25.
O'Malley, J. M. & A. U. Chamot. 1990. *Learning Strategies in Second Language Acquisition*. Cambridge: Cambridge University Press.
Oxford, R. & A. Cohen, A. 1992. "Language Learning Strategies: Crucial issues of concept and classification". *Applied Language Learning* 3.1-35.

Pinker, S. 1989. *Learnability and Cognition: The acquisition of argument structure.* Cambridge, MA: MIT Press.
Plough, I. 1994. *A Role for Indirect Negative Evidence in Second Language Acquisition.* Unpublished doctoral dissertation, Michigan State University.
Pollock, J.-Y. 1989. "Verb Movement, Universal Grammar, and the Structure of IP". *Linguistic Inquiry* 20.365-424.
Raven, J. 1976. *Raven's Standard Progressive Matrices* (Sets A, B, C, D & E). Oxford: Oxford Psychologists Press.
Raven, J., J. C. Raven & J. H. Court. 1991. *Raven Manual.* Section 1: *General overview.* Oxford: Oxford Psychologists Press.
Saleemi, A. 1990. "Null Subjects, Markedness, and Implicit Negative Evidence". *Logical Issues in Language Acquisition* ed. by I. M. Roca, 235-258. Dordrecht: Foris.
Saleemi, A. 1992. *Universal Grammar and Language Learnability.* Cambridge: Cambridge University Press.
Schachter, J. 1988. "Second Language Acquisition and its Relationship to Universal Grammar". *Applied Linguistics* 9.219-235.
Schwartz, B. 1993. "On Explicit and Negative Data Effecting and Affecting Competence and Linguistic Behavior". *Studies in Second Language Acquisition* 15.147-163.
Schwartz, B. & M. Gubala-Ryzak. 1992. "Learnability and Grammar Re-organization in L2A: Against negative evidence causing the unlearning of verb movement". *Second Language Research* 8.1-38.
Sharwood Smith, M. 1990. "Second Language Learnability". *Logical Issues in Language Acquisition* ed. by I. M. Roca, 259-273. Dordrecht: Foris.
Sternberg, R. J. 1988. *The Triarchic Mind.* New York: Viking Press.
Trahey, M. & L. White 1993. "Positive Evidence and Preemption in the Second Language Classroom". *Studies in Second Language Acquisition* 15.181-204.
Trusted, J. 1979. *The Logic of Scientific Inference.* London: Macmillan Press.
Valian, V. 1990. "Null Subjects: A problem for parameter-setting models of language acquisition". *Cognition* 35.105-122.
White, L. 1989. *Universal Grammar and Second Language Acquisition.* Amsterdam: John Benjamins.
White, L. 1991a. "Adverb Placement in SLA: Some effects of positive and negative evidence in the classroom". *Second Language Research* 7.133-161.
White, L. 1991b. "The Verb-Movement Parameter in Second Language Acquisition". *Language Acquisition* 1.337-360.
White, L. 1992a. "Long and Short Verb Movement in Second Language Acquisition". *Canadian Journal of Linguistics* 37.273-286.
White, L. 1992b. "On Triggering Data in L2 Acquisition: A reply to Schwartz & Gubala-Ryzak". *Second Language Research* 8.120-137.

The negative effects of 'positive' evidence on L2 phonology

Martha Young-Scholten
University of Durham

Introduction

The past decade has seen the intensifying of a debate regarding post-puberty (=adult) second-language (L2) access to the syntactic principles and parameters of Universal Grammar (UG) (see Chomsky 1981). In L2 phonology, the access issue is only just starting to be addressed;[1] investigations of interlanguage (IL) phonology have typically aimed (1) to predict first-language (L1) transfer with more precision; (2) to identify IL processes which are unrelated to L1 transfer; and (3) to account for the variability with which transfer and non-L1-based processes operate during acquisition. Much less attention has been devoted to the question of eventual attainment, since it *seems* quite obvious that the ultimate outcome for the great majority of post-puberty learners is not native or even native-*like* competence in the L2 phonology. The generalization that it is impossible for the adult learner to achieve success in acquiring an L2 phonology is not weakened by the existence of a select few who are successful, as such examples can be dismissed as cases of extraordinary talent or atypical cerebral organization.[2]

Yet, along with the observed pervasive lack of eventual attainment, recent L2 phonology studies suggest that adults have continued access to the phonological principles of UG, if not the parameters of UG as well (for discussion, see Young-Scholten forthcoming)–a situation which parallels L2 syntax findings (see, e.g., White 1989). Why, then, the observed lack of eventual complete attainment–or even near attainment? When we subject the process of L2 phonological acquisition to closer scrutiny, we may well find that assumptions regarding the levels of phonological proficiency possible for adults turn out to be unfounded. In any case, a more critical examination of L2 phonology must be undertaken before we can address the issue of access to the phonological principles and parameters of Universal Grammar.

It is not clear that we are currently prepared to answer questions regarding ultimate attainment and access to UG because variables relating to the input the learner has received are generally not controlled for when data are collected. For example, even though the effect of formal instruction on the acquisition of morphosyntax in a second language may turn out to be inconsequential, a number of researchers have taken pains to use data collected from untutored learners (who have received no classroom instruction) when offering claims regarding post-puberty access to the principles and parameters of UG (see, e.g., Clahsen and Muysken 1986 or Vainikka and Young-Scholten 1994). However, the majority of L2 phonology data is collected from tutored learners. That the role of classroom input in the acquisition of an L2 phonology is not inconsequential becomes glaringly obvious when one considers the nature of the phonological input a good many L2 learners typically receive.[3] My claim is that while much of the L2 phonology research carried out up to now has indeed provided valuable insights into the factors which influence interlanguage phonology, the studies involved are problematic in terms of addressing the issues of ultimate attainment and access to UG. I explain below why these studies are problematic in general and offer as a specific example the acquisition of syllable structure.

Access to the phonological principles and parameters of UG

In investigating the L2 acquisition of phonology in terms of what we take to be the phonological principles and parameters of Universal Grammar, the question of ultimate attainment becomes much more relevant. For L2 syntax the logic is as follows: If both principles and parameters are accessible to adult learners, they will develop native syntactic competence in the L2. Conversely, if adult L2 speakers show evidence of native competence, then this is because they have access to UG. There may, however, exist various contravening factors connected to a learning situation arising from a particular combination of native and target language which will block progress towards native competence (see, e.g., White 1989).

At first glance, it might appear that the Joseph Conrad phenomenon discussed in Scovel (1969)[4] holds for adult second language learners, and that while adult learners have access to the syntactic principles of UG, they do not have access to the phonological principles and parameters. As mentioned above, there is evidence of post-puberty access to the phonological component of UG. Although most of the studies from which this evidence comes do not address the access-to-UG issue as such, asking the question first posed by Eckman (1981) "Are interlanguage phonology rules 'natural'?" is tantamount to asking whether adults have access to (at least) the principles of UG. More recent research within the principles and parameters framework provides evidence that not only are L1 phonological parameter settings transferred by learners (Archibald 1993), but parameters are also reset to a new value (Broselow and Finer 1991; Pater 1993; Young-Scholten 1994). Even though learners may arrive at a parameter setting which is not that of the L2, the fact that they progress beyond the L1 setting is evidence that the learner has access to the parameter involved. Research has not yet answered the question of whether adults eventually reset phonological parameters to the correct L2 values. One might presume that the inability to reset parameters to the target language value is our explanation for incomplete phonological attainment, but we would need to explain why, given access to the phonological parameters of UG, learners do not eventually reset them at the correct L2 values.

Possible explanations for lack of attainment

If adults have access to the phonological principles and parameters of UG, shouldn't we have more evidence of complete attainment? Perhaps the solution lies in the performance/competence dichotomy; for some reason adult second language learners who have near-native or native L2 phonological competence are unable (for reasons unrelated to UG) to translate this into performance. Given that it is production data upon which most claims in L2 phonology are based perhaps we are underestimating learners' phonological competence. Alternatively, a number of non-linguistic factors which could account for lack of native L2 production (and also for general lack of attainment) have been discussed in the literature, from anxiety to the reluctance to take on a new identity to the misinterpretation of neural signals by the articulators. However, based on the evidence we have, none of these explanations turns out to be adequate.

A number of researchers have investigated the ability of adult learners to produce L2 sounds when exposed to aural input in a language laboratory setting and have arrived at more encouraging conclusions. For example, Olson and Samuels (1973) found older learners actually performed better than younger learners on audio-taped instruction in German phonemes. Similarly, Snow and Hoefnagel-Höhle (1977) found that adults were better at imitating Dutch segments. And Neufeld (e.g., 1977) designed 18-hour audio-visual courses on Chinese, Japanese and Eskimo pronunciation with which he was able to bring English speakers to such a high level of proficiency that some of them convinced native-speaker judges they, too, were native speakers.

An input-based explanation. It seems that while we do not have a ready explanation for the inability of adults to acquire native or near-native competence in an L2 phonology, these laboratory experiments may be telling us something. Let us consider the process of adult L2 phonological acquisition from an angle from which it is infrequently examined–that of input. If we look closely at the input received by the overwhelming majority of learners in studies discussed in the literature, it is immediately apparent that the input received by older second language learners is of a fundamentally different nature than that received by first language learners–and by younger second language learners.

Input and language acquisition

The interaction of the input the learner receives with the innate linguistic knowledge the learner brings to the task of language acquisition has been a topic of increasing interest (see Hornstein and Lightfoot 1981). The general idea within the principles and parameters framework for L1 acquisition is that the only input which the child uses–and indeed which the child is able to make use of–consists of utterances in the ambient language, that is, the primary linguistic data (PLD). PLD functions as positive evidence in that it clues the child in to what is possible in the language, but not what is impossible. Second language learners receive positive evidence, but also typically receive negative evidence in the form of corrective feedback and explicit evidence in the form of explanation, within the context of formal instruction. While adult L2 learners often receive a considerable amount of negative and explicit evidence, it is by no means a given that such evidence has any impact on the learner's L2 linguistic competence. Schwartz (1993) argues that negative and explicit evidence cannot act on linguistic competence because metalinguistic knowledge and linguistic competence are separately encapsulated in the mind. In other words, it is not simply the fact that negative evidence is not positive, but rather that such data do not constitute PLD, which means that negative evidence will be ineffective.

Although the details of how PLD guide phonological competence will differ from what has been proposed for syntax, we can adopt as null hypothesis the idea that negative and explicit evidence also have no role to play in the acquisition of phonological competence. With this hypothesis in mind, let us consider the sort of phonological data second language learners are exposed to.

Positive evidence with negative consequences

The aural input learners in a foreign language classroom receive from their teachers and their peers is primary linguistic data and functions as positive evidence. A problem arises with positive evidence in the classroom when the input constitutes an accent which deviates from whatever standard the learners are expected to acquire. While classroom L2 learners are often also exposed to recorded input which represents the variety of L2 (or varieties, e.g. American and British English) to be acquired, the aural input received from the teacher and especially the learner's classmates is typically L1-accented. Whether the situation depicted here represents sound pedagogical practice is not relevant; rather, the focal issue is whether it is legitimate to base claims in L2 phonology on data collected from learners whose principal initial exposure was to such input. For example, L2 English data are typically collected from individuals who began to learn English in secondary school in their native countries from non-native (and non-native-like) speakers of English. Data collection begins not long after the learner's arrival in the English-speaking country and subsequent entry into an intensive ESL program. Is it any wonder that such learners' IL phonologies are not native-like? The interesting research question, then, is to what extent exposure to native speaker L2 input following exposure to non-native-accented L2 input results in changes in the learner's interlanguage phonology.

Non-native-accented input is thus positive evidence with a negative effect, at least in terms of the researcher's desire to measure whether the L2 phonology has been acquired. Assessing L2 phonological competence is an even riskier endeavor when a nativized variety of the L2 exists, as it does for English in India or Malaysia. Edge (1991) warns against the use of data from speakers of such varieties to investigate IL processes—easily "a questionably valid procedure [since] these speakers may be operating in terms of an alternative target" (1991:391).

But let us suppose that learners who are not in the target language country are blessed with native speaking teachers. The classroom input could nonetheless be misdirective if the teacher engages consistently in 'teacher-talk'. The phonological characteristics of teacher talk in, for example, English include an absence of the assimilations, reductions and deletions typical of running speech (i.e., postlexical phenomena). Word boundaries may be marked by release and/or aspiration of consonants and the vowels in unstressed syllables may not be reduced. The standard reduction in American English of the question "Did you eat yet?" shown in (1a) below becomes exaggeratedly careful, as shown in (1b).

(1) a. [dʒitʃet]
 b. [dɪd#ju#it#jet]

If learners rarely or never hear the reduced and assimilated alternates, there is no reason to assume they will acquire them. Indeed, there is evidence that instruction is a factor in the acquisition of postlexical phenomena. Young-Scholten (1993b) found that German guestworkers who had received no teacher-talk input (because they were uninstructed) followed the same route in their acquisition of weak pronouns in German as children do, while instructed learners who were none-

theless receiving naturalistic input at the time of testing still followed a different route.
 These two variants of PLD (i.e., NL-accented TL and teacher-talk) constitute variables that should be controlled for when collecting data. If, for example, one wishes to investigate whether Spanish-speaking learners acquire the rhythmic structure of English, one should collect data from learners who have received input from speakers with native or native-like English who do not regularly engage in teacher-talk.[5] However, even such learners will still receive a type of input which may impede their L2 acquisition of phonology.

Orthographic input in L2 phonology

A classroom learner who receives input which is non-native accented or input which is native-accented, but displays characteristics associated with teacher-talk will typically also be receiving a good deal of written input. Whether this input is transmitted via textbooks, 'authentic' materials such as the daily newspaper or the teacher's blackboard scrawl, the written word will be omnipresent in most second language classrooms. More importantly, lessons will be devoted to helping the second language learner to read the L2 with a good accent.
 What is a common classroom practice has a simple flaw. Literacy in the first language does not precede, but rather follows the establishment of phonological competence. Indeed, it has been noted by researchers like Gorosch (1960) that "already existing associations between written symbols and the speech sounds of the native language [...] inhibit the acquisition of a good pronunciation" (cited in Ekstrand 1978:137). It follows that the natural sequence of events is the establishment of L2 phonological competence prior to the introduction of literacy in the L2. Yet the teaching of L2 speech is essentially instruction in the pronunciation of target language graphemes, since learners are usually taught to read in the L2 from the very start, before they have begun to acquire the L2 phonology. Two decades after Gorosch's remark, Taylor (1981) again urges us to consider the influence of the written word, as it is "overwhelming and all pervasive for most literate people (and assuming in consequence a dominant position in most processes of teaching English, even those aimed primarily at establishing oral competence)" (1981:240). Yet influence of the written word typically has been noted only in passing in L2 studies, usually as a source of error when no other explanation can be found.
 Thus even when the learner receives native-accented, non-teacher-talk PLD, the potential for positive evidence to have negative consequences still exists. Premature exposure to orthographic input (at or near the initial stages of L2 phonological development) can be expected to impede progression to native phonological competence in the L2. Furthermore, as it is usually the case that the

PLD classroom L2 learners receive displays all three characteristics discussed above, controlling for input variables becomes imperative if one seeks to determine the learner's potential for achieving native competence in the target language.

The negative effects of orthographic input

It is difficult to argue against the view that input in an accent other than the target accent will not result in acquisition of the target accent. However, it is not immediately obvious why it should be the case that orthographic input impedes the acquisition of the target phonology, particularly if the learner is also receiving at least some aural input from native speakers.[6] In order to see why this form of positive evidence might have negative consequences, we need to consider the nature of orthographic input.

The nature of orthographic input

In that the development of literacy involves the parallel development of the metalinguistic awareness of various phonological and morphological constituents (Goswami and Bryant 1990; Gombert 1992), orthographic input relates to the acquisition of phonology in much the same way that grammatical explanations relate to the acquisition of syntax. Orthographic evidence can in a sense be classified as explicit evidence. The process of learning to read an alphabetic script such as English involves the connection of pre-established phonological constituents to their graphemic representations. When the L2 learner confronts the graphemes of a new language at the start of acquisition, prior to the establishment of the L2 phonology, the learner will be compelled to search for the phonological constituents which these graphemes might represent. Because the L2 phonology has not yet been established, the learner will only be able to access the L1 phonology.[7]

What would constitute evidence in support of the hypothesis that premature orthographic exposure results in (increased) L1 transfer? With respect to the acquisition of phonemes in the L2, one might examine the orthographic representation of phonemes in the learner's L1 and L2 to ascertain whether, when the phoneme is realized differently in the L2 or undergoes a rule the learner–perhaps unexpectedly–ignores the PLD (because orthographic evidence fails to reveal such facts). Leaving aside what would doubtless be a fruitful search for confirming evidence, we will turn to the question of how orthographic input affects the acquisition of prosodic structure, since recent L2 research in this area has resulted in the strongest claims with respect to access to the principles and parameters of UG.

First language acquisition and PLD

Before we address how orthographic input affects the L2 acquisition of prosodic structure, let's consider how the child learning its first language initially makes sense of the PLD. The child receives aural input for at least six months before canonical babbling commences, and receives a further six months of input before uttering its first real words. It is not until the child has received an additional three to five years of input that its attention is directed to graphemic symbols for sounds. Although graphemic input is omni-present in the child's environment, most children do not learn to read until their attention is directed to this input; unlike the situation with respect to PLD and the acquisition of language, the acquisition of literacy typically involves a certain amount of formal instruction.

Yet before they learn to read, children are able to make use of the PLD to gain information regarding the location of words, for example. However, in their research on young children's early segmentation of the sound stream in English, Gleitman, Gleitman, Landau and Landau (1988) found that before they are able to determine word boundaries, children first demonstrate the ability to identify stressed syllables. Unstressed syllables take longer to analyze–and are typically omitted in early English, later to be uttered as dummy syllables. What this indicates is that children are able to make use of prosodic cues regarding the approximate location of a word, but not where the word begins and ends.

Gleitman et. al.'s analysis provides us with a fairly detailed account of how the child's nervous system seems to be designed to deal with the PLD. Although claiming that adults have access to UG is not the same as claiming they make use of precisely the same processing mechanisms as children do, it becomes apparent that comparable processing mechanisms which adult L2 learners may still have at their disposal would equip the learner to deal with PLD rather than orthographic input. In other words, if adults have continued access to UG and remain able to process the PLD in ways similar to children, the mechanisms specifically geared to acquiring language are not even tapped by orthographic input.[8]

We are now in a position to look at an example of the possible negative consequences of premature exposure to orthographic input on the acquisition of an L2 phonology.

The L2 acquisition of syllable structure

Studies of the L2 acquisition of syllable structure do indeed suggest that the route of the acquisition of syllable structure in English is affected by orthographic exposure. While the claim has been made above that orthographic input and phonological input cannot act in tandem to act to result in phonological competence, it appears that orthographic knowledge can act as an input filter.

It is well-documented that L2 learners transfer a less elaborated L1 syllable structure in the process of acquiring a second language with a more complex syllable structure. For example, learners whose L1 canonical syllable structure is CV engage in syllable simplification strategies to replicate the CV syllable structure of their L1 when imposing their L1 syllable structure on the L2. Strategies which have been attested are deletion of one or more initial or final consonant, the word-initial and word-final insertion of a glottal stop and the epenthesis of a vowel to break up initial and final consonant clusters. While such interlanguage rules may often be the result of transfer from the learner's L1, researchers such as Tarone (1980) and Eckman (1981) have noted that epenthesis may occur when no such rules exist in the learner's L1. Use of epenthesis by L2 learners is difficult to explain on the grounds of universal strategies since children's early phonologies show little evidence of epenthesis (see, e.g., Oller 1974; Weinberger 1987).

Why should second language learners prefer epenthesis and children prefer deletion? In order to apply a rule of epenthesis, the learner has to have a sense of what the underlying representation of a given word is. Young children do not have a sense of where words begin and end at the early stages of first language acquisition, whereas second language learners who have access to the written representation of words are able to identify word boundaries and thus have access to information regarding initial and final consonants/consonant clusters in words.

According to Oller (1974), adult L2 learners rarely omit unstressed syllables. This is quite a curious fact, for two reasons. To begin with, omission of unstressed syllables is quite common among children acquiring their first language. Moreover, adult L2 learners seem to experience persistent difficulties with the production of the reduced, centralized vowels in unstressed syllables in languages such as English (see Major 1987) and German (see Young-Scholten 1993a), typically producing tense vowels instead. Thus one would expect adults to omit unstressed syllables at least at the initial stages of development, and perhaps later to produce the same sort of dummy unstressed syllables children do.

Access to the written representation of words from the start can account for the non-omission by L2 learners of unstressed syllables and their preference for epenthesis. It is worth noting that choice of data elicitation task may influence the frequency of epenthesis. Data collected using tasks which involve reading isolated words or sentences would be expected to contain a higher frequency of epenthesis. Simply categorizing such tasks as 'formal' fails to explain patterns observed in the data.

If one considers research on the L2 acquisition of syllable structure and use of syllable simplification strategies (e.g., Eckman 1981; Tarone 1980), one finds that the learners involved were schooled, since they were students in ESL programs at the universities where the researchers collected data. Data from the rare studies in which learners had received little or no formal instruction and hence considerably less orthographic input (e.g., Sato 1984; Tropf 1987; Verma, Firth and Corrigan 1992) suggest that deletion is quite common. Sato's subjects, for example, were two Vietnamese learners of English, aged 10 and 12, with no previous English upon their placement with foster parents in the US. These children did not participate in any ESL classes, but they did attend school. One can therefore surmise that the majority of the input they received (i.e., from their foster parents, classmates and teachers) was not orthographic. Not surprisingly, these learners exhibited no epenthesis.

The preceding discussion raises a number of questions which will need to be answered through empirical investigation. It is not likely that the strong form of a hypothesis relating to orthographic input will be borne out, that is, that any exposure at all to the written word will result in an altered route of acquisition. On the one hand, it would be of value to empirically test the influence of orthographic input. On the other hand, however, researchers would be advised to acknowledge the probable effect of orthographic input and to control for this variable when investigating the development of an L2 phonology by adult learners.

Input and ultimate attainment

One of the hypotheses related to orthographic input which could be proposed is that without the negative influence of such input (i.e., in a naturalistic/untutored acquisition context), adults will eventually attain native competence in their L2 phonology. As soon as one formulates such a hypothesis, a number of studies carried out on age of arrival and ultimate attainment immediately come to mind. These studies all suggest that there is a critical period for eventual attainment of an L2 phonology.

From the late 1960s a number of studies were carried out to address the question of why adults so rarely attain native competence in an L2 phonology, but children much more frequently do (see, e.g., Asher and Garcia 1969; Olson and Samuels 1973; Oyama 1976; Patkowksi 1990; Suter 1976; Thompson 1991). The usual explanation is a neurological one, related to the termination of the critical period around puberty (see, e.g., Scovel 1969). Adult second language learners are thus beyond the critical period within which it is still possible to acquire native competence in an L2 phonology. However, not all researchers are convinced. Major, for example, states that "it has not been sufficiently demonstrated that age is truly the causal factor" (1987:186), and Flege observes that "the age of L2 learners is inevitably confounded with other conditions that co-vary with chronological age" (1987:167).

Orthographic input is certainly one of the factors that typically co-varies with age. Indeed, when one reads between the lines in the various studies, there is no counter evidence that literacy is not a decisive factor. Moreover, these studies suggest that greater exposure to PLD in the L2 in general, but especially prior to exposure to orthographic input, leads to a higher level of eventual attainment. In fact, there is evidence that formal instruction (which involves orthographic input) correlates negatively with pronunciation achievement.

Conversely, if one does find situations in which adult L2 learners are not exposed to orthographic input, then one should find much higher achievement. There are several studies which appear to bear this out. Hill (1970) is a well-known contribution to the issue of ultimate attainment, although it is regarded as somewhat anecdotal since we lack empirical verification of Hill's claim that adults in the Amazon and New Guinea attain native competence in the phonology of their second languages. However, we can assume that, since these second language learners were pre-literate, they had not received orthographic input. Furthermore, we can surmise that they did not receive non-native-language-accented target language input.

Empirical evidence does exist which points to the conclusion that at least near-native phonological competence can be achieved by non-exceptional adult L2 learners, for example, Ioup, Boustagvi, El Tigi and Moselle's (1994) assessment of the syntactic and phonological competence of two English speakers of Arabic. Of interest here is that one of the two speakers had received only PLD as input and had never developed any literacy in the L2.

Conclusion

What I hope to have shown is that the influence of the input most adult L2 learners receive cannot be ignored if the continued investigation of the acquisition of a second phonology within a principles and parameters framework is to bear fruit. Unless orthographic input and native-language-accented target language input are controlled for, conclusions regarding transfer and developmental processes and especially access to UG must be questioned. In addition, the type of elicitation technique must also be taken into account; tasks which involve the reading of lists of words, sentences or even passages are more likely to result in pronunciation which reflects access to orthographic representations.

There are two ways in which one might proceed in seeking evidence to support these claims. One can control for the aforementioned variables in much the same way that L2 syntax researchers have controlled for input variables: by collecting data from groups of learners who have received no formal instruction and commence their acquisition only upon arrival in the target language country. Another way in which we might proceed to determine the precise influence of orthographic input is through the manipulation of orthographic input as an independent variable. Once the effects of such input are known, one could continue to collect data from instructed learners, and factor out orthographic interference. In any case, the serious consideration of this not altogether positive evidence is bound to uncover many more answers regarding the L2 acquisition of phonology than we currently have.

Acknowledgments

This is a revised version of the paper presented at the IV. EUROSLA conference in Aix-en-Provence, September 1994. I am grateful to the members of that audience, particularly Bonnie Schwartz, Robert Bley-Vroman, Ocke-Schwen Bohn and Ana Parrondo for their insights, and in addition, to Anne Vainikka, Lynn Eubank and an anonymous reviewer for their helpful suggestions.

Notes

1. What the access issue essentially (re)addresses is the existence of a sensitive/critical period; that this period for the L2 acquisition of phonology might begin to terminate well before puberty (say, at age six; see Long 1990) does not alter the argument presented here.

2. See, for example, Obler (1989).

3. As we will see, this pertains to most of the data upon which conclusions regarding L2 phonology are based.

4. The Joseph Conrad phenomenon takes its name from the author whose L2 syntactic competence stood in marked contrast to his Polish-accented English.

5. I leave aside questions relating to the timing of native-accented input and the amount required of such input; these are empirical questions which can only be answered by further research.

6. Indeed, the opposite claim has been made, that orthographic input has a facilitative effect. For example, Dickerson (1991) suggests that orthographic cues can overcome pronunciation difficulties. Yet it is far from clear that orthographic evidence, for example, of the phonemic status in Engish of /p/ and /b/ or /r/ and /l/ is of use to Arabic speakers or to Japanese speakers, respectively.

7. This point raises a good many questions that must be left to future research. Among these are whether orthographic evidence as explicit evidence is indeed powerless to alter phonological competence. And if, for example, when the grapheme is one which does not exist in the L1 writing system, the learner receives instruction about how to pronounce the L2 graphemes (additional explicit evidence), does this result in what can be termed L2–or IL–phonological competence? If not, that would mean that the linguistic behavior of classroom learners, for whom the above scenario is typical, does not represent L2 *phonological competence*, but only *learned knowledge*.

8. There is some evidence that older learners do not process input in the same manner as do young children. In her study of very young, older and post-puberty first language learners of American Sign Language, Newport (1993) found that even the older pre-puberty children did not acquire all of the complex morphology of ASL. Newport's proposal is that the limited short-term memory of younger learners actually aids them in their acquisition of morphology. Older learners' increased short-term memory may well strenthen the tendency for these L2 learners to make use of epenthesis as a syllable simplification strategy (see below).

References

Archibald, J. 1993. *Language Learnability and L2 Phonology: The acquisition of metrical parameters*. Dordrect: Kluwer.
Asher, J. J. & R. Garcia. 1969. "The Optimal Age to Learn a Foreign Language". *Modern Language Journal* 38.334-341.
Broselow, E. & D. Finer. 1991. "Parameter Setting in Second Language Phonology and Syntax". *Second Language Research* 7.35-59.
Chomsky, N. 1981. "Principles and Parameters in Syntactic Theory". *Explanation in Linguistics: The logical problem of language acquisition* ed. by N. Hornstein & D. Lightfoot. London: Longman.
Clahsen, H. & P. Muysken. 1986. "The Availability of Universal Grammar to Adult and Child Learners. A study of the acquisition of German word order". *Second Language Research* 2.93-119.
Dickerson, W. 1991. "Orthography as a Pronunciation Resource". *Teaching English Pronunciation* ed. by A. Brown, 159-172. London: Routledge.
Eckman, F. 1981. "On the Naturalness of Interlanguage Phonological Rules". *Language Learning* 31.195-216.
Edge, B. A. 1991. "The Production of Word-Final Voiced Obstruents in English by L1 speakers of Japanese and Cantonese". *Studies in Second Language Acquisition* 13.377-393.
Ekstrand, L. H. 1978. "English Without a Book Revisited: The effect of age on second language acquisition in a formal setting". *Didakometry*. Department of Educational and Psychological Research, School of Education. Malmo, Sweden..
Flege, J. E. 1987 "A Critical Period for Learning to Pronounce Foreign Languages?" *Applied Linguistics* 8.162-177.

Gleitman, L., H. Gleitman, B. Landau & E. Landau. 1988. "Where Learning Begins: Initial representations for language learning". *Language: Psychological and biological aspects* ed. by F. Newmeyer, 150-193. Cambridge: Cambridge University Press.
Gombert, J. E. 1992. *Metalinguistic Development*. London: Harvester Wheatsheaf.
Gorosch, M. 1960. "English Without a Book: A bilingual experiment in primary schools by audio-visual means". Preliminary Report. Ms., University of Stockholm.
Goswami, U. & P. Bryant. 1990. *Phonological Skills and Learning to Read*. Hove: Lawrence Erlbaum.
Hill, J. 1970. "Foreign Accents, Language Acquisition and Cerebral Dominance Revisited". *Language Learning* 20.237-248.
Hornstein, N. & D. Lightfoot, eds. 1981. *Explanation in Linguistics: The logical problem of language acquisition*. London: Longman.
Ioup, G., E. Boustagvi, M. El Tigi & M. Moselle. 1994. "A Case Study of Successful Adult Second Language Acquisition in a Naturalistic Environment". *Studies in Second Language Acquisition* 16.73-98.
Long, M. 1990. "Maturational Constraints on the Acquisition of Language". *Studies in Second Language Acquisition* 12.251-285.
Major, R. 1987. "Foreign Accent: Recent research and theory". *IRAL* 25.185-202.
Neufeld, G. 1977. "Language Learning Ability in Adults: A study on the acquisition of prosodic and articulatory features". *Working Papers in Bilingualism* 12.45-60.
Newport, E. 1993. "Maturational Constraints on Language Learning". *Language Acquisition: Core readings* ed. by P. Bloom, 543-560. London: Harvester Wheatsheaf.
Obler, L. 1989. "Exceptional Second Language Learners". *Variation in Second Language Acquisition, Volume II: Psycholinguistic issues* ed. by S. Gass, C. Madden, D. Preston & L. Selinker. Clevedon: Multilingual Matters.
Oller, D. K. 1974. "Toward a General Theory of Phonological Processes in First and Second Language Learning". Paper presented at the Western Conference on Linguistics, Seattle, WA.
Olson, L. & S. J. Samuels. 1973. "The Relationship between Age and Accuracy of Foreign Language Pronunciation". *Journal of Educational Research* 66.263-267.
Oyama, S. 1976. "A Sensitive Period for the Acquisition of a Non-native Phonological System. *Journal of Psycholinguistic Research* 5.261-285.
Pater, J. 1993. "Theory and Methodology in the Study of Metrical Parameter (Re)setting". *McGill Working Papers in Linguistics* 9.211-244.
Patkowski, M. S. 1990. "Age and Accent in a Second Language: A reply to James Emil Flege". *Applied Linguistics* 11.73-89.
Sato, C. 1984. "Phonological Processes in Second Language Acquisition: Another look at interlanguage syllable structure". *Language Learning* 34.43-57.
Schwartz, B. D. 1993. "On Explicit and Negative Data Effecting and Affecting Competence and Linguistic Behavior". *Studies in Second Language Acquisition* 15.147-163.
Scovel, T. 1969. "Foreign Accents, Language Acquisition and Cerebral Dominance. *Language Learning* 19.245-253.

Suter, R.W. 1976. "Predictors of Pronunication Accuracy in Second Language Learning". *Language Learning* 26.233-253.
Tarone, E. 1980. "Some Influences on the Syllable Structure of Interlanguage Phonology". *IRAL* 18.139-152.
Taylor, D. S. 1991. "Non-native Speakers and the Rhythm of English". *Teaching English Pronunciation* ed. by A. Brown, 235-244. London: Routledge.
Thompson, I. 1991. "Foreign Accents Revisited: The English pronunciation of Russian immigrants". *Language Learning* 41.177-204.
Tropf, H. 1987. "Sonority as a Variability Factor. *Sound Patterns in Second Language Acquisition* ed. by A. James & J. Leather, 172-192. Dordrecht: Foris.
Vainikka, A. & M. Young-Scholten. 1994. "Direct Access to X'-Theory: Evidence from Korean and Turkish adults learning German". *Language Acquisition Studies in Generative Grammar* ed. by T. Hoekstra & B. D. Schwartz, 265-316. Amsterdam: Benjamins.
Verma, M., S. Firth & K. Corrigan. 1992. "The developing system of Panjabi/Urdu Speaking Children Learning English as a Second Language in Britain". *New Sounds 92*, 174-199. Amsterdam: University of Amsterdam.
Weinberger, S. 1987. "The Influence of Linguistic Context on Syllable Simplification". *Interlanguage Phonology* ed. by G. Ioup & S. Weinberger, 401-417. Rowley, MA: Newbury House.
White, L. 1989. *Universal Grammar and Second Language Acquisition*. Amsterdam: John Benjamins.
Young-Scholten, M. 1993a. *The Acquisition of Prosodic Structure in a Second Language*. Tübingen: Narr.
Young-Scholten, M. 1993b. "The L2 Acquisition of Informal Speech in German". *Current Issues in European Second Language Acquisition Research* ed. by B. Kettemann & W. Wieden, 111-124. Tübingen: Narr.
Young-Scholten, M. 1994. "On Positive Evidence and Ultimate Attainment in L2 Phonology". *Second Language Research* 10.193-214.
Young-Scholten, M. Forthcoming. "A New Research Programme for the L2 Acquisition of Phonology". *Issues in Second Language Acquisition: An introduction* ed. by P. Jordens & J. Lalleman. The Hague: Mouton.

German plurals in adult second language development
Evidence for a dual-mechanism model of inflection

Harald Clahsen
University of Essex

Introduction

I will investigate the acquisition of the German plural system in adult second language (L2) learners whose native languages (L1) are Romance. My focus will be on the nominal plural system. This involves many irregularities and can be expected to be acquired late in L2 development.

The general background for this study is the question of how to represent regular and irregular inflectional morphology. This issue has recently come up in psycholinguistics, particularly in the connectionist-vs.-symbolist debate. I think that the acquisition data we have are relevant to this debate. Recall that the connectionist approach proposes a *unitary representation* of inflection, as for example in Rumelhart and McClelland's (1987) model of past tense forms in English, where regular, semiregular and irregular morphology is handled in a single associative network. This view stands opposed to the *dual-mechanism model* proposed, among others, by Pinker and Prince (1988), which assumes two qualitatively different ways of inflection; one is rule-based, whereas the other is rote-based and involves storing inflected word forms in the lexicon. The most important difference between the two models has to do with the way regular morphology is represented. In the dual-mechanism model, regular forms are generated by a productive mental operation that adds an affix to a stem. In a unitary model, by contrast, regular inflectional affixes do not have a special representation; they are rather members of a single network just like any other (irregular) affix.

The system of noun plurals in German has some properties which make it particularly interesting as a test case in the debate over regular and irregular morphology. In contrast to English, where the plural affix -*s* is used with nearly all nouns, plural formation in German is much less systematic. There are eight possible plural allomorphs, most of which are highly irregular. Only the plural allomorph -*s* has properties that are typical of a regular default affix. The -*s* morpheme is used with new words and names, for example. However, the most frequent plural allomorph in German is -*n* (see Köpcke 1988), and since most nouns have irregular plurals, the plural -s is less frequent in any stretch of discourse than any of the several irregular plural allomorphs. This means that it is not at all obvious for a language learner to determine whether German has a default plural at all, and, if so, what form it has.

The results we have on the acquisition of noun plurals in German, both on L1 acquisition (Clahsen, Rothweiler, Woest and Marcus 1992) and on adult L2 development, suggest that even in this case, where learners are confronted with a highly irregular system in the input, qualitative distinctions between regular and irregular plurals are made quite early on. Note, for example, that in German, compounds can contain irregular plurals (e.g., *Kindergarten*, literally 'children garden'), but not regular plurals (**Autoswaschanlage*, 'cars wash'). Similarly, in our language acquisition data (both L1 and L2), we found that those plural allomorphs which are used in overregularizations are left out within compounds. This shows that regular and irregular inflected forms differ qualitatively in terms of their relation to other grammatical processes (e.g., compounding) and that language learners respect these grammatical distinctions. Given a unitary representation of plural morphology, these results are hard to account for. Under the dual-mechanism model, however, they have a straightforward explanation: A regular plural form created by an inflectional rule may not enter into a compound, whereas irregular plurals, which are stored in the lexicon, are accessible for compounding.

A short description of the German plural system

In German the plural can be marked on the noun as well as on the determiner (e.g., *die*, 'the-PL'). Here I will only deal with noun plurals. Plural morphology on the noun is highly irregular and complex. There are five plural allomorphs, -(*e*)*n*, -*s*, -*e*, -*er* and ⌀, three of which also allow a variant with an umlaut (e.g, ü). The examples in (1a-e) show the eight possible plural allomorphs.

(1) a. -⌀   das Segel   die Segel   'the sail/sails'
            der Lehrer   die Lehrer   'the teacher/teachers'
        ¨-⌀   die Mutter   die Mütter   'the mother/mothers'
            der Apfel   die Äpfel   'the apple/apples'

b. -e	der Hund	die Hunde	'the dog/dogs'
	das Bein	die Beine	'the leg/legs'
¨-e	die Kuh	die Kühe	'the cow/cows'
	die Maus	die Mäuse	'the mouse/mice'
c. -er	das Kind	die Kinder	'the child/children'
	der Geist	die Geister	'the spirit/spirits'
¨-er	der Wald	die Wälder	'the forest/forests'
	das Huhn	die Hühner	'the hen/hens'
d. -(e)n	die Strasse	die Strassen	'the street/streets'
	die Frau	die Frauen	'the woman/women'
e. -s	das Auto	die Autos	'the car/cars'
	der Park	die Parks	'the park/parks'
	die Kamera	die Kameras	'the camera/cameras'

The use of these allomorphs with specific nouns is to varying degrees arbitrary. There are preferred combinations of nouns and plural allomorphs which are determined by the gender and/or the morphophonological characteristics of the noun; however, the list of exceptions is quite long (see, among others, Köpcke 1988; Mugdan 1977). The only exceptionless rule is that feminine nouns ending in -e form the plural with -n. All other patterns can be only described as tendencies. Within the system of plural allomorphs, the affix -s is special in several ways. First, the use of -s is phonologically underdetermined; that is, -s appears when the phonological environment does not permit any other plural allomorph. The suffix -s is, with few exceptions, the sole plural marker for names as in (2a) below, newly created expressions such as clippings as in (2b) and acronyms as in (2c) and with borrowed and foreign words as in (2d). This illustrates that -s always appears when the noun does not yet have a lexical entry for the plural form.

(2) a. die Müllers 'the Mullers'
    b. Loks (Lokomotiven) 'locomotives'
       Sozis (Sozialisten) 'socialists'
       Unis (Universitäten) 'universities'
    c. GmbHs 'corporation,' 'Inc'
    e. kiosks 'newsstands'

In general, plural formation in German is much less systematic than, for example, in English, where only a few rules account for nearly all plural formation. Mugdan's attempt to account for plural formation in German through structuralist IP-rules led to ten rules and 17 lists of exceptions (Mugdan 1977:87).

Wunderlich (1986) and Wiese (1988) have analyzed the German plural system within the framework of Lexical Morphology (see Kiparsky 1982, 1985) and have argued that -s is the default affix in the system of German noun plurals. One reason for assigning -s default status is that it is found with all nouns which do not yet have a marked lexical entry for plural as in the examples in (2). This can be accounted for by the *Elsewhere Condition* (see Kiparsky 1982); if a morphological rule such as plural formation can be realized through a specific lexical entry, then this takes precedence over a general rule. This means that the default form only occurs when there is no idiosyncratic entry available. The second observation concerning the distribution of -s is that it does not occur in compounds, whereas all other (irregular) plural forms are frequently used in compounds. This regular/irregular distinction holds for root compounds as well as for synthetic compounds. Consider the examples in (a-h) below. The distribution in these examples follows from the general constraint that a regular plural form created by an inflectional rule may not enter into a compound, whereas irregular plurals, which are stored in the lexicon, are accessible for compounding. Thus, the plural -s may not occur inside a compound as shown in (3a) and (3b), whereas the other (irregular) plurals may enter compound formation on Level 2. Note in particular the contrast between the -s plural of the clipped noun in (3b) and the -(e)n plural of same noun, now in its full form, in (3c). The examples in (3d) and (3e) also illustrate plural inside compound for the -(e)n affix, and those in (3f), (3g) and (3h) illustrate it for the -e affix and the regular and umlauted varieties of the -er affix, respectively.

(3) a.*Autosberg   'car heap'
    b.*Sozistreffen   'socialists' meeting'
    c. Sozialistentreffen   'socialists' meeing'
    d. Professorenkränzchen 'professors' circle'
    e. Frauenladen   'women's center'
    f. Schweinestall   'pigsty'
    g. Kindergarten   'kindergarten'
    h. Bücherregal   'book shelf'

Noun plurals in adult L2 learners

Let us now turn to L2 acquisition. Table 1 presents an overview of previous studies on the acquisition of noun plurals in German. As the table shows, elicited data as well as spontaneous speech corpora from tutored and untutored L2 learners with various language backgrounds have been studied with respect to plurals. However, other than a few remarks on noun plurals in the longitudinal study of Meyer-Ingwersen, Neumann and Kummer (1977) on Turkish learners of German, all the previous studies are cross-sectional. To fill this gap, I studied the use of noun plurals in the learners of the ZISA longitudinal data; see Clahsen (1984) for an initial description of the ZISA longitudinal project.

Table 1: Previous studies on noun plurals in German L2 acquisition

study	group	L1	tutoring	design	elicitation
Heidelberger Projekt Pidgin-Deutsch (1975)	foreign workers	Spanish, Italian	no	cross sectional	interviews
Mugdan (1977)	students	various	yes	cross sectional	formal test
Orlovic (1978)	foreign workers	Serbo-Croatian	no	cross sectional	interviews
Phillips & Bouma (1980)	students	English	yes	cross sectional	formal test

In the ZISA longitudinal study, eleven immigrants from Italy, Spain, and Portugal were interviewed every two weeks for at least 57 weeks, some for well over 80 weeks, usually starting within a few weeks after immigration to Germany. The data consist of informal interviews and free conversations which were audiotaped and subsequently transcribed and analyzed. At the time of the first interview, the learners were between 14 and 37 years of age. Most of them had had little formal education; their social and cultural background was fairly homogeneous. Background information on these learners can be found in Table 2.

For the results reported below, an analysis of all obligatory contexts was carried out. The description below has two parts. First, all nouns that occurred in obligatory contexts for plural marking will be analyzed; imitations were not included here. Then, plurals within nominal compounds will be investigated.

Plural allomorphs

Table 3 provides an overview of the plural allomorphs that occur in the data. The table displays a clear difference between the Italians, on the one hand, and the Spaniards and Portuguese, on the other. Whereas the latter make use of all the allomorphs available in German, most of the Italians do not have the -*s* plural. Only Bruno produces one (correct) instance with -*s* (*fotos*) in a later recording. For the other Italian learners, -*s* does not occur, although there are obligatory contexts in which -*s* is required in German. In these cases, errors such as those in (4a-c) below occur. The observed difference with respect to the occurrence of -*s* plurals coincides with how plurals are marked in the learners' L1. In Italian plurals are marked through vowel changes, whereas in Spanish and Portuguese -*s* is the regular plural marker. Thus, the plural marker -*s* is familiar to Spanish and Portuguese learners, whereas it is not to Italian learners.

(4) a. bone (Bongiovanni) correct: Bons, 'tickets'
    b. kilen (Lina) correct: Kilos, 'kilograms'
    c. bonbon (Lina) correct: Bonbons, 'sweets'

Table 2: Social-demographic information on the ZISA longitudinal learners

name	date of birth	origin	education	date of immigration	employment in Germany	tutoring
Ana	1956	Spain	HS, TS	1978	cleaning lady	rarely
José	1961	Spain	ES, convent school	1977	waiter	no
Leonor	1945	Portugal	U, medical school	1979	doctor	yes
Maria	1946	Portugal	ES	1977	cleaning lady	no
Zita	1960	Portugal	ES	1978	cleaning lady	no
Alfio	1956	Sicily	TS	1977	factory worker	rarely
Bongiovanni	1960	Sicily	ES	1978	unskilled factory worker	no
Bruno	1962	Sicily	ES, HS (1 year)	1978	factory worker	no
Giovanni	1955	Sicily	HS, U (2 years)	1978	grinder	rarely
Lina	1945	Sicily	ES	1978	unskilled factory worker	no
Salvatore	1941	Sicily	ES	1978	unskilled factory worker	rarely

Note: Information under Education indicates highest level completed: Elementary school (ES), high school (HS), technical school (TS), university (U).

Table 3: Inventory of plural allomorphs

learner-language	¨-∅/-∅	¨-e/-e	-(e)n	¨-er/-er	-s
Alfio I(talian)	+	+	+	+	-
Bongiovanni I	+	+	+	+	-
Bruno I	+	+	+	+	(+)
Giovanni I	+	+	+	+	-
Lina I	+	+	+	+	-
Salvatore I	+	+	+	+	-
Ana S(panish)	+	+	+	+	+
José S	+	+	+	+	+
Leonor P(ortuguese)	+	+	+	+	+
Maria P	+	+	+	+	+
Zita P	+	+	+	+	+

Table 4 presents a quantitative overview of the proportion of correct plural marking and the kinds of errors that occur in the data. The first two columns provide frequencies of correct plural marking, the first column provides the absolute number of correct plural markings, and the second column shows the percentage of correct plural markings in obligatory contexts. The third column contains the number of errors, including both singular forms and overregularizations. The fourth column shows in how many cases singular forms were used in plural contexts. The last four columns contain forms that are wrong in German. The cases with -*n* and -*s* are overregularizations of German plural allomorphs. The cases with -*e*, however, are particular, since errors with -*e* also occur in singulars. It will be argued that -*e* is not a plural allomorph for the learners and that its use has to do with phonotactic differences between German and the learners' L1. The last column contain plural allomorphs that do not exist in German.

As can be seen from the second column in Table 4, the proportion of correct plural marking is around 50% (∓10%) for all learners except Ana S. There are many errors in plural inflection, and it seems that this part of German grammar is quite hard for L2 learners to acquire. With respect to the *development* of plural marking, we made a comparison with the stages of word order acquisition that were previously studied in the ZISA project (see, e.g., Clahsen 1987). We found that for some learners the percentage of correct plural forms increases as they are developing along these stages. For example, Giovanni produced 31% correct plural forms at Stage 1 of word order development, and 41% correct plurals at Stage II while José produced 37% correct plural forms at Stage I and 61% at Stage 4. However, for other learners (e.g., Bongiovanni, Bruno and Ana), the proportion of correct plurals does not increase, even though they make progress in other grammatical areas. Even on the highest developmental stage, the percentage of errors in plural inflection is still around 30%. This shows that although the plural is marked early, none of the learners acquire the correct system of plural marking during the two-year period of observation.

Table 4 also shows that the majority of errors are the result of singular forms used in plural contexts. This accounts for more than 80% of the errors for most of

Table 4: Plural marking in adult L2 learners

learner-language	correct ∑	%	errors ∑	singular forms -ø	overregularizations -n	-s	-e	other
Alfio I	27	59	19	16	1	0	2	0
Bongiovanni I	37	40	56	46	3	0	7	0
Bruno I	125	61	80	66	4	0	10	0
Giovanni I	56	46	67	60	1	0	5	1
Lina I	38	40	57	39	2	0	11	5
Salvatore I	20	54	17	15	0	0	2	0
Ana S	25	29	60	47	4	6	3	0
José S	70	54	60	56	0	3	1	0
Leonor P	86	60	55	36	11	7	1	0
Maria P	58	56	46	37	2	4	2	1
Zita P	35	44	45	36	2	3	4	0

the learners; only for Lina with 68% (39 singular forms out of 57 errors; see Table 4) and Leonor with 65% (36 singular forms out of 55 errors) are the percentages of unmarked forms in plural contexts slightly lower. Again, there is no developmental change in this regard, even for those learners with the highest values for correctness. Whenever there is an error, it is most often the case that a plural marking is missing in an obligatory context.

With respect to overregularizations, Table 4 displays a clear difference between the Italians, on the one hand, and the Spaniards and Portuguese, on the other. Whereas the latter use -s (in addition to -n) in overregularizations, the Italians never produce errors with -s. This coincides with what we saw previously, namely, that except for one instance with -s from Bruno in a later recording, no other Italian learner acquires the plural allomorph -s during the period of observation. In (5a-g) below, some examples of overregularizations of -s are given. The examples illustrate that there is no restriction on the use of -s; thus, -s may replace -n as in (5a), (5b) and (5f), umlaut as in (5c), -e as in (5d), -⌀ as in (5e) or -er as in (5g). This suggests that -s is a default plural marking for the Spanish and Portuguese learners.

(5) a. grupps (Ana S)   correct: Gruppen, 'groups'
    b. saches (Ana S)   correct: Sachen, 'things'
    c. vaters (Ana S)   correct: Väter, 'fathers'
    d. freundes (José S) correct: Freunde, 'friends'
    e. fingers (Zita P)   correct: Finger, 'fingers'
    f. names (Maria P)   correct: Namen, 'names'
    g. länders (Leonor P) correct: Länder, 'countries'

With respect to overregularizations of -n, there is no difference between the three groups of L2 learners. We found errors with -n for Italian, Spanish and Portuguese learners. Consider the examples in (6a-f) below. As with -s, there do not seem to exist restrictions on the use of -n; it is used instead of -⌀ as in (6a), -e as in (6b), (6c) and (6d), -er as in (6e) and -s as in (6f). The only case that is not documented are overregularizations of -n when an umlaut is required, such as (5c) with respect to -s. This, however, seems to be an accident, since overall the umlaut plural is quite rare.

(6) a. arbeitern (Bongiovanni) correct: Arbeiter, 'workers'
    b. papieren (Alfio)   correct: Papiere, 'papers'
    c. besuchen (Giovanni)   correct: Besuche, 'visits'
    d. gesprächen (Bruno)   correct: Gespräche, 'talks'
    e. büchen (Ana)   correct: Bücher, 'books'
    f. spaghetten (Leonor)   correct: Spaghettis

Consider now errors with the form -e. Table 4 shows that this is the most frequent error type for the Italians, whereas with the Spanish and Portuguese learners, it occurs just in a few examples. Notice, however, that the affix -*e* also occurs for the corresponding singulars. Thus, Ana and Zita, for example, say *persone* when referring to several persons, but they also say *persone* when referring to one person. Examples of this kind can be found for all of the Italian learners as well as for the Portuguese; José uses -*e* only once (*touriste*), and there is no context in which the corresponding singular form could be used. This suggests that -*e* is, in most cases, not a plural allomorph for the learners. Most probably, the occurrences of -*e* have to do with phonotactic differences between German and the learners' L1, that is, with the use of closed syllables, which are more restricted in the Romance languages, particularly in Italian.

Let us finally look at a particular subtype of overregularization in which the endings -*n* or -*s* are used, although the noun is already marked for plural. There are some instances for 'double' markings of this kind in the available data; The examples in (7a-h) give a full list of this sort. We find that only -*s* and -*n* are used in these cases; -*e*, however, is never used. This confirms that -*n* and -*s*, but not -*e*, are default plural forms for the learners. In most cases, -*n* or -*s* are added to nouns that are marked with umlaut and/or -*er*. (7d) is a *pluralia tantum* noun, and (7e) is a double marking that is possible in the local dialect.

(7) a. männen (Bruno I)   correct: Männer, 'men'
    b. büchern (Ana S)   correct: Bücher, 'books'
    c. büchen (Ana S)   correct: Bücher, 'books'
    d. elterns (Ana S)   correct: Eltern, 'parents'
    e. jungens (José S)   correct: Jungen, 'boys'
    f. männers (Zita P)   correct: Männer, 'men'
    g. länders (Leonor P)   correct: Länder, 'countries'
    h. kinders (Maria P)   correct: Kinder, 'children'

Summarizing these results, we have seen that the plural is marked early in development, but that none of the learners in our study acquired the complete system. We also saw that there are differences between the learners' acquisition of plural, particularly with respect to the use of the -*s* allomorph, that depend on their first language, that is, early use of -*s* (including overregularizations) with Spaniards and Portuguese, but not with Italians. Finally, there is evidence that the learners have two kinds of plural markings: Irregular forms, which are restricted in use and do not occur in overregularizations, and regular affixes, which may replace any other plural allomorph. The allomorphs -*n* and, for the Spaniards and Portuguese, also -*s* may be regarded as regular, that is, as default plural forms. These forms are used in overregularizations with no recognizable restrictions. Also, in cases of double marking, only -*n* or -*s* are added to an otherwise correct irregular plural form, as shown in the examples in (7). Notice further that these properties of the default forms -*n* and -*s* even hold for the earliest stage of grammatical development. This suggests that the distinction between regular and irregular morphology, in this case plurals, does not have to be acquired in L2 development.

Plural marking in compounds

To test the proposed interpretation, I will now look at plural formation in compounds. Recall that irregular plural forms may occur within compounds in German, whereas the default plural may not. Does such a feeding relationship also hold for the noun plural system of L2 learners?
 The ZISA longitudinal corpus contains a total number of 119 compounds. All of these compounds are so-called root compounds (N+N). In contrast to German, N+N compounding is not productive in the learners' first languages. There are only very few (probably lexicalized) cases of N+N compounds, and there is no basis for establishing a clear regular/irregular distinction. Hence, the source of the learners' knowledge of the regular/irregular distinction in German root compounds cannot be direct positive transfer from their L1.
 The distribution of plural markings on the first noun of these 119 nominal compounds is as in (8) below.

(8) a. The plural allomorphs *-e*, *-er* and *-n* occur in nominal compounds.
  b. The plural *-s* never occurs within a compound.
  c. The plural *-n* is sometimes left out in compounds, even in cases in which it is required in German.

With respect to (8a), the examples in (9a-j) illustrate that all the plural allomorphs except *-s* are used within compounds. There are no errors in the use of these forms. More important with respect to the feeding relationships between compounding and inflection is which plural allomorphs are left out in compounds. Notice with respect to (8b) that there are several instances of compounds in which the first noun, if it occurs outside a compound, takes the plural allomorph *-s*; see the examples in (10a-e) below. This means that there were chances to use the *-s* plural. In the available data, however, the *-s* plural never occurs in a compound.

(9) a. kindergarten (José S)
  b. getränkekarte (José S)   'beverage menu'
  c. wochenende (José S)   'weekend'
  d. wörterbuch (Bruno I)   'dictionary'
  e. schraubenzieher (Bruno I)   'screwdriver'
  f. kindergeld (Lina I)   'family allowance'
  g. arbeitslosengeld (Lina I)   'unemployment compensation'
  h. arbeiterfamilie (Leonor P)   'working-class family'
  i. faschistenzeit (Leonor P)   'era of fascism'
  j. schweinefleisch (Leonor P)   'pork'

(10) a. kilometer (Giovanni I) plural: Kilos
b. autobahn (Giovanni I) 'highway'; plural: Autos
c. kontonummer (Bongiovanni) 'account number'; colloquial pl: Kontos
d. fotokurs (Alfio) 'photography course'; plural: Fotos
e. babymuscheln (José S) 'baby mussels', 'vongole'; plural: Babys

Concerning missing plural markings in compounds, (11a-i) below lists all examples in which a plural marking that is required in German has been left out. Examples of this type are not very frequent; all of them, however, are largely similar in that the only plural allomorph that is left out within compounds is -*n*. In other words, whenever a plural marking is required on the first noun of a compound, the learners have it, except for the cases with -*n* listed in (11). Notice also that these cases cannot be taken directly from the input, since they are ungrammatical in German.

(11) a. zitronetee (Giovanni I) correct: Zitronentee, 'lemon tea'
b. olivesalat (Giovanni I) correct: Olivensalat, 'olive salad'
c. krankkasse (Giovanni I) correct: Krankenkasse, 'health insurance'
d. tapetefabrik (Giovanni I) correct: Tapetenfabrik, 'wallpaper factory'
e. kerzschlüssel (Bongiovanni I) correct: Kerzenschlüssel, 'sparkplug wrench'
f. straßebahn (José S) correct: Straßenbahn, 'street car'
g. gaststätteküchen (Maria P) correct: Gaststättenküchen, 'restaurants' kitchen'
h. fraueklinik (Zita P) correct: Frauenklinik, 'women's hospital'
i. wocheende (Leonor P) correct: Wochenende, 'weekend'

There are differences between the learners in terms of the use of compounds and the occurrence of -*n* inside compounds. Some learners use -*n* inside compounds whenever it is required (Bruno, Alfio, Lina, Ana). All of these compounds, however, occur in later recordings. At the beginning, compounds requiring the plural -*n* do simply not occur in the data of these four learners. Nothing can be said about Salvatore, since he has only one (correct) compound (*kindergeld*, 'family allowance'). The remaining learners leave out the -*n* (see the examples in (11)) and sometimes produce the -*n* inside compounds. Giovanni's data on compounds show a clear developmental pattern: In early recordings, -*n* is omitted in compounds; later in development -*n* occurs in compounds. I used the stages of L2 word-order acquisition (Clahsen 1987) to determine the developmental level of Giovanni's knowledge of German. The four examples in which -*n* is left out inside a compound (see (11)) occur during stage I, whereas the examples in which the plural -*n* is used inside a compound are at later stages; examples of the latter are provided in (12a-g) below. A similar pattern holds for Bon-Giovanni and Maria. The examples without -*n* are in stage I (see (11)), whereas in later stages -*n* is used whenever required (see (12)). The data of Zita, José and Leonor are less clear, because they do not have compounds requiring -*n* in stage I. The errors in (11) occur in later recordings, at which -*n* also occurs in compounds.

(12) a. schraubenzieher (Giovanni I)   'screw driver'
     b. kohlensäure (Giovanni I)   'carbonic acid'
     c. wochenende (Giovanni I)   'weekend'
     d. augenblick (Giovanni I)   lit. 'eyes look', ' moment'
     e. krankenwagen (Giovanni I)   lit. 'patients car', 'ambulance'
     f. kerzenschlüssel (Bongiovanni I) 'sparkplug wrench'
     g. olivenöl (Maria P)   'olive oil'

These data are too scanty to make any strong claims on the development of compounding in L2 acquisition. The available data in this area lead to the following preliminary conclusions: (i) Only -*n* (and -*s*) are left out inside compounds; (ii) The use of the plural -*n* inside compounds seems to change during development: In early stages it is left out, and in later stages it is supplied in most cases. These conclusions, however, have to be tested on the basis of more specific data on compounds.

Before turning to a morphological analysis of the data, let us consider an alternative way to account for the data. We might say that in examples such as (11) -*n* is left out for phonological reasons. It could be that the learners simply delete a word-final consonant to end up with an open syllable. This implies that -*n* (and other word-final consonants) are left out in compounds irrespective of whether they are plural allomorphs or not. In other words, we would expect to find compounds such as *wageheber ('lifting-jack') instead of *wagenheber* and *streifekarte ('streetcar ticket') instead of *streifenkarte*. We would also expect that sometimes the final consonant of the -*er* plural allomorph is omitted; thus, we should get *kindegeld ('family allowance') or *wörtebuch ('dictionary'). However, such cases do not occur in the data. We found that only -*n* is left out in compounds and that this only happens if -*n* is a true plural marker. Consider, for example, the compounds used by Giovanni. At the same stage at which he produced the incorrect compounds (11a), (11b) and (11c), he also produced the correct compounds in (13). This means that -*n* is left out in case it is a plural allomorph, and that it is maintained otherwise. Thus, a purely phonological explanation of the data in (11) can be ruled out. I maintain the claim that it is the plural -*n* that is sometimes left out in compounds.

(13) a. streifenkarte (Giovanni I, stage I)   'streetcar ticket';
                                              sing./pl.: Streifen, 'strip(s)'
     b. lohnsteuer (Giovanni I, stage I)   lit. 'salary tax';
                                              sing.: der Lohn, 'salary'

In order to account for the observations made above in the dual-mechanism model, we could say that in early L2 development, that is, in stage I, -*n* and/or -*s* are default affixes in the L2 learners' plural system, and that the other allomorphs are irregular. This means that in case the learner does not find a stored plural entry for a particular noun, either it will not be inflected for plural, or it will receive a default plural marking. This accounts for the overregularizations of -*n* and -*s*. In the case of 'double' markings such as those in (7), there are marked plural entries in the lexicon (e.g., *Männ(er)-, Büch(er)-,Kind(er)-*) to which a regular plural affix can be added. This is similar to the so-called mixed inflection of verbs (e.g., *rannte*, 'ran'; *brachte*, 'brought') where a regular affix (-*te*) is added to an irregular stem which is already marked for past tense.

If the feeding relationships between inflection and compounding also hold for L2 learners' grammatical systems, and if -*n* and/or -*s* are default affixes at the beginning, then we would expect these two affixes to be left out in compounds. This is in fact the case. Later in development this changes, namely, as soon as the learner discovers that the plural -*n* may occur inside compounds in German. In this way, the observations noted above can be accounted for. The L2 plural system differs from the German one in that for some learners -*n* is a default affix. Most probably, this results from the high frequency of -*n* in the input. More important, however, is that, despite this error in assigning -*n*, the feeding relationships between inflection and compounding also hold for the L2 learners' system of plural marking. Thus, the constraint that compounding can be fed by irregular plurals, but not by default plurals, is not violated in the L2 learners' plural system. Moreover, the *Elsewhere Condition*, specifying that a specific rule or (irregular) entry takes precedence over a general rule, also holds for the L2 learners' plural system; this was shown in the results on overregularizations. Thus, L2 learners have to learn which affixes have default status, but like child language, the general constraints do not have to be learned.

Summary and conclusion

The general background for the present study is the current psycholinguistic debate on the representation of regular and irregular morphology. The specific question under investigation was whether or not the grammatical systems created by L2 learners exhibit qualitative differences between regular and irregular inflected forms. My test case was the system of noun plurals in German. I found that, out of the set of German plural allomorphs, L2 learners use two affixes, namely -*n* and -*s*, in overregularizations; the preference for using either -*n* or -*s* depends on the learners' native language. More importantly, those affixes that are overregularized are left out in compounds, even in cases in which the corresponding compound does have an internal plural marking in German. This shows that the learners have two qualitatively different kinds of plural forms: (i) irregular forms, which are not used in overregularizations, but which do occur in compounds; and (ii) default plurals, which are overregularized and which do not occur in compounds. In other words, a grammatical process, namely compounding, is sensitive to the distinction between regulars and irregulars. This result clearly favors a dual-mechanism model, which offers ways of qualitatively distinguishing between regular and irregular morphology over any unitary network.

Moreover, I found that in the longitudinal data investigated here there were no drastic developmental changes in the use of overregularizations in noun plurals and in plural formation in compounds. At all stages, overregularizations comprise a small minority of the noun plurals used by the learners, and also at all stages, those plural allomorphs that are overregularized can be left out in compounds. Similar results were obtained in Clahsen et al. (1992) for German child language. Taken together, these results support the view that the two modes of inflection and the constraints on the interaction of compounding and inflection are present from the beginning of the acquisition of morphology.

Acknowledgments

I would like to acknowledge the work of Andreas Collings, who, as part of a larger study on the development of plural marking, analyzed the ZISA data reported here. In Collings' study, a wide range of data, including elicitation tests with tutored L2 learners, is being analyzed. This present paper is a revised version of a paper that was written and researched in 1990/1991 and presented at the Twelfth Second Language Research Forum, University of California, Los Angeles, in March 1991. During the conference, I had the pleasure of staying at Bill Rutherford's house, listening to his marvelous spinet performances and enjoying his hospitality.

References

Clahsen, H. 1984. "The Acquisition of German Word Order: A test case for cognitive approaches to L2 development. *Second Languages: A crosslinguistic perspective* ed. by R. Andersen, 219-242. Rowley, MA: Newbury House.
Clahsen, H. 1987. "Connecting Theories of Language Processing and (Second) Language Acquisition". *First and Second Language Acquisition Processes* ed. by C. Pfaff, 103-116. Cambridge, MA: Newbury House.
Clahsen, H., M. Rothweiler, A. Woest & G. Marcus. 1992. "Regular and Irregular Inflection in the Acquisition of German Noun Plurals". *Cognition* 45.225-55.
Heidelberger Projekt Pidgin-Deutsch. 1975. *Untersuchung zur Erlernung des Deutschen durch ausländische Arbeiter*. Report No. III, University of Heidelberg.
Kiparsky, P. 1982. "From Cyclic Phonology to Lexical Phonology". *The Structure of Phonological Representations, Part I* ed. by H. v. d. Hulst & N. Smith, 131-175. Dordrecht: Foris.

Kiparsky, P. 1985. "Some Consequences of Lexical Phonology". *Phonology Yearbook 2* ed. by C. Ewen & J.Anderson, 85-138.
Köpcke, K.-M. 1988. "Schemas in German Plural Formation". *Lingua* 74. 303-335.
Meyer-Ingwersen, J., R. Neumann & M. Kummer. 1977. *Zur Sprachentwicklung türkischer Schüler in der BRD*. Kronberg: Scriptor.
Mugdan, J. 1977. *Flexionsmorphologie und Psycholinguistik*. Tübingen: Gunter Narr.
Orlovic, M. 1978. *Zum Gastarbeiterdeutsch jugoslawischer Arbeiter im Rhein-Main-Gebiet: Empirische Untersuchungen zur Morphologie und zum ungesteuerten Erwerb des Deutschen durch Erwachsene*. Wiesbaden: Steiner.
Philipps, B. & L. Bouma. 1980. "The Acquisition of German Plurals in Native Children and Non-native Adults". *IRAL* 18.21-28.
Pinker, S. & A. Prince. 1988. "On Language and Connectionism: Analysis of a parallel distributed processing model of language acquisition". *Cognition* 28.73-193.
Rumelhart, D.E. & J. L. McClelland. 1987. "Learning the Past Tenses of English Verbs: Implicit rules or parallel distributed processing". In B. MacWhinney (ed.), *Mechanisms of Language Acquisition* ed. by B. MacWhinney, 195-248. Hillsdale, N.J: Erlbaum.
Wiese, R. 1988. *Silbische und lexikalische Phonologie: Studien zum Chinesischen und Deutschen*. Tübingen: Niemeyer.
Wunderlich, D. 1986. "Zum Aufbau lexikalischer Repräsentationen". Paper at the Department of Linguistics, University of Düsseldorf.

Universal Grammar in L2 acquisition
Some thoughts on Schachter's Incompleteness Hypothesis

Sascha W. Felix
University of Passau

Introduction

In her keynote address at the Conference on Generative Approaches to Language Acquisition in 1993, Lydia White urged second-language (L2) researchers not to become too obsessed with the question of the accessibility of Universal Grammar (UG) in L2 acquisition, but to focus rather on more detailed descriptions of the way in which L2 learners master the target language. Nevertheless, it appears that the question of whether or not L2 learners have access to principles of Universal Grammar is still very much alive; in fact, the basic problem of which cognitive modules govern and control both first- and second-language acquisition seems to be the very *raison d'être* of much L2 acquisition research. It is thus not very surprising that in a recent paper on "Maturation and the issue of Universal Grammar in L2 acquisition" Jacquelyn Schachter (forthcoming) reinvestigated the issue and forcefully argued against the view that Universal Grammar is not only responsible for first-language (L1) acquisition, but also for L2 acquisition.

Since Schachter's excellent and very stimulating paper provides a detailed and critical summary of a wide variety of arguments that have been advanced against the idea of Universal Grammar operating in L2 acquisition, supplemented by a specific proposal of her own, it seems worthwhile to take a fresh look at the underlying issues and controversies. For reasons of space, I will not be able to consider all of Schachter's arguments in detail, but will rather focus on those ideas which–as far as I can tell–are shared by a substantial number of people in the *no-access* community.

What makes the starting point of the discussion relatively easy is that, in general, L2 researchers, no matter what theoretical position they subscribe to, at least agree on certain basic facts. That is, it is largely uncontroversial that much of what characterizes child L1 acquisition does not apply–at least not in the same way–to L2 acquisition. To my knowledge, nobody has claimed that L2 acquisition is totally indistinguishable from L1 acquisition. Schachter focuses on four major differences between child L1 and adult L2 acquisition. The most obvious difference concerns the level of success. While all L1 learners attain native speaker competence in their mother tongue, adult L2 learners typically do not reach a comparable level. The second difference concerns what Schachter calls *fossilized variation*, that is, the phenomenon that L2 learners typically use both grammatical and ungrammatical structures simultaneously. The third difference relates to the L1 learner's equipotentiality for language acquisition and the L2 learner's lack of it. In other words, L1 learners will acquire any language with equal success, while L2 learners typically find some languages more difficult than others.[1] And finally, the well-known interference phenomena, namely, L2 learners' tendency to transfer structures from their mother tongue to the L2.

While none of these observations is–as far as I can see–truly controversial, it is the types of conclusions that may be drawn from these facts where L2 researchers tend to disagree. In what follows I will look at some of the conclusions that Schachter draws, in particular with respect to the UG-accessibility issue.

Universal principles on the basis of L1

Before we proceed, it should be noted that there is a second set of facts which appear to be largely, though not totally uncontroversial.[2] Past research on L2 acquisition has determined a number of structural domains in which L2 learners seem to acquire intuitive knowledge about the target language which is in some sense comparable to that of L1 learners. A considerable number of studies (e.g., Bley-Vroman, Felix and Ioup 1988; Flynn 1987, 1989; Felix 1988; White 1988, 1989a, 1989b) have demonstrated that L2 learners do show a considerable degree of sensitivity to UG-based constraints even in those domains which structurally differ from their native language. However, there are also domains in which L2 learners typically do not display such knowledge (e.g., Clahsen and Muysken 1986). In other words, all those who favor a *UG for all*-view need to explain why L2 learners fail to observe UG constraints in certain domains, while conversely those who hold a *UG not at all*-position have to explain how L2 learners acquire UG-based intuitive knowledge in some other domains. With respect to the latter case, the standard answer is that they do so because their mother tongue is, of course, an instantiation of UG principles; therefore–so the argument runs–they know what is universal on the basis of their native linguistic knowledge.

Before I look at this argument in detail, I would like to draw the reader's attention to a point that is frequently forgotten in the comparison between L1 and

UNIVERSAL GRAMMAR IN L2 ACQUISITION

L2 achievements. As Schachter (forthcoming:4) notes, "the facts of adult L2 acquisition are not anywhere near as impressive as those of child L1 acquisition". It is, of course, a matter of personal taste how much one is impressed by facts of language acquisition. Nevertheless, it seems to me that the achievements in L2 acquisition are frequently underestimated. Even though L2 acquisition is undoubtedly inferior to L1 acquisition with respect to ultimate attainment, it is nevertheless possible to reach a fairly advanced level of linguistic competence in a second language. Despite well-known deficiencies, especially at the phonological and morphological level (e.g., Meisel 1991), L2 learners frequently attain a level of competence that allows them to communicate in a second language both effectively and adequately. In other words, L2 learners are not like chimps with respect to language acquisition. If Universal Grammar plays no role whatsoever in L2 acquisition–such that this process was exclusively controlled by the learner's general intelligence–then we would expect L2 learners to be better than chimps just to the same degree that they are more intelligent than these animals. Although I do not know of any direct evidence to support such a claim, it is at least my intuition that L2 learners are much more like L1 learners than they are like chimpanzees.

Returning to the question of how L2 learners acquire UG-like knowledge in some domains, Schachter notes:

> granted there are the same deficiencies in the input as in the L1 case, but the adult L2 learner does not overcome them in the same way the child L1 learner does. And to the extent that she does, it can reasonably be argued that *the learner's L1 knowledge, combined with knowledge gained from the input, was the source* (unless it can be shown that she cannot have known it from either source) (forthcoming:8-9, emphasis mine)

As noted above, this is the standard argument to explain the fact that at least in some domains L2 learners appear to possess a type of intuitive knowledge of the target language that is fairly similar to that of an L1 learner. What this argument essentially boils down to is the following claim: Due to the fact that the L2 learner already knows one language and that this language–among other things–represents properties of Universal Grammar, it is possible to know what Universal Grammar looks like at least in a specific domain. Although this argument has been around for some time, I believe it is untenable not so much for empirical, but for logical reasons. What I would like to argue is that it is logically impossible to derive properties of Universal Grammar from a single instantiation of UG.

Suppose that my native language–the only natural language I know– has two properties P and Q, where P is a universal property of all natural languages and Q is language-specific. We might imagine P being the property of structure dependency, and Q the property of overt Wh-movement. The crucial question is this: Is it possible for me, by virtue of being a native speaker of this language, to know that P is a universal property and Q is not? As far as I can see, the answer is straightforward: no. From the perspective of a native speaker who knows just this one language, all its properties are created equal; there is nothing in my native language that tells me that some properties are universal while others are not.

To take a more specific example: Suppose a speaker of French is to learn Japanese as a second language. In French Wh-questions may be formed by either syntactic Wh-movement, or the Wh-phrases may remain *in situ*. Consequently, (1) and (2) below are equally grammatical options.

(1) tu vas où?
    you go where
    "Where are you going?"
(2) où vas-tu?
    where go-you
    "Where are you going?"

As is well known, Japanese does not permit overt syntactic Wh-movement, but only Wh-movement at LF. Consequently, the Japanese analogue to (2) is ungrammatical, while the analogue to (1) is grammatical. In order to find out that Japanese does not permit overt syntactic Wh-movement, French-speaking L2 learners must either have access to negative evidence, or they must know that syntactic Wh-movement is not a universal property of natural languages, but rather a language-specific property of French. The point I would like to emphasize is that there is nothing in French that permits learners to determine that LF movement as in (1) is a universal property of all natural languages, while overt syntactic Wh-movement is French-specific. In other words, combining learners' native knowledge of French and the Japanese input data they are exposed to, there is nothing to prevent the (incorrect) conclusion that the analogue of (2) is a grammatical structure in Japanese.

At a more general level, we can observe that, of all the properties in a given language, a specific subset is universal, while some other subset is language-specific. However, for each individual property of that language the native speaker has no possibility of knowing which subset this property is an element of. Consequently, the idea of deriving universal properties from the knowledge of one's mother tongue is–as far as I can tell–without much empirical substance and logically untenable.

At the empirical level, Kellerman (1978) has shown that native speakers of Dutch do have very strong intuitions about those properties of their native language which appear to be universal in contrast to those which are Dutch-specific. Again, this observation is interesting precisely because there is nothing in Dutch itself that allows the native speaker to make this distinction. To put it differently: There must be something on top of speakers' knowledge of the native language that permits them to distinguish between what is universal and what is language-specific in their mother tongue. It thus appears to be an empirical fact that native speakers are able to distinguish between universal and language-specific properties of their native language. At the same time, it is a matter of pure logic that they cannot derive this distinction from knowledge of their mother tongue alone. Given these considerations, I do not see how it can be "reasonably" argued that learners' L1 knowledge provides them with information about universal properties of natural languages.

Given the differences between L1 and L2 acquisition, Schachter (forthcoming:9) notes further that "the proponent of the *UG for all* language learning positions is in the difficult situation of trying to explain why UG does not produce the same results in the adult case that it does in the child L1 case". I admit that the proponent of the *UG for all*-position is in a difficult situation, but this situation is no more difficult than the one of the proponent of a *UG not at all*-position. Either party has something important to explain: The proponent of the *UG for all*-position has to explain why L2 acquisition does not work better than it does, and the proponent of the *UG not at all*-position has to explain why L2 acquisition works as well as it does. Given this situation, there are numerous options of which Schachter mentions only two. Apart from the *UG for all* and *UG not at all*-positions, one could imagine, for example, *UG in part*, *UG+general problem solver*, *UG with interfering factors*, and the like.[3]

What I am trying to argue for is that the mere fact of differences between L1 and L2 acquisition does not favor any of these positions. It is a purely empirical question whether or not UG plays a role in L2 acquisition and, if it does, why it is not as successful as in L1 acquisition. Since Schachter strongly favors the *UG not at all*-position I will look at some of her arguments in detail.

Biology in L2 acquisition

Citing Keenan (1988, 1991), Schachter (forthcoming:11) notes that "the brain of a child at the outset of language acquisition is distinct from the brain of the same individual when the language has been learned". This observation is both true and irrelevant as little, if anything, follows from it. It is likewise true that the brain of a four-year old child is distinct from the brain of the same individual at the age of two. But as far as we know, this has no deep effect on the individual's L1 acquisition capacity. Consequently, the observation that the child brain is different from the adult brain is only relevant to the extent that this difference can be shown to correlate and to be causally linked to a corresponding difference in the individual's L1 learning capacity. Whether or not such a correlation or, better, causal link exists is a truly empirical question. Therefore, it is incorrect to say that "those maintaining that UG subserves adult L2 acquisition must maintain that language acquisition capability is like perceptual adaptation, plastic through life" (forthcoming:13).

Contrary to Schachter's statement, I do not see any logical entailment between these two claims. It is easy to imagine that the language acquisition capability may degenerate as people grow older, or that the language acquisition capability differs even during the prepuberterian phase, for example, in a child of two versus a child of four. Similarly, one could imagine that while UG subserves L2 acquisition after puberty, it only does so until the age of, say, 50. All of these are empirical questions that need to be investigated. As far as I can see, all the proponents of the *UG for all*-position are compelled to argue for is that language acquisition is possible in the adult with a level of attainment that cannot be accounted for without reference to principles of Universal Grammar. In other words, the *UG for all*-position would be disconfirmed if it could be shown that adult L2 learners can only reach a level of competence that can be explained by mechanisms of a general problem solver. As far as I know, this has not been shown yet.

Schachter then continues to review some of the literature dealing with the critical period for L1 acquisition, pointing out that there is little doubt that such a critical period does, in fact, exist.[4] Again, I feel that these observations are both true and irrelevant. As far as I know, none of the *UG for all*-proponents seriously argues that L2 acquisition after puberty is exactly like L1 acquisition. In fact, the challenging aspect about L2 acquisition is precisely that adult L2 learners may attain a surprisingly high level of competence and yet typically fail in specific domains. In other words, even though adult L2 learners are worse than child L1 learners, they are significantly better than chimps.

It seems to me that the challenge that proponents of the *UG not at all*-position like Schachter are facing is precisely to explain why L2 acquisition is as successful as it is, and where L2 learners get the type of knowledge from that is standardly assumed to derive from the operation of Universal Grammar. As far as I can see, the only argument that Schachter presents to account for similarities between L1 and L2 learning is that L2 learners "know what a language should look like and that their L1 grammars have many UG characteristics incorporated into them" (forthcoming:19). As I already pointed out, this argument fails for logical reasons. On the basis of their native language, adult L2 learners do not know what *language* should look like; they only know what *their* language looks like.

Of course, much of the argument depends on how one visualizes the nature of the adult speaker's competence. As far as I know, there are at least two standard views. One view (e.g., Frazier 1985) holds that there need not be any direct relationship between a native adult's competence and the system of UG that the child is born with. That is, the adult's grammar may well be a rule system of a very different type from the system of Universal Grammar. In this view, UG is just a kind of vehicle whose input is the child's linguistic experience and whose output is some kind of a rule system. The more traditional view which–as far as I can see–most people in generative linguistics hold is that there is, in fact, a very close relationship between Universal Grammar as the initial state and an adult's competence as the final state. In fact, according to this view, the only difference between the initial state and the final state is that parameters are fixed in the final state whereas in the initial state they are still unspecified. Note incidentally that under this view the question of whether or not adults have access to Universal Grammar does not even arise because by definition the answer is positive. That is, an adult speaker's competence is nothing but the system of Universal Grammar with fixed parameters.

Interestingly, Schachter develops a third scenario of what the adult's grammar might look like. The basic assumption of Schachter's idea is that in each particular natural language some principles of Universal Grammar are instantiated while others are not. Schachter continues:

> ... certain principles of UG are triggered in L1 acquisition only as certain properties are found in the input to the child; if, in the course of development, such properties are not found in the input and incorporated into the grammar, the principles dependent on them do not subsequently form part of the adult grammars of speakers of these languages. (forthcoming:24)

To illustrate her point, Schachter mentions subjacency:

> It [subjacency] is triggered only if the input data provide the child with evidence that there is overt extraction in the language; if subjacency is not triggered in this way in the course of first language acquisition, then the principle will never be called forth and the subsequent adult grammar of the language will not contain that principle. (forthcoming:25)

As far as I can see, there are two problems with this view, one logical, the other empirical. At the logical level, it seems to me that under this view the distinction between the *UG for all* and *UG not at all*-positions simply collapses; or, rather, the *UG for all*-position becomes true almost by definition. Notice that under this view an adult English speaker's knowledge that, say, extractions from complex NPs are ungrammatical consists in knowing that they violate subjacency. Crucially, however, you can only know that extractions from complex NPs violate subjacency if you know subjacency. And that is tantamount to saying that subjacency as a principle of Universal Grammar is part of adult speakers' knowledge of their language. Put differently, with respect to the phenomenon under discussion, an adult speaker's knowledge consists of two parts:

(a) the abstract principle of subjacency, and
(b) the language specific parametrization of this principle.

It seems obvious that if you hold this view, the question of whether or not adult speakers of English have access to subjacency doesn't even make sense, because the only logically possible answer is positive. This is trivially so because you cannot claim simultaneously that an adult knows subjacency and doesn't know subjacency.

Furthermore, one might claim that while an adult speaker of English knows subjacency, this knowledge is somehow blocked–for whatever reason–when it comes to learning a second language. In other words, one might want to claim that knowledge of subjacency is somehow constrained to knowledge of one's native language, but cannot be transferred or applied to the acquisition of a second language. However, this is precisely what Schachter does not claim. In fact, she argues that those principles of Universal Grammar that have been triggered during L1 acquisition and thus constitute part of adults' knowledge of their native language are indeed accessible during second language acquisition. This knowledge accounts for those domains in which we find that L2 learners come up with judgments similar to those of L1 learners.

According to Schachter, to the extent that L2 learners overcome the same deficiencies in the input as L1 learners, "it can reasonably be argued that the learner's L1 knowledge combined with knowledge gained from the input was the source" (forthcoming:8-9), then this is at best a very metaphorical use of the term *learner's L1 knowledge*. What is crucial about this knowledge with respect to overcoming deficiencies in the input is not the fact that L1 learners know their language–that is, they are native speakers of the language–but rather that this knowledge consists of principles of Universal Grammar (and their parametric values). I do not see that this view is anything but a very specific version of the *UG for all*-position. At least, it is fundamentally different from the view that L2 acquisition is guided and controlled exclusively by principles of general problem solving. In other words, Schachter claims that the L2 learner's accessibility to principles of Universal Grammar is restricted to a specific subset of these principles, namely, those that are instantiated in the learner's native language. In this sense, Schachter is much closer to the *UG for all*-proponents than to the *UG not all*-proponents.

Nevertheless, there appears to be a crucial distinction between the position advocated by Schachter and the one that I believe researchers like White or Flynn would hold. Schachter explicitly claims that while it is true that L2 learners have access to Universal Grammar in general, they only have access to a specific subset of principles, namely, those that have been triggered during the process of L1 language development and are thus instantiated in the learner's L1. To illustrate her point, Schachter uses subjacency again. In a language like English, which has a wide variety of extraction phenomena as in NP- and Wh-movement, the principle of subjacency is relevant and thus triggered during the English speaking child's language development. Thus, by Schachter's hypothesis, the adult speaker of English does have knowledge of subjacency and therefore can utilize this knowledge in the case of L2 acquisition. This situation would sharply contrast with a speaker of a language which does not have any extraction phenomena, so that subjacency would not be instantiated. For example, since Korean and Japanese are standardly believed not to have either NP-movement or Wh-movement, subjacency would not be triggered during the Korean and Japanese child language development process. As a consequence, an adult native speaker of Korean or Japanese would not have knowledge of subjacency and thus could not utilize subjacency in the case of learning, say, English. Schachter terms this view the *Incompleteness Hypothesis*, which means that adult speakers and thus adult L2 learners have incomplete knowledge of Universal Grammar: They only know those principles which are instantiated in their native language.

I believe that it is at this point where the empirical problem begins. The subjacency principle, which Schachter uses merely for illustration, is clearly wrong. It is empirically not true that there are no subjacency phenomena in Japanese or Korean. While it is true that there is no overt Wh-movement or NP-movement in Japanese, Watanabe (1992), for example, has shown that there are other types of structures–free relatives, for example–in which subjacency effects occur. That is, while English and Japanese differ with respect to the type of extractions or movements that are grammatical in each language, they do not differ with respect to the instantiation of subjacency. In other words, subjacency is instantiated in both languages, but in the context of different types of constructions.

It should be acknowledged, however, that Schachter uses subjacency merely as an illustrative example, so even if the subjacency example is wrong, it might still be the case that there are other principles which are instantiated in some languages, but not in others. Consequently, the question is whether there are such principles. As far as I can see–at least at our current state of knowledge–the answer is clearly negative. Obviously, the principles generally subsumed under X-bar theory are instantiated in all languages. Subjacency, as Watanabe (1992) has shown, is not constrained to languages with overt Wh- and NP-movement, but occurs also in languages with Wh-*in situ*. Further, the Empty Category Principle seems to hold in some way or another in all languages. The principles of Binding Theory would need to be checked, but I do not know of any languages that have no binding phenomena whatsoever. In other words, it seems that at least all the 'big' principles hold for all languages. The only possible counterexample that comes to mind has to do with null subjects. Clearly, there are languages with *pro*-drop, and languages without *pro*-drop. However, even though *pro*-drop has been a favorite example in studies on both L1 and L2 acquisition, it is clearly not a principle. Rather it seems to be a manifestation of the interplay of various other principles. The same would be true for scrambling or Verb Second (V2). For a long time, the standard view seemed to be that there are scrambling languages like German or Russian, and non-scrambling languages like English or French (see, e.g., Fanselow 1987). However, as research went on, it became all too apparent that this dichotomy is empirically wrong (see Haider 1993). It seems that there are languages that scramble more, and other languages that scramble less. Whatever happens to be the case does not seem to be a reflection of whether or not a given principle is present in one language, but not in another; rather, observable variation seems to be a consequence of particular parameters that are set to different values in different languages. The same is true for V2-phenomena. Again, V2 is surely not a principle of Universal Grammar, but a language-specific phenomenon which derives from a specific parametric setting in conjunction with the operations of principles of Universal Grammar. In other words, even in languages which are generally considered to be typically non-V2, we find remnants of V2-phenomena as illustrated by, for example, the English *do*-paraphrase.

To summarize, I do not currently see any strong evidence to suggest that languages not only differ with respect to parametric values, but also with respect to which principles of Universal Grammar are instantiated. At least it seems to be the case that most of the traditional principles that have dominated much discussion in theoretical syntax are manifested in all natural languages. The same seems to hold true of those principles which Chomsky recently proposed in the Minimalist Program (Chomsky 1993). It is fairly obvious that principles like *Procrastinate* or *Greed* apply to all natural languages. In fact, this is almost what the concept of Universal Grammar refers to. Languages may differ with respect to parametric values and peripheral options, but Universal Grammar specifies what is common to all natural languages.

Nevertheless, it might still be the case that there are some minor principles which are instantiated in some languages, but not in others. However, if this could be shown to be true, then obviously this subset would be so small as to be not of much empirical substance. At least, it would not be too convincing to try to explain some crucial differences between L1 and L2 acquisition with a distinction in Universal Grammar which is at best peripheral.

Conclusion

Given these considerations, it seems to me that rather than advocating a non-UG accessibility position, Schachter has, in fact, provided some very strong arguments for the idea that L2 learners do indeed have access to Universal Grammar, not by virtue of already knowing a native language, but rather by virtue of possessing a type of knowledge which is an instantiation of parametrized principles of Universal Grammar.

If all this is true, we are back where we started. The crucial question is this: If second language learners have knowledge of principles of Universal Grammar, why is it that UG does not work as effectively in L2 acquisition as it does in L1 acquisition. I believe to have shown that the Incompleteness Hypothesis is not an empirically tenable position, because it crucially relies on the assumption that natural languages may instantiate only a subset of UG principles, an assumption which does not seem to be compatible with what we currently know about Universal Grammar. Consequently, something else must be responsible for differences between L1 and L2 acquisition. To find out exactly what it is should keep L2 researchers in business for a long time to come.

Notes

1. An anonymous reviewer pointed out that at least the phenomena of equipotentiality and fossilized variation may be controversial for child L2 acquisition. Though this is certainly true, Schachter's remarks seem to relate exclusively to adult L2 acquisition. For some arguments emphasizing the relevance of child L2 data for an adequate theory of L2 acquisition see Schwartz (1992).

2. Proponents of a more uncompromising *UG for all* or *UG not at all* position will presumably find these 'facts' dubious and will argue that the opposing view is simply wrong. Nevertheless, in much of the UG-accessibility literature researchers take great pains at explaining away data of the opposing view, so that at least at the level of observational data certain 'facts' seem to be generally acknowledged.

3. For a detailed discussion of these and similar issues, see Felix (1988), Hilles (1991), Jenkins (1988), and White (1989b).

4. The question of whether or not there is, in fact, a fixed critical period for acquisition remains, however, controversial. While most researchers tend to agree that there are age-dependent effects on L2 acquisition, the precise nature of these effects and their (possible) biological correlates are still unclear. For some discussion, see, e.g., Birdsong (1991), Coppieters (1987), Flynn & Manuel (1991) and Long (1988).

References

Birdsong, D. 1991. "On the Notion of 'Critical Period' in UG/L2 Theory: A response to Flynn and Manuel". *Point Counterpoint* ed. by L. Eubank, 147-165. Amsterdam: John Benjamins.
Bley-Vroman, R., S. Felix & G. Ioup. 1988. "The Accessibility of Universal Grammar in Adult Language Learning". *Second Language Research* 4.1-32.
Chomsky, N. 1993. "A Minimalist Program for Linguistic Theory". *The View from Building 20* ed. by K. Hale & S. J. Kayser, 1-52. Cambridge, MA.: MIT Press.
Clahsen, H. & P. Muysken. 1986. "The Availability of Universal Grammar to Adult and Child Learners: A study of the acquisition of German word order". *Second Language Research* 2.92-119.
Coppieters, R. 1987. "Competence Differences between Native and Near-Native Speakers". *Language* 63.544-573.
Fanselow, G. 1987. *Konfigurationalität*. Tübingen: Narr.
Felix, S. 1988. "UG-Generated Knowledge in Adult Second Language Acquisition". *Linguistic Theory in Second Language Acquisition* ed. by S. Flynn & W. O'Neil, 277-294. Dordrecht: Kluwer.
Flynn, S. 1987. *A Parameter-Setting Model of Second Language Acquisition: Experimental studies in anaphora*. Dordrecht: Reidel.
Flynn, S. 1989. "The Role of the Head-Initial/Head-Final Parameter in the Acquisition of English Relative Clauses by Adult Spanish and Japanese Speakers". *Linguistic Perspectives on Second Language Acquisition* ed. by S. Gass. & J. Schachter, 89-108. Cambridge: Cambridge University Press.
Flynn, S. & S. Manuel. 1991. "Age-Dependent Effects in Language Acquisition: An evaluation of 'critical period' hypotheses". *Point Counterpoint* ed. by L. Eubank, 117-145. Amsterdam: John Benjamins.
Frazier, L. 1985. "Syntactic Complexity". *Natural Language Parsing* ed. by D. Dowty, L. Karttunen & A. Zwicky, 129-189. Cambridge: Cambridge University Press.
Haider, H. 1993. *Deutsche Syntax-Generativ*. Tübingen: Narr.
Hilles, S. 1991. "Access to Universal Grammar in Second Language Acquisition". *Point Counterpoint* ed. by L. Eubank, 305-338.Amsterdam: John Benjamins.
Jenkins, L. 1988. "Second Language Acquisition: A biolinguistic perspective". *Linguistic Theory in Second Language Acquisition* ed. by S. Flynn & W. O'Neil, 109-116. Dordrecht: Kluwer.
Kean, M.-L. 1988. "The Relation between Linguistic Theory and Second Language Acquisition: A biological perspective". *Learnability and Second Languages* ed. by J. Pankhurst, M. Sharwood Smith & P. Van Buren, 61-70. Dordrecht: Foris.
Kean, M.-L. 1991. "Learnability and Psychological Reality". Ms., University of California at Irvine.
Kellerman, E. 1978. "Giving Learners a Break: Native speaker's intuitions as a source of predictions about transferability in second language learning". *Working Papers on Bilingualism* 15.

Long, M. 1988. "Maturational Constraints on Language Development". *University of Hawai'i Working Papers in English As a Second Language* 7.1-53.

Meisel, J. 1991. "Principles of Universal Grammar and Strategies of Language Use: On some similarities and differences between first and second language acquisition". *Point Counterpoint* ed. by L. Eubank, 231-276. Amsterdam: John Benjamins.

Schachter, J. Forthcoming. "Maturation and the Issue of Universal Grammar in L2 Acquisition". To appear in *Handbook of Language Acquisition* ed. by W. Ritchie & T. K. Bhatia. New York: Academic Press.

Schwartz, B. 1992. "Testing between UG-Based and Problem-Solving Models of L2A: Developmental sequence data". *Language Acquisition* 2.1-19.

Watanabe, A. 1992. "Wh-in situ, Subjacency and Chain Formation". *MIT Occasional Papers in Linguistics*, 2. Cambridge, MA: MIT Working Papers in Linguistics.

White, L. 1988. "Island Effects in Second Language Acquisition". *Linguistic Theory in Second Language Acquisition* ed. by S. Flynn & W. O'Neil, 144-168. Dordrecht: Kluwer.

White, L. 1989a. "The Principles of Subjacency and Second Language Acquisition". *Linguistic Perspectives on Second Language Acquisition* ed. by S. Gass & J. Schachter, 134-158. Cambridge: Cambridge University Press.

White, L. 1989b. *Universal Grammar and Second Language Acquisition*. Amsterdam: John Benjamins.

White, L. 1993. "Interlanguages as Natural Languages: Implications of parameter missetting in second language acquisition". Plenary address at the Conference on Generative Approaches to Language Acquisition. Durham University, September 18.

Acquiring linking rules and argument structures in a second language
The unaccusative/unergative distinction

Antonella Sorace
University of Edinburgh

Introduction

This paper presents a unified account of a series of studies recently conducted on the acquisition of intransitive verbs in Italian as a second language (L2; Sorace 1993a, 1993b, 1995a, in preparation). The particular interest of this class of verbs lies in the fact that it subdivides into the two much-studied subclasses of unaccusative and unergative verbs, which have distinct syntactic and semantic properties. Languages differ in the extent to which they exhibit a regular mapping between syntax and semantics in this domain; from the point of view of the learner, the more regular such a mapping, the easier it is to acquire the unaccusative/ unergative distinction. It has been argued that there are further language-internal differences among the syntactic properties of these verbs: Some properties depend entirely on the structural position of the argument of the verb, whereas others can also be put in systematic correspondence with lexical-semantic features. Two of the most important manifestations of unaccusativity in Italian–*ne*-cliticization and auxiliary selection–have often been quoted as examples of purely syntactic vs. syntactic and semantic properties, respectively (Grimshaw 1991). The empirical findings reviewed in this paper indicate that both of these properties are acquired by L2 learners according to developmental paths which can be characterized in lexical-semantic terms. These developmental regularities can be explained by assuming that the acquisition of the syntax of unaccusatives crucially depends on the internalization of linking rules which govern the mapping of lexical-semantic representations onto lexical-syntactic representations at the level of argument structure. It is argued that such rules may be the main locus of crosslinguistic variation, and that they have to be acquired by language learners on the basis of the available evidence. It is further suggested that the acquisition of linking rules in an L2 raises peculiar problems of learnability, and that argument structure is a non-obvious source of transfer in L2 acquisition that deserves serious investigation.

The paper is in five sections. The first presents the linguistic facts and the theoretical background to the problem; the second introduces a different approach in terms of syntax-semantic interfaces; the third outlines the main learnability issues; and the fourth summarizes the empirical evidence obtained in the studies, offering a comprehensive interpretation. Finally, the fifth section draws some general conclusions.

Theoretical background

Since the formulation of the Unaccusative Hypothesis (Perlmutter 1978; Burzio 1986), it has been generally accepted that the two subclasses of intransitive verbs are differentiated along structural lines: The single argument of an unergative verb is a subject at all levels of representation, whereas the single argument of an unaccusative verb is an object at d-structure which may or may not move to the subject position at s-structure. This structural difference is responsible for the syntactic behavior of unaccusative verbs, whose subjects tend to display some of the same properties as the objects of transitive verbs. The range of such properties is not exactly the same cross-linguistically, since they interact with other syntactic constraints operating on individual languages. There are, however, striking parallels among the manifestations of unaccusativity/unergativity in different languages, which justifies the attempt to derive them from a simple generalization at the level of underlying syntactic structure (see Grimshaw 1987; Rappaport and Levin 1988). We shall consider two ways languages may vary with respect to these properties.

First, languages vary with respect to the degree of surface differentiation between unergative and unaccusative verbs. The internal argument of an unaccusative verb in a language like English obligatorily moves to the preverbal subject position: The two verb types therefore end up having identical surface structures. In languages with a more flexible word order, like Italian, the argument of an unaccusative verb may remain in its base position (although such a position may also be the landing site of movement for the external argument of transitive and unergative verbs). What further differentiates English and Italian is that Italian has other overt morphosyntactic cues that systematically distinguish the two classes of intransitive verbs, such as auxiliary selection and *ne*-cliticization, whereas English has fewer, and less obvious, cues (see examples in (8) below).

Second, languages also vary in their degree of internal consistency of unaccusative/unergative syntactic behavior. Italian is one of the most consistent languages from this point of view. This is because, unlike many other languages, unaccusative verbs participate as a class in most of the syntactic diagnostics of unaccusativity. These include the selection of perfective auxiliary *essere* and the cliticization of partitive *ne*, as shown in (1) and (2) below.

(1) a. Molti turisti sono partiti   *unaccusative*
    many tourists are left
    'Many tourists have left'
  b. Ne sono partiti molti (di turisti)
    Of-them are left many
    'Many of them have left'

(2) a. I professori hanno parlato a lungo   *unergative*
    the professor have talked for a long time
  b.*Ne hanno parlato due (di professori)
    of-them have talked two

In French, by contrast, the selection of *être* 'be' as perfective auxiliary is restricted to a narrow set of unaccusative verbs, and the cliticization of *en* 'of-them'–the equivalent of Italian *ne*–does not systematically separate unaccusative from unergative verbs. In fact, there are no syntactic properties in French that, alone, identify the whole class of unaccusative verbs (Legendre 1989).

(3) a. Les touristes sont arrivés   *unaccusative*
    the tourists are arrived
    'The tourists have arrived'
  b. Il en est arrivé beaucoup
    it of-them is arrived many
    'Many of them have arrived'
  c. L'argent a disparu   *unaccusative*
    the money has disappeared
  d. Il en a disparu beaucoup
    it of-it has disappeared a lot
    'A lot of it has disappeared'
  e. Les enfants ont dormi jusqu'à midi   *unergative*
    the children have slept until noon
  f. *Il en a dormi beaucoup
    it of-them has slept many

Modern Spanish has only one perfective auxiliary–*haber*–and no constructions equivalent to *ne*-cliticization. However, unaccusative verbs allow adjectival participles, as in Italian and French, and tend to be characterized by other syntactic properties such as the possibility of having bare plurals in post-verbal position (Schroten 1986; Torrego 1989; Hoekstra and Mulder 1990), which is disallowed by unergative verbs.

(4) a. Los chicos salidos de la casa a las nueve no han llamadoun *accusative*
   The children gone out from home at nine have not called
 b. *Los chicos gritados a las nueve no han llamado   *unergative*
   The children shouted at nine have not called

(5) a. Llegaron invitatos a la fiesta   *unaccusative*
   Arrived some guests to the party
 b. *Hablen representativos maûana   *unergative*
   (will) talk some representatives tomorrow

Unaccusative verbs in English appear in particular constructions, such as the resultative construction (in which the resultative phrase is predicated of the surface subject as in (8b) below) and the *there*-construction as in (8d). In contrast, they are not permitted in other structures such as the *X's way* construction (Rappaport 1988; Levin and Rappaport Hovav 1994). The availability of numerous counterexamples, however, suggests that once again these diagnostics apply to subsets of unaccusative verbs, rather than to the whole class. The *there*-construction, for example, seems to be restricted to monadic verbs denoting a change of state, and to presentational contexts: Dyadic verbs entering into unaccusative/transitive alternations give much less acceptable results in this construction (see Burzio 1986; Haegeman 1994; Napoli 1988; Zubizzarreta 1987).[1]

(8) a. John wiped the table clean   *transitive*
 b. The river froze solid   *unaccusative*
 c. *He talked hoarse   *unergative*
 d. There appeared another book by Chomsky   *unaccusative*
 e. *There sank three boats   *unaccusative*
 f. He worked his way to the top   *unergative*
 g. *Mary went her way to the office   *unaccusative*

The apparent inconsistency exhibited by most languages has been one of the principal arguments against a definition of unaccusativity in purely structural terms, the assumption being that if unaccusativity derives from the particular syntactic property of certain verbs of having their argument in object position, then all unaccusative verbs should satisfy all diagnostics in the same way. This situation would be expected in particular of those diagnostics–such as *ne*-cliticization–which depend straightforwardly on this particular structural configuration. The fact that, within the same language, some verbs behave more regularly than others with respect to individual diagnostics clearly requires an explanation. Explanations in the literature tend to divide neatly between those rejecting a syntactic characterization of unaccusativity (and therefore the Unaccusative Hypothesis *tout court*; see Centineo 1986; van Valin 1990; Seibert 1993) and those maintaining the validity of the Unaccusative Hypothesis but attempting to identify lexical or semantic constraints on its implementation. According to the latter position, "unaccusativity is syntactically represented but semantically determined" (Levin and Rappaport 1989: 316).

Syntax-semantics interfaces

But what is the meaning of "semantically determined"? Traditional semantic accounts are a first step towards finding an answer. It is widely acknowledged that, from a semantic point of view, the unergative/unaccusative distinction is associated with a difference between the thematic function realized by the single argument of the verb: The argument of unergative verbs typically, but not always, presents agentive properties, such as protagonist control and intentionality, whereas the argument of unaccusative verbs typically, but not always, displays the characteristics of a theme, that is, of an entity affected by an unintentional and/or uncontrolled change of state or location (for more extensive discussion, see Sorace 1993b; in preparation). The two verb classes are also differentiated in aspectual terms: Unergative verbs tend to refer to atelic events–or activities, in terms of the Vendler/Dowty classification (Vendler 1967; Dowty 1979; van Valin 1990; on the related notion of event structure, see Grimshaw 1991; van Hout forthcoming). Unaccusative verbs mostly denote a telic event (i.e., one with a specified endpoint or resulting state). The point of controversy concerns the relationship between thematic roles and syntactic positions. While focusing on structural differences, the original version of the Unaccusative Hypothesis (e.g., Perlmutter and Postal 1978) had the ambitious aim of establishing a bi-directional direct correspondence between the roles of agent and theme and the positions of subject and object, respectively. As it is not difficult to find counterevidence to such a strong claim (see Rosen 1984), there has been a tendency to abandon the attempt to find a systematic relationship between syntax and semantics in the domain of intransitivity, and to concentrate on either purely syntactic or the purely semantic definitions of the phenomenon.

Our position is in line with Levin and Rappaport's: A proper understanding of the variation displayed both cross-linguistically and language-internally by intransitive verbs requires a fine-grained specification of the lexical-semantic determinants of verb classes and of how they are syntactically encoded. The idea is that there may be indirect correspondences between a non-homogeneous lexical-semantic level and the syntactic level. Consistent with much recent work on the lexicon (e.g., Guernssel et al. 1985; Hale and Keyser 1986; Marantz 1984), we assume the existence of three levels of representation: a conceptual structure, which is a formal representation of the meaning of lexical items, including the thematic roles of a verb; an argument structure, which specifies the number of arguments required by a verb, and whether they are external or internal, by means of abstract variables (the only ones that the syntax can 'see'); and a syntactic structure, which encodes grammatical relationships. The thematic roles of a verb are projected from conceptual structure onto variables in argument structure, which are in turn projected onto grammatical positions at the syntactic level of representation. Any correspondences between the levels of conceptual and syntactic structure are mediated by argument structure, and the mapping between levels is governed by a set of linking rules.

From our point of view, what deserves particular attention are the linking rules that create lexical-syntactic representations at argument structure from lexical-semantic representations at conceptual structure. Our approach is that within this multi-dimensional (and potentially universal) semantic 'space', languages may choose different semantic primitives as the ones relevant for encoding the grammatical features of unergativity/unaccusativity.[2] We maintain that lexical-semantic representations are defined in multi-dimensional and gradable terms, rather than as homogeneous and discrete thematic roles. The basic problem is to explain how gradable representations are mapped onto necessarily discrete syntactic representations. One of the consequences of this position is that there is no discrete distinction between unergative and unaccusative verbs at the lexical-semantic level, although there necessarily is one at the syntactic level. The other consequence is that linking rules are language-specific and may in fact be regarded as the main locus of cross-linguistic variation.[3] Let us now examine in some more detail how the underlying, multi-dimensional semantic space may be structured.

The role of theme, or 'affected entity'–which unifies the semantic features of the single argument of unaccusative verbs–can be decomposed according to the type of event affecting the subject, in terms of the dimensions *dynamic/static*, *telic/atelic*, and *concrete/abstract*. The intersection of these dimensions generates a hierarchy of intransitive verbs (henceforth 'unaccusative hierarchy') whose core consists of monadic verbs denoting a directed change of location (i.e., the most inherently telic/dynamic/concrete) and where other verbs are placed at more and more peripheral positions depending on their degree of distance with respect to the core.[4] The most peripheral positions along this hierarchy are occupied by change-of-condition verbs paired with a transitive counterpart and by change-of-location verbs paired with an atelic counterpart, to which telicity may be added compositionally by means of a directional phrase: These verbs are different from monadic verbs in various respects and the intransitive telic alternant is derived from the basic transitive alternant, or from the atelic alternant, respectively.[5] Table 1

LINKING RULES AND ARGUMENT STRUCTURES 159

Table 1: Unaccusative hierarchy

Unpaired (monadic) verbs
    Change of location
        andare ('go')   <*y* comes to be at a different *location*>
    Change of condition
        sparire ('disappear')   <*y* comes to be in a different *condition*>
    Continuation of a pre-existing condition
        durare ('last')   <*y* continues to be in a pre-existing *condition*>
    Existence of a condition
        esistere ('exist')   <*y* is in a certain *condition*>

Paired (dyadic) verbs
    With a transitive alternant
        aumentare ('increase')   <*y* comes to be in a different *condition*>
                                     (with the counterpart *aumentare*: <aumentare *y,x*>)
    With an atelic alternant
        correre ('run')   <*y* comes to be in a different *location*>
                                     (with the counterpart *correre*: <correre *x*>)

Note: The symbols *x* and *y* refer to the external and the internal arguments, respectively.

Table 2: Unergative hierarchy

Unpaired (monadic) verbs
    Non-motional activity
        dormire ('sleep')   <*x* is engaged in a *non-motional activity*>
    Motional activity
        nuotare ('swim')   <*x* is engaged in a *motional activity*>

Paired (dyadic) verbs
    With a telic alternant
        correre ('run')   <*x* is engaged in a *motional activity*>
                                     (with the counterpart *correre*:
                                     <*y* comes to be at a different *location*>)

Note: The symbols *x* and *y* refer to the external and the internal arguments, respectively.

shows the unaccusative hierarchy for Italian, with a specification of the relevant semantic sub-structures.[6]

    The thematic role of agent, which is regarded as the common denominator of the features characterizing the argument of unergative verbs, can be decomposed in a similar way in terms of the dimensions *telic/atelic* and *dynamic/ static*. The result is 'unergative hierarchy' shown in Table 2, which consists of three subtypes, corresponding to three types of activity denoted by the verb.[7] The table shows that the core of unergativity consists of monadic verbs denoting static, atelic activities. Further away from the core one finds monadic verbs denoting physical, though still atelic, movement, whereas the most distant position from the core is occupied by atelic verbs of movement paired with a telic counterpart. Across languages, the linking rules governing the correspondence between conceptual structure and argument structure select different components as the crucial determinants of unaccusativity and unergativity. Dutch and German, for example, differ with respect to the linking rules determining unaccusativity: As several studies have suggested (Brinkmann 1992; van Hout, Randall and Weissenborn 1993; Randall, van Hout, Weissenborn and Baayen 1994), the factor relevant for unaccusativity in Dutch is telicity (or 'change with an endpoint'). This means that whenever the only argument of an intransitive verbs denotes an entity undergoing a telic change, such argument is linked to the internal argument position in argument structure.[8] German, on the other hand, has a wider-range linking rule which relies on the semantic concept of transition (Seibert 1993). While a telic change necessarily involves a transition, a transition between locations or conditions does not necessarily involve telicity, because it may refer to an event with no specified endpoint, as shown by the examples in (9).

(9) a. Die Jungen sind stundenlang durch den Saal getanzt.
    The youths are for hours through the room danced
    'The youths danced in the room for hours.'
  b. Paul ist stundenlang über den Strand gejoggt.
    Paul is for hours over the beach jogged
    'Paul has jogged on the beach for hours.'

Along similar lines, we are proposing that the relevant linking rule for Italian selects 'existence of a state' as the semantic component that is sufficient to trigger the mapping of a verb's single argument onto the internal argument position in argument structure, and therefore unaccusative syntax (see van Valin 1990 on the importance of 'state' for unaccusativity). In the absence of this 'stative' component, the single argument of a verb is linked to the external argument position, which ensures that the verb displays unergative syntax. In contrast, the semantic component selected in French as the determinant of unaccusativity is not the presence of a stative element, but rather the change that leads to a new location. The presence of this component in the semantics of a verb triggers the linking of its single argument to the internal argument position; its absence determines the linking of the argument to the external position.[9] As a result of this difference in range between the French and the Italian linking rules, the class of French verbs displaying unaccusative syntax is narrower than the corresponding Italian class. The class of syntactically unaccusative verbs in English seems to be slightly larger than in French. Taking into account the few identifiable diagnostics, the linking rule determining unaccusative syntax in English singles out 'change-of condition' as the grammatically relevant factor. However, this is not the whole story. If our account is correct, these crucial semantic components are at the same time the most general and the least salient among those subsumed by the meaning of a verb: They are the minimal triggers of unaccusative syntax. Among the Italian verbs which subsume a stative component in their semantics, for example, existence-of-state verbs instantiate only the minimal stative component and therefore satisfy diagnostics to a lesser degree than verbs denoting a change of state, which are closer to the core in terms of telicity and dynamicity. More generally, verbs within an individual language may satisfy the typical diagnostics of unaccusativity/unergativity to varying degrees depending on the relative position of the minimal trigger on the hierarchy. This has important consequences for language acquisition, as will be argued in the following sections.

Issues of learnability

The acquisition of the syntax of intransitive verbs poses interesting problems for language learners. One of the problems that has often been discussed in the literature arises when learners acquire a language such as English, which presents a scarcity of morphosyntactic reflexes of the unaccusative/unergative distinction. Baker (1983) has argued that semantic factors play a crucial role in this case, because they are the only cues the learner can rely on. Within our approach, semantic factors influence syntactic acquisition in a more general way. If the learners' task is to infer what portion of the semantic space underlying intransitive verbs is linked to what position in argument structure (in other words, the linking rules instantiated by the target language), then (a) we would expect the acquisition of all syntactic manifestations of unaccusativity/unergativity to be affected by lexical-semantic factors; (b) we would expect this to happen in all languages, even in one such as Italian, which has an array of overt reflexes of the unaccusative/ unergative distinction; (c) if the hierarchies discussed above have any validity, we would furthermore expect the acquisition of syntactic properties to be sensitive to the relative hierarchical position of a verb, and therefore to take place in an order consistent with the hierarchy (e.g., first with core verbs and at later stages with peripheral verbs); and (d) we would also expect the advanced learners' knowledge of the unaccusative/unergative distinction to be characterized by more indeterminacy with respect to peripheral verbs. This could also result from the increased variation in the target language input relative to these verbs.

While these predictions may apply to both L1 and L2 learners, a different kind of learnability problem may arise in L2 acquisition as a consequence of the fact that L2 learners already have knowledge of the set of linking rules instantiate d by their L1. We would expect that, depending on the relative range of the L1 and the L2 linking rules with respect to each other, learners might face acquisition tasks of different magnitude. Particularly problematic would be the situation of learners who have to acquire linking rules for unaccusativity of a narrower scope than the ones instantiated in the L1, because they may have to reconsider the syntactic status of verbs that are close to the core. This problem is related to the more general issue of learners' retreat from incorrect generalizations. Assuming initial transfer of L1 knowledge, will positive evidence always suffice to abandon the transfer route? If negative evidence is available, will it be taken on board by L2 learners? What kind of knowledge representation of unaccusativity do learners have if they reach a near-native level of command of the L2?

The relevance of second language acquisition data

The empirical studies reviewed in this section were conducted in order to test the predictions formulated above.[10] Since they are similar with respect to objectives, methodology, research design, and data analysis, these are summarized here for convenience.

Objectives. The studies are concerned with the acquisition of the syntax of unaccusativity in Italian L2 (one of the studies also deals with French L2), and make specific reference to auxiliary selection and *ne*-cliticization with intransitive verbs belonging to the different lexical-semantic types represented in the hierarchies.

Methodology. All of the studies are based on acceptability judgments and do not consider production data. The method of elicitation employed is a timed version of magnitude estimation of linguistic acceptability.[11]

Research design. Sentences in different lexical versions were constructed around each of the intransitive verb types, of which half contained the canonical, or 'correct' auxiliary (e.g., *essere* for unaccusatives and *avere* for unergatives) and the other half contained the alternative, or 'incorrect' auxiliary. Sentences were of two syntactic types: basic word order (i.e., simple declarative sentences; used in all the studies), and with *ne*-cliticization (used in one of the studies).

Data analysis. The differences were calculated, for each sentence type, between the mean acceptability value assigned to the sentence with the correct auxiliary and the value assigned to the sentence with the alternative auxiliary. The relative size of this difference represents the strength of the subjects' preference for one auxiliary over the other, whereas its sign indicates the direction of preference: positive if the correct auxiliary is preferred; negative if the alternative auxiliary is preferred.[12] The assumption behind this analysis was that the strength of auxiliary preferences would be proportional to the position of a verb along the hierarchy to which it belongs: Verbs closer to the core would elicit stronger preferences for the canonical auxiliary.

Study 1: Developmental data

This cross-sectional study (reported in Sorace 1995a) involved four groups of English-speaking learners of Italian L2, ranging in proficiency from beginning to near-native, and a group of native Italian speakers. The test materials were 32 sentence types, which included the three verb types represented on the unergative hierarchy and five verb types represented on the unaccusative hierarchy, each presented in two syntactic versions (basic and *ne*-cliticized) and with *essere* and *avere*.[13]

Let us first look at the results for unergative verbs displayed in Figures 1 and 2. Recall that unergatives select auxiliary *avere* and do not allow *ne*-cliticization; auxiliary preferences were calculated by subtracting the acceptability value assigned to sentences with *essere* from the values assigned to the corresponding sentences with *avere*. Figure 1, relative to auxiliary preferences in basic sentences, shows that the judgments on auxiliary choice, for all subject groups, are differentiated according to verb type. In conformity with the prediction, the strength of preference f or the canonical auxiliary *avere* is more marked for verbs denoting non-motional activities (such as *dormire* 'sleep') than for monadic verbs denoting motional activity (*camminare* 'walk'), particularly in the judgments of non-native subjects. (The difference between the two is negligible in the native judgments). The most indeterminate judgments are elicited by motional activity verbs alternating with a telic counterpart (e.g., *volare* 'fly'), even for the native subject group. The non-native judgments gradually approximate native judgments with respect to strength of preferences, at the same time preserving the same pattern of differences among verb types.

The results obtained for *ne*-cliticization, represented in Figure 2, indicate a more irregular pattern. (Recall that *ne*-cliticization is not allowed by unergative verbs regardless of auxiliary). One can notice that there is little differentiation among verb types at lower proficiency levels, but that near-native and native subjects do not completely reject the combination of *avere* and *ne*-cliticization with verbs of non-motional activity (e.g., *Ne hanno parlato molti* 'Many of them have talked'). While auxiliary differences are close to zero for motional activity verbs (thus indicating no preference for any of the two ungrammatical sentences), *ne*-cliticization with paired verbs of motional activity (as in *Ne sono corsi molti di*

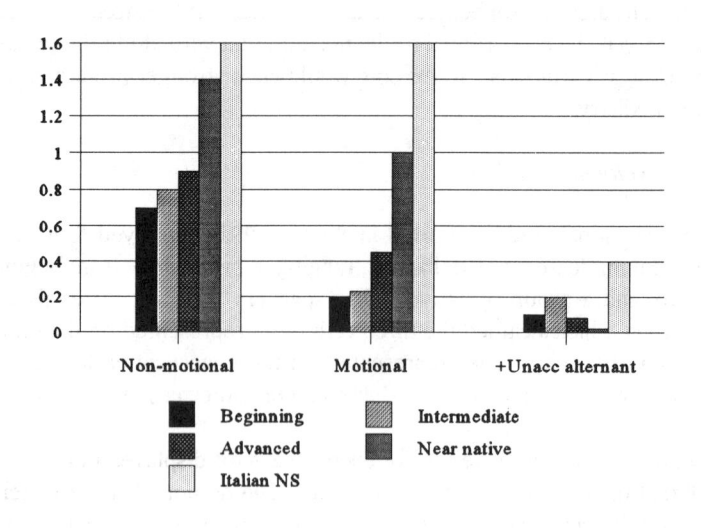

Figure 1: Unergative verbs—mean auxiliary preferences for avere *on basic sentences (in logs)*

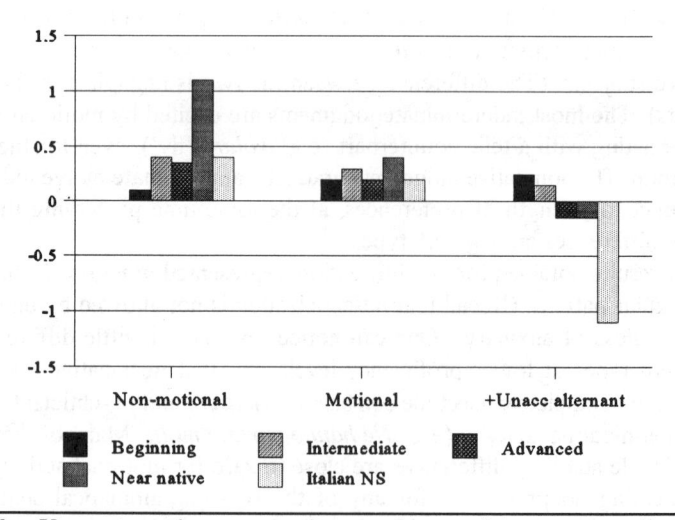

Figure 2: Unergative verbs—mean auxiliary preferences for avere *on* ne-*cliticized sentences (in logs)*

atleti 'Many of them have run') is marginally judged as acceptable by the native group. Moreover, their preference is definitely in favor of *essere*, as shown by the negative sign of the auxiliary difference. This rather surprising result confirms the ambiguous status of these verbs with respect to unergative syntax, which may be ascribed to their semantic proximity to unaccusative verbs.

Let us now consider the pattern of judgments obtained for unaccusative verbs. (Recall that these verbs select auxiliary *essere* and permit *ne*-cliticization; auxiliary preferences were calculated by subtracting the acceptability values assigned to sentences with *avere* from the values assigned to the corresponding sentences with *essere*.) This pattern is displayed in Figures 3 and 4. Figure 3 suggests that, in basic sentences, verbs denoting change of location (e.g., *arrivare* 'arrive') elicit stronger preferences for *essere* at all proficiency levels, confirming our hypothesis that places these verbs at the core of unaccusativity. The size of auxiliary differences is a function of the degree of proximity of verb types to the core, and change-of-location verbs are the most determinate in all subject groups. However, lower proficiency subjects give indeterminate judgments on most of the other verb types; the perception of the full verbal hierarchy becomes clear only at the highest levels. The acquisition of unaccusativity in Italian involves a growing sensitivity to the relative influence of lexical-semantic factors on its syntactic manifestations.

Figure 4, which shows the results for the *ne*-cliticized sentences, displays a similar, albeit slightly more irregular, pattern. Once again, the strength of auxiliary preferences is proportional to the coreness of verbs; preferences are strongest for *ne*-cliticized sentences occurring with *essere* and change-of-location verbs (e.g., *ne sono arrivati molti* 'Many of them have arrived') at all proficiency levels and weaker for peripheral verbs. (The order of preferences for the two most peripheral verb types is the opposite from that in basic sentences, but the difference is statistically not significant.) Subjects at lower proficiency levels are unable to provide determinate judgments on *ne*-cliticization with the most peripheral verb types, and they have a very marginal preference for *avere*. This supports the view that these verbs are marked with respect to unaccusative linking and thus more difficult to acquire. Finally, the fact that preferences becomes progressively stronger across proficiency levels suggests that the syntactic development of unaccusativity in interlanguage grammars involves growing knowledge of the link between auxiliary *essere* and *ne*-cliticization, despite the fact that neither of these properties are instantiated in the learners' L1. Overall, the results bear out our prediction that not only auxiliary selection but also *ne*-cliticization, as syntactic manifestations of unaccusativity, would be sensitive to lexical-semantic properties of verbs.

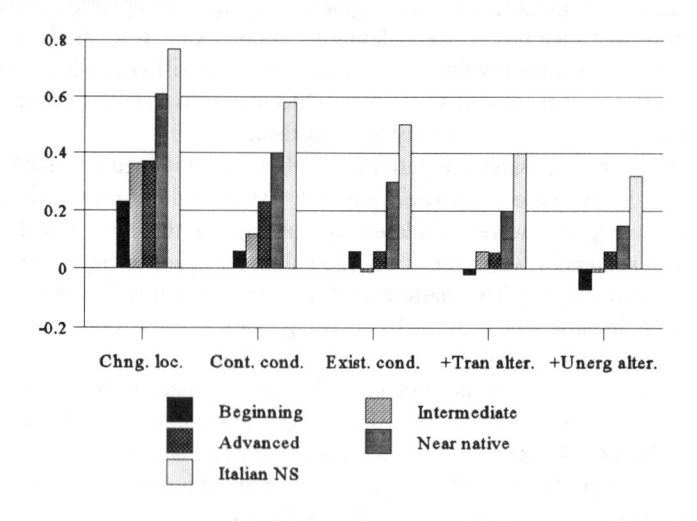

Figure 3: Unaccusative verbs–mean auxiliary preferences for essere *on basic sentences (in logs)*

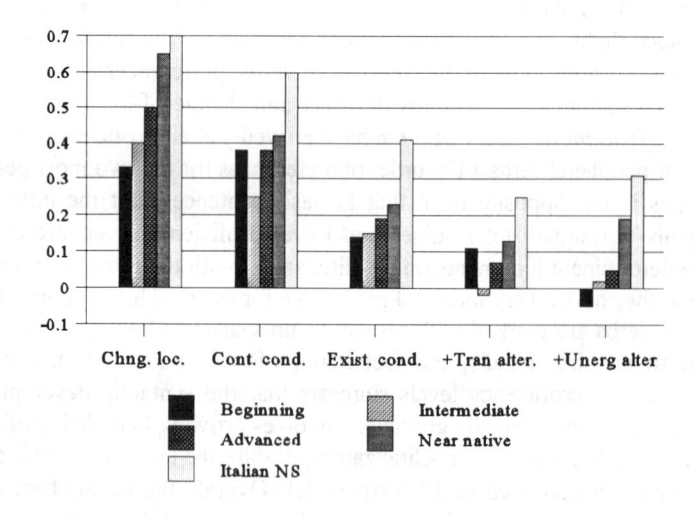

Figure 4: Unaccusative verbs–mean auxiliary preferences for essere *on* ne-*cliticized sentences (in logs)*

Study 2: Near-native data

This study (reported in Sorace 1993a) was conducted with two groups of near-native speakers of Italian, one consisting of native English speakers and the other of native French speakers. A control group of native Italian speakers also participated in the experiment. The results reviewed here are concerned with auxiliary selection in basic sentences presenting the same five verb types as in Study 1 (other structures were tested but will not be discussed here; see Sorace 1993a for a full account). The mean auxiliary preferences expressed by the three subject groups are shown in Figure 5. As the figure makes clear, the pattern of judgments obtained from the three language groups are remarkably similar. The near-native subjects, regardless of their native language, express strongest preferences for *essere* as an auxiliary with change-of-location verbs, and progressively weaker preferences for *essere* with the more peripheral verb categories (although the French subjects do not clearly differentiate among the three most peripheral verb types). Recall that both English and French have a linking rule of a narrower scope–and therefore a more restricted class of syntactic unaccusatives–than Italian. Native speakers of these languages with near-native command of Italian end up having a perception of the hierarchy which is virtually

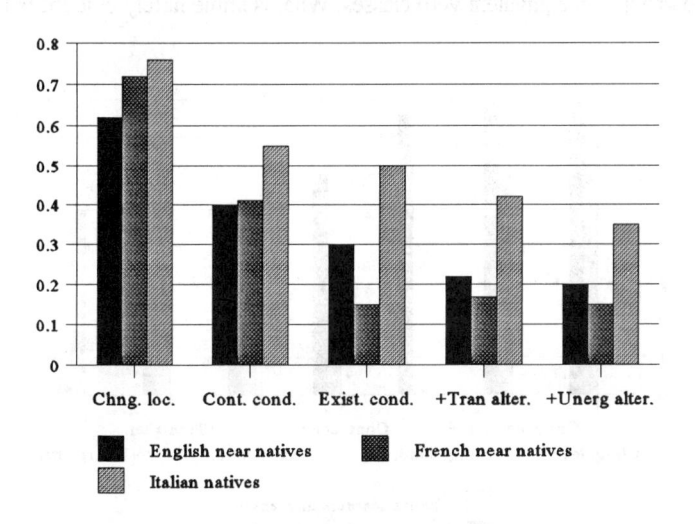

Figure 5: Unaccusative verbs–mean auxiliary preferences for essere on basic sentences (in logs)

the same as that of native Italians, with the same areas of indeterminacy. What makes this achievement possible? Since positive evidence plays an obvious role, but is often insufficient to guarantee successful acquisition, the nature of the relationship between the L1 and the L2 linking rules must also be a determinant factor in the explanation.[14] Study 3 sheds more light on this aspect.

Study 3: Learning asymmetries

The last set of results are drawn from a study conducted with two groups: one of Italian-speaking learners of French L2 and one of French-speaking learners of Italian L2 (see Sorace 1993b). Subjects in both language groups were at an advanced proficiency level and comparable with respect to a variety of factors. The test required them to judge sentences exemplifying six categories of verbs corresponding to positions on the unaccusative hierarchy in Table 1. The 'change-of-condition' class included both verbs that select the same auxiliary in Italian and French, and verbs that select different auxiliaries (i.e., *essere* in Italian and *avoir* in French). All sentences were presented in two versions, one with the canonical auxiliary and one with the alternative auxiliary.

Figure 6 depicts the auxiliary preferences in the judgments of the two language groups on equivalent verb classes. What is immediately evident is the fact

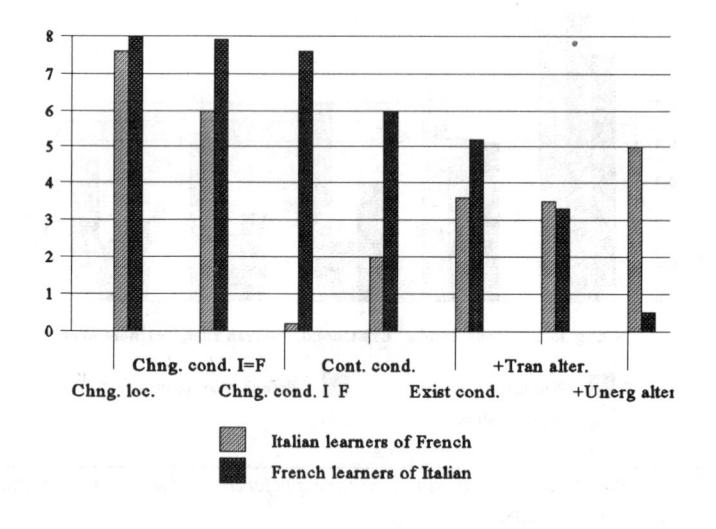

Figure 6: Unaccusative verbs—mean auxiliary preferences for the correct auxiliary on basic sentences

that preferences for the canonical auxiliary are equally strong in the two groups for change-of-location verbs and change-of-state verbs that select the same auxiliary in Italian and French (i.e., *venire/venir* 'come'; *diventare/devenir* 'become'), but radically different for change-of-state verbs that select opposite auxiliaries (i.e., *sparire/disparaître* 'disappear'). The judgments of the French subjects on Italian verbs are consistent with the unaccusative hierarchy, whereas the judgments of the Italian subjects on French verbs are conditioned by the hierarchy but in the reverse order: Sentences constructed with *avoir* instead of *être* are judged as significantly less unacceptable with core verbs than with peripheral verbs. The data reveal a surprisingly asymmetrical pattern in the acquisition of auxiliary choice with unaccusative verbs, a pattern that cannot be explained on the basis of exposure to input since both groups had received quantitatively and qualitatively comparable amounts of it. A plausible explanation resides in the fact that while both groups have knowledge of the semantic space underlying intransitivity (and of what counts as core or periphery in it), the French learners start from a more restricted linking rule and move towards a wider-range rule. They are assisted in the process by the consistency of the Italian system. The Italian learners, in contrast, face the task of restricting the range of their linking rule, changing the assignment to argument structure positions (from internal to external) for verbs which are close to the core. They encounter further obstacles in the frequent internal inconsistencies exhibited by the French system. The data show that the degree of indeterminacy in the judgments of Italians on French verbs is directly proportional to the proximity of a verb to the core. This suggests that change-of-condition verbs are perceived as the most inherently associated with unaccusative syntax and therefore as the most difficult to re-categorize; this is why, in our view, Italian learners are reluctant to abandon the L1 linking rule with these verbs, despite the counterevidence in the input.

Conclusions

To sum up, this paper has proposed an alternative approach to unaccusativity, according to which (a) the lexical-semantic components of intransitive verbs indirectly determine their syntactic status as unaccusative or unergative verbs, through the mediation of argument structure; (b) these lexical-semantic components, which belong to a potentially universal 'semantic space', may be placed in hierarchical orders which identify verbs that are central (core) from the perspective of linking to the internal or external argument positions, and verbs that are more peripheral; (c) within the common semantic space, languages may select different 'minimal triggers' of unaccusativity, which determines cross-linguistic variation at the level of linking rules.

With these theoretical assumptions, we argued that the acquisition of the syntax of unaccusativity crucially depends on the internalization of the linking rules that relate the conceptual structure underlying intransitive verbs to their argument structure. L2 data provide critical evidence for this hypothesis. To demonstrate this, we focused on the acquisition of unaccusativity in Italian L2 by English-speaking and French-speaking learners, and specifically on two of the most important grammatical properties that distinguish unergative and unaccusative verbs: auxiliary choice and the distribution of *ne*-cliticization. The data reviewed indicate that both properties are acquired gradually and according to developmental paths which are sensitive to the lexical-semantic hierarchies that subdivide intransitive verbs. The data also reveal learning asymmetries which depend on the relationship between the relative scope of the L1 and L2 linking rules and suggest a plausible explanation for the persistence of transfer among Italian learners of French. More generally, the data point to the intimate connection between lexical knowledge and syntactic knowledge in acquisition. Undoubtedly, more research is needed to give further insight to the numerous aspects of the work discussed here, such as the cross-linguistic validity of lexical-semantic hierarchies and the universality of the developmental routes in the acquisition of unaccusativity.

Notes

1. Among the other Germanic languages, both Dutch and German have a choice of perfective auxiliary which is similar, but not identical, to that of Italian (Grewendorf 1987; Hoekstra 1984; Seibert 1993). These languages also display syntactic differences between unergatives and unaccusatives which are not found in Romance languages, such as the impersonal passive construction, allowed only with unergative verbs (Perlmutter 1978; Zaenen 1988). In neither language, however, does any diagnostic consistently apply to unaccusatives or unergatives as whole verb classes: In a significant number of cases further specifications, often of a semantic nature, are necessary beyond the purely structural ones in order for a particular diagnostic to apply (see Seibert 1993 for a discussion of German).

2. See Randall et al. 1994 for a similar view. We are in agreement with Jackendoff (1990: 285-286), who argues that linking rules may be regarded as an autonomous component of linguistic knowledge, characterized by its own properties and typology which are largely independent of conceptual and syntactic structures. Regarding linking rules as the main locus of cross-linguistic variation implies that there are no 'unaccusative mismatches', i.e., verbs showing unaccusative semantics and unergative syntax, or vice versa. Strictly speaking, the terms 'unaccusative' and 'unergative' apply only to the syntactic level, i.e., to refer to verbs whose single argument is linked to the direct object position or to the subject position, respectively.

LINKING RULES AND ARGUMENT STRUCTURES 171

3. As an anonymous reviewer points out, there is a risk of increasing the descriptive power of lexical conceptual structures without a corresponding increase in explanatory adequacy. The notion of 'hierarchy' in the context of this paper represents a constraint on what might appear as a proliferation of lexical-conceptual categories. Much more work is needed, however, to construct a properly constrained formal theory of argument structure which does not sacrifice the richness of the semantic level (see Hale & Keyser 1993 for an attempt to interpret argument structure as a syntax, subject to general syntactic principles).

4. Our account predicts that if a language has any syntactic reflexes of unaccusativity, these are more likely to occur (and be retained) with core verbs than with peripheral verbs. The existence of gradients of acceptability with respect to diagnostics of unaccusativity has been recognized by several authors, e.g., Rappaport (1988), Levin & Rappaport Hovav (1994), and Legendre, Miyata & Smolensky (1991).

5. The status of dyadic verbs is somewhat heterogeneous with respect to the semantic dimensions discussed here, and therefore difficult to represent in hierarchical terms. In both cases, the 'unaccusative' member of these alternations seems to be more peripheral with respect to monadic verbs. Verbs entering the causative alternation, such as *break* (e.g., Keyser & Roeper 1984; Pinker 1989; Burzio 1986; Levin & Rappaport Hovav 1994), may be regarded as inherently dyadic verbs of change of condition (as opposed to inherently monadic verbs, such as *disappear*), because they denote externally caused events: The intransitive member of the pair is usually seen as derived from the basic transitive alternant by means of a process of 'detransitivization' (but see Zubizarreta 1987 for the opposite view, in which the basic form is the intransitive one, from which the transitive alternant is derived by a process of 'anti-causativization'). Haegeman (1994) treats these verbs as intransitives which project their theme argument in the subject position in d-structure. Zubizarreta (1987) argues that the lexical representation of these verbs (in French) specifies a form of irregular linking, which makes them syntactically comparable to unergatives (see Labelle 1990). Verbs entering unaccusative/unergative alternations, such as *run*, are inherently atelic verbs of movement (as opposed to inherently telic verbs, such as *arrive*) to which telicity can be compositionally added by means of a directional phrase (see Note 7).

6. See Sorace (1993a, 1993b, forthcoming) for diachronic and synchronic evidence in support of the unaccusative hierarchy.

7. The differences between verbs denoting motional activity and verbs denoting non-motional activity has been the object of several studies (e.g., Torrego 1989; Saccon 1991; Hoekstra & Mulder 1990). In Italian, and in other languages that have a two-auxiliary system, intransitives denoting motional activity (the most peripheral on the hierarchy) display unaccusative syntax in the presence of a locative phrase (which may or may not be directional). Even more revealingly, monadic verbs of motional activity (those occupying the middle position on the hierarchy) also show unaccusative syntactic behavior when there is a locative phrase. In contrast, monadic intransitive denoting non-motional activities (defined as 'core' in terms of the hierarchy) do not easily participate in these shifts from unergative to unaccusative syntax.

8. The centrality of the concept of telicity in Dutch is demonstrated by the fact that all Dutch intransitive verbs of manner of motion may (compositionally) enter ±telic alternations, which results in regular shifts from unergative to unaccusative syntax. This means that Dutch, unlike Italian, has no distinction between monadic and dyadic intransitives denoting motional activity.

9. It is only change-of-location verbs that exhibit consistent unaccusative syntactic behavior in (European) French. Isolated counterexamples such as *rester* 'stay' do not invalidate this generalization: Continuatives involve the negation of a potential change, and therefore subsume the notion of change in their semantics (interestingly, *rester*–the only continuative verb that displays unaccusative syntax in French–involves the negation of a change of location). Other verbs, such as *disparaître* 'disappear' or *exister* 'exist' are syntactically inconsistent (for example, they select auxiliary *avoir* but allow *en*-cliticization). This is also to be expected within our approach.

10. Since all of the studies reviewed here are published elsewhere, the review will not include a full discussion of the statistical significance of the results, which can be found in the original sources.

11. The advantage of the magnitude estimation technique is that it enables one to measure acceptability on an interval scale and therefore to apply the full range of parametric statistics to the data (see Bard, Robertson & Sorace 1994; Sorace 1995b for details). In the studies reviewed in this paper, subjects were presented with a series of randomized sentences, one at a time. They were instructed to assign any number to the first sentence and thereafter to assign numbers reflecting the acceptability of each subsequent sentence relative to the first. It is customary in the analysis of magnitude estimation data to transform numerical responses into logs and to carry out calculations on the log-transformed data. The means shown in Figures 1-5 are given as arithmetic means of logs. The means in Figure 6 are given as geometric means (i.e., arithmetic means of exponentiated logs) in order to be consistent with the original source.

12. Separate analyses were also conducted on the judgments obtained on each auxiliary. In general, these show that the canonical auxiliary is judged as acceptable by both native and non-native subjects across verb types, whereas the alternative auxiliary is more or less unacceptable depending on verb type. For this reason, two of the original sources (Sorace 1993a, 1993b) discuss only the judgments relevant to the incorrect auxiliaries. In this paper, however, we have decided to show the data in the form of auxiliary differences because this analysis takes into account the judgments on both auxiliaries and therefore provides a more complete picture of the subjects' knowledge of unaccusativity.

13. The test materials on change-of-condition verbs in studies 1 and 2 had to be discarded because of an error in the administration of the test.

14. The English and the French near-native speakers produced radically different judgments from those of Italians on phenomena related to restructuring in Italian, such as optional auxiliary change and clitic climbing. We defined the English state of knowledge as incomplete and the French state of knowledge as divergent (see Sorace 1993a). Both of them indicate that the available evidence had not be processed for the purpose of acquisition.

References

Baker, M. 1983. "Objects, Themes, and Lexical Rules in Italian". *Papers in Lexical-Functional Grammar* ed. by L. Levin, M. Rappaport & A. Zaenen. Bloomington: Indiana University Club.
Bard, E. G., D. Robertson & A. Sorace. 1994. "Magnitude Estimation of Linguistic Acceptability". Research paper HCRC/RP-52, Human Communication Research Centre, University of Edinburgh.
Brinkmann, U. 1992. "Choice of Auxiliary with Intransitive Verbs of Motion: An analysis of an unaccusative diagnostic". Ms., Max Planck Institute for Psycholinguistics, Nijmegen.
Burzio, L. 1986. *Italian Syntax: A government-binding approach*. Dordrecht: Foris.
Centineo, G. 1986. "A Lexical Theory of Auxiliary Selection in Italian". *Davis Working Papers in Linguistics* 1.1-35.
Dowty, D. R. 1979. *Word Meaning and Montague Grammar*. Dordrecht: Reidel.
Fillmore, C. J. 1968. "A Case for Case". *Universals in Linguistic Theory* ed. by E. Bach & R. J. Harms, 1-90. New York: Holt, Rinehart, and Winston.
Gougenheim, G. 1951. *Grammaire de la Langue Française du Seizième Siècle*. Lyon: Editions I. A. C.
Grewendorf, G. 1989. *Ergativity in German*. Dordrecht: Foris.
Grimshaw, J. 1987. "Unaccusatives: An overview". *NELS* 17.244-258.
Grimshaw, J. 1991. *Argument Structure*. Cambridge, MA: MIT Press.
Gruber, J. 1965. *Studies in Lexical Relations*. Dissertation, MIT.
Guernssel, M., K. Hale, M. Laughren, B. Levin & J. White Eagle. 1985. "A Cross-linguistic Study of Transitivity Alternations". *Papers from the Parasession on Causatives and Agentivity* ed. by W. H. Eilfort, P. D. Kroeber & K. L. Peterson, 48-63. Chicago: Chicago Linguistic Society.
Haegeman, L. 1994. *Introduction to Government and Binding Theory*. Second edition. Oxford: Blackwell.
Hale, K. & S. J. Keyser 1986. "Some Transitivity Alternations in English". *Lexical Project Working Paper* 7. Center for Cognitive Science, MIT.
Hale, K. & S. J. Keyser 1993. "On Argument Structure and the Lexical Expression of Syntactic Relations". *The View from Building 20* ed. by K. Hale & S. J. Keyser, 53-110. Cambridge, MA: MIT Press.
Hoekstra, T. 1984. *Transitivity: Grammatical relations in government-binding theory*. Dordrecht: Foris.
Hoekstra, T. & R. Mulder. 1990. "Unergatives as Copular Verbs: Locational and existential predication". *The Linguistic Review* 7.1-79.
Jackendoff, R. 1972. *Semantic Representations in Generative Grammar*. Cambridge, MA: MIT Press.
Jackendoff, R. 1983. *Semantics and Cognition*. Cambridge, MA: MIT Press.
Jackendoff, R. 1990. *Semantic Structures*. Cambridge, MA: MIT Press.
Labelle, M. 1990. "Unaccusatives and Pseudo-unaccusatives in French". *NELS* 20. 303-317.

Legendre, G. 1989. "Unaccusativity in French". *Lingua* 79.95-164.
Legendre, G., Miyata, Y. & P. Smolensky 1991. "Unifying Syntactic and Semantic Approaches to Unaccusativity: A connectionist approach". *Proceeedings of the 17th Annual Meeting of the Berkeley Linguistic Society*. Berkeley: Berkeley Linguistic Society.
Levin, B. & S. Pinker, eds. 1992. *Lexical and Conceptual Semantics*. Cambridge, MA: MIT Press.
Levin, B. & M. Rappaport. 1989. "An Approach to Unaccusative Mismatches". *NELS* 19.314-328.
Levin, B. & M. Rappaport Hovav. 1992. "The Lexical Semantics of Verbs of Motion: The perspective from unaccusativity". *Thematic Structure: Its role in grammar* ed. by I. M. Roca. Dordrecht: Foris.
Levin, B. & M. Rappaport Hovav. 1994. "A Preliminary Analysis of Causative Verbs in English". *Lingua* 92.35-77.
Marantz, A. P. 1984. *On the Nature of Grammatical Relations*. Cambridge, MA: MIT Press.
Napoli, D. J. 1988. "Review of Burzio 1986". *Language* 64.130-142.
Perlmutter, D. 1978. "Impersonal Passives and the Unaccusative Hypothesis". *Proceedings of the Fourth Annual Meeting of the Berkeley Linguistic Society*. Berkeley: Berkeley Linguistics Soceity.
Perlmutter, D. 1989. "Multiattachment and The Unaccusative Hypothesis: The perfect auxiliary in Italian". *Probus* 1.63-119.
Perlmutter, D. & P. Postal. 1984. "The 1-Advancement Exclusiveness Law". *Studies in Relational Grammar 2* ed. by D. Perlmutter & C. Rosen. Chicago: University of Chicago Press.
Pinker, S. 1989. *Learnability and Cognition*. Cambridge, MA: MIT Press.
Randall, J. H. 1990. "Catapults and Pendulums". *Linguistics* 28.1381-1406.
Randall, J. H., A. Van Hout, J. Weissenborn & H. Baayen. 1994. "Approaching Linking". Paper at the BU Conference on Language Development, Boston, MA.
Rappaport, M. 1988. "Unaccusativity and Verbs of Motion". *Proceedings of the Second Symposium on English and Greek*. Thessaloniki: Aristotle University.
Rappaport, M. & B. Levin 1988. "What to Do with Theta-roles". *Syntax and Semantics: Thematic relations* ed. by W. Wilkins. New York: Academic Press.
Rosen, C. 1984. "The Interface between Semantic Roles and Initial Grammatical Relations". *Studies in Relational Grammar 2* ed. by D. Perlmutter & C. Rosen. Chicago: University of Chicago Press.
Schroten, J. 1986. "Ergativity, Raising and Restructuring in the Syntax of Spanish Aspectual Verbs". *Linguisticae Investigationes* X.439-465.
Seibert, A. J. 1993. "Intransitive Constructions in German and the Ergative Hypothesis". *Trondheim Working Papers in Linguistics* 14. University of Trondheim.
Sorace, A. 1993a. "Incomplete vs. Divergent Representations of Unaccusativity in Non-native Grammars of Italian". *Second Language Research* 9.22-47.

Sorace, A. 1993b. "Unaccusativity and Auxiliary Choice in Non-native Grammars of Italian and French: Asymmetries and predictable indeterminacy". *Journal of French Language Studies* 3.71-93.
Sorace, A. 1995a. "Contraintes Sémantiques sur la Syntaxe: L'acquisition de l'inaccusativité en italien L2". To appear in *Acquisition Intéraction en Langue Etrangére*.
Sorace, A. 1995b. "The Use of Acceptability Judgments in Second Language Acquisition Research". To appear *Handbook of Language Acquisition* ed. by T. Bathia & W. Ritchie. New York: Academic Press.
Sorace, A. In preparation. "Lexical Hierarchies in the Domain of Unaccusativity".
Torrego, E. 1989. "Unergative-unaccusative Alternations in Spanish". *MIT Working Papers in Linguistics* 10.253-269.
Van Hout, A. Forthcoming. "Projection Based on Event Structure". To appear in *Lexical Specification and Lexical Insertion* ed. by P. Coopmans, M. Everaert & J. Grimshaw. Hillsdale: Lawrence Erlbaum Associates.
Van Hout, A., J. Randall & J. Weissenborn 1993. "Acquiring the Unergative-unaccusative Distinction". *The Acquisition of Dutch* ed. by M. Verrips & F. Wijnen. Publikatie n. 60, Universiteit van Amsterdam.
Van Valin, R. D. 1990. "Semantic Parameters of Split Intransitivity". *Language* 66. 221-260.
Vendler, Z. 1967. "Verbs and Times". *Linguistics in Philosophy*. Ithaca, NY: Cornell University Press.
Zaenen, A. 1988. "Unaccusativity in Dutch: An integrated approach". Ms., Stanford University.
Zubizarreta, M.-L. 1987. *Levels of Representations in the Lexicon and in the Syntax*. Dordrecht: Foris.

Data, evidence and rules

Maria Beck
University of North Texas

Bonnie D. Schwartz
University of Durham

Lynn Eubank
University of North Texas

Introduction

The point of this three-part paper is to address the notion of 'evidence' as it relates to generative linguistics, and in particular to the Principles and Parameters approach applied to nonnative language (L2) acquisition. What we attempt is, first, to provide a general overview to the way different types of input data can be conceived to cause the building of a grammar and then, secondly, to propose–by way of specific exemplification–that there is good reason to believe that (unfortunately) not all data can actually be used in L2 grammar building. In short, the position we take is that only some input data can in fact serve as evidence by the grammar-building process in the construction of an Interlanguage 'grammar'. What is important to note here is that we are differentiating the term 'data' from the term 'evidence'; as we attempt to show, the different types of data are only *potential* evidence for grammar building: While all evidence for constructing a grammar comes from data, not all data turn out to be evidence–for a variety of reasons.[1] In addition, we also explore one way–here involving morphosyntactic 'rules'–to explain the difficulties nonnative speakers have. Importantly, this explanation does not presuppose the inaccessibility of Universal Grammar in L2 acquisition. And finally, we also speculate on what alternatives there might be to data-driven grammar construction, in order to get nonnative speakers' linguistic behavior to more closely match native-speaker linguistic behavior.

Background

We first need to review some assumptions made within the Principles and Parameters approach to native language (L1) acquisition. As is well known, the primary motivation for positing an innate Universal Grammar is to provide an answer to what has been called 'The Logical Problem of Language Acquisition' (Baker 1979; Hornstein & Lightfoot 1981). In brief, the 'Logical Problem' points out that there are certain things that native speakers come to know concerning their language for which they have had no evidence and which 'inductive learning' or 'general problem solving' can also not explain. For example, as has often been noted, part of the knowledge that native speakers eventually gain tells them that certain phenomena in their language are not possible. Compare the sentences in (1a) and (1b) below.

(1) a. Norm has often eaten a whole banana pie.
 b. *Norm ate often a whole banana pie.
 (cf. Norm often ate a whole banana pie; Norm ate a whole banana pie often.)

It is due to the particular form of UG that native speakers of English know that (1b) is not allowed. Importantly, it is not by way of being told that certain phenomena are impossible that we all gain knowledge of ungrammaticality. We return below to the phenomenon illustrated in the pair of sentences in (1), for not all languages manifest such a grammaticality contrast.

Indeed, within the tradition of generative linguistics, the only kind of input data that is assumed to be used in the L1 grammar-building function is 'positive data'. Positive data consist of utterances that the acquirer is exposed to in the ambient language—that is, what the acquirer hears; this is in opposition to 'negative data', which consist of explicit information about the impossibility of a form, utterance or sentence. There is also a third type of data, namely, 'explicit data', which consist of descriptive information *about* the language. Thus, there are in principle three different types of data that should be considered as potential evidence for the process of grammar construction. These are listed in (2) below.

(2) a. Positive data: (contextualized) utterances in the ambient language;
 b. Negative data: explicit (and perhaps implicit) information about the impossibility of a form, utterance or sentence;
 c. Other explicit data: descriptive information about the language.

While the role of negative data has been the subject of intensive research in native language acquisition, the potential usefulness of explicit data has not been addressed, for perhaps obvious reasons. The reasons that negative data are assumed to be irrelevant to grammar building in L1 acquisition are of both a conceptual and an empirical nature. Conceptually, L1 children do not produce the kinds of errors that require negative data in order to be overcome; in other words, all errors in L1 acquisition are un-doable because there will always be further positive data to force reorganization of the developing L1 grammar. At the empirical level, it has been shown that not all children are even exposed to negative data. Thus, if just a single child can acquire the final-state grammar without negative data, then negative data cannot be necessary for grammar building. In short, the puzzle confronted by L1 acquisition researchers is how to account for language development in the face of only positive data (i.e., (2a)) in combination with, of course, Universal Grammar.

Data vs. evidence in L2A

The situation is somewhat different in L2 acquisition, where both negative data and explicit data–more typically called 'correction' and 'grammar instruction', respectively–are at times plentiful, especially in the context of the foreign-language classroom. In light of the brief summary of L1 acquisition and different types of data, an obvious question arises: Does the depiction of grammar construction in L1 acquisition carry over to L2 acquisition? In other words, is it also the case that in L2 acquisition there is a restriction on the type of data that can serve as evidence in the grammar-building process? What we attempt to show in the remainder of this paper is that the answer is 'yes'–only positive data can be used as evidence in nonnative grammar construction (see Schwartz 1993 for more detailed discussion). In addition, however, we also show that perhaps not even all positive data can serve as evidence in the grammar-building process of L2 acquisition.

Eubank: What kind of evidence?

While there are different types of data that might potentially be involved in grammar building, the data that are commonly held to be basic yet necessary to language acquisition are positive data, those arising simply from exposure to utterances in the ambient language. As narrow as such data seem, however, it turns out that not even all positive data may be relevant to acquisition. Perhaps the best way to demonstrate this further restriction on data is to review how generative grammar has changed over the years and how these changes have affected the relevance of data to acquisition.

In the 1960s and early 1970s, acquisition research of a formal nature was concerned primarily with the notion of linguistic rules. Thus, for example, in regard to the English passive, the so-called 'Standard Theory' of Chomsky (1965) included a series of phrase-structure rules that would produce something like an active sentence and a passive transformational rule that would rework the active sentence to produce the passive. What is important to understand about the Standard Theory is that such rules were specific both to particular languages and to particular structures within languages: The passive transformation, for example, could apply only under very restricted conditions, and it could result only in an English passive sentence. Implicit knowledge of such rules was assumed at the time to constitute one's linguistic competence.

How was acquisition to proceed under this type of theory? In particular, what evidence did the learner need in order to acquire, for example, the English passive transformation? In actual fact, not that much was made explicit early on, but the work of Wexler & Culicover (1980) suggested that the relevant input to acquire the passive transformation was itself a passive sentence. In effect, to acquire the passive, learners needed exposure to positive data that included passive sentences. Of course, this depiction vastly oversimplifies the nature of acquisition under the Standard Theory, but it does indicate an important generalization: In this theory, there was a clearly isomorphic relationship between structural changes brought about by particular rules and the relevant evidence to learn these rules.

As interesting as it was, Standard Theory presented a multitude of conceptual difficulties (for discussion, see Atkinson 1992); what came to replace the Standard Theory is what we now know as the Principles and Parameters (P&P) theory (Chomsky 1981). And among the many characteristics that differentiate P&P theory from Standard Theory, one that is important for the present discussion is the notion of parameterized principles. Thus, unlike the language- and structure-specific rules of the Standard Theory, P&P in general has no such rules. Indeed, for any particular parametric selection, one would expect to observe a variety of superficial, observable effects. It was once thought, for example, that the Italian-like selection on the '*pro*-drop parameter' would result in several different visible consequences: missing subjects, post-verbal/VP subjects, long Wh-movement of subjects, empty resumptive pronouns in embeddings, and apparent *that*-trace violations (Chomsky 1981). In other words, rather than having particular rules which were associated isomorphically with particular structural results, specific values of parameters were expected to be associated with a number of different manifestations.

So acquisition proceeds via the selection of appropriate parametric values in this framework, but which of the observable data are relevant to parameter selection? One might think that any of the observable manifestations of a particular parametric value could serve as evidence to select the appropriate value for that language. Hence, if a particular value of some parameter resulted in five observable manifestations, then any of those five manifestations could serve the learner in determining the value of the parameter. However, such a conception turns out to be somewhat too ambitious, because considerations of learnability show that not all of the superficial manifestations of a particular value can, in turn, constitute the relevant evidence in parameter setting.

An example can illustrate the role of learnability in determining the relevance of positive data. Here we concentrate only on L1 acquisition; we turn below to L2 acquisition. For the example, consider again the null-subject phenomenon, where in many languages we find the apparent optionality of lexical subjects in tensed clauses. On the assumption of such a parameter, we might imagine, roughly following Rutherford and Sharwood Smith (1988), an analysis such as that in (3) below, where the two values of the parameter ('A' and 'B') are listed along with the observable results of these values for subjects.

(3) Value   Result
    A   Optional subjects (e.g., SVX or VX)
    B   Obligatory subjects (e.g., only SVX)

Hence, according to (3), selection of value 'A' results in declarative sentences in which we may or may not observe a lexical subject, but selection of 'B' has the result of making lexical subjects mandatory. Further, one might assume (for L1 development) that one or the other of these two values is a default value, that is, that the child begins acquisition with this value already in mind.

Now to the relevance of data. Of course, if the default value and the value of the ambient language are the same, then we have nothing of interest to examine. The situation is more challenging when the default value and that of the ambient language happen to be different. Assume, for example, that 'B' (obligatory subjects) is the default value and that the ambient language has value 'A' (optional subjects). What the child will thus be exposed to during the course of acquisition is positive data in which lexical subjects may or may not be present. Importantly, data that include lexical subjects are irrelevant to this situation because the child already knows from the default setting 'B' that subjects are obligatory. The only relevant data in this example comprise utterances without lexical subjects, because these strings are impossible in setting 'B'. In other words, given a default of 'B', exposure to utterances that do not include lexical subjects will show that the default 'B' value must be incorrect, hence that 'A' must be the correct value.

Assume, however, that 'A' is the default and that the ambient language has value 'B'. In other words, the child's default grammar allows optional subjects while the language of exposure will appear to have obligatory subjects.[2] What is important in this case is that exposure to utterances that have lexical subjects is irrelevant because such utterances only confirm what the child already knows from value 'A': Subjects may be present. In order to change from value 'A' to value 'B', the child will have to notice that the ambient language does not include any sentences in which lexical subjects are missing. In other words, the relevant data here would comprise not what the child observes, but what the child does *not* observe. It is here that one finds a problem of learnability: Positive data only tell the child what strings exist in the language, not what strings do not exist. As a result, the child would be faced with an impossible learning situation if she is assumed to have 'A' as the default value on (3), and 'B' is the value associated with the language of exposure.

More generally, even though particular parametric values may result in a variety of superficial manifestations, not all of these manifestations may be relevant evidence for parameter setting since particular values of parameters may be unlearnable from positive data. In other words, such considerations of learnability make it clear that positive data may consist of data that are relevant for acquisition (parameter setting) and data that are irrelevant. In effect, not all positive data are positive evidence.

From considerations of learnability like that discussed above come the kinds of questions that have been considered for L2 development, specifically, where a learner begins acquisition with a parametric value derived from transfer from the L1 and not as a default. In some cases, one would expect parameter 're-setting' to be impossible on the basis of positive data, and so, logically, in order for L2 parameter selection to proceed, it would seem to have to take place (if at all) on the basis of negative data and/or explicit data (see, e.g., White 1991a, 1992b; Schwartz and Gubala-Ryzak 1992; see also Rutherford and Sharwood Smith 1988).[3] Yet, again, with regard to the relevance of data to parameter setting, this view of L2 acquisition and the particular studies guided by it were informed by the basic framework of the Principles and Parameters theory. As one might imagine, however, time has not stood still in linguistics since the advent of P&P in the early 1980s. More recently, a number of conceptual shifts seem to have enjoyed wide acceptance, and some of these would appear to have the effect of restricting even further what data would be relevant for setting parameter values (see, e.g., Pollock 1989; Chomsky 1991, 1992). One such view seems crucial in this regard. The idea is that parametric values are determined by evidence that is lexical in nature, in effect, that all parameters are lexical parameters.[4]

Consider an example of this view of parameters. For this, we employ the well-known data on the placement of finite (thematic) verbs vis-à-vis medial adverbs that Lydia White has examined (see White 1989b for a broad review). The contrasting placements for English and French are shown below in (4a-b) and (5a-b), respectively.

(4) a. Marie always takes the metro.
    b. *Marie takes always the metro.

(5) a. *Marie toujours prend le métro.
   b. Marie prend toujours le métro.

One widely accepted explanation for the contrast between (4) and (5), following work by Emonds (1978), involves movement of the finite verb, or more specifically, (thematic) verb movement, in French, versus no such movement in English. For English and French, respectively, such movement is illustrated in the two trees in (6) and (7) below (both simplified for expository purposes).

(6)
```
         IP
        /  \
       NP   I'
       |   / \
       |  I   VP
       |     / \
       |   Adv  VP
       |    |  / \
       |    | V   NP
     Marie always takes the metro
```

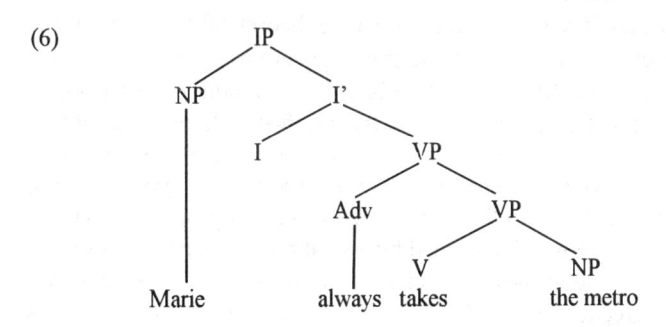

(7)
```
         IP
        /  \
       NP   I'
       |   / \
       |  I   VP
       |  |  / \
       |  | Adv VP
       |  |  |  / \
       |  |  | V   NP
     Marie prend toujours   le métro
```

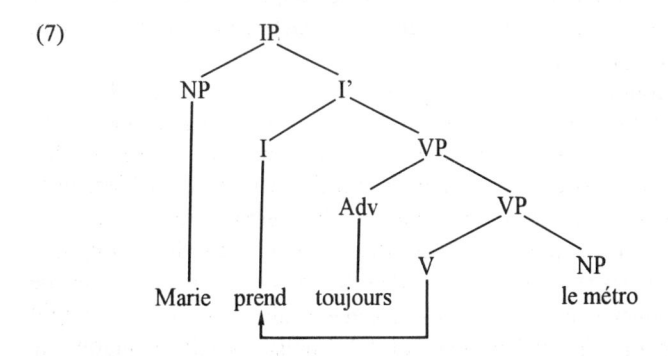

As shown in (6), the English finite, thematic verb remains in VP, and the result is that the medial adverb precedes it. In the French tree in (7), the finite verb moves up to I, and so the medial adverb follows the finite verb. In effect, then, we have a parameter, with one setting requiring verb movement as in French and the other setting forbidding thematic verb movement as in English.

How can the L2 learner discern which value is correct for the language she is learning? In other words, what data are relevant evidence to set this parameter correctly? As is well known, White, focussing on native French learners of English, has looked at this from several perspectives (e.g., White 1989a, 1991a), but the only perspective we examine in this section of the paper is one that involves positive data. In recent work, Trahey & White (1993) massively expose their French-speaking learners to English sentences in which the adverb precedes the verb, hence to sentences like (4a) above. Their results indicate that the learners still accept English sentences like (4b), even though they also accept sentences like (4a). Such results are very puzzling because parameters of UG principles are generally assumed to be exclusive.

Given such findings, it is useful to reexamine the theoretical backdrop of the Trahey & White study. Again, they assume that exposure to sentences like (4a) will force a switch in parametric values. In effect, the assumption is that purely syntactic data are relevant evidence to re-set the parameter. Is this assumption correct? The theoretical research in which the movement parameter was originally proposed, Pollock (1989) and Chomsky (1991), seems to suggest that the assumption may be flawed. The idea that Pollock and Chomsky propose is that the possibility of moving the verb is determined by lexical affairs, in particular, what they call the 'strength' of subject-verb agreement. In this view, if a language has robust subject-verb agreement (as in the case of French), then verb movement is allowed; if a language has impoverished subject-verb agreement (as in English), then verb movement is prohibited. In other words, perhaps the relevant evidence to set this parameter involves not data on ordering characteristics, but rather data on verbal agreement inflection, which is lexical.

White is, of course, aware of this possibility, and in White (1992a) she includes data on the status of English subject-verb agreement among such learners. Unfortunately, however, these data turn out in the end not to be terribly informative because what they seem to show is that the learners get subject-verb agreement right only for a subset of verbs and thus that verbal agreement has yet to be acquired as a morphological rule by these learners. Ideally, though, if Chomsky and Pollock are right in assuming that the relevant evidence to set the verb-movement parameter involves verbal agreement inflection, then we might expect to find that the French speakers of L2 English would abandon the possibility of moving the verb at just that point where they acquire English subject-verb agreement.

There is, however, a more important point here, and it goes back once again to the relationship between data and evidence: If UG parameters are associated with items located in the lexicon, and, more importantly, if paraticular parametric values are determined on the basis of simple lexical data such as the verb-movement example suggests, then the relative positions of adverbs and verbs are data that *result* from the values, but they would not constitute the critical evidence for parameter setting. Put differently, what we find is a dissociation of cause and effect: Positive evidence, that is, data that may bring about parameter setting, may not even consist of the same thing as the data that are brought about through parameter setting.

Schwartz: What kind of data?

So far we have looked at a case in which a particular type of positive data may be insufficient to force the desired change in parameter setting from the L1 French value (see (6)) to the English value (see (7)). Whether this necessarily implies that there are no positive data available in principle to force such a change lies beyond the scope of this paper. However, logically, there are still two other types of data that are potential evidence for forcing the parameter to switch to the English setting, namely, negative data and explicit data. In fact, from a common-sense perspective, this seems quite reasonable: If the problem for the Interlanguage 'grammar' lies in moving the thematic verb across the adverb, then why not just give L2 acquirers the necessary evidence that such movement is prohibited in English? In other words, common sense would tell us that all that needs to be done is to point out to these acquirers, first, that in English the order SVAdvO is not possible, and second, that in order for an adverb to be in sentence-medial position in English, it must precede the verb–this is to say that, unlike in French, the order SAdvVO is allowed in English.

Telling acquirers what is not possible is negative data and providing them with the order that is possible is explicit data. And indeed, this is just what Lydia White and her associates did in another study (1991a, 1991b). Specifically, there were two groups of French-speaking L2 subjects: One group was not given any special instruction on adverb placement, but the other group was taught both what is and what is not possible in English. These possibilities are schematically represented in (8) below.

(8) a. * S V Adv O
    b. S Adv V O
    c. S V O Adv
    d. Adv S V O

So, (8a) exemplifies negative data, and (8b) through (8d) exemplify explicit data. There is also one other aspect of the adverb-instruction worth emphasizing: The only verbs used in the instruction sessions were transitive verbs.

The details of the testing need not concern us. What is important is that whereas the pre-test results show the two groups to be (basically) indistinguishable, the results of two post-tests clearly reveal that the instruction definitely changed the linguistic behavior of the subjects in the adverb-instruction group. The subjects not receiving instruction on adverb placement continued to (incorrectly) allow the order SVAdvO, but those exposed to instruction (correctly) rejected this sequence (at least, in both short-term testing sessions).

There was in addition an unexpected finding–and this will prove to be crucial to reinterpreting the data: The adverb-instruction group–but not the other group–(incorrectly) disallowed sentences of the type SVAdvPP. An example of this kind of sentence is given in (9) below.

(9) John walks slowly to school

Recall that the adverb instruction dealt with transitive verbs exclusively. Thus, the testing of adverb placement on intransitive verbs with a PP (as in (9)) is the only aspect of the testing that went *beyond* what the acquirers had been explicitly taught. Note also that sentences such as (9) are grammatical in English. And so, if it were the case that the L2 subjects had simply switched their verb-movement parameter from the French value to the English value, then there would be no reason for them to disallow sentences in which an adverb comes between a verb and a PP.

It was this observation that led to the reanalysis by Schwartz and Gubala-Ryzak (1992) of White's data. Space considerations require that we only briefly summarize the logic of that reanalysis. What should be pointed out is that there are multiple derivations for the order SVAdvPP, which depend in part on where the adverb and PP are base-generated. These are schematized in (10) below, in which the origin of moved elements is indicated by co-indexed traces (t).

(10) a. S V_i [$_{VP}$ Adv [$_{VP}$ t ... PP ...   →S V Adv PP (see (4b))

b. i. S V_i [$_{VP}$ t_i t_j Adv] ... PP_j ...   →S V Adv PP

ii. S [$_{VP}$ V t_j Adv] ... PP_j ...   →S V Adv PP (no V-to-I movement)

c. i. S V_i [$_{VP}$ [$_{VP}$ [$_{VP}$ t_i] Adv] PP]   →S V Adv PP

ii. S [$_{VP}$ [$_{VP}$ [$_{VP}$ V] Adv] PP]   →S V Adv PP (no V-to-I movement)

Of the five derivations for SVAdvPP, only (10a) depends on raising a verb across an adverb (see the tree in (7)). So, then, the question arises as to what is guiding the L2 subjects to disallow the order SVAdvPP. In other words, even if the L2 acquirers did switch the parameter to the 'no movement' value, there are still two derivations for SVAdvPP that do not depend on raising the verb, namely, (10bii) and (10cii). As Schwartz & Gubala-Ryzak noted, in order to disallow SVAdv PP, two other things–that is, two other things in addition to no verb movement–are required: not base-generating the adverb to the right of the verb, and not base-generating or extraposing PP to the right of the VP. In short, the Interlanguage 'grammar' would have to consider all possible derivations in (10) to be impossible in order to get sentences like (9) to be out–and neither the negative data nor the explicit data could be the evidence for the L2 acquirers' grammar to make such deductions. So, if it is not the Interlanguage grammar that lies behind the L2 acquirers' rejection of SVAdvPP, what is?

What Schwartz & Gubala-Ryzak suggest instead is that part of the post-instruction linguistic behavior is not the product of an Interlanguage grammar; descriptively-speaking, the result of the instruction was that the L2 acquirers did only two things (at least, in the short-term): First, they behaved in accordance with what they had been taught, accepting SAdvVO, SVOAdv, and AdvSVO but rejecting SVAdvO (see (8)); second, they then extended what they were told was an impossible English pattern to subsume SVAdvPP as well. In sum, the only thing these L2 acquirers–but not their 'grammars'–inferred from the instruction is that the pattern SVAdvPP (or perhaps even SVAdvXP) is not possible in English.[5]

This conclusion is further supported by the findings in the long-term post-test, carried out one year later on a subset of the subjects in the adverb-instruction group:

> ... [R]esults from the follow up study suggest that classroom instruction of the kind tried here has only short-term effects on the learner's knowledge of language. ... [S]ubjects reverted to an [SVAdvO] error score which was not significantly different from their score prior to instruction a year earlier. (White 1991a:157)

The fact that the change in linguistic behavior was short-lived is–in and of itself–significant, since it, too, independently suggests that grammar reorganization–that is, parameter re-setting–was never effected. A theoretically more economical (and plausible) way to view the results is to simply say that negative data and explicit data had led to no restructuring of the Interlanguage grammar. It is however important to note that we are not saying that negative data and explicit data do nothing in L2 acquisition; what we are saying, instead, is that these types of data cannot be used as evidence in the construction of an L2 grammar. (For further elaboration, see Schwartz 1993.)

We next explore in more detail why certain data might not serve as evidence in L2 grammar building. Following this we turn to possible implications for language instruction that seem to stem from this hypothesis.

Beck: What rules?

As discussed above, Pollock (1989) and Chomsky (1991) suggest that subject-verb agreement provides the evidence that determines, in a parametric sense, whether or not main verbs can move out of their underlying position. A growing body of research on L1 acquisition appears to suggest that this idea holds true. For example, the early analysis in Clahsen (1988a) showed for the L1 development of German that the acquisition of the verbal agreement paradigm coincided with the acquisition of verb raising. More recently, Meisel (1994), working on the simultaneous acquisition of two first languages (French and German), also shows that when the children acquire the verbal agreement paradigm, verb raising occurs. In L1 development, then, the acquisition of subject-verb agreement seems to provide evidence for verb movement.

On the other hand, this normal acquisition pattern seems to contrast with L1 development in dysphasics, that is, children with Specific Language Impairment (SLI). For example, Clahsen (1988a, 1989), investigating grammatical development among German SLI children, suggests a dissociation between the acquisition of verbal inflection and verb raising. Eubank (1993), analyzing the German SLI corpus in Clahsen (1988a), finds that the occurrence of verbal inflectional morphology and the position of the verb seem unrelated to one another. More specifically, the German SLI data include instances of both raised and unraised verbs, but, in sharp contrast to normal acquisition (see, e.g., Wexler 1994), the raised and unraised positions include both inflected and uninflected verbs. This difference between normal and dysphasic development evokes a question: If verbal inflection is the information that controls verb movement, and if the SLI children do indeed acquire this inflection, then why, in the SLI case, isn't verb raising also determined by verbal inflection?

One possible answer to this question is suggested by the recent work of Pinker and Prince (1991). According to their proposal, inflection of regular verbs is created on-line by means of a linguistic rule that appends an inflectional affix to a stem, whereas irregular verb forms (e.g., *go* → *went*) are not created on-line but rather are stored separately in associative memory. In cases of normal language development, then, regular verbal agreement inflection would thus be the result of the acquisition of a linguistic rule. However, for cases of SLI development, Gopnik and Crago (1991), following Pinker and Prince (1991), argue that dysphasics do not have such linguistic rules but instead store both irregular and regular inflectional forms as unanalyzed wholes in associative memory. Hence, on the assumption that these proposals obtain, the necessary evidence that determines verb movement can now be defined more precisely: It is not merely the acquisition of verbal inflection, but rather the acquisition of the relevant inflectional *rules* that constitutes evidence for verb raising. In the case of SLI development, where inflectional rules are lacking–as Gopnik and Crago argue–the observed dissociation between verbal inflection and verb movement is predicted.

A similar line of reasoning can be pursued for adult L2 acquisition, where a variety of studies have indicated difficulties with verb raising (e.g., Clahsen 1988a,

1988b; Clahsen and Muysken 1986; duPlessis et al. 1987; White 1991b). One possible explanation for these difficulties might be that adult L2 learners are incapable of acquiring the inflectional rule, that is, the inflectional information that determines whether or not verbs can move out of their underlying position. In other words, verb raising may occur when it shouldn't or, conversely, it may not occur when it should. If this view turns out ultimately to be correct, L2 acquisition could be seen to class more naturally with impaired L1 development than with normal L1 development.[6]

Note that such a view is not without precedent. For example, in their 1974 morpheme-order study, Bailey, Madden and Krashen report that the order in adult L2 acquisition more closely matched the order found for adult non-fluent aphasia than it did the order for normal L1 development. In addition, the adult L2 morpheme order–but not the L1 order–seems to be best predicted by frequency of input (for discussion, see Larsen-Freeman and Long 1991). This relationship between frequency of input and order of acquisition is precisely the type of relationship one would predict if the morphemes are all being maintained in associative memory. Such a relationship should be contrasted with normal L1 acquisition, in which the morphemes are differentiated on the basis of bound versus free morphology such that linguistic rules can then be applied to the bound morphemes to create words.

The possibility is, then, that L2 inflectional knowledge is impaired. Investigating this idea, Beck (1995) reports on a series of experiments involving reaction times which were conducted in order to determine whether or not L2 learners actually do employ morphological rules. In these experiments, nonnative speakers of English are visually presented with an English verb stem (e.g., *laugh*) on a computer monitor and asked to say the simple past form into a microphone (e.g., *laughed*). The reaction times record the elapsed time between the presentation of the stimulus and the onset of the oral response. In this matched-pair design (see Beck 1995 for details), the verb stems that were included vary according to frequency (i.e., some are high-frequency and some are low-frequency stems). If the L2 subjects employ morphological rules, then one would predict that there will be no difference in reaction times between the inflected high-frequency and the inflected low-frequency verb forms, since the operation of the rule would not be affected by the frequency of the verb stem. Results to date are consistent with the use of an on-line morphological rule, at least for the English regular past tense.

Such results were at first somewhat surprising, given the input-frequency/ morpheme-order correlations of the research summarized above. However, among the many differences between the reaction-time experiments and the L2 morpheme-order studies, one difference is particularly noteworthy. In all of the morpheme-order studies, results were tabulated on the basis of subjects' contextualized production data. In other words, subjects were producing sufficiently well-developed morphosyntactic contexts so that researchers could calculate the usual obligatory-occasion statistic (see, e.g., Dulay, Burt and Krashen 1982). In contrast, the reaction-time experiments utilize data from completely decontextualized production. The importance of this difference is brought out in the discussion of native-language impairments by Pinker and Prince (1991). They point out that native-language deficits "...do not appear [to] extend to the pure morphotactic operation of concatenating stem and affix" (1991:244). In terms employed here, inflectional deficits would not necessarily be apparent in the kind of decontextualized production employed in the reaction-time experiments. Such deficits would, however, appear when production necessitates the application of inflectional rules over a syntactic context. As Pinker and Price put it, "...systematic encoding of grammatical features in less-than-word-size morphemes can be dissociated from handling the phonological material expressing those morphemes, and ... it is the encoding process that is the neurologically vulnerable computation" (1991:244). In short, then, the fact that the results of the L2 reaction-time experiments were consistent with the use of on-line inflectional rules is an outcome one could well expect from a decontextualized task.

At this point, then, the crucial question that needs to be investigated is whether L2 learners have access to the morpho-syntactic mechanism that applies rules over a syntactic context. Current work involves redesigning the reaction-time experiment to probe for the use of inflectional rules over just such syntactic contexts. Given the more specific proposals by Pinker and Prince for this domain of linguistic performance, it is these follow-up experiments that are expected to locate a deficit in L2 competence—if there is one. If L2 knowledge is deficient in that it involves a selective impairment to the subsystem that governs inflection in syntax, then one predicts for these experiments that reaction times from native-speaking subjects will distinguish between sentences that have inflected versus uninflected verbs, but that reaction times from L2 subjects will fail to distinguish between these types of sentences.

A relevant question at this juncture would be whether such an impairment could be compensated for in L2 learning and teaching, either through exposure to explicit data, or drilling, or other kinds of instructional therapy. In other words, could some kind of focussed L2 therapy supplant or at least complement an impaired mechanism and thereby provide the necessary evidence that determines, in this particular case, verb raising? Of course, at present one can only speculate as to the potential usefulness of such intervention. On the one hand, *a priori* considerations suggest the following: While instructional therapy might well result in the appearance of inflection-like verb forms in "Learned Linguistic Knowledge"

(Schwartz 1993) during tasks requiring the utilization of rules over a syntactic context, it seems less plausible to think that these therapy-supported forms could actually constitute the necessary evidence that determines verb raising. First of all, instruction is and always has been designed to promote the storage and utilization of knowledge in associative memory. In other words, if such therapy only results in inflection-like verb forms maintained in associative memory, then—as in the case of native-language impairment—we would not expect any cross-over from associative memory to the rule-based system, thereby denying UG the evidence necessary to control verb raising. The evidence may simply not be available. In addition, while there is a lack of empirical data, anecdotal observation seems to suggest that exactly this may be the case. For example, in many foreign-language classroom situations, we find an early preoccupation with inflectional paradigms, including the verbal agreement paradigm. However, if it were the case that rule-like verbal behavior of L2 learners could constitute evidence for verb raising, then one would expect to find no problems with verb placement in target languages where verb movement is relevant. Informal observation seems to incidate quite the opposite, however: We find continuing verb-placement difficulties even after the verbal agreement paradigm appears to have been mastered in the traditional pedagogical sense. In short, standard morphology-focussed instruction does not seem to be able to supplant the impaired mechanism.[7]

We do not want to suggest here that explicit evidence or instructional therapy is of no practical use. The only claim we want to make is that this kind of activity cannot engage UG. However, if there is indeed a selective impairment connected with L2 acquisition, then the "Learned Linguistic Knowledge" of Schwartz (1993), gained via exposure to negative data or other explicit data, may well be the only means by which nonnatives can take on the appearance—even though not the substance—of the native speaker.

Conclusion

In this three-part contribution, we have attempted to lay out some of the fundamental notions that underlie our (different) research agendas. After differentiating among positive, negative and explicit data, we argued that it is important to recognize the difference between mere 'data' and 'evidence', the latter defined as information from the ambient language that can effect change in the grammar. Crucially, such evidence is strictly theory-dependent; as linguistic theory develops, our understanding of what comprises evidence may change. In addition, we argued that evidence seems to be restricted to positive data. In other words, formal instruction, defined as the provision of explicit and negative data, seems to result in "Learned Linguistic Knowledge" rather than in 'true' grammatical knowledge. Finally, we speculated on the limits of positive data themselves. In particular, it was suggested that if verb raising is tied to the morphosyntactic rules of regular verbal inflection, these rules may not be accessible to the L2 learner–which would in turn explain problems with verb placement in interlanguage. In summary, the relationship between, on the one hand, the various kinds of data and, on the other, the building of interlanguage grammars may not be as obvious and direct as once was assumed.

Notes

1. As an anonymous reviewer points out, some readers may be more familiar with the difference between 'input' and 'intake'. In fact, what we will discuss below is related, at least to a limited degree: 'Intake' would comprise 'evidence' while 'data' comprise 'input'. Perhaps the central difference is the role of linguistic theory in determining what comprises mere 'data' and what comprises 'evidence', as we shall see.

2. There is an idealization here, too, since we assume that the child knows the difference between, e.g., finite declarative clauses, which will have lexical subjects, and imperatives or nonfinite clauses, which may not have lexical subjects.

3. Indeed, Rutherford & Sharwood Smith (1988) examine, in an L2 context, the very null-subject phenomenon discussed above. The point they make is that the impossible learning situation created by the necessity of negative or explicit data might be alleviated by "explicit" consciousness raising in L2 acquisition. They point out, of course, that the idea requires empirical validation. See the discussion below by Schwartz ("What kind of data?") for related concerns.

4. The idea of lexical parameters was actually proposed much earlier in work by Hagit Borer (1984).

5. Readers who are unaccustomed to thinking in such terms might consider a simple, lexical example. Suppose that a speaker of English is told ('instructed') to avoid expletive expressions like *damn it*. The result is that such expressions are no longer observed in the speaker's speech. One understanding of this observation would be that the speaker's lexicon has undergone some fundamental change, perhaps by expunging such expressions from the lexical repertoire. Common sense suggests, of course, that this possiblility is not correct. A more reasonable understanding would be that the speaker still 'knows' ('cognizes'; see Chomsky 1975) terms like *damn it*, but also 'believes' that one is not supposed to use the expression.

6. An anonymous reviewer felt uncomfortable with "the notion of L2 learners being 'impaired'" and "needing 'therapy'" (see below). In fact, however, what is suggested here–that there may be an impairment to the morphosyntactic system that appends bound affixes to stems–is rather mild in comparison to suggestions that Universal Grammar may be 'unavailable' to the L2 learner. If anything, the inaccessibility of Universal Grammar would amount to a very massive impairment to the language capacity.

7. On the other hand, in a preliminary experimental study reported by Clahsen, Hansen and Rothweiler (1994), four German-speaking SLI children who received explicit instruction on subject-verb agreement appear, as a result, to have acquired more native-like verb placement. In other words, morphology-focussed instruction seems to have been able to supplant the impaired mechanism in the case of SLI. Whether Clahsen's preliminary findings will obtain in a more fully developed study–and whether the possibility would extend at all to L2 knowledge–remains to be seen.

References

Atkinson, M. 1992. *Children's Syntax: An introduction to principles and parameters theory.* Oxford: Blackwell.
Bailey, N., C. Madden, C. & S. Krashen. 1974. "Is There a 'Natural Sequence' in Adult Second Language Learning?" *Language Learning* 24.235-43.
Baker, C. L. 1979. "Syntactic Theory and the Projection Problem". *Linguistic Inquiry* 10.533-81.
Beck, M. 1995. "Tracking Down the Source of Native Speaker and Non-native Speaker Differences in Syntactic Competence". Ms., University of North Texas. Submitted to *Second Language Research.*
Borer, H. 1984. *Parametric Syntax.* Dordrecht: Foris.
Chomsky, N. 1965. *Aspects of the Theory of Syntax.* Cambridge, MA: MIT Press.
Chomsky, N. 1981. *Lectures on Government and Binding.* Dordrecht: Foris.
Chomsky, N. 1975. *Reflections on Language.* New York: Random House.
Chomsky, N. 1991. "Some Notes on Economy of Derivation and Representation". *Principles and Parameters in Comparative Grammar* ed. by R. Freidin, 417-54. Cambridge, MA: MIT Press.
Chomsky, N. 1992. "A Minimalist Program for Linguistic Theory". *The View from Building 20* ed. by K. Hale & S. J. Keyser, 1-52. Cambridge, MA: MIT Press.
Clahsen, H. 1988a. *Normale und gestörte Kindersprache.* Amsterdam: John Benjamins.
Clahsen, H. 1988b. "Parameterized Grammatical Theory and Language Acquisition: A study of the acquisition of verb placement and inflection by children and adults". *Linguistic Theory in Second Language Acquisition* ed. by S. Flynn & W. O'Neil, 47-75. Dordrecht: Kluwer.
Clahsen, H. 1989. "The Grammatical Characterization of Developmental Dysphasia". *Linguistics* 27.897-920.
Clahsen, H., D. Hansen & M. Rothweiler. 1994. "The Missing Agreement Account of Specific Language Impairment: New evidence from longitudinal studies and therapy experiments". Paper at the BU Conference on Language Development, Boston, MA.
Clahsen, H. & P. Muysken. 1986. "The Availability of Universal Grammar to Adult and Child Learners–A study of the acquisition of German word order". *Second Language Research* 2.93-119.
Dulay, H., M. Burt. & S. Krashen. 1982. *Language Two.* Oxford: Oxford University Press.
duPlessis, J., D. Solin, L. Travis & L. White. 1987. "UG or Not UG, That is the Question: A reply to Clahsen and Muysken". *Second Language Research* 3.56-75.

Emonds, J. 1978. "The Verbal Complex V'-V in French". *Linguistic Inquiry* 9.151-75.
Eubank, L. 1993. "Verb Placement and Inflection in German SLI". Paper presented at the conference on Generative Approaches to Language Acquisition. University of Durham, Durham, England.
Gopnik, M. & M. Crago. 1991. "Familial Aggregation of a Developmental Language Disorder". *Cognition* 39.1-50.
Hornstein, N. & D. Lightfoot. 1981. "Introduction". *Explanation in Linguistics: The logical problem of language acquisition* ed. by N. Hornstein & D. Lightfoot, 9-31. London: Longman.
Larsen-Freeman, D. & M. Long. 1991. *An Introduction to Second Language Acquisition Research*. London: Longman.
Meisel, J. 1994. "Getting FAT: Finiteness agreement and tense in early grammars". *Bilingual First Language Acquisition* ed. by J. Meisel, 89-129. Amsterdam: John Benjamins.
Pinker, S. & A. Prince. 1991. "Regular and Irregular Morphology and the Psychological Status of Rules of Grammar". *Proceedings of the Seventeenth Annual Meeting of the Berkeley Linguistics Society* ed. by L. Sutton & C. Johnson, 230-251. Berkeley, CA: Berkeley Linguistics Society, Inc.
Pollock, J.-Y. 1989. "Verb Movement, Universal Grammar, and the Structure of IP". *Linguistic Inquiry* 20.365-424.
Rutherford, W. & M. Sharwood Smith. 1988. "Consciousness Raising and Universal Grammar". *Grammar and Second Language Teaching* ed. by W. Rutherford & M. Sharwood Smith, 107-116. New York: Newbury House.
Schwartz, B. D. 1993. "On Explicit and Negative Data Effecting and Affecting *Competence* and *Linguistic Behavior*". *Studies in Second Language Acquisition* 15.147-63.
Schwartz, B. D. & M. Gubala-Ryzak. 1992. "Learnability and Grammar Re-organization in L2A: Against negative evidence causing the unlearning of verb movement". *Second Language Research* 8.1-38.
Trahey, M. & L. White. 1993. "Positive Evidence and Preemption in the Second Language Classroom". *Studies in Second Language Acquisition* 15.181-204.
Wexler, K. 1994. "Optional Infinitives, Head Movement and the Economy of Derivations". *Verb Movement* ed. by D. Lightfoot & N. Hornstein, 305-350.
Wexler, K. & P. Culicover. 1980. *Formal Principles of Language Acquisition*. Cambridge, MA: MIT Press.
White, L. 1989a. "The Adjacency Condition on Case Assignment: Do L2 learners observe the Subset Principle?" *Linguistic Perspectives on Second Language Acquisition* ed. by S. Gass & J. Schachter, 134-58. Cambridge: Cambridge University Press.
White, L. 1989b. *Universal Grammar and Second Language Acquisition*. Amsterdam: John Benjamins.
White, L. 1991a. "Adverb Placement in Second Language Acquisition: Some effects of positive and negative evidence in the classroom". *Second Language Research* 7.133-61.
White, L. 1991b. "The Verb-Movement Parameter in Second Language Acquisition". *Language Acquisition* 1.337-60.

White, L. 1992a. "Long and Short Verb Movement in Second Language Acquisition". *Canadian Journal of Linguistics* 37.273-86.
White, L. 1992b. "On Triggering Data in L2 Acquisition: A reply to Schwartz and Gubala-Ryzak". *Second Language Research* 8.120-37.

Markedness aspects of case-marking in L1 French/L2 English interlanguage

Helmut Zobl
Carleton University

Introduction

Recent case-theoretic proposals by Roberts (1993) to account for historical changes in French offer an attractive framework for the analysis of certain syntactic structures in L1 French/L2 English interlanguage. The interlanguage structures concerned are I°–to–C° movement (subject-auxiliary inversion) in interrogative contexts and the dative shift construction. Both exhibit a salient distributional contrast involving lexical NPs and pronominal NPs (henceforth [±pron]). Specifically, the following distribution occurs (see Zobl 1979). With interrogatives, I°–to–C° movement is far more frequent with [+pron] subjects. Subjects that are [-pron] overwhelmingly lack inversion, occurring with declarative syntax. Examples from the data illustrating the contrast are given in (1-2) below.[1]

(1) The woman was happy?
(2) Are they very happy?

Yet another construction containing [-pron] subjects employs double auxiliary marking, as in (3) below.

(3) Is this two boys are twins?
  'Are these two boys twins?'

The individual data from oral interviews with 58 adult-age informants showed a strict implicational relationship:

> The occurrence of [-pron] subjects with I°–to–C° movement in an informant's speech entails the presence of [+pron] subjects with I°–to–C° movement.

The converse relationship, I°–to–C° movement with [-pron], but not [+pron] subjects, did not obtain.

Turning now to the second interlanguage structure, the dative shift construction, we find an analogous pattern. LeCompagnon (1984) reports that in the English speech of two adult French speakers, [+pron] NPs in dative shift constructions (i.e., V NP NP) were in complementary distribution with [-pron] NPs, which occurred in the nonshifted, V NP PP subcategorization. Examples from LeCompagon (1984) illustrating this distributional contrast are given below.

(4) They used this device to show many different levels of space to the spectators.
(5) We could show her some interesting things in New Hampshire.

The data revealed, moreover, that overgeneralization of dative shift to verbs disallowing it only occurred with [+pron] indirect objects. In a judgment task carried out with four additional subjects, sentences with dative shift verbs occurring in [NP PP$_{[+pron]}$] contexts were deemed ungrammatical, as were sentences with dative shift verbs in [__NP$_{[-pron]}$ NP] contexts. Two distinct subcategorization frames exist, then, for dative shift verbs and dative shift-like verbs: [V NP NP] for [+pron] and [V NP PP] for [-pron] indirect objects.

The interlanguage distributions described in the preceding paragraphs reflect patterns in French involving lexical NPs and clitic pronouns (*je, tu, me*, etc.). In interrogatives, I°–to–C° movement is only possible when the subject is [+clitic pron] as the examples in (6) and (7) demonstrate.

(6) Est-elle sortie hier soir?
    'Did she go out last night?'

(7) *Est Simone sortie hier soir?
    'Did Simone go out last night?'

Similarly, dative shift verbs in French disallow V NP[-pron] NP as shown in (8) below.

(8) *Simone explique Pierre le problème
    'Simone is explaining Pierre the problem'

When the indirect object is [+pron], the clitic appears in a position immediately preceding the verb, as (9) illustrates.

(9) Simone lui explique le problème.

These, briefly, are the distributional facts in French.

To appreciate the case-marking system which gives rise to the distributional contrasts in French and in the interlanguage data, we next consider some case-theoretic proposals by Koopman and Sportiche (1991) and Roberts (1993). After briefly summarizing these, we address the question of why the [±pron] subject asymmetry in French-English interlanguage recurs as well in the L2 German of an adult Turkish speaker (Schwartz and Sprouse 1994). The L2 input in both cases leads to the adoption of a case-marking system which fails to generate the full range of 'inverted' structures contained in the primary data available to the learners. This case of undergeneration will be explored on the working assumption that the conjunction of ample positive evidence coupled with a failure to adopt L2 values is often a signal for the existence of a marked L2 system or parametric option.

Case-marking configurations

Koopman and Sportiche (1991) propose that two types of structural case-marking are possible–via agreement and via government. The second of these can occur in two configurations, making for three case-marking configurations. These are shown in Figure 1. (Inherent case-marking, not being structural, is left out of consideration.) The configuration in (A) in Figure 1 represents the case-marking found in contemporary French and English for assignment of nominative case to the subject NP. It is case-marking via agreement and occurs in declarative syntax. The configuration in (B1) represents the configuration for assignment of object case, by the verb, to the object NP. The configuration in (B2), according to Koopman and Sportiche (1991), is the one found in English for case-marking the subject NP in interrogative contexts. Case-marking is assumed to occur at S-structure. After I°–to–C° movement, the configuration for case-marking via agreement in (A) is no longer available. Inversion has altered the specifier-head configuration required for agreement (Roberts 1993:26). Observe that in configuration (B2), after movement of I°–to–C°, the subject is separated from I° by the maximal projection, IP. For nominative case-marking to take place, I° must case-mark into the IP. Case-marking configuration (B2) is thus the one required for nominative marking of subject NPs in inversion contexts. Roberts (1993) details how French went from a system with all three configurations to one having only (A) and (B1). As the sentences in (6) and (7) illustrated, subject-auxiliary inversion is only possible when the subject NP is [+pron]. The same is of course true for subject-main verb inversion.

Agreement		Government			
(A)	IP	(B1)	V'	(B2)	C'
NP	I'	V	NP	C	IP
	I				NP

Figure 1: Case-marking configurations (adapted from Koopman and Sportiche 1991)

In Koopman and Sportiche's (1991) and Robert's (1993) account of case-marking, Baker's (1988) notion of 'incorporation' plays an important role. Clitic pronouns are able to attach to, or incorporate, with I° in C°, thereby receiving nominative case-marking. (Strictly speaking, the clitic would incorporate with the verb in C°, which bears the I°-features for tense and agreement.) Lexical NPs are ineligible for this process. The incorporation proposal can be extended to indirect objects in French. Clitic pronouns escape the restriction limiting direct case-marking to one complement NP, the direct object NP (see Baker 1988). Indirect objects that are [-pron] require indirect case-marking with *à*; clitic complements, however, can receive dative case from the verb by incorporating with it. Thus, incorporation of clitic pronouns with I° and V represents an important means of case-marking in French, given the absence of the configuration in (B2).

A markedness account for the acquisition of case

A question that poses itself is why French-speaking learners appear to attribute to English pronominals the movement mobility that characterizes French clitics. As discussed in the introduction, the L2 primary data contains abundant evidence that I°–to–C° movement and dative shift are possible with [-pron] NPs. Also, the input contains abundant evidence to refute a mistaken identification of English pronominals with French clitics. While pronouns in English do cliticize (e.g., *give'em hell*), there is ample positive evidence confirming that English pronominals are unlike clitics. For example, [+pron] NPs can be stressed and other material can intervene between subject pronouns and the verb. Given this wealth of evidence, what might account for the difficulty in moving to an English system?

The [±pron] asymmetry in the French-English interlanguage acquires wider significance when put in the context of developmental data reported by Schwartz and Sprouse (1994) for an adult Turkish speaker of German. The authors report a [±pron]asymmetry for sentences in which a nonsubject constituent has been topicalized to the Spec of CP position, that is, XVS. The subject-verb 'inversion' created by this movement of a nonsubject constituent is initially restricted to subject NPs that are [+pron]. Schwartz and Sprouse (1994) account for this asymmetry with reference to Koopman and Sportiche's (1991) case-marking configurations and suggest that, when the specifier-head agreement configuration is not available, nominative case-marking is first carried out through incorporation rather than through structural government. For them, the implementation of 'inversion' with [+pron] subjects represents a case of conservative, subset, learning. (According to their analysis, Turkish does not provide a model for this form of case-marking.) An approximation to the target data is achieved without the addition of a new case-marking configuration for nominative case.

According to Koopman and Sportiche (1991) and Rizzi and Roberts (1989), Universal Grammar makes available three mechanisms for checking case, these being (a) specifier-head agreement, (b) structural government and (c) incorporation. As stated above, Schwartz and Sprouse (1994) interpret the [± pron] asymmetry in the Turkish speaker's XVS utterances as evidence for subset learning. While it is correct that the learner's recourse to incorporation allows the grammar only to generate a subset of the sentences generated by a grammar with structural government, this extensional notion of subset learning has come under criticism (Fodor 1989). On an intensional definition, by contrast, the learner's grammar for case-marking does not appear to be a subset grammar of the target grammar. Of the three mechanisms identified above, German has structural government for nominative and accusative case and specifier-head agreement. (We again ignore inherent case.) The interlanguage grammar would have structural government for accusative case, specifier-head agreement and incorporation. Intensionally, then, the learner's grammar of case marking has three mechanisms although it undergenerates relative to the target grammar. It would seem that the Turkish speaker's grammar has taken on added complexity to at least partially accommodate the input data.

The interlanguage data raise the question whether these mechanisms stand in a markedness relationship. More precisely, could it be that case-checking via incorporation represents the default option, in the sense of Lebeaux (1988)? Unable to implement structural government for nominative case-marking, both the francophones and the Turkish speaker fall back on the computationally less complex process of incorporation. In this connection, Baker (1988:108ff) makes the important observation that incorporation is actually a means of circumventing standard case-marking. Through incorporation, for example, a verb's case-marking potential is not used up. (This observation is relevant for the [±pron] asymmetry found with dative shift constructions.) This suggests that with recourse to incorporation, case-marking comes for free, so to speak.

Consider now the option that is avoided—nominative case-marking via structural government. In configuration (B2), case marking takes place across the (finite) IP boundary. This configuration has an interesting parallel in the case marking found with so-called 'exceptional case-marking verbs' like *expect*, *believe* and *consider*, as illustrated in the example in (10) below.

(10) Brett expects [$_{IP}$ Scarlet to chase after him]

In this example, *expect* case-marks *Scarlet* across the IP boundary via structural government. Thus, English permits case-marking via government across a finite IP for nominative case and a nonfinite IP for accusative case. French disallows both, exceptional case-marking into a nonfinite IP being impossible (Kayne 1984).[2] Given that the configuration under which exceptional case marking takes place has traditionally been deemed marked, the structural parallel provided by the nominative case-marking configuration suggests that it, too, should be considered marked. More generally, we can say that whenever case-marking occurs across a maximal projection, we are dealing with a marked configuration. This assumption explains the infrequency, cross-linguistically, of 'exceptional case-marking' structures and 'inversion' structures, as well as the marginal status of VSO word order compared with SOV and SVO in the known languages (10% for VSO vs. 40% and more for the other two).[3] In VSO, the raised verb in I° presumably must case-mark, across the VP projection, the subject NP in the Spec of VP.

Conclusion

This paper has sought to explain [±pron] asymmetries in L1 French/L2 English interlanguage with reference to the case-marking configurations and mechanisms proposed by Koopman and Sportiche (1991) and Roberts (1993). These data as well as developmental data from a Turkish learner of German raise the question why structural government for nominative case-marking, amply evidenced in the L2 primary data, does not appear to be accessible to the L2 learners at first. Instead, they resort to the process of incorporation, which enables pronominals, but not lexical NPs, to appear in structures conforming to the L2 input. The paper has suggested that structural government for nominative case-marking represents a marked configuration, requiring as it does case-marking or checking across a (finite) IP boundary. Building on suggestions by Baker (1988), it is proposed that incorporation represents a default mechanism for case-marking, an option that can be resorted to whenever a marked form of case assignment is called for by the primary data. Its occurrence in interlanguage grammars, both in cases where the L1 provides a model (French), and where it does not (Turkish), argues that recourse to default options for dealing with computational complexity may be an acquisitional universal.

Notes

1. The data stem from two oral tasks, interviews in which S's were invited to ask questions about a cartoon strip and the location where the interview took place. The data base consisted of about 380 interrogatives. Questions containing the subject pronoun *you* were excluded since many of these appear to have been formulaic.

2. Kayne (1984) in fact assumes that, in French, complements of the equivalents of exceptional case-marking verbs are CPs, not just IPs. This is suggested by the possibility of using verbs like *croire* 'believe' in control structures.

3. The assumption that nominative case-marking into a finite IP is marked may also shed light on the absence of subject-auxiliary inversion in L1 English at a time when WH-movement is productive. The absence of inversion can therefore not be due to the lack of a complementizer projection. It may also shed light on the occurrence of dummy auxiliary marking in L1 English interrogatives, as illustrated by the example in (3). If the fronted auxiliary is a dummy question marker, then there would be no need for nominative case-marking via structural government. It is significant that the dummy auxiliary construction occurs in the L2 interlanguage with lexical NPs. In L1 English, though, it occurs with pronominal subjects as well.

References

Baker, M. 1988. *Incorporation: A theory of grammatical function changing.* Chicago: Chicago University Press.
Fodor, J. 1989. "Learning the Periphery". *Learnability and Linguistic Theory* ed. by R. Matthews & W. Demopoulos, 129-54. Dordrecht: Kluwer.
Kayne, R. 1984. "On Certain Differences between English and French". *Connectedness and Binary Branching* by R. Kayne, 103-23. Dordrecht: Foris.
Koopman, H. & D. Sportiche. 1991. "The Position of Subjects". *Lingua* 85.211-258.
Lebeaux, D. 1988. *Language Acquisition and the Form of the Grammar.* Indiana University: Indiana University Linguistics Club.
LeCompagnon, B. 1984. "Interference and Overgeneralization in Second Language Acquisition: The acquisition of English dative verbs by French speakers". *Language Learning* 34.39-67.
Rizzi, L. & I. Roberts. 1989. "Complex Inversion in French". *Probus* 1.1-30.
Roberts, I. 1993. *Verbs and Diachronic Syntax: A comparative history of English and French.* Dordrecht: Kluwer.
Schwartz, B. D. & R. Sprouse. 1994. "Word Order and Nominative Case in Non-Native Language Acquisition". *Language Acquisition Studies in Generative Grammar* ed. by T. Hoekstra & B. D. Schwartz, 316-68. Amsterdam: John Benjamins.
Zobl, H. 1979. "Nominal and Pronominal Interrogation in the Speech of Adult Francophone ESL Learners". *SPEAQ Journal* 3.69-93.

Language transfer
What do we really mean?

Gita Martohardjono
Queens College, City University of New York

Suzanne Flynn
Massachusetts Institute of Technology

Introduction

Most, if not all, second language (L2) researchers would agree that an L2 learner's first language (L1) plays a role in the acquisition of an L2. We know that L2 learners, in contrast to L1 learners, do not start at the initial state, S_0; the L1 is in some way available to the L2 learner. However, while there is consensus at this level of discourse about the L2 acquisition process, there is little agreement concerning the precise nature of the L1 in the L2 target grammar construction (see related discussions in Gass and Selinker 1983; 1992). Can we account for the construction of the L2 grammar in terms of the grammatical features particular to the L1–the Transfer Hypothesis (TH)–or in terms of more general linguistic principles which, while guiding L1 acquisition, transcend the particular instantiation of the L1 grammar–the Universal Grammar (UG) approach?

Within the framework of the TH, it is assumed that the L2 learner relies primarily, if not solely, on the end product, viz., a steady state L1, to construct the grammar of the L2. Such a position implies that the principles that underlie the L1 acquisition process are no longer available to the L2 learner in the construction of the target L2 in a form other than as instantiated in the L1. Within a UG framework, both L1 and L2 acquisition are constrained by the same set of linguistic principles. That is, during the course of L1 acquisition, UG does not itself become the L1 grammar. Rather, it remains available to determine the course of subsequent language acquisition as well, viz., L2 acquisition.

Our purpose in this chapter is to highlight findings that will contribute to the development of a principled definition of 'transfer'. Our end goal is to develop one that is explanatory and consistent with a unified theory of both the L1 and L2 learning processes although we will not fully achieve this goal in this paper. We will briefly consider results from two different kinds of constructions in English: control and movement. These data suggest that during L2 acquisition, learners do not rely primarily on their L1 grammars in the construction of the target L2. Interestingly, this can be shown to be the case both when L2 learners manifest knowledge that is not exemplified in the L1 as well as in the case when the L1 does manifest a particular structure.

Control structures

Let us begin with a brief consideration of control structures in English. They all involve some form of anaphora, which we define in a general sense to characterize the relation between a 'proform' (either the null argument, PRO, or a lexical pronoun like *he*) and another term. Consider the examples in (1-3) below, in which coindexation indicates the anaphoric possibilities.

(1) a. John$_i$ promised Henry$_j$ PRO$_i$ to go to the store.
    b. John$_i$ reminded Henry$_j$ PRO$_j$ to go to the store.
    c. John$_i$ told Henry$_j$ PRO$_j$ to go to the store.

(2) a. John$_i$ promised Henry$_j$ that he$_{i,j,k}$ will go to the store.
    b. John$_i$ reminded Henry$_j$ that he$_{i,j,k}$ will go to the store.
    c. John$_i$ told Henry$_j$ that he$_{i,j,k}$ will go to the store.

(3) a. *John promised Henry that PRO will go to the store.
    b. *John promised Henry he to go to the store.

The set of sentences in (1) above involve an infinitive complement; those in (2) have tensed, finite complements. The sentence structures exemplified in (1) are subject to some type of Control theory which restricts both the distribution and interpretation of the empty category PRO. The starred sentences in (3) indicate that the lexical pronoun may not appear in what has been characterized as the 'control domain'. The interpretation of the PRO subjects are constrained to be obligatorily coreferential with one unique name in the sentence. In this way, PRO is unlike the lexical pronouns which are 'free'.

In control structures, the verb of the main clause is involved in determining the choice of the antecedent of the PRO subject. For example, as the indices indicate, when the matrix verb is *tell* or *remind*, the antecedent of PRO is the matrix object, *Henry*. When the matrix verb is *promise*, the antecedent of PRO is the matrix subject, *John*. Thus, a full grammatical analysis of control involves a number of different factors: structural configurations, intrinsic properties of verbs,

LANGUAGE TRANSFER: WHAT DO WE REALLY MEAN? 207

and other semantic and pragmatic considerations as noted by Chomsky (1981). In UG theory, numerous proposals have been made for a theory of control. The principal features of these proposals concern the fact that in these sentences there is a structural domain which involves c-command, in some version, of PRO by an antecedent where the antecedent and PRO satisfy certain structural restrictions.

In terms of these restrictions, the crucial difference between sentences containing a non-finite, infinitival clause and those containing a finite *that* clause is the fact that sentences with infinitivals provide a domain within which the reference of the PRO can be fixed to a minimal antecedent. By contrast, in the sentences with finite clauses, the presence of a complementizer, *that*, obstructs the definition of a minimal command domain containing a possible antecedent; hence, the reference of the proform cannot be fixed by the minimal controller and it is free by Principle B of the Binding Theory (see extended discussion in Sherman and Lust 1993).

In this context, let us consider what a strict version of the TH would predict for the L2 acquisition of these structures in English by adult Japanese, Chinese and Spanish speakers. We will begin with a brief description of the relevant facts in Japanese, Chinese and Spanish.

Japanese

The relevant sentences for Japanese are shown in (4) below. The sentences in (4a), (4b) and (4d) indicate that Japanese clearly has finite clauses. It has also been argued that Japanese does not have an infinitive although there is a form of the verb *yoo ni* that attaches to a verb form that cannot inflect for tense as shown in (4c). It is unclear what the nature of the null element is in these sentences, although we have written it as PRO. Japanese does have pronouns, but they behave more like NPs in English than like pronouns. With respect to specific control properties, the verb *yakusoku* 'promise' in Japanese takes a tensed clause and PRO can either be subject or object controlled as in (4a). Pronouns in these sentences tend to be strongly subject controlled.

(4) a. John$_i$-ga Henry$_j$-ni [PRO$_{i,j}$ eraberu to] yakusoku-sita.
   John-NOM Henry-DAT PRO will be chosen COMP promised
   John$_i$ promised Henry$_j$ that PRO$_{i,j}$ will be chosen.

   b. John$_i$-ga Henry$_j$-ni [kare$_{i,j}$-ga/PRO$_{i,j}$ eraberu to] itta.
   John-NOM Henry-DAT he/PRO will be chose COMP told
   John$_i$ told Henry$_j$ that he/PRO$_{i,j}$ will be chosen.

c. John$_i$-ga Henry$_j$-ni [PRO$_{*i,j}$ MIT-ni iku-yoo ni] itta.
John-NOM Henry-DAT PRO MIT-to go told
John$_i$ told Henry$_j$ Pro$_{*i,j}$ tto go to MIT.

d. John$_i$-ga Henry$_j$-ni [PRO$_{i,j,k}$ iku koto]-o omoidas-ase-ta.
John-NOM Henry-DAT PRO go fact-ACC remember-CAUSE-PAST
John$_i$ made Henry$_j$ remember the fact that PRO$_{i,j,k}$ will go.

The verb *itta* 'tell' in Japanese can take either a finite clause or a form of the verb *yoo ni*. With a finite clause for the verb *itta*, control is ambiguous as in (4b) above. But with the *yoo ni* form there seems to be a preference for object control as in (4c). Tentatively, it appears that with a finite subordinate clause, control is ambiguous, with *yoo ni* it is not, and at least in the case of *itta* it is solely object-controlled. *Omoidas* 'remind' in Japanese, as in (4d), is a causative type verb that takes a full tensed clause with the nominalizer *koto* 'fact'. The null pronoun is three-way ambiguous in this sentence.

Chinese

As in Japanese, Chinese clearly has finite clauses with an aspect marker *-le*. However, Chinese does not seem to have an infinitive. There is no morphological marking to determine this. In addition, as in Japanese, the status of the null pronominal element is not clear; it also appears that it is not the same element as in English regardless of its status.

As seen in the examples in (5) below, Chinese allows both a null and an overt pronoun. With respect to control properties, *daying* 'promise' in Chinese, as in English and Japanese, is subject controlled as seen in (5a-b); *pro* is object controlled with *jiao* 'tell' and *tixing* 'remind' as in (5c) and (5e); with an overt pronoun, control is free as shown in (5d) and (5f).

(5) a. John$_i$ daying Henry$_j$ pro$_{i,*j}$ qii shangdian.
John promise Henry pro go to store
John$_i$ promises Henry$_j$ pro$_{i,*j}$ to go to the store.

b. John$_i$ daying Henry$_j$ ta$_{i,*j}$ qii shangdian.
John promise Henry he go to store
John$_i$ promises Henry$_j$ that he$_{i,j}$ will go to the store.

c. John$_i$ jiao Henry$_j$ pro$_{*i,j}$ qii shangdian.
John tell (shout) Henry go to store
John$_i$ tells Henry$_j$ pro$_{*i,j}$ to go to the store.

d. John$_i$ gaosu Henry$_j$ ta$_{i,j,k}$ bu-neng chi dao.
John tell Henry he not-can be late
John$_i$ tells Henry$_j$ he$_{i,j,k}$ cannot be late.

e. John$_i$ tixing Henry$_j$ pro$_{*i,j}$ qii shangdian.
John remind Henry go to store
John$_i$ reminds Henry$_j$ that he$_{*i,j}$ to go to the store.

f. John$_i$ tixing Henry$_j$ ta$_{i,j,k}$ huei qii shagdian.
John remind Henry he would go to store
John$_i$ reminds Henry$_j$ that he$_{i,j,k}$ would go to the store.

Spanish

In contrast to Japanese and Chinese, Spanish clearly has both finite and non-finite clauses, as seen in the examples in (6) below. Spanish also has PRO, like English, as shown in (6a) and a *pro* in finite clauses, like Chinese and Japanese as in (6c-d). All three verbs, *prometer* 'promise', *recordar* 'remind' and *decir* 'tell', allow finite clauses; however, no infinitive is allowed with *tell* or *remind*. *Promise* is subject controlled with PRO as in (6a) and free with pronouns.

(6) a. Juan$_i$ le$_j$ promete a Henry$_j$ PRO$_{i,*j}$ ir a la tienda.
Juan him promise to Henry to go to the store
Juan$_i$ promises Henry$_j$ PRO$_{i,*j}$ to go to the store.

b. Juani le$_j$ promete a Henry$_j$ que pro irç a la tienda.
Juan him promise to Henry that will go to the store
Juan$_i$ promises Henry$_j$ that he$_{i,*j}$ will go to the store.

c. Juan$_i$ le$_j$ dice a Henry$_j$ que pro vaya a la tienda.
Juan him tell to Henry that go to the store
Juan$_i$ tells Henry$_j$ pro$_{i,*j}$ to go to the store.

d. Juani le$_j$ recuerda a Henry$_j$ que pro$_{i,j}$ irç a la tienda.
Juan him remind to Henry that will go to the store
Juan$_i$ reminds Henry$_j$ that he$_{i,j}$ will go to the store.

To summarize, Japanese, Chinese and Spanish all have pronouns as in English; all three languages also have some form of a null pronoun although this matches most closely between Spanish and English. Spanish has infinitives; however, though it appears that the grammars of Japanese and Chinese have a finite verb form, they do not instantiate infinitives. Overall, then, if L2 acquisition is indeed constrained by principles of UG, then we would predict that patterns of acquisition for all three groups should be comparable; moreover, we would also predict that the patterns should correspond to those isolated for L1 acquisition of

Table 1: ESL proficiency levels (Michigan Test score range: 0-50)

Level	Japanese	Language Chinese	Spanish
Mid	29.6 (n=13)	29.18 (n=11)	32.2 (n=9)
High	44.4 (n=22)	44.1 (n=10)	45.17 (n=12)
Overall	37.0 (n=35)	36.7 (n=21)	38.6 (n=21)

Table 2: Mean ages of ESL learners

Level	Japanese	Language Chinese	Spanish
Mid	28.7	25.4	23.8
High	30.6	24.9	27.0
Overall	29.7	25.1	25.4

English.[1] However, if L2 learners were relying on L1 alone, we would have the following prediction: In the acquisition of control structures, native speakers of Chinese and Japanese should prefer finite over non-finite clauses. Native speakers of Spanish should show a preference for finite clauses with *tell* and *remind* as those verbs do not take infinitives in the L1.

To test these predictions, we tested three groups of language learners at two distinct stages of ESL proficiency. Leveling was determined by the results of the listening comprhension and the grammar subtests of the Michigan Test, which was administered to all learners prior to testing. Levels were independently determined based on norms established by the the Michigan Test. Learners at the beginning level were not tested as they did not not have the minimal required syntax to complete the tasks. The results for each of the three language groups is shown in Table 1. Mean scores indicated that the learners were equated in terms of their general ESL abilities as measured by the placement test. Mean ages of these learners are shown in Table 2.

The learners were administered an elicited imitation task in which they were asked to repeat the sentence verbatim as given by the experimenter. All subjects were given bilingual lists of the words to be used in the experimental sentences before the actual testing. All sentences were equalized in syllable length and approximately in number of words; they were also pragmatically neutral.

Sentences administered to the subjects are exemplified in (7) below. We used three verbs: subject-controlled *promise* and the object-controlled *remind* and *tell*. (see related discussion in Flynn, Foley and Lardiere 1991). Sentences in (7a) involve infinitivals and a PRO in subject position of the subordinate clauses. Sentences in (7b) involve tensed *that*-clauses with a pronoun in subject position.

(7) a. Infinitives
   The worker reminds the woman to inform the engineer.
   The gentleman tells the teacher to introduce the owner.
   The lawyer promises the doctor to prepare the message.

   b. Finite *that*-complements
   The boss reminds the man that he will finish the assignment.
   The owner tells the architect that he will prepare the lunch.
   The owner promises the boss that he will review the test.

Overall results are shown in the graph in Figure 1. There are no significant differences between the mid and high ESL levels; thus, we have conflated the results as illustrated in the graph. All subjects indicate an overall preference for the infinitival structures (sentences in (7a) above) over their finite counterparts (sentences in (7b)), clearly a result which contradicts those made by the TH. Results for amount correct for all three groups indicate more correct productions for the infinitival structures than the tensed structures. In addition, as illustrated in

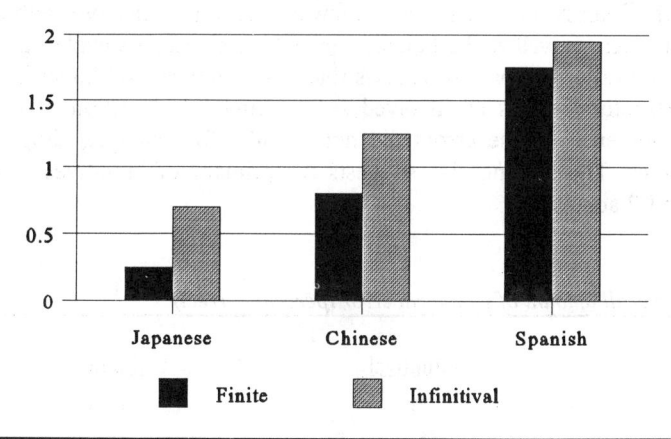

Figure 1: Mean amount correct

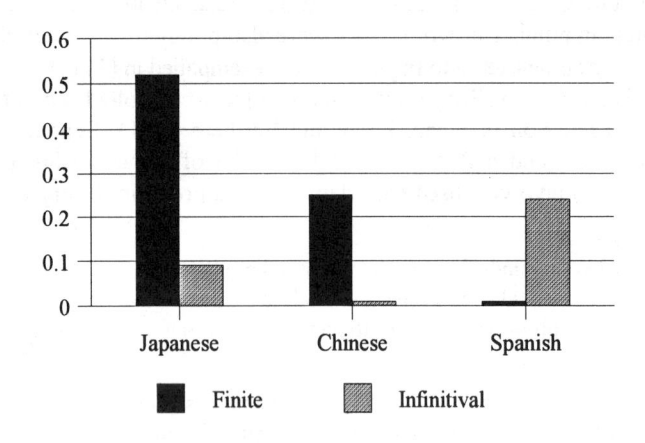

Figure 2: Mean amount of conversion errors

Figure 2, results of the error analyses indicate more conversions of the finite *that*-clauses to infinitival complements than conversions of the infinitives to finite *that*-clauses for the Japanese and Chinese. For example, when given the sentence *The boss reminds the man that he will finish the assignment*, the learners would often convert this sentence to *The boss reminds the man to finish the assignment* in their imitations, but they would rarely convert infinitives to finite *that*-clauses. By contrast, the Spanish speakers made very few conversions of this type although the Spanish speakers as well as the Japanese and Chinese speakers made significantly more structural errors on *that*-clauses than on infinitives, as shown in Table 3 below. Structural errors all involved some structural alteration of the initial stimulus sentence. These errors did not include, for example, simple lexical substitutions. This finding also suggests the primacy of infinitives over finite clauses in L2 acquisition.

Table 3: Overall amount of structural error (percent correct)

Language	Infinitival	Finite
Spanish	2%	12%
Japanese	9%	29%
Chinese	21%	43%

How do we account for these results? As we have seen, the overall preference for infinitival structures cannot be accounted for in terms of the L1s of the adult learners tested. A solution suggests itself, however, if we go back to the minimality condition outlined above. Recall that sentences with infinitivals lend themselves to the definition of a minimal domain with a fixed antecedent for the proform, while in the case of finite clauses, minimality cannot be applied to fix the reference of the proform. We suggest that the preference for infinitival structures over their finite counterparts reflects the crucial role of minimality–and not the L1– in constraining L2 grammar construction. Simply stated, L2 learners follow a UG principle which will allow them to fix the reference of the proform. This explanation also coheres with data from other studies in both L1 and L2 acquisition (e.g., C. Chomsky 1969; Sherman and Lust 1993; d'Anglejan and Tucker 1975; Cooper, Olshtain, Tucker and Waterbury 1979) which show a marked preference for object control, which again follows from the principle of minimality. It seems that L2 learners resort to the principle of minimality in the acquisition of control structures. Further research is needed to determine the extent of the application of this principle in second language acquisition.

Acquisition of Wh-structures

Consider now another example, the acquisition of Wh-structures, illustrating that L2 grammars are not collections of transferred L1 structures but rather reflect generation via an invariant computational system. Cross-linguistically there are at least two ways in which question-formation can be instantiated at surface structure: either with overt Wh-movement or without.

At least three principles of Universal Grammar have been proposed to constrain the instantiation of overt movement: Subjacency, the Constraint on Extraction and the Empty Category Principle. In somewhat more recent versions of the theory (e.g., Chomsky 1986), these have been subsumed under the notion 'barrier'. We will here only be concerned with two aspects of movement constraints determined by barriers. The first one accounts for the difference between sentences (8a) and (8b) below; the other explains the difference in degree of acceptability between the starred (unacceptable) sentence in (9a) and the question-marked (marginally acceptable) sentence in (9b). Note that the extraction site is indicated by a trace (t) in the examples.

(8) a. What did Tom fix t that the man had broken?
  b.*Who did Tom fix the door that t had broken?

(9) a.*Which soup did the man leave the table after the waiter spilled t?
  b. ?Which car did John spread the rumor that the neighbor stole t?

The difference between (8a) and (8b) derives from the fact that in (8a), where the head of a relative clause is questions, extraction of the Wh-word doesn't cross any barriers. In (8b), on the other hand, extraction out of the relative clause crosses two barriers and results in a violation (see extended discussion in Martohardjono 1993). The difference between (9a) and (9b) is more subtle, one involving degree of acceptability. The difference derives from the fact that (9a) involves extraction out of an adjunct clause, which results in a strong violation because it involves crossing two invariant barriers. In contrast, the extraction out of a noun complement in (9b) results in a weak violation because here only one barrier is crossed, and, furthermore, barrierhood depends on the particular properties of the verb, namely, whether it assigns a thematic role or not. The sentences in (9a-b) represent differences between strong and weak violations.

What would a TH predict in terms of the acquisition of these structures in English by L2 learners whose L1s do not instantiate overt Wh-movement in questions? Indonesian and Chinese are two such languages (Huang 1982; Martohardjono and Gair 1993); hence, the L1 grammar for speakers of these languages does not provide structures from which knowledge of movement constraints can be derived. In addition, the Wh-questions in these languages do not provide knowledge about varying degrees of acceptability as in the examples in (9a-b) above. The TH would therefore predict the following: If L2 learners are guided by transfer from the L1 in their acquisition of Wh-questions, they should not evidence knowledge of movement constraints. That is, they should accept sentences like (8b) to the same degree as sentences like (8a). Furthermore, they should not evidence knowledge of differential violations (i.e., strong vs. weak) since in their L1s questioning a Wh-word in any of these domains results in grammaticality. Knowledge that (8b) is ungrammatical in English can only be derived from UG. Similarly, knowledge that (9a) is stronger violation than (9b) is also provided by UG. The UG prediction for these learners is therefore that they should evidence (a) knowledge of ungrammaticality of violations in general and (b) knowledge of relative acceptability in particular.

For this experiment, testing involved a group of native-speaking controls (n=10) and two groups of L2 learners of English, one with L1 Chinese (n=16) and the other with L1 Indonesian (n=17). The sentence-types in the experiment included extractions out of relative clauses and adjunct clauses (strong violations) and extractions out of Wh-islands and noun complements (weak violations). Ungrammatical extractions were matched with grammatical extractions out of the same domains. The task was a paced grammaticality judgment task. Subjects were presented sets of Wh-questions preceded by a declarative sentence as in (10) below.

LANGUAGE TRANSFER: WHAT DO WE REALLY MEAN? 215

Table 5: Mean percent correct rejection of all ungrammatical sentences

Chinese	65%
Indonesian	74%
English	92%

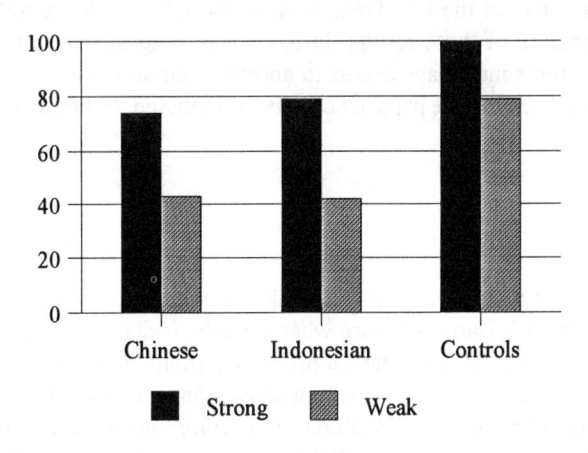

Figure 3: Knowledge of strong vs. weak violations

(10) The man left the table after the waiter spilled the soup

They were told that this declarative was a grammatical sentence in English. They then heard four questions which were derived from the declarative sentence: one grammatical extraction, one violation, and two filler sentences. Examples of the grammatical and ungrammatical extractions are given in (11a-b) below.

(11) a. Which man left the table after the waiter spilled the soup?
b. Who did the man leave the table after spilled the soup?

They were asked to judge each question as a 'good' or a 'bad' sentence in English and were instructed to respond 'yes' in the former case or 'no' in the latter. They were also given the choice of 'not sure' and 'don't understand'. All sentences were taped and presented twice. The task was paced so that subjects had six seconds in which to respond to each sentence.

Table 5 provides the results for mean percent correct rejection of all the ungrammatical sentence-types. As can be seen from these results, both the Indonesian and the Chinese groups showed general knowledge that sentences like (8b), (9a) and (9b) above (i.e., violations of movement constraints in English) are ungrammatical. Furthermore, they evidenced the more subtle ability to differentiate between the different types of violations. This can be seen in the graph in Figure 3, which shows that, like the control group, both the Chinese and the Indonesian groups rejected the strong violations (relative clause and adjunct clause) to a higher degree than weak violations (Wh-islands and noun complements). Critically, the type of knowledge evidenced by these learners cannot be derived from the equivalent structures in the L1. Transfer from the L1, in other words, is not a possible explanation of these results. Instead, they suggest that in L2 grammar construction learners must have access to another source of knowledge, namely, to UG principles, even if these happen not to be instantiated in the same way in the L1.

Conclusion

To summarize, we have presented data which suggest that in the acquisition of control structures L2 learners ignore what is made available to them in the L1, both in terms of particular grammatical properties (finite/non-finite) as well as in terms of lexical properties (Spanish does not allow infinitives in control structures). Instead, they resort to a principle of UG, minimality, which results in a marked preference for sentences with infinitival clauses. In the acquisition of Wh-questions, L2 learners clearly evidence knowledge of movement constraints in spite of the fact that movement is not instantiated in the equivalent structures in the L1. In addition, they evidence a more subtle and differentiated knowledge of strong and weak violations, again not derivable from the L1. These data then lead us to the following conclusions:

- L2 learners do not assume that the L2 is like the L1.
- The Transfer Hypothesis fails to explain L2 learners' knowledge of deeper principles as well as systematic errors.
- Theories that ignore such data will ultimately fail to provide a full account of L2 learners' process of grammar construction and at best provide only superficial descriptions of peripheral phenomena in L2 acquisition.

Thus it seems that L2 learners do not assume that the L2=L1. Transfer theories are inadequate in that they fail to explain both L2 learners' knowledge of what is not instantiated in the L1 (movement) as well as their preferences and systematic errors (control). We argue that at best transfer theories describe peripheral phenomena in L2 acquisition and that a principled theory of second language acquisition needs to incorporate a theory of Universal Grammar.

Notes

1. It is important to note that the UG position does not necessarily hypothesize for all areas of L2 acquisition that the patterns of acquisition for L2 learners with distinct L1s learning a common L2 will be the same. Other work (e.g., Flynn 1983, 1987; Flynn and Martohardjono 1994) suggests, for example, that differences will emerge among learners in terms of a match/mismatch of the head-direction/head-complement parameter. The goal of the present paper is to highlight at least two ways in which we cannot make predictions about the role of the L1 in L2 acquisition in terms of surface structure contrasts between the L1 and the L2.

References

Chomsky, C. 1969. *The Acquisition of Syntax in Children from 5 to 10*. Cambridge, MA: MIT Press.
Chomsky, N. 1981. *Lectures on Government and Binding*. Dordrecht: Foris.
Chomsky, N. 1986. *Barriers*. Cambridge, MA: MIT Press.
Cooper, R., E. Olshtain, R. Tucker & M. Waterbury. 1979. "The Acquisition of Complex English Structures by Adult Native Speakers of Arabic and Hebrew". *Language Learning* 29.255-275.
d'Anglejan, A. & R. Tucker. 1975. "The Acquisition of Complex English Structures by Adult Learners". *Language Learning* 25.281-296.
Flynn, S. 1983. *A Study of the Effects of Principal Branching Direction in Second Language Acquisition: The generalization of a parameter of Universal Grammar*. Dissertation, Cornell University.
Flynn, S. 1987. *A Parameter-Setting Model L2 Acquisition*. Dordrecht: Reidel.
Flynn, S. & G. Martohardjono. 1994. "Mapping from the Initial State to the Final State: The separation of universal principles and language specific properties". *Syntactic Theory and First Language Acquisition: Crosslinguistic perspectives*, Vol.1 ed. by B. Lust, J. Whitman & J. Kornflit, 319-336. Hillsdale, NJ: Lawrence Erlbaum.
Flynn, S., C. Foley & D. Lardiere. 1991. "The Minimality Principle in Adult Second Language Acquisition". Paper at the Second Language Research Forum, University of Southern California.
Gass, S. & L. Selinker. 1983. *Language Transfer in Language Learning*. Rowley, MA: Newbury House.
Gass, S. & L. Selinker 1992. *Language Transfer in Language Learning*. Amsterdam: John Benjamins.
Huang, J. 1982. *Logical Relations in Chinese and the Theory of Grammar*. Dissertation, MIT.
Martohardjono, G. 1993. *Wh-Movement in the Acquisition of a Second Language: A crosslinguistic study of three languages with and without movement*. Dissertation, Cornell University.

Martohardjono, G. & J. Gair. 1993. "Apparent Inaccessibility in Second Language Acquisition: Misapplied principles or principled misapplications?" *Confluence: Linguistics, L2 acquisition, and speech pathology* ed. by F. Eckman, 79-104. Amsterdam: John Benjamins.

Sherman, J. C. & B. Lust. 1993. "Children Are in Control". *Cognition* 46.1-51.

Age before beauty
Johnson and Newport revisited

Eric Kellerman
University of Nijmegen

One of the most enduring and fascinating problems confronting researchers of second language acquisition (SLA) is whether adults can ever acquire native-like competence in a second language (L2), or whether this is an accomplishment reserved for children who start learning at a relatively early age. As a secondary issue, there is the question of whether those rare cases of native-like success reported amongst adult learners are indeed what they seem, and if they are, how it is that such people can be successful when the vast majority are palpably not.[1]

In the by now substantial literature on the age question in SLA, there are a small number of papers which are constantly cited as having provided crucial evidence for the existence of a critical period for second language acquisition. Of the newer crop, one, Johnson and Newport (1989), has been singled out for particular praise. Johnson and Newport (henceforth JN89) studied the English performance of Korean and Chinese migrants to America in terms of the age at which they arrived. They postulate that the critical period ends at roughly age 7, with performance then declining in linear fashion until age 15, after which it continues its decline, though subject to considerable variation. Long (1990:271), in his survey of the age literature, labels JN89 "The least ambiguous evidence to date of maturational constraints operating in the morpho-syntactic domain"; Strömquist and Day (1993:136) claim that "Johnson and Newport (1989) found substantial support for the critical period hypothesis"; Hawkins, Towell and Bazergui (1993:190) consider this study to be "particularly" representative of those demonstrating the failure of late-starting learners to attain completeness; Towell and Hawkins (1994) devote several appreciative pages of their book to the findings of the Johnson and Newport study; Lightbown and Spada (1993) use it in illustration of the 'younger is better' position; Gass and Selinker (1994:241) describe it as carefully designed, and so on.

To my knowledge, JN89 has so far had few detractors,[2] and their subsequent work (Johnson 1992; Johnson and Newport 1991) has supported their own and other people's earlier findings. Yet I am doubtful whether their 1989 paper or the virtual replication by Johnson (1992)[3] really have very much to contribute to the important 'critical period for L2 acquisition' debate (Bley-Vroman 1989). My reservations concern the method and materials they use and the way they (and others) interpret their data. I will look at each of these problems in turn. I will also consider the arguments and evidence of those who have expressed reservations about JN89 (e.g., Bialystok and Hakuta 1994; Percival, Howerd and Hill 1994; and van Wuijtswinkel 1994). I should say here that I have no personal axe to grind with respect to the critical period hypothesis (CPH), and I do not wish by implication to cast doubt on Johnson and Newport's other work, nor to hold Johnson and Newport in any way responsible for accolades that they have received.

Problem 1: Method

The Johnson and Newport method of establishing knowledge of any of twelve grammatical categories is to make use of learner judgments either of spoken stimuli (JN89) or written ones (Johnson 1992). The same stimuli (with one or two small exceptions) are used in both papers. In each case, subjects are presented with pairs of sentences where one is correct in terms of the particular grammatical category, and the other erroneous. These pairs are not presented contiguously; each member appears in a different half of the task, and each half is randomized for presentation. That the data were randomized rather than presented in pairs may be of consequence, as we shall see.

The instruction to subjects in JN89 was to listen to, and in Johnson (1992) to read, each stimulus sentence and

> ... [to] make a judgement as to whether or not it was a grammatical sentence in English, guessing if they were unsure. The subjects recorded their responses by circling *yes* or *no* next to each test item. (Johnson 1992:224-225)

This is where the trouble starts, I think. It has been argued elsewhere (e.g., Kean 1986; Kellerman 1984, 1985) that this method of obtaining data is problematic, since it assumes an unspoken contract between subject and researcher to focus exclusively on the research object (i.e., the error). That is, if an ungrammatical sentence is marked as incorrect (i.e., judged *no*), the subject who rejects it must be doing so for the same reason a native speaker would. But one simply cannot know what is being judged in the sentence without supplementary information via think-aloud protocols, underlining or correction.

One way of finding out if subjects tend to judge stimuli as the researchers required would be to examine the patterns of acceptance and rejection across both grammatical and ungrammatical sentences. If learners were sometimes making judgments on faulty apprehensions of what was or was not English (as learners often do), then we should see substantial numbers of rejections of grammatical sentences as well. However, JN89 and Johnson (1992) scored responses to the *ungrammatical* sentences alone, since "only ungrammatical items can be said to be testing any particular rule type" (Johnson 1992:230). Johnson justifies this decision by claiming that if a grammatical sentence is marked as incorrect, there is no way of knowing what it is that the learner is having a problem with; but if an ungrammatical sentence is marked as correct, "she or he must have failed to represent *the structure under test* as a native speaker would" (note 5:247; italics added). This is true, but this does *not* mean that all responses to ungrammatical items are necessarily transparent either, since there can be no such certainty as to what part of an ungrammatical sentence the learner has adjudged incorrect. It is quite conceivable that a subject may fail to recognize the ungrammaticality of the researcher's target structure, while some other irrelevant (and perfectly grammatical) aspect of the sentence could be unjustly considered wrong. But JN89's scoring method means that such a response would be considered evidence of a *correct* judgement, and the learner would be credited with the appropriate knowledge. And here we see a potential disadvantage to pseudo-randomizing the order of stimuli, since pair-wise presentation of grammatical and ungrammatical sentences is more likely to draw the learner's attention to the target structures (since it will be there that the sentences differ). For this reason it is vital to have an item analysis showing patterns of rejection and acceptance over all the stimuli. No doubt it could be done, but it has not been.

Problem 2: The stimuli

JN89 claim to test twelve simple "rules" of English, representing "a wide variety of the most basic aspects of English sentence structure" (72; also Johnson 1992: 231). I will consider five of these (*Plural, 3rd Person Singular, Past Tense, Present Progressive,* and *Determiner*) to illustrate what I see as problematic about the structure of the stimuli.[4] It is unfortunate that neither JN89 nor Johnson (1992) present the full list of stimuli they used in their experiments. There is some discussion of them with examples in JN89, but for a reasonable selection from the actual study one must go to Johnson's 1988 thesis or, as I have done, Appendix I of van Wuijtswinkel (1994), an unpublished partial replication using Dutch learners of English (of which more anon). From the latter source[5] it is evident that the term 'rule' is to be taken lightly, since certain 'rules' seem to be testing more than basic morphology or syntax. Take the example of the 'rule' labeled *Past*

Tense. According to JN89, this category and three others (*Plural, Determiner, 3rd Person Singular*) "dealt specifically with English morphology" (p. 72). In fact, this is not the whole story. The past-tense sentences and subheadings in (1-3) below come from van Wuijtswinkel (1994, Appendix I), but originate from JN89.

(1) Irregular to regular
   a.*Last night the books falled off the shelves.
   b. Last night the books fell off the shelves.

(2) Morpheme omission
   a.*Last night the old lady die in her sleep.
   b. Last night the old lady died in her sleep.

(3) Inappropriate contexts
   a.*At this moment Mr. Thompson watched a baseball game.
   b. At this moment Mr. Thompson is watching a baseball game.

While the pair in (1a-b) clearly does test knowledge of the relatively minor issue of irregular past-tense morphology, the pairs in (2a-b) and (3a-b) could be said to test rather different matters. The pair in (2a-b) raises the question of whether the subject knows that past time is to be marked on the verb in English at all (it might be seen as a 3rd person singular problem by the learner, but any response of *incorrect* will do). The pair in (3a-b), on the other hand, tests understanding of the meaning of simple past versus present progressive tenses, or even of whether *at this time* is a time adjunct that refers only to the present. This is a matter of function first and morphology very much second, I would submit.

This intermingling of the semantic and morphological considerations is repeated through several other items gathered under the heading of particular rules. In (4-6) below are stimuli cited in van Wuijtswinkel (1994) for *Plural* (I shall generally provide only ungrammatical versions from now on).

(4) Irregular to regular
   *Two mouses ran into the house this morning

(5) Morpheme omission
   *The farmer bought two pig at the market

(6) Mass nouns with plural marker
   *The girl's swimsuit is full of sands

Again, it seems that the sentences in (5) and (6) have as much to do with function as form. The sentence in (5) raises questions of grammaticalization again. Does the learner know about plural marking on nouns? Does the learner know about the distinction between mass and count nouns as in (6)? Knowledge of this distinction has wider repercussions than merely the presence or absence of plural marking. Only the sentence in (4) can be said to test knowledge of morphology (Johnson and Newport's avowed target), pure and simple.

The *3rd Person Singular* category follows the same pattern. Here, in addition to stimuli like the one in (7) below, we also have sentences like the one in (8).

(7) Morpheme omission
 *John's dog always wait for him at the corner

(8) Inappropriate contexts
 *Yesterday the hunter shoots a deer (versus *shot a deer*)

The availability of non-target judgments in (7) notwithstanding (*dogs, waited, is waiting*), (8) has nothing to do with the 3rd person singular at all; it deals with the appropriate tense to use with a past-time adjunct. The presence or absence of the bound morpheme -*s* is irrelevant since it has no role in determining tense choice (as would be obvious if the sentence had been *Yesterday the hunters shoot a deer*). Therefore this sentence (and presumably others) are just variants on (3a) above, which is supposed to test knowledge of the *Past Tense*.

The same pattern pervades the category *Present Progressive*. Compare the sentence in (9) with the one in (10) below.

(9) Morpheme omission
 *The little boy is speak to a policeman

(10) Inappropriate contexts
 *Yesterday the man is standing in the rain for his bus (as opposed to *stood in the rain*)

Quite apart from the possibility that some subjects might want to change *Yesterday* into *Today* (for which they would receive full credit) or *is speak* into *speaks*, (9) and (10) test quite different aspects of what it is to know the present progressive. (10) could be said not to test it at all–all that would be needed is the change from *is* to *was*.

The stimuli testing knowledge of *Determiners* are also of both kinds, as indicated in (11) and (12) below.

(11) Determiner omission
 *Tom is reading book in the bathtub.[6]

(12) 'A' in place of 'the': Determiners in places where they shouldn't be
 *Mary opens a windows in her room every night.

Judgment of (11) requires knowledge that there is such a thing as a determiner in English (which one would not matter, of course; it is sufficient to reject (11) to show knowledge of *Determiners*, though the presence of *the bathtub* might confuse). By contrast, (12) seems multi-interpretable. Is the target *the window, the windows, a window* or just plain *windows*? The paired stimulus has *the windows* although this seems an arbitrary choice. Again, one wonders how 'morphological' the relevant knowledge required is. If the learner's beliefs about what is wrong do not necessarily coincide with the native speaker's knowledge of what is wrong, it does not seem plausible to treat what may be fortuitously correct judgements of ungrammatical sentences as the mark of 'acquisition' (as must be the case, given the scoring method). In any case, correctly identifying the locus of error without offering some evidence of appropriate correction also raises the question of what it means to know a 'rule'. Here again we see why it is important to have an error analysis of all the stimuli.

An obvious question to raise now is whether the blending of formal and functional in these 'rule' types actually matters in the pursuit of the validity of age-related effects. After all, it could be argued that the coherence of the categories is not really a central issue, as long as the overall error scores and the subsequent thorough statistical treatment show a clear advantage for the subjects who were youngest upon arrival. Or, alternatively, it could be argued that the categories test *all* aspects relating to the acquisition of a particular morpheme, including the ability to make judgments about inappropriate use of target structures and their functions. Exactness in terminological use may not be a strong requirement.[7]

Problem 3: How universal is universal?

But clearly the fudging of form and function does matter in the end, and it matters because the adult arrivals (17-39 age group) differ from the early arrivals (3-7 age group) only in their worse performance on some categories. In fact, in Johnson (1992), the written replication of JN89, the differences between the early arrivals (3-7) and the adult arrivals (17-39) boil down to only three of the twelve rule types: *Determiners*, *Plural* and *Subcategorization* (which I have not illustrated, since it is a lexico-syntactic category).[8] So what is it about these three categories that makes their successful acquisition seem age-dependent? That problem begs for attention and requires, at the very least, the proper construction of experimental stimuli.

As JN89 themselves rightly state (p. 88), those rules that divide late arrivals from early arrivals cannot just be attributed to contrasts between the native language (L1) and the L2, since a number of the categories with no L1 counterparts appear relatively easy to acquire. To which I would add that ascribing any variation in performance to L1-L2 differences would be of little value in this case since the language backgrounds of JN89's early and late arrivals were identical.[9]

For the sake of argument, however, let us accept Johnson and Newport's methodology and findings, and move on to a discussion of the significance of their results. In JN89, a good deal of space is devoted to the question of whether there is a role for the first language in a consideration of age-related effects. As they themselves admit, there is such a thing as transfer,[10] but they deny it any significance in terms of their own results. Furthermore, from the results of "studies currently underway" using learners with different L1s, "it is already clear that the strong correlation between age of arrival and test performance replicates with subjects from these other first-language backgrounds" (JN89:93). This leads Johnson and Newport to speculate:

> [The] strong effects of age of acquisition may be accompanied by effects of input, first language typology, or other variables that do not appear in our data on Chinese and Korean learners. Most importantly, however, we have reason to expect, on the basis of our data, that *these effects of age of acquisition will persist.* (p. 94)

This assumption has been vigorously challenged by Percival, Howerd and Hill (1994), who predicted that learners with L1 backgrounds typologically similar to English and who had begun learning at around age 12 (some five years after JN89's principle 'acquire-by' date) would perform like native speakers on the JN89 stimuli even in a *foreign* language context, simply because they would find the stimuli too easy (see also Long 1993 for this same point, though less vociferously expressed). This prediction has since been tested (and confirmed) by van Wuijtswinkel (1994), using a subset of the stimuli JN89 themselves used, as well as sentences from Johnson and Newport (1991) on subjacency, and some material from other sources testing knowledge of pied-piping and preposition stranding. The latter material was included because of the need to specifically isolate the potential effects of differences and similarities between Dutch and English, since subjacency does not distinguish them.

Table 1 shows the percentage of successful judgments (i.e., a response of incorrect to an ungrammatical stimulus) made by various kinds of Dutch learners of English and a group of English native speakers for the stimuli selected by van Wuijtswinkel (that is, including scores for subjacency, pied-piping and *pro*-drop). It should be pointed out here that, unlike JN89, van Wuijtswinkel scores responses to all stimuli, correct or incorrect, but she does not provide separate figures for the JN89 stimuli. Thus we cannot see if there is any tendency on the part of subjects to mark grammatical stimuli as ungrammatical. However, given the very high scores presented in Table 1 as well as Table 2, we can reasonably assume that tendency does not exist. Only the high school group was (minimally) exposed to English before the age of twelve as part of the elementary school curriculum. However, this group also performed worst, despite having had the earliest start.

Table 1: Success rates for all items (adapted from van Wuijtswinkel 1994)

N	Group	age ($\bar{x}$)	correct ($\bar{x}$)	SD
19	high school students	16;8	82%	4.6
26	2nd year English majors	21;7	88%	2.6
8	English professors	35;1	90%	2.3
10	Native speakers	-	92%	1.5

Note: Of the original 72 subjects, 9 were subsequently omitted for producing surprisingly low scores (less than 75%) on a preliminary test consisting of simple 'filler' sentences of the active declarative type; two of these subjects came from the professors' group, three from the English majors' group and four from the high school students' group. Van Wuijtswinkel does not discuss why anyone should have failed to achieve even 75% on this test, but given the simplicity of the material, incentive to concentrate may have occasionally been lacking.

Table 2: Success rates on a subset of the JN89 stimuli (adapted from van Wuijtswinkel 1994)

N	Group	correct ($\bar{x}$)	SD
19	high school students	87%	4.9
26	2nd year English majors	93%	2.3
8	English professors	95%	2.2
10	Native speakers	95%	1.5

Table 3: Performance on grammar test of natives and non-natives (adapted from Johnson and Newport 1989)

N	Age of arrival	correct ($\bar{x}$)
23	17-39	76.2
8	11-15	85.5
8	8-10	92.8
7	3-7	97.6
23	(natives)	97.4

Table 2 shows the percentages of successful judgements on 150 representative items from the original 276 (54%) of the JN89 study. Scores on this part of the test are even higher than in Table 1. For the sake of comparison, Table 3 is taken from JN89. It shows the percentage of 'correct' judgments made by each 'age of arrival' group of ungrammatical stimuli. These results suggest that for these features of English (a) Dutch subjects are no more likely than Korean and Chinese subjects to accept sentences which are ungrammatical; (b) age of onset of learning is irrelevant; (c) years of exposure to the target language via the school and university curricula may be critical;[11] and (d) residence in the country where the target language is spoken is not necessarily an advantage.

Since performance in all age groups is consistently high, the Dutch subjects seem not a whit disadvantaged in these tasks by their relatively late start. We must therefore consider the possibility that the similarity of Dutch and English plays an important role in their performance, and it is thus interesting to see how van Wuijtswinkel's subjects perform on stimuli drawn from Johnson and Newport's study of subjacency (Johnson and Newport 1991). *No* statistical differences emerge between the English professors' group and the native speakers on such sentences, though there are some statistically significant differences between these two groups and the other two. Success rates are again generally high, however. Once more, it seems as if exposure (or talent) is the crucial factor. Anyway, since subjacency works in the same way in Dutch and English, we can always put these high scores down to crosslinguistic influence (as Schachter 1990 does).

Success in judging sentences with pied-piping and preposition stranding proved to be greater all round when Dutch and English worked in identical fashion than when they were divergent, again supporting a role for first language influence. However, the native speakers of English *also* performed worse on these divergent sentences, even though they were supposed to be grammatical. Since none of the native speakers of English were living in the Netherlands, we cannot invoke language attrition here. It is therefore instructive to note, as van Wuijtswinkel (1994:52) reports in her summary, that "no [statistically] significant differences were found between the [university professors] and native speakers on any aspect of English syntax tested in this study. Among the high school students, ... one of the 19 performed in the range of the native speakers on all items; 15 subjects among the English majors and professors (out of 34) performed within this range". As we have already seen, the scores are more impressive still for the original JN89 stimuli. There is little comfort for Johnson and Newport here, as all the Dutch learners have clearly passed their critical 'acquire-by' dates.

Bialystok and Hakuta's re-analysis

A further question has been raised as to the interpretation of JN89's data. JN89 claimed that whereas children arriving before age 7 were clearly native-like on the test items, there was a strong inverse linear relationship ($r = -.87$) between age of arrival and performance up to the age of 15. However, with the older learners (17 upwards), there was no such correlation ($r = -.16$). This would support some 'younger is still better, but youngest is best' position, with puberty as a sort of rough cut-off point. However, Bialystok and Hakuta (1994) reanalyze JN89's data, showing that the critical period cut-off point can easily be shifted to age 20, whereby the strong inverse correlation between age and performance is maintained (i.e., $r = -.87$), but with the result that there is now a substantially larger (and significant) inverse correlation between age of arrival and performance for the post-20 group ($r = -.49$).

Bialystok and Hakuta offer their own suggestions why 20 should form a performative watershed. These relate to amount of exposure to formal grammar (younger arrivals will have had more exposure) and the linguistic status of learners who arrived before age 7, who may have behaved like native speakers because they *were* native speakers. The information that they were not derives from the subjects themselves and, given temporal distance and the nature of self-report, may be unreliable.

Conclusion

If it is conceivable that typological considerations may override the predictions of the CPH in given areas of grammar, then clearly the CPH as it is usually stated is too crude and is in need of some refinement.

We are still searching for an explanation of the fact that some types of English rules are more difficult to master than others, at least when the L1s of the learners are Chinese and Korean (see also Kellerman 1989). It is true that the written presentation of stimuli reduces the number of rule types that distinguishes Chinese and Korean early and late arrivals to three, but when the L1 is Dutch and the L2 English, differences between native speakers and L2 learners who started learning after 12 almost totally disappear. It is tempting to ascribe these results to typological facts, pure and simple. But it would be wrong to merely consign results like van Wuijtswinkel's to the curiosity cabinet on the grounds that they only refer to a limited collection of L1-L2 pairings (Indo-European languages, for instance). If we marginalize these and similar data in order to maintain an attractive hypothesis, we fall into the same erroneous ways as Dulay and Burt did when they tried to blind us to the existence of crosslinguistic influence in the early 1970s. Anyway, it is hard to know where to stop: The most diverse languages may share typological features (head direction, for instance), and if we begin by ignoring the performance of learners of related languages just because they are related, before we know it we will be back doing contrastive analysis again and setting up complex hierarchies of difficulty in the manner of Stockwell, Bowen and Martin (1965).

There remains, as always, it seems, the possibility of a compromise hypothesis spanning rank universalism (*if you don't start young enough, there are rules you won't acquire*) and rank particularism (*thank your L1 for the L2 rules you do acquire*), one that will perhaps guide any future research of mine in this complex area. It is this:

There is an interaction between L1 and L2 features and age of acquisition, such that learners attempting to acquire certain (but not all) features in the L2 which have no L1 equivalents must have acquired those features by the age of x^{12} or they will never acquire them. Features of the L2 with clear L1 analogues, on the other hand, can in principle be mastered whatever the age of onset of learning.

This suggestion offers a refinement of the CPH which takes account of previous evidence in its favor as well as according an important place to the L1 in the acquisition process. This compromise position still leaves the hard work to be done: It requires us to search for an explanation for the variable difficulty of particular L2 rules (reminiscent of Brown's attempts at an explanation for the order of acquisition of the Famous Fourteen morphemes; see Brown 1973). I leave that problem, which I believe should also be guiding future research on the critical period, for another occasion.[13] But anyway, the moral of this chapter is that we should not allow ourselves to be uncritically seduced by the shimmering trappings of golden youth.

Acknowledgments

My thanks go to Ellen Bialystok, Theo Bongaerts, Clive Perdue and an anonymous reviewer for helpful remarks on an earlier version of this chapter.

Notes

1. Selinker (1972) put the number of successful learners at 5%, though this figure was intended to be taken as a metaphor for a "very small number indeed" and not as a reliable estimate (Larry Selinker, personal communication).

2. I do not mean to suggest that everyone believes that there is a critical period for SLA–only that specific criticism of this paper is thin on the ground.

3. Using written rather than the spoken material of the original. Results are very similar.

4. The others are *Pronominalization, Particle Movement, Subcategorization, Auxiliaries, Yes/No Questions, WH-Questions,* and *Word Order* (JN89:72).

5. Van Wuijtswinkel uses 150 of Johnson and Newport's original 276 sentences, so I am assuming that the stimuli she chose are representative of the original set.

6. Why is *the bathtub* included in this stimulus?

7. As supporting evidence, it should be noted that Johnson and Newport (1989:78) maintain that their results show that only early arrivals can achieve native "fluency".

8. See Figure 2 in Johnson (1992:231).

9. I thank an anonymous reviewer for the following important points: (1) It is not correct to lump the Chinese and Korean learners together as if they were dialect speakers of some pan-Asiatic language; there are clear differences between the languages (see, e.g., Comrie 1987), some of them relevant to the rule categories studied by JN89; (2) We do not know how many of JN89's subjects were Korean and how many were Chinese in each of the groups they identify by age of arrival in the USA.

10. Though they cite surprising and somewhat ancient sources.

11. Only 'may be critical' as it is perfectly possible to interpret these results as correlating with language aptitude, since high school students have obligatory English classes while English majors, though not exactly screened for their abilities before entering English departments in Holland, are self-selecting. University professors have, of course, been through the entire academic mill and usually are where they are because of their language gifts.

12. Fill in your own favored upper bound for the CPH.

13. Some suggestions could be made in the direction of Snow's "semantically strongly- and weakly-based systems" (Snow 1976), Rivers' "interlingual conceptual contrast" (Rivers 1983), and Slobin's "thinking for speaking" (Slobin 1993).

References

Bialystok, E. & K. Hakuta. 1994. *In Other Words: The science and psychology of second language acquisition*. New York: Basic Books.
Bley-Vroman, R. 1989. "What is the logical problem of foreign language learning?" *Linguistic Perspectives on Second Language Acquisition* ed. by S. Gass & J. Schachter, 41-68. New York: Cambridge University Press.
Brown, R. 1973. *A First Language*. Cambridge, MA: Harvard University Press.
Comrie, B. 1987. *The World's Major Languages*. London: Croom Helm.
Hawkins, R., R. Towell & N. Bazergui. 1993. "Universal Grammar and The Acquisition of French Verb Movement by Native Speakers of English". *Second Language Research* 9.189-233.
Johnson, J. 1988. *Critical Period Effects on Universal Properties of Language: The status of subjacency in the acquisition of a second language*. Dissertation, University of Illinois at Urbana-Champaign.
Johnson, J. 1992. "Critical Period Effects in Second Language Acquisition: The effect of written versus auditory materials on the assessment of grammatical competence". *Language Learning* 42.217-248.

Johnson, J. & E. Newport. 1989. "Critical Period Effects in Second Language Learning: The influence of maturational state on the acquisition of ESL". *Cognitive Psychology* 21.60-99.
Johnson, J. & E. Newport. 1991. "Critical Period Effects on Universal Properties of Language: The status of Subjacency in the acquisition of a second language". *Cognition* 39.215-258.
Kean, M. 1986. "Core Issues in Transfer". *Crosslinguistic Influence in Second Language Acquisition* ed. by E. Kellerman & M. Sharwood Smith, 80-90. Oxford: Pergamon.
Kellerman, E. 1984. "The Empirical Evidence for the Influence of the L1 in Interlanguage". *Interlanguage* ed. by A. Davies, C. Criper & A. Howatt, 98-122. Edinburgh: Edinburgh University Press.
Kellerman, E. 1985. "Dative Alternation and the Analysis of Data: A reply to Mazurkewich". *Language Learning* 35.91-101.
Kellerman, E. 1989. "The Imperfect Conditional". *Bilingualism Across the Lifespan* ed. by K. Hyltenstam & L. Obler, 87-115. Cambridge: Cambridge University Press.
Lightbown, P. & N. Spada. 1993. *How Languages are Learned*. Oxford: Oxford University Press.
Long, M. 1990. "Maturational Constraints on Language Development". *Studies in Second Language Acquisition* 12.251-285.
Long, M. 1993. "Second Language Acquisition as a Function of Age: Research findings and methodological issues". *Progression and Regression in Language* ed. by K. Hyltenstam & Å. Viberg, 196-221. Cambridge: Cambridge University Press.
Percival, V., F. Howerd & B. Hill. 1994. "Age of Arrival vs. Time of Arrival: A reconsideration of Johnson and Newport 1989. *University of Hawai'i Working Papers in ESL* 12.141-151.
Rivers, W. 1983. *Communicating Naturally in a Second Language*. Cambridge: Cambridge University Press.
Schachter, J. 1990. "On the Issue of Completeness in Second Language Acquisition". *Second Language Research* 6.93-124.
Selinker, L. 1972. "Interlanguage". *IRAL* 10.209-231.
Slobin, D. 1993. "Adult Language Acquisition: A view from child language study". *Adult Language Acquisition: Cross-linguistic perspectives* ed. by C. Perdue, 239-252. Cambridge: Cambridge University Press.
Snow, C. 1976. "Semantic Primacy in First and Second Language Acquisition". *Interlanguage Studies Bulletin* 1(2 & 3).137-165.
Stockwell, R., J. Bowen & J. Martin. 1965. *The Grammatical Structures of English and Spanish*. Chicago: University of Chicago Press.
Strömquist, S. & D. Day. 1993. "On the Development of Narrative Structure in Child L1 and Adult L2 Acquisition". *Applied Psycholinguistics* 14.135-158.
Towell, R. & R. Hawkins. 1994. *Approaches to Second Language Acquisition*. Clevedon, UK: Multilingual Matters.
Wuijtswinkel, K. van. 1994. *Critical Period Effects on the Acquisition of Grammatical Competence in a Second Language*. BA thesis, Nijmegen University.

Style-shifting in oral interlanguage
Quantification and definition

Jean-Marc Dewaele
Birkbeck College, University of London

Introduction

While the notion of style may be intuitively understood by all speakers, it seems to have escaped every attempt by linguists at theoretical and empirical definition.[1] In this squib I will discuss the problem of identifying a particular speech-style in interlanguage speech and native speech, as a base. Using data from advanced Dutch-French interlanguage, I will then present a quantified variable (a measure of 'formality') that reflects the degree of explicitness of speech, working within the theoretical framework of Levelt (1989) and de Bot (1992). A number of theoretical arguments will be proposed to explain why degree of explicitness can be considered as the essential characteristic of interlanguage speech styles.

The concept of style

In his discussion of styles, Labov (1972) writes that styles "can be ranged along a single dimension, measured by the amount of attention paid to the speech. The most important way in which this attention is exerted is in audio-monitoring one's own speech, though other forms of monitoring also take place" (p. 208). The continuum of styles for Labov thus ranges from the highly formal to the vernacular: "the style in which minimum attention is given at the monitoring of speech" (*ibid.*). The main indication one has about the amount of attention paid to speech is the task or the situation in which the speech is produced. For Labov, however, "it is of course not enough to set a particular context in order to observe casual speech. We also look for some evidence in the type of linguistic production that the speaker is using a speech style [A] that contrasts with speech B" (pp. 94-95). The problem Labov faces is thus to find a fundamental linguistic variable reflecting the formality of speech. The use of phonological variables, which he found to vary systematically in different styles, is not taken into consideration "because the values of these variables in Styles A and B are exactly what we are trying to determine by the isolation of styles" (p. 95).

Considering the lack of a global linguistic measure reflecting formality, Labov presents a number of characteristics of speech, channel cues, that covary with the degree of formality. These channel cues are "modulations of the voice production which affect speech as a whole" (p. 95). Four of them are fluency indicators: volume, speech rate, pitch, rhythm; the last one is the presence of laughter in the speech extract. Labov presents no strict criteria about these channel cues. He admits that they are crude and subjective indicators of style since he underlines the necessity of a better quantified variable: "the most immediate problem to be solved in the attack on sociolinguistic structure is the quantification of the dimension of style" (p. 245).

Labov's principle of "attention to form" came increasingly under attack in the late 1980s (e.g., Bell 1984; Rampton 1987; Young 1989; Gradol and Swann 1989). Bell (1984:117), who reanalyzed the data in Labov (1972) upon which Labov based his principle, concludes that the concept of "attention to form" is "a non-starter". The influence of Labov's definition of formality still lingers, however. *The Longman Dictionary of Applied Linguistics* (Richards, Platt & Weber 1985), for example, defines "formal speech" as "the type of speech used in situations when the speaker is very careful about pronunciation and choice of words and sentence structure. This type of speech may be used, for example, at official functions, and in debates and ceremonies" (p. 109). It is striking to note the circularity in this definition, since it provides only a few vague linguistic characteristics of what formal speech is.

Tarone's "Chameleon Model" (1979) adapts Labov's theory to the study of English interlanguage. In her view every learner possesses a number of speech styles that can be tapped using different tasks: "A grammaticality judgment task provides information about only the more formal, or careful style, (...) the description of entities, or narration of a story, must be assumed to tap different styles of the IL continuum (Tarone 1988:40). Tarone (1988) refers explicitly to Labov's principle of "attention to form" in her definition of formality, thereby falling into the same circular argument that formal speech is the speech produced in a formal situation. Since her hypothesis that formality–and thus attention to form–should be linked to morphological accuracy was not upheld, Tarone (1987, 1989) started to downplay the role of attention to form. Tarone (1987:36) writes, "attention to form can at best be only an intermediary factor: We are still left with establishing what it is in the task and the situation that causes learners to pay attention to form".

I believe that Tarone's concern raises a series of crucial questions for interlanguage research:

- What is it that makes interlanguage speakers style-shift?
- Do the principles that apply to native speakers also apply to speakers of an interlanguage?
- Why does there appear to be a correlation between formal style and particular events like debates or ceremonies?
- Given that there will be strong individual variation, how can speech-styles be measured in interlanguage?

In order to begin to answer such questions, it is my basic assumption that one needs to develop a sound quantified measure of style.

The explicitness-implicitness dimension

In two earlier studies (Dewaele forthcoming a, b), I found identical patterns of variation in word-class proportion at the token level between different genres of written speech in native Italian and native Dutch and between different oral styles (ranging from informal to formal) in native French, in Dutch-French interlanguage, and in native Dutch.[2] The variation found was not one of content words versus function words, as predicted by Halliday (1985); rather–and interestingly–variation cut across both categories. It appears that the proportion of nouns, determiners (articles and adjectives) and prepositions is higher in the corpora of written and formal oral speech, whereas pronouns, verbs and adverbs are found to be more frequent in the corpora of oral and informal speech. Variation appears to be significant for every category except for the conjunctions. Similar variation also exists in native English, which was confirmed by Hudson (1994). Recent research suggests that the same pattern also emerges in Somali (Biber & Hared 1992) and Korean (Kim 1990). One can thus conclude that written speech and more formal situations lead to an increase in nouns, determiners and prepositions. This pattern of variation, which seems to be of an universal nature, could be one of a "general sort of processes [which] must intersect in some as yet unknown way" (Selinker 1992:214).

Subsequent research reported in Dewaele (forthcoming c) presents the results and interpretation of a principal-components factor analysis[3] performed on the proportion of nouns, determiners, prepositions, verbs, pronouns, adverbs, and conjunctions in two styles of the Dutch-French interlanguage of 27 Flemish university students. For each of two situations (informal conversation, formal oral examination), a separate factor analysis was performed. Each time, two main orthogonal factors appeared. The first dimension, which explains over 50% of the variance, was *implicitness/explicitness*. Nouns, modifiers and prepositions obtained strong negative loadings on this factor, as opposed to the pronouns, adverbs, and verbs, which obtained high positive loadings (see Table 1).[4] Nouns, modifiers and prepositions are thus situated near the explicit end of this dimension, in contrast to pronouns, adverbs, and verbs, which are near the implicit end of the continuum. The factor analysis also yielded a second factor, which I called *complexity*. As this is not of interest to the present discussion it will be ignored here.

Table 1: *Factor analysis on 'implicitness/explicitness' as applied to the proportions of word classes in the speech extracts of 27 speakers in formal and informal situations*

Variable	Informal	Formal
noun	-.90	-.89
determiner	-.89	-.70
pronoun	-.73	-.77
verb	.78	.40
adverb	.66	.86
conjunction	-.24	-.29
Variance Explained:	55%	53%

A theoretical explanation of the implicitness/explicitness factor

I believe that the perception speakers have of the formality of a situation leads them to produce more or less formal speech. It is my view that choice of speech style depends on the need of speakers to be unambiguously understood. The main characteristic of formal speech would therefore be a high degree of explicitness. As a result, if speakers wish to avoid ambiguity and misinterpretation of their words, they relie as little as possible on the spatio-temporal context they share with their interlocutor(s). This is apparently achieved by explicit and precise description of the elements of the context needed to disambiguate the expression. For example, Levelt (1989:58) writes, "Interlocutors anchor their contributions steadily in the spatio-temporal context of their conversation". Such anchoring is known as *deixis*. By anchoring their utterances in a shared spatio-temporal context, speakers can transmit much more information than what is literally said. There is thus less need for precision since the context shared by sender and receiver will provide the additional information lacking in the linguistic expression itself. If, on the other hand, senders and receivers do not share the same spatial or temporal context–like a journalist talking to an invisible audience or writing for imaginary readers–they will have to add more details to make tacit understandings explicit, and their style will thus become more formal and less deictical.

Distinguishing deixis, Levelt (1989:45) distinguishes four types: deixis of person, deixis of place, deixis of time, and deixis of discourse. In the data I have analyzed, the words that are used to produce such 'deictic' speech belong mainly to the classes of pronouns, adverbs and verbs. It follows for interlanguage that the relative proportion of these word-classes is bound to increase in more informal speech. Particularly pronouns are essentially context-dependent. Words that are typically independent of the (spatio-temporal) context are nouns, prepositions and the majority of the determiners.[5]

I found that the most frequent adverbs (*before, yesterday*) are context-dependent. In this sense, they are similar to possessive or demonstrative pronouns. Finite verbs are deictic in the sense that they refer implicitly to a particular time through their tense (time deixis; see Levelt 1989:55) and to a particular subject through their conjugation (person or object deixis). The latter feature is especially important in languages such as Spanish or Italian, in which a pronoun does not have to be stated as subject, since it can be inferred directly from the form of a verb. This makes an expression with a finite verb much more context-dependent than a corresponding expression without a finite verb.

Using individual factor scores, the degree of explicitness or formality of individual speech extracts can be measured and located on the continuum of styles. We thus have a reliable and empirical second-order measure, based on the proportions of word-classes, to analyze style-shifting.

Conclusion

At this stage an answer can be put forward about the motivations of speakers who style-shift. I believe the answer lies primarily in a decision about optimal communication. Informal or implicit speech is much more economical than its explicit, formal variant. In Zipf's (1949) terms, speakers respect the principle of least effort–as long as they do not violate the maxim of quantity that every co-operative speaker is supposed to respect in a particular situation (Grice 1975). This means that a speaker will, if possible, avoid a formal style which is rigid, heavy and cognitively more demanding since this style involves the use of nouns that require more lexical searching due to their relatively infrequent use. Less formal speech is more dynamic, more elliptical and cognitively less demanding because, among other reasons, this style uses high-frequency lemmas which are more easily and quickly retrieved. This is particularly important in a second language situation where there already is a larger cognitive load in play. Speakers, if they can control this dimension, rely maximally on the spatio-temporal context and use non-verbal communication–which is also less demanding than explicit speech. Speakers in informal situations need not worry too much about being misinterpreted because of the possibility of immediate feedback and restatement. If possibilities of feedback and quick correction are not present, as is the case in more formal situations like debates or ceremonies, speakers will invest more energy in trying to be as clear as possible, to avoid deictical speech and hence to minimize the risk of misinterpretation.

I can thus summarize the answers to the questions raised at the beginning of this squib as follows:

- The style-shifting of interlanguage speakers reflects the degree to which they anchor their utterances in the spatio-temporal context (ranging from highly deictical to context-independent utterances).
- The same principle also applies to native speech and appears to be of a universal nature.
- The choice of a particular speech-style is motivated by a principle of economy. One will only invest more energy in the production of speech when one feels the need to be unambiguously understood in a situation that is perceived as formal. Typical examples of such situations are ceremonies or conferences.

Acknowledgment

I wish to thank Larry Selinker for his comments on an earlier version of this squib.

Notes

1. A good review of the different meanings of 'style' is presented in Azuike (1992).

2. For Italian, I used the data of Zampolli (1975) and for Dutch the frequency dictionaries of Uit de Bogaart (1975) and de Jong (1979). I constituted a small corpus of native French discourse (3.245 word-tokens) consisting of two written genres and two oral styles. The Dutch-French interlanguage corpus consists of 14 hours of conversation (65,000 words) between the researcher and 27 Flemish students in two situations.

3. The basic idea of principal-components analysis is that different variables (in casu the proportions of seven word classes in the oral speech extracts of 27 subjects) can be expressed by a minimum number of new variables ("principal components"). the extraction of principal components amounts to a *variance maximizing (varimax) rotation* of the original variable space. When there are seven original variables, they must be defined as a *space*, and the factor will then be a line running through this seven-dimensional space and finding maximal variance. More information on this subject can be found in Stevens (1987).

4. A loading is the value of the correlation between an original variable and the new factor.

5. The demonstrative adjectives are the only context-dependent determiners.

References

Azuike, M. N. 1992. "Style: Theories and practical application". *Language Sciences* 14.109-127.
Biber, D. & Hared, M. 1992. "Dimensions of register variation in Somali". *Language Variation and Change* 4.41-75.
Bell, A. 1984. "Language style as audience design". *Language in Society* 3.145-204.
de Bot, K. 1992. "A bilingual production model: Levelt's 'speaking' model adapted" *Applied Linguistics* 13.1-24.
de Jong, E. D. 1979. *Spreektaal. Woordfrequenties in gesproken Nederlands*. Utrecht: Bohn, Scheltema & Holkema.
Dewaele, J. M. Forthcoming a. "La Composition Lexicale de Styles Oraux et Écrits". To appear in *Language and Style*.
Dewaele, J. M. Forthcoming b. "Variation dans la Composition Lexicale de Styles Oraux". To appear in *International Review of Applied Linguistics*.
Dewaele, J. M. Forthcoming c. "How to Measure Formality of Speech? A model of synchronic variation". To appear in *Proceedings of the Second Conference of the European Second Language Association* ed. by K. Sajavaara. Jyväskylä, Finland.
Gradol, D. & J. Swann. 1989. *Gender Voices*. Cambridge: Basil Blackwell.
Grice, H. P. 1975. "Logic and Conversation". *Syntax and Semantics: Speech acts* ed. by P. Cole & J. L. Morgan, 41-58. New York: Academic Press.
Halliday, M. A. K. 1985. *Spoken and Written Language*. Oxford: Oxford University Press.
Hudson, R. 1994. "About 37% of Word-Tokens are Nouns". *Language* 70.331-339.
Kim, Y. J. 1990. *Register Variation in Korean*. Unpublished Ph.D. Dissertation, University of California at Los Angeles.
Labov, W. 1972. *Sociolinguistic Patterns*. Philadelphia: University of Pennsylvania Press.
Levelt, W. J. M. 1989. *Speaking: From intention to articulation*. Cambridge, MA: MIT Press.
Rampton, B. 1987. "Stylistic Variability and Not Speaking 'Normal' English: Some post-Labovian approaches and their implications for the study of interlanguage". *Second Language Acquisition in Context* ed. by R. Ellis, 47-58. London: Prentice Hall.
Richards, J., J. Platt & H. Weber. 1985. *Longman Dictionary of Applied Linguistics*. London: Longman.
Selinker, L. 1992. *Rediscovering Interlanguage*. London: Longman.
Stevens, J. 1986. *Applied Multivariate Statistics for the Social Sciences*. Hillsdale, NJ: Erlbaum.
Tarone, E. 1979. "Interlanguage as a Chameleon". *Language Learning* 29.181-191.
Tarone, E. 1987. "Methodologies for Studying Variability in Second Language Learning". *Second Language Acquisition in Context* ed. by R. Ellis, 35-36 London: Prentice Hall.

Tarone, E. 1988. *Variation in Interlanguage.* London: Edward Arnold.
Tarone, E. 1989. "Accounting for Style-Shifting in Interlanguage". *Variation in Second Language Acquisition* ed. by S. Gass, C. Madden, D. Preston & L. Selinker, 13-21. Clevedon: Multilingual Matters.
Uit den Bogaart, P. C. 1975. *Woordfrekwenties in Geschreven en Gesproken Nederlands.* Utrecht: Oosthoek, Scheltema & Holkema.
Young, R. 1989. "Ends and Means: Methods for the study of interlanguage variation". *Variation in Second Language Acquisition* ed. by S. Gass, C. Madden, D. Preston & L. Selinker, 65-90. Clevedon: Multilingual Matters.
Zampolli, A. 1975. "Statistique Linguistique et Dépouillements Automatiques". *Lexicologie: Feestbundel de Tollenaere* ed. by P. G. J. Van Sterkenburg, 325-358. Groningen: Wolters-Noordhoff.
Zipf, G. K. 1949. *Human Behavior and the Principle of the Least Effort.* Cambridge, MA: Addison-Wesley.

Observations of language use
in Spanish immersion classroom interactions

Susana Blanco-Iglesias
Joaquina Broner
Elaine Tarone
University of Minnesota

The most successful program for teaching second languages in the public schools in both Canada and the United States has been the language immersion approach.[1] However, after more than 20 years of immersion education in North America, and research documenting superior outcomes for immersion students, there appears to have been little systematic research documenting, through direct observation, immersion students' use of their first as well as their second languages in the classroom. (In fact, second-language "classroom research" which is "actually grounded in the classroom itself" is fairly rare (Nunan 1991:265).)[2] There have been persistent but poorly documented reports from teachers and students alike that indicate that students do not exclusively speak in the second language (L2) in immersion classrooms during periods when they are supposed to be immersed in L2, but rather make extensive use of their native language (L1) in those classrooms, particularly in the upper grade levels (Broner 1991; Heitzman 1993; Parker, Heitzman, Fjerstad, Babbs and Cohen forthcoming).[3]

Tarone and Swain (1995) suggest that such reports make sense if we view immersion classrooms as speech communities which become increasingly diglossic[4] over time. They hypothesize that in immersion classroom interactions, the L2 may function as a superordinate language variety, used predominantly for academic topics in conversations with the teacher or for 'public' discourse addressed to the class as a whole. They hypothesize that the L1 may be used as a vernacular by older children for more private peer-peer social interactions. They conclude with a call for research on children's patterns of language use in immersion classrooms to assess the validity of their hypotheses.

The study

In this paper we report on a preliminary case study in which we document our observations of the way in which Spanish immersion students in grades K through 5 in a US school used their first and second languages over a period of six weeks in interacting with teachers and with one another in the classroom.

Research questions

Do children in kindergarten through fifth grade Spanish immersion classrooms use English (L1) or Spanish (L2) when
(a) conversing with their teacher?
(b) responding to the teacher in teacher-fronted discussions?
(c) conversing with their peers in desk work?

Subjects

The subjects in this study were all students in the same Spanish immersion school in a large Midwestern (US) city. The program is a total immersion program in which students are taught entirely in Spanish in kindergarten and first grade; English language arts are gradually introduced in grades two through five.[5] At this school site the immersion program runs from kindergarten through fifth grade. Observations were made of students in kindergarten through fifth grade, with particular focus on second through fifth-grade classes, during the portion of their day in which students were supposed to be hearing and using Spanish exclusively.

Data collection

For six weeks during Spring 1994, fourteen different classes were observed, with most of the observations focusing on second through fifth grade classes. Three second-grade classes were observed, one of them several times. Three third-grade classes were observed, one of them twice. Three fourth-grade and three fifth-grade classes were observed (two of the fifth-grade classes three times each). Each observation lasted 10-50 minutes.

Data were gathered using notebooks. Beebe (1994:3) argues for the need to use notetaking as a valuable data-gathering technique in situations where tape-recording is not possible (i.e., a courtroom, a CEO meeting, a classroom, a marital argument, among others). The data reported here are described as natural spontaneous notebook data and were hand transcribed using immediate facilitated recall using the procedures outlined in Beebe (1994).

OBSERVATIONS OF LANGUAGE USE

One purpose of this study is to evaluate the success of our use of natural spontaneous notebook data using immediate facilitated recall in recording bilingual interactions in classrooms. It is very difficult to obtain permission to audiotape classroom interactions; school personnel are far more likely to permit observation and notetaking in classrooms than audiotaping. We found that we were able to make certain adjustments to Beebe's method. In fact, in collecting our data, we had an advantage over Beebe in that there were always two observers, both native speakers of Spanish, present to gather the data, and those observers could and did make a point of checking their observations with one another. Thus, there was a check on the immediate perceptions of the notetaker. Usually, the notetaker sat behind the second observer so that she could make discreet notes, writing down the utterances she heard using memory techniques described by Beebe (1994:15-16), while the second observer watched the class. (Memory techniques used included use of shorthand for note taking, memorization of pragmatic force perceived, speedy onset of transcription, and transcription of core act first.) Watcher and observer whispered periodically, asking for confirmation or confirming the form of particular utterances. The notebook data were keyboarded in detail with accompanying commentary within two days of the observation; usually the two observers would divide up the task of keyboarding in order to be able to get the task done within two days of the observation to ensure accuracy of transcription as much as possible.

At times the observers keyboarded the same set of observations; at those times the details of the typescripts were not always the same. The watcher might include nonverbal information that the notetaker did not have, or the notetaker might include information she had heard but which had not been entered in the notes. Thus, the details of the utterances written down using the notetaking technique cannot always be relied upon; however, we are confident in the ability of the technique to pick up the general patterns of L1 and L2 use specified in our research questions.

Another shortcoming, or weakness, to the use of notebook data in bilingual situations such as this one is that the observers' background and general research purpose tended to influence the amount of detail provided in the notes with regard to the actual utterances produced in L1 or L2. The notetakers were native speakers of Spanish and were particularly 'tuned in' to the use of Spanish in these classrooms because they had been told that the children did not use Spanish very much, and so they were interested in documenting those cases where Spanish *was* used. They were also interested in noting down what grammatical structures the children were using in Spanish. The observers often did not transcribe exactly the English utterances produced by these immersion students and so were often reduced to noting that the children spoke to each other in English, without recording what exactly they had said. This problem was of course exacerbated by the fact that the children's Spanish utterances were intended for the class as a whole or the teacher, while many of their English utterances to each other were not always meant to be overheard and so were often whispered, and furthermore, incorporated slang expressions with which these native speakers of Spanish were at times not familiar. Perhaps in future studies using this technique for data collection in bilingual situations, there should be two observers who are native speakers of *each* of the languages being used, and an effort made accurately to transcribe in detail utterances from both languages.[6]

A more obvious shortcoming to the use of notebook data, and one discussed at some length by Beebe, is that notebook data do not lend themselves as easily as tape-recorded data to quantitative analysis. That is, notebook data can only provide an indication of patterning in the data. Where such patterns appear to occur, then additional studies using tape-recorded and transcribed data are called for in the target situation in order to verify the existence and the strength of those patterns. In spite of these problems, the use of notebook data seems to be very productive in generating likely hypotheses on general patterns of language use, with anecdotal documentation of some individual utterances, to be subjected to more systematic and quantitative study using more rigorous methodologies.

Data analysis

The notebook data from each observation were organized using the categories in (1) through (8) below.

(1) grade
(2) total time observed
(3) classroom setting (the physical layout)
(4) activity (the teacher-structured task(s) in which the students were engaged)
(5) teacher (whether male/female, native speaker of L2, substitute/permanent)
(6) language used by teacher to students, by students to teacher, and by students to each other
(7) examples of interactions (utterances recorded in the notebooks)
(8) overall comments on the tone of the class

Results

Table 1, showing categories (1) grade, (2) time observed, and (6) language use, shows the general tendencies of children and teachers to resort to either English or Spanish when addressing one another. In discussing these general tendencies below, we will give examples from the observers' notebook data and add information from observer comments as these seem relevant. (In our presentation

Table 1: Classes observed in a Spanish immersion elemetary school in terms of English (L1) and Spanish (L2) use

grade	time observed[7]	language(s) used[8] teacher-students	students-teacher	students-students
K	15 min	Spanish	Spanish/English	English
1	30 min	Spanish	Spanish	Spanish/English
2a	1 hr 30 min	Spanish	Spanish	English/Spanish
2b	10 min	Spanish	Spanish	Spanish/English
2c	10 min	Spanish	Spanish	Spanish/English
3a	15 min	Spanish	Spanish	Spanish
3b	1 hr 15 min	Spanish	Spanish	Spanish
3c	20 min	Spanish	Spanish	Spanish
4a	20 min	Spanish	English/Spanish	English
4b	25 min	Spanish	Spanish	Spanish
4c	45 min	Spanish	Spanish/English	Spanish/English
5a	1 hr 25 min	Spanish	Spanish/English	English/Spanish
5b	1 hr 45min	Spanish	Spanish/English	Spanish/English
5c	1 hr	Spanish	Spanish/English	Spanish/English

of results we have changed all the names of the students to pseudonyms and given each class a designator number.)

We see that teachers consistently used Spanish to address the children in every grade level. The children's use of Spanish and English, however, varies from grade to grade. We review below the language use patterns grade by grade.

Kindergarten

In responding to the teachers in kindergarten, the children use English (presumably because they do not yet know much Spanish). In talking to each other, we see that in kindergarten the children remain in English.

First, second and third grades

From first through third grades, the children used Spanish in addressing their teachers. Examples of such interactions are shown in (9) though (11) below.

(9) First grade
Teacher: ¿Qué hay en el poster?
What's in the poster?
Students: autobuses, flores, basura, una un abuelo ...
buses, flowers, garbage, a, a grandfather ...

(10) Second grade
Teacher: ¿Qué cantidad de leche dan las vacas?
How much milk do cows give?

Child: Depende de las vacas.
It depends on the cows.

(11) Third grade (teacher reading a sentence written by a girl)
Teacher: "... me enseñó China." ¿acerca de China? ¿sobre China?
"... he showed me China." about China?
Girl: Yo ya estaba en China, me enseñó China.[9]
I was already in China. He showed me China.

The observers' comments note that in these exchanges, the students were typically on task, discussing academic topics: doing their schoolwork. By the third grade, the children's Spanish was usually very good, with good pronunciation and surprisingly good mastery of such difficult grammatical distinctions as the imperfect and preterit tenses, as in (11) above.

In talking with each other in the first and second grade, we see that the children varied somewhat from class to class. In the first-grade class observed, the children tended to use Spanish, though the observers did hear a little English in those contexts. In the second-grade classes, the children remained in Spanish fairly well both when addressing the teacher and each other. However, some English[10] was heard when the children were addressing each other, particularly when they were in transition, as shown in (12) below, recorded when these second-graders were lining up to go outside for recess.

(12) Second grade
Child 1: ¿Vas a ir al recreo?
You going to recess?
Child 2 (throwing a football):
I'm passing the ball!
Child 1: Nice catch!

In the third grade, however, much less English was heard in child-child interactions. Primarily Spanish seemed to be used in such interactions, across all three classrooms observed. For example, in the interaction in (13) below, the third-grade children were playing a game of Bingo in Spanish.

(13) Third grade
Child 1: Más despacio
(slower)
Child 2: ¿Treinta y qué?
Thirty and what?
Child 1: Treinta.
Thirty.
Child 2: Treinta y cero.
Thirty and nothing.

And in the interaction in (14) below, one child was teasing[11] another, who was a little shy because the observers were sitting nearby.

(14) Third grade
    Child 1:   ¡Mira, él no puede hablar!
                 Look, he can't talk!
                 (the rest giggle)
    Child 2:   ¡Te dije!
                 I told you!

Thus, in some sense, these children's use of Spanish in all contexts appears to increase steadily through the third-grade level.

Fourth grade

However, patterns of language use begin to change in the fourth and fifth grades. Table 1 shows that the fourth-grade children used more English in conversations with one another and in addressing the teacher. The pattern was mixed in the three fourth-grade sessions observed; one fourth-grade class (Class 4b) appeared to use Spanish to a much greater extent than the others, thus perpetuating the pattern found in the third-grade classes. But language use patterns were changing in *all* the fourth-grade classes—and quite radically in one of these classes (Class 4a).

We need to provide some background information about Class 4a. This class had had another teacher for the first part of their school year, and had had a very hard time adjusting to their current teacher. The observers' notes show that there was a general atmosphere of lack of discipline and respect for the teacher the day they observed, the students whispering to one another and ignoring the teacher while she was talking. The class observation began with the teacher introducing the observers to the class, telling her students that the observers were there to see how they spoke Spanish and how they behaved. "Cool" said one child out loud, beginning a session of whispering. The teacher then asked "Jane" a question (in Spanish) and "Jane" responded in English. The exchange[12] in (15) was then observed.

(15) Fourth grade (Class 4a)
    Teacher: ¡Muy mal Jane! Todavía lo puedes mejorar si lo dices en español.
                  Very bad, Jane! You can only improve this situation [speaking
    English in front of observers] if you speak in Spanish.
    Jane: Tú hablas inglés.
                  You speak English. (very ironic tone)
    Others: ¡Muy mal, muy mal!
                  Very bad, very bad!

In Class 4c, the atmosphere was more respectful and more Spanish was used, but even here English turned up in children's language addressed to each other. In the discussion in (16), the fourth-grade class was in a teacher-fronted discussion planning a program the class would present to a senior citizens' center.

(16) Fourth grade (Class 4c)
    Teacher: ¿Cuál era la canción?
               What was the song?
    Child 1: Yo sabe uno.
               (I knows one)

(Teacher begins to converse in Spanish with some students; others begin to talk to each other in English)

    Child 2: Ah! Everybody knows that ...
    Child 3: It's short.
    Child 4: It's stupid.
    Child 5: I will never forget the lyrics to that song!
    Teacher: ¡No te olvides en qué idioma estamos hablando!
               Don't forget what language we're speaking in!

The observers noticed that when the children in this fourth-grade class addressed one another, they used Spanish for academic topics, but did not ever seem to use Spanish to socialize with each other; they switched to English when they drifted away from school topics.

The most Spanish in the fourth grade was used in Class 4b. The teacher had set up a system of cooperative groups in which the leader of each group was responsible to keep a record when students in his/her group used English (a system which apparently led to quite a bit of in-group discussion). Yet even in this class, the observations show that the students used some English with each other in desk work when the teacher was not monitoring them. This is illustrated in (17) below.

(17) Fourth grade (Class 4b)
    Child 1: ¡Elisa! No sabes ... (whispered)
              Elisa! You don't know ...
    Child 2: Maybe, maybe not. Have fun on Friday! (teasing)
    (Teacher asks Child 2 to sit alone.)

So we see that the overall trend in the fourth-grade classes observed was for the children to use more English in speaking with each other and even at times in full-class, teacher-fronted discussions, but not when addressing the teacher.

Fifth grade

The fifth-graders in this school are the 'seniors' of the school. In Table 1 we see that in the three fifth-grade classes the children continued this trend of mixed

OBSERVATIONS OF LANGUAGE USE 249

Spanish/English use when addressing each other and the teacher. Observer comments indicate that the students were using mostly English to talk to each other, particularly on social topics, and mostly Spanish (though also some English) in teacher-fronted discussions focusing on schoolwork. The conversational exchanges in (18) illustrate the sorts of language use patterns observed during more than three hours of observation of these fifth-grade classes.

(18) Fifth grade
Mary to teacher: ¿Qué era el número 13, 14, 15?
                   What was number 13, 14, 15?

(Teacher responds to Mary)

Student to Mary: You messed up, Mary!

In many instances, the English speech style used in the fifth-grade student-student interactions was clearly vernacular and apparently tied to pre-adolescent expressiveness. In the example in (19), for instance, a very popular Spanish-speaking aide called on three students to leave the classroom to work with her in a separate area.

(19) Fifth grade
Aide: Necesito a Pablo, Juan y Pedro.
         I need Pablo, Jan and Pedro.
Pedro: Yes!! (leaps up, with arm gesture)[13]

In the exchange in (20) below, the students were doing desk work. While the teacher was paying attention, they commented on the assignment in (somewhat mixed) Spanish, but when another teacher came in and the two teachers began to converse in Spanish, the children switched to a more vernacular English as their conversation veered off-topic.

(20) Fifth grade
Child 1: No pueden hacer nada más, entonces.
          We can't do any more, then.
Child 2: Sí, eso es Omar. Es muy ugly.
          Yes, that's Omar. He's very ugly.

(Second teacher enters; teachers converse in Spanish)

Child 1: No, jerk!
Child 2: Ok, Ok, no mira.
          Ok, ok, don't look.

In (21) below, we see the same pattern again in another fifth-grade class, in an exercise where the children were reading aloud to the same Spanish-speaking aide as in (19) some questions they had previously written about Mexico.

(21) Fifth grade
    Child: "¿Hay bonitas niñas?" (reading aloud)
              "Are there pretty girls?"
    Aide: Guapísimas.
              Gorgeous.
    Boy 1:   I got two dimes ... (whispered)
    Boy 2:   C'mon everybody! Let's do the funky thing!
    Girl: You guys are sick.

Clearly, in the examples in (20) and (21), it does seem as if the fifth-grade children were using a great deal of English slang, the function of which was for in-group communications of a pre-adolescent nature. It does not seem likely that these children would know equivalent Spanish vernacular expressions to use for expressions like "the funky thing". Even if they did, the Spanish equivalents might not have the same expressive force for them.

At times it seemed in the fifth-grade desk work interactions that one student would hold out for Spanish, against a rising tide of English usage. In the example in (22) below, the children were working in groups at different tables with microscopes.

(22) Fifth grade
    Girl 1:   Why don't we just try that? (said to another child before plugging
                 the microscope into the wall)
    Girl 2:   Sí, podemos enchufarlo.
             Yes, we can plug it in.
    Girl 1:   Turn this so that we can ... (meaning so that we can plug it in)
    Girl 3:   There we go.
    Girl 2:   Apagálo (rather than apágalo)
             Turn it off.
    Boy: What did you do? (talking to one of the girls)
             This is cool, can I look? Can I look?

If in fact these children are using English as a vernacular speech style for in-group purposes, it is possible that single students' use of Spanish in such situations marks them as "lames", in Labov's (1972) terms: individuals whose use of more standard language marks them as peripheral to the core adolescent group. It is not possible to investigate this possibility without more systematically-gathered tape-recorded data.

Discussion

Clearly, the language of transitions from one classroom to another–the language of the hall–was English at all grade levels (with the possible exception of third grade). This is illustrated in the example in (23) below.

(23) Fifth grade
    Teacher: Los de la banda se tienen que irse.
                    Band members have to go.
    Student: It's pouring outside. (said while leaving)

And in the example in (24) below, a fourth-grade class was lining up in the hall before recess.

(24) Fourth grade
    Child 1:   Three outfields, shortstops, second base.
    Child 2:   What about marbles?
    Child 3:   No more than 6.
                 He's a pain in the ...
    Teacher (announcing penalty for speaking English):
                 Tienen cinco minutos menos para el lunes.
                 You have 5 fewer minutes for Monday recess.
    Children: Five minutes less!! (whispered)

Possibly future studies will show that English is simply the language of relaxation, while Spanish is the language of the school task. In other words, when the children are "on duty", as it were, focused on their schoolwork, they speak Spanish. When they relax, they speak English.[14]

However, we feel that there is more than just relaxation involved in English language use. Especially in the fifth-grade conversations, there appears to be an additional function of the language, as hypothesized by Tarone and Swain (1995)–the use of highly vernacular language forms to mark the speakers as in-group members of a pre-adolescent speech community.

> Pre-adolescents and adolescents need a vernacular style as a way of signaling their identities. They tend to mark their identity and identification with one another as adolescents in a number of ways: in their mode of dress, their hairstyles, their music preferences–and their use of vernacular language. It becomes important to most pre-adolescents and adolescents to present the right image and to "talk the right talk". The "right talk" is constantly changing as older adolescents move out of this particular age group and younger adolescents move in. The use of the accepted current vernacular terms ("cool it" vs. "squash it" or "that's cool" vs. "that's fresh") is central to the emerging adolescent's image and identity. (p. 30)

Such vernacular terms are common in many of the English utterances noted down by the observers in the fifth-grade class: "you messed up" in example (18) above, "Yes!!" in example (19), "jerk!" in (20), "the funky thing" in (21), "This is cool" in (22), and "He's a pain in the ..." in (24). We are reminded of interviews with immersion students who indicate that such are the second-language expressions they felt they needed but did not have in immersion programs. An example of this kind of comment is in (25) below, from Tarone and Swain (1995).

(25) Suzannah: ...when ... [we] get older..., we start speaking in a way that they don't teach us, in French, how to speak. So I don't know if it's slang or just the way kids speak.... I speak differently to my friends than I do to my parents. It's almost a whole different language, and...they don't teach us how to speak [French] that way.

The data recorded in this study certainly support the view, articulated here by Suzannah, that at least one reason why these older children may be switching to English may be that they need to use a vernacular 'kid-speak' with each other, and they do not have such a vernacular in the L2–only an L1 vernacular.

Obviously not all the English utterances recorded here are in such a vernacular, though many are. It is possible that more than one force may be at work to encourage these children to use English with one another. More systematic research is needed to investigate this possibility.

Acknowledgments

We would like to thank the staff, teachers and students of the Spanish immersion school we observed for their support and help. We are also grateful to Carol Klee for her input and to Helen Jorstad for her assistance with this study.

This study is funded by grants from the Department of Education and the University of Minnesota, and was carried out under the auspices of the Center for Advanced Research on Language Acquisition (CARLA), University of Minesota, Mpls 55455. The views and opinions expressed in this paper are those of the authors and do not reflect those of the funders, nor are they the official position of CARLA unless otherwise designated.

Notes

1. A language immersion program is a school program in which children are taught through the medium of the second language. French immersion programs predominate in Canada, while the US has set up immersion programs in Spanish, French and German, among others.

2. Nunan's (1991) review of the literature concludes, "little second language research is actually carried out in language classrooms, and ... we know comparatively little about what does or does not go on there" (p. 265).

3. Heitzman (1993) and Parker et al. (forthcoming) were focused on documenting the languages used in thinking by children in immersion programs. Occasional observations were made of the language overheard in those classrooms, but these observations were incidental to the main focus of the study and anecdotal in nature.

4. Ferguson (1959) first introduced the term "diglossia" to describe the situation that obtains in Arabic-speaking countries in which a local version of Arabic is learned at home as a first language, but a quite different variety, Standard Arabic, is learned at school and used exclusively in formal public situations. Fishman (1971:74) extends the term diglossia to include any society in which two or more languages are used under distinct circumstances as, for example, High and Low varieties.

5. Children learn to read in English in grade 2. They are given 30 minutes of English instruction per day in grade 2, 45 minutes in grade 3, 60 minutes in grade 4 and 90 minutes in grade 5.

6. The observers felt that they got better at accurately recording detailed utterances in both languages as the study progressed, so that the data on the three fifth-grade classes, which were recorded in the last three weeks of the observation period, contains a great deal more detail of which the observers are much more confident.

7. The length of time we were able to observe in each classroom varied. However, we were able to observe classes from second through fifth grade for a total of at least an hour and a half at each grade level. Thus, we are fairly confident that we had sufficient time at each grade level to use as a basis for comparison across grade levels.

8. Where two languages are listed in the table, the first language listed was produced more frequently by the children; hence, the entry "English/Spanish" means that more English than Spanish was used during the period of the observation. As noted previously, the notetaking methodology does not allow us to measure how much more English or Spanish was used in any given context; future studies using tape-recorded data will be needed for this purpose.

9. This particular girl was considered by her teachers to have an exceptionally good mastery of Spanish; her accurate use of the Spanish imperfect and preterit here certainly supports her teachers' view of her.

10. As noted above, the note-taking methodology does not allow us to measure *how much* more English vs. Spanish was used.

11. It is particularly interesting that for these third graders, teasing was done in Spanish. As we shall see, in the later grades, the tendency was to switch to English for this sort of student-student teasing, as in the interaction in (17) in the text.

12. There is evidence of cultural miscommunication in the example in (15) in the text. This teacher, who was from Spain, was being very direct, as is the norm in Spain, in informing the children of their misbehavior ("¡Muy mal!"). These American children, however, were used to a more 'positive' style of discipline (e.g., "No entiendo. Otra vez."). They clearly reacted very negatively to the teacher's comment here. Rampton (1987) documents a similar case of student refusal to accommodate to classroom language norms.

13. This is an exclamation which is almost always accompanied by a nonverbal arm gesture familiar to most Americans. The immersion children at this school have also been observed to use a direct 'translation' of the exclamation ("¡Sí!") into Spanish, accompanied by the same gesture. We suspect that native speakers of Spanish from other cultures would be mystified by this.

14. Helen Jorstad notes (personal communication) that in her obsrvations of immersion classrooms, it appears to be very common for students who are usually sitting at their desks and paying attention to speak Spanish. When they are allowed to relax, however, they get up, move around, switch to English, and increase the general energy level of the group.

References

Beebe, L. 1994. "Notebook Data on Power and the Power of Notebook Data". Paper at the TESOL Conference, Baltimore, Maryland, March 11, 1994.
Broner, J. 1991. "Report on Observations on the Use of Spanish at an Immersion School". Manuscript, University of Minnesota.
Heitzman, S. 1993. "Language Use in Full Immersion Classrooms: Public and private speech". Undergraduate Summa Thesis, University of Minnesota.
Labov, W. 1972. "The Linguistic Consequences of Being a Lame". *Language in the Inner City*, ed. by W. Labov, 255-292. Philadelphia: University of Pennsylvania Press.
Nunan, D. 1991. "Methods in Second Language Classroom-Oriented Research". *Studies in Second Language Acquisition* 13.249-274.
Parker, J., S. Heitzman, A. Fjerstad, L. Babbs & A. D. Cohen. Forthcoming. "Exploring the Role of Foreign Language in Immersion Education". To appear in *Second Language Acquisition Theory and Pedagogy*, ed. by F. Eckman, D. Highland, P. Lee, J. Mileham & R. Weber. Hillsdale, NJ: Lawrence Erlbaum.
Rampton, B. 1987. "Stylistic Variability and Not Speaking 'Normal' English". *Second Language Acquisition in Context*, ed. by R. Ellis, 47-58. London: Prentice-Hall.
Tarone, E. & M. Swain. 1995. "A Sociolinguistic Perspective on Second-Language Use in Immersion Classrooms". *Modern Language Journal* 79(2).24-46.

Some neurolinguistic evidence regarding variation in interlanguage use
The status of the 'switch mechanism'

Marjorie Perlman Lorch
Birkbeck College, University of London

In intercultural situations, interlanguage (IL) speakers may switch between their native language (NL) and IL and between various ILs depending on context and a variety of other factors (e.g., Selinker 1992). Little discussion has appeared in the literature which addresses the cognitive processes that subserve this behavior. Evidence from bilingual aphasia and neurolinguistic research can contribute to the way in which the cognitive description of the ability to switch between different language systems in spoken production must be developed in order to contribute to a comprehensive account of IL performance.

The term 'switching' is applied here in its broadest sense. The notion of code-switching is used to describe the performance of one or more speakers who shift between their various languages and ILs in listening and speaking, alternating between codes at the clause, sentence or discourse level or in response to situational or psycholinguistic constraints.

'Code-switching' is commonly employed in the bilingual literature to describe speakers and situations in which there is mixing or switching between more than one language (e.g., Grosjean 1982). Sociolinguists have demonstrated the range of social and situational variables which affect code-switching behavior and the concomitant linguistic constraints on producing utterances with language mixing (see Nishimura 1986; Gardner-Chloros forthcoming and references therein). Switching and mixing of languages in interlingual situations may be due to variability in target language (TL) competence reflected in re-emergence of production of fossilized forms in certain contexts or discourse domains (Selinker 1992).

The origin of the concept of a mechanism for switching between language systems lies in the realm of neurolinguistics.[1] The neurologist Wilder Penfield (1959) provided the modern formulation of the idea of

... [a] curiously effective automatic switch that allows each individual to turn from one language to another. What I have referred to as a 'switch' would be called, by experimental physiologists, a conditioned reflex. When child or adult turns to an individual who speaks only English, he speaks only English, and, turning to a man who speaks French and hearing a word of French, the conditioning signal turns the switch over and only French words seem to come to mind. (p. 253)

Penfield makes specific neurolinguistic claims, stating that

the [linguistic] mechanism that is developed in the brain is the same whether one, two or more languages are learned...the cortico-thalamic speech mechanism serves all... languages [known to the speaker] and there is no evidence of anatomical separation... (p. 253)

This neurolinguistic issue has obvious implications for patterns of bilingual aphasia as Penfield himself points out. He states that descriptions in the literature of bilingual aphasics who lost one language and preserved another as the result of a stroke must have been inadequately studied or be due to psychological (i.e., emotional rather than cognitive) reasons why one language was preferred during recovery.[2]

Penfield's shift from a neurological to psychological account for the ability or inability to switch between languages is unsatisfactory. Detailed descriptions of bilingual aphasia have been published throughout this century (see Paradis 1983) and a major monograph on the subject was produced by Albert and Obler in 1978. These authors detailed the variety of patterns exhibited by polyglot aphasics with respect to the language production and comprehension abilities in their two (or more) languages. More rigorously investigated recent cases of bilingual aphasia have continued to show patterns of differential recovery of one language over another. A case in point will be discussed in detail below.

Bilingual speakers who suffer neurological impairment to dominant perisylvian cortex have impaired language functions which are manifest in a variety of ways. Of the various possibilities for patterns of impairment in languages and ILs, most of the logically possible permutations have been described. These descriptions document patterns of impairment where the various languages are affected equally in degree and kind, and those where the languages are differentially affected: better or selective recovery of one of the languages, or even two different aphasia types (Albert and Obler 1978; Paradis 1977, 1983). The question that is often asked by neurolinguists is this: Is the differential or selective recovery sometimes seen in cases of bilingual aphasia an example of an impaired switch mechanism?

New evidence

A recently published case of bilingual aphasia (Aglioti and Fabbro 1993) may be interpreted as evidence of impairment to the 'switch mechanism'. The paper documents a case where L2 Italian, studied formally in school and to a fairly low level of proficiency, was the IL produced spontaneously by the patient in preference to her NL Venetan, which was her home language.[3] The patient produced her Italian IL preferentially, even when explicitly asked to speak her NL. She even produced her IL Italian in contexts where she knew that her listeners were monolingual Venetan speakers who could not understand it. In instances where she started off speaking in her NL Venetan, she would soon switch back to Italian IL, even in formal examinations where she was explicitly instructed only to speak Venetan.

This patient could be described as suffering from an impaired ability to switch to and from one of her two languages and maintain spoken production in a given language. What was significant about her impaired ability to produce language was that her choice of language was often inappropriate to a particular discourse context. She may be said to have lost what Penfield described as the "conditioned reflex" to switch to and produce the appropriate language for the context and conversational partner.

Models of language switching

Paradis (1989) has offered an explanation of bilingual performance, both normal and aphasic, which denies the need for some mechanism to account for language switching. In his activation model of language processing (based in part on Green 1986), Paradis posits the same cognitive form and neurological function for monolingual and bilingual speakers. In Paradis' model there is no switch mechanism dedicated to shifting between language systems. All differences seen in bilingual aphasics' language production and code-switching in normal bilingual and IL speakers are accounted for with reference to "inhibition" of a particular language process or store.

The most significant aspect of this model is the determination that the ability to switch between languages (and ILs) is considered to be cognitively and neurolinguistically identical to monolinguals' ability to shift between the various speech registers required in different discourse domains. The Venetan-Italian bilingual aphasic case described above would therefore be interpreted in Paradis' model as an example of an impairment in the ability to use the appropriate social language register in speech production.[4] However, a Paradis-type account is not consistent with the current neurolinguistic picture of aphasic production. The general characterization of aphasia based on the hundred year history of Western literature in language disorders does not include inappropriate use or failure to effectively modulate the social aspects of speech register (e.g., Goodglass 1993).

Patients with lesions restricted to the cortical dominant hemisphere language zone are not impaired in the use of and ability to switch between social registers. However, patients with lesions outside the cortical language zone, either in homologous areas of the right hemisphere or in proximity to the language zone, may demonstrate difficulties in producing socially appropriate language. Head Injury patients with fronto-limbic dysfunction often use inappropriately informal, joking or lewd language in formal contexts and may not be able to switch to an appropriate register even when explicitly requested to do so. Certain right hemisphere damaged patients have paralinguistic, pragmatic problems in their use of language as well (Code 1987).[5]

In addition, it has been reported that certain right (but not left) hemisphere damaged patients have difficulty expressing, in their language and tone, emotions appropriate to context (Borod et al. 1984). But patients of this type would not be classified as aphasic–that is, their central linguistic system and linguistic competence is intact.

Significantly, Aglioti and Fabbro's patient discussed above has a lesion located in a subcortical area adjacent to the classical left cortical language zone.[6] Note that one of the difficulties resulting from this lesion was the inability to maintain and switch appropriately between languages as context demanded. Monolingual patients with lesions in this area are not described as producing socially or pragmatically inappropriate language, but are in fact aphasic (Damasio et al., 1982).[7]

Evidence for the production of context-dependent language

There is neurolinguistic evidence, to be discussed below, which suggests that people's ability to know what particular language they are listening to is situated outside the left hemisphere cortical language zone, and that this ability is quite impervious to disruption from the kind of damage that leads to aphasia. There seems to be something very fundamental in auditory processing which enables people to discriminate whether they are hearing their own native language or another. In aphasic patients with severe auditory comprehension disorders, the ability to discriminate their native language from another language is preserved (Boller and Green 1972). The ability to discern which language is being spoken is preserved in these patients even though there is little demonstrable indication that they can extract any meaning from listening to their NL.

There is also evidence that determining which language one is being addressed in and producing that language in return may be dissociated. A polyglot aphasic who demonstrated an inability to produce speech in a specified language, producing spontaneous translations and language mixing, could always identify what language was being spoken to him even if he could not produce a response in that language (Perecman 1984). Indeed, he would often spontaneously produce language identity tags to repetitions of utterances.

Other aspects of primary auditory-verbal processing appear to have a different neurolinguistic status. Discrimination of emotional affect in voices conveyed by suprasegmental changes in pitch appears to be affected along with the comprehension and production of other context-sensitive aspects of communication by right hemisphere disruption (Borod et al. 1985).

The ability to identify a speaker and therefore to know with whom you are speaking has also been investigated. Van Lancker and Kreiman (1987) and Van Lancker, Kreiman and Cummings (1985) report that both non-aphasic right and aphasic left hemisphere brain damaged patients do poorly on voice discrimination and speaker identification tasks. While the normal control subjects found the task of unknown voice discrimination an extremely easy one, a study by Lorch and Meara (forthcoming) suggests that the task of unknown language discrimination is a relatively difficult one for monolingual subjects. Unknown language identification appears to be somewhat easier (Lorch and Meara 1989a; 1989b). The cognitive ability to apprehend aspects of the language context generally (and, indeed, which language you are hearing specifically) is still poorly understood.

Taken together, the evidence from normal and neurologically impaired subjects begins to build a picture of the complex organization of the multitude of auditory-verbal linguistic and cognitive processes implicated in listening to and producing languages and ILs. The notion of a unitary 'switch mechanism,' used to describe the speaker/hearer's variation in language performance in interlingual situations, is not supported by the evidence under review. Neurolinguistic evidence also fails to support models of language processing which treat switching between languages and switching between different social registers of one language in the same fashion.[8] The ability or inability to produce *gentleman* rather than *bum* does not appear to be neurolinguistically equivalent to the ability or inability to produce *homme* rather than *man*.

The conceptualization of this problem has crucial bearing on the larger issue of the nature of linguistic processes and their relation to other cognitive processes in IL systems which are sensitive to contextual information. The formulation of the modularity question for descriptions of the cognitive status of IL learning and use will ultimately need to be addressed. Neurolinguistic evidence can contribute to the understanding of the organization of contextually-based language production. The considerations of cases of variation in bilingual aphasic language production and psycholinguistic evidence of extralinguistic functions in normal monolingual subjects as described above can contribute to considerations of speakers' capacity to produce variation in interlingual contexts.[9] The simplistic notion of a 'switch mechanism' requires refinement and, especially in interlingual situations, may fractionate into distinct and separate (extra)linguistic functions.

Interlanguage 'switching'

In IL use, a form of switching can be considered to be inherent in spoken productions in non-native contexts. Phonological, lexical, morphological and syntactic selections occurring in 'on-line' language production are necessarily drawing on different NL and IL linguistic resources. The psycholinguistic implications of this ability clearly must be central to descriptions IL speakers' language behaviour. Variation in an invidividual's IL production will be modulated by factors of discourse domain and context (Selinker and Douglas 1985). If this general perspective proves empirically valid, how this range of IL genres is selected and switched between in the language production process requires a cognitive level of description. Only then will a comprehensive model of IL performance be obtained.

If both register switching and language switching can be described as being triggered by the perception of contextually based cues, then both will have direct implication for on-line linguistic processes–word choice, syntactic structure, phonological form, and so forth. What has to be explained then is why the neurolinguistic evidence should not reflect these parallels?

The currently considered models either (1) describe both language and register switching as internal to the language system (e.g., Paradis) or (2) place language switching between languages under the modulation of a 'switch mechanism' (e.g., Penfield). The aphasia evidence suggests that the neurolinguistic organization of the ability to draw on different language systems can be impaired centrally. In order to produce contextually sensitive speech, cognitive systems external to the central linguistic system are required. The notional 'switch mechanism' must be developed and refined. An explanatory account must include the complex interaction and integration of several distinct psycholinguistic processes: identifying which language is being spoken, accessing the appropriate lexicon and parser, and indeed knowing what language your listener knows and what the situation requires.

SOME NEUROLINGUISTIC EVIDENCE REGARDING VARIATION

Acknowledgments

An early form of this argument was presented at the meeting of the International Association of Logopedics and Phoniatrics Aphasia Committee Meeting, in Bordeaux, France, August 1994. The author wishes to thank Loraine Obler, Michel Paradis, Franco Fabbro, Valeria Daro, Yvan Lebrun, Louisa Springer, and Nina Dronkers for their comments, all of which contributed to the development of the ideas expressed here.

Notes

1. Earliest reports, which appeared in the German literature, are reviewed in Perecman (1984).

2. Aglioti & Fabbro (1993:1362) cite Poetzl (1930) as referring to an alteration in the switch mechanism being responsible for the permanent 'tuning' on one language only.

3. Though the authors do not use the concept of 'interlanguage,' it is clear from their report that the L2 behavior described can be interpreted in this manner.

4. The work of Jakobson (1956) on 'similarity disorders' and Goldstein (1948) on the impairment in the 'abstract attitude' reflected in some aphasic patients may be seen as possible precursors to this notion.

5. The case of Christopher, the 'Polyglot Savant' who has extrodinary language learning abilities while demonstrating severe cognitive limitations in all other intellectual domains (Smith & Tsimpli 1991, 1995), is also a germane demonstration of the dissociation between linguistic competence and extralinguistic functions. This developmentally disordered individual has attained remarkable linguistic performance in sixteen languages, which he flawlessly and rapidly translates into English, but he can not respond appropriately to non-literal meta-representational language meanings like cartoons and jokes.

6. The lesion is reported to be located in the left subcortical basal ganglia, an area dedicated to language motor programming.

7. The explanation given by Aglioti and Fabbro for their patient's difficulty is couched in terms of a distinction in implicit and explicit memory. They argue that access to implicit memory (i.e., one's NL) is controlled by the basal ganglia while explicit memory (i.e., formally acquired L2) is not.

8. Models discussed in this paper are only illustrative examples. There are numerous language processing models which include provision for switching in bilingual circumstances (see Green 1993).

9. The considerations raised here may parallel the debate on variation in interlanguage (see papers by Gregg 1990; Ellis 1990; Tarone 1990).

References

Albert, M. & L. Obler. 1978. *The Bilingual Brain*. New York: Academic.
Aglioti, S. & F. Fabbro. 1993. "Paradoxical Selective Recovery in a Bilingual Aphasic following Subcortical Lesions". *NeuroReport* 4.1359-1362.
Boller, F. & E. Green. 1972. "Comprehension in Severe Aphasics". *Cortex* 8.382-394.
Borod, J., E. Koff, M. [Lorch] Perlman & M. Nicholas. 1984. "Channels of Emotional Communication in Patients with Focal Lesions". Paper presented at the meeting of the International Neuropsychological Society, Houston, Texas.
Borod, J., E. Koff, M. [Lorch] Perlman & M. Nicholas. 1985. "Channels of Emotional Expression in Patients with Unilateral Brain Damage". *Archives of Neurology* 42.345-348.
Code, C. 1987. *Language, Aphasia and the Right Hemisphere*. Chicester: Wiley.
Damasio, A., H. Damasio, M. Rizzo, N. Varney & F. Gersh. 1982. "Aphasia with Nonhemorrhagic Lesions in the Basal Ganglia and Internal Capsule". *Archives of Neurology* 39.15-20.
Ellis, R. 1990. "A Response to Gregg". *Applied Linguistics* 11.384-392.
Gardner-Chloros, P. Forthcoming. "Code Switching in Community, Regional and National Repertoires: The myth of the discreteness of linguistic systems". To appear in *One Speaker, Two Languages* ed. by L. Milroy & P. Muysken. Cambridge: Cambridge University Press.
Goldstein, K. 1948. *Language and Language Disturbances*. New York: Grune and Stratton.
Goodglass, H. 1993. *Understanding Aphasia*. New York: Academic.
Gregg, K. 1990. "The Variable Competence Model of Second Language Acquisition and Why It Isn't". *Applied Linguistics* 11.364-384.
Green, D. 1986. "Control, Activation, and Resource: A framework and model for the control of speech in bilinguals". *Brain and Language* 27.210-223.
Green, D. 1993. "Towards a Model of L2 Comprehension and Production". *The Bilingual Lexicon* ed. by R. Schreuder & B. Weltens, 249-277. Philadelphia: John Benjamins.
Grosjean, F. 1982. *Life with Two Languages*. Cambridge, MA: Harvard.
Jakobson, R. 1956. "Two Aspects of Language and Two Types of Aphasic Disturbances". *Fundamentals of Language* ed. by R. Jakobson & M. Halle, 49-73. The Hague: Mouton.
Lorch, M. & P. Meara. 1989a. "How People Listen to Languages They Don't Know". *Language Sciences* 11.343-353.
Lorch, M. & P. Meara. 1989b. "What Makes a Language Easy to Recognize?" Manuscript, Birkbeck College, University of London.
Lorch, M. & P. Meara. Forthcoming. "Can People Discriminate Languages They Don't Know?" To appear in *Language Sciences*.

Nishimura, M. 1986. "Intrasentential Code-Switching: The case of language assignment". *Language Processing in Bilinguals* ed. by J. Vaid. Hillsdale, NJ: Lawrence Erlbaum.
Paradis, M. 1977. "Bilingualism and Aphasia". *Studies in Neurolinguistics* ed. by H. Whitaker & H. Whitaker, 3.65-121.
Paradis, M., ed. 1983. *Readings on Aphasia in Bilinguals and Polyglots*. Montreal: Didier.
Paradis, M. 1989. "Bilingual and Polyglot Aphasia". *Handbook of Neuropsychology* ed. by F. Boller & J. Grafman, 117-140. Amsterdam: Elsevier.
Penfield, W. 1959. "Epilogue–The learning of languages". *Speech and Brain-Mechanisms* ed. by W. Penfield & L. Roberts, 235-255. New York: Antheum.
Perecman, E. 1984. "Spontaneous Translation and Language Mixing in a Polyglot Aphasic". *Brain and Language* 23.43-63.
Poetzl, O. 1930. "Über die parietal bedingte Aphasie und ihren Einfluss auf die Sprecher mehrerer Sprachen". *Zeitschrift für die Gesamte Neurologie und Psychiatrie* 96.100-124.
Selinker, L. 1992. *Rediscovering Interlanguage*. New York: Longmans.
Selinker, L. & D. Douglas. 1985. "Wrestling with 'Context' in Interlanguage Theory". *Applied Linguistics* 6.190-24.
Smith, N. & I. Tsimpli. 1991. "Linguistic Modularity? A case study of a 'savant' linguist". *Lingua* 84.315-351.
Smith, N. & I. Tsimpli. 1995. *The Mind of a Savant*. Oxford: Blackwell.
Tarone, E. 1990. "On Variation in Interlanguage: A response to Gregg". *Applied Linguistics* 11.392-400.
Van Lancker, D. & J. Kreiman. 1987. "Voice Discrimination and Recognition are Separate Abilities". *Neuropsychologia* 25.829-834.
Van Lancker, D., J. Kreiman & J. Cummings. 1985. "Voice Recognition and Discrimination: New evidence for a double dissociation". *Journal of Clinical and Experimental Neuropsychology* 7.609.

Beyond 2000
A measure of productive lexicon in a second language

Batia Laufer
University of Haifa

Learning vocabulary means an increase in the vocabulary size

Second-language (L2) acquisition has often been described and discussed in terms of the learner's progress along the Interlanguage continuum, from almost a non-existent knowledge of L2 towards native-like competence, without necessarily reaching this level. By the same token, L2 vocabulary development can be regarded as a gradual approximation to the native speaker's lexical system. Such a process will entail qualitative and quantitative changes in the learner's lexicon. Whatever the importance of improving qualitative knowledge like the word's connotations, non-core meanings, or collocations, the obvious mark of progress in lexical development is in the increase in the learner's vocabulary size. It can hardly be disputed that the most striking difference between the vocabulary of native speakers and that of L2 learners, or between the vocabulary of beginners and that of advanced learners is in the number of words each one controls, particularly in free production. When learners are stuck for a word, or literally lost for words, it is not the case that a specific shade of meaning is unavailable to them. It is the word in its core meanings that is unknown. An example of the gap between the vocabulary of learners and that of native speakers is reflected in the following figures: Learners at the Cambridge FCE proficiency level, which is also the level of many high school graduates in English in the Western world, are supposed to know around 3000 lexical items. 18 year old native speakers of English are reported to know about 18 000 words, according to modest estimates (Nation 1990).

Examining vocabulary learning requires measuring the productive lexicon

If vocabulary learning means a gradual increase in the number of words in the learner's lexicon, then it is reasonable to expect L2 researchers to investigate this phenomenon. For example, it would be interesting to find out what conditions (of input, or learner) affect the growth or lack of growth of vocabulary size; whether the passive and the active vocabulary developments are related; whether there is some kind of ceiling beyond which active vocabulary size does not grow; what changes in lexical size occur during the language attrition process.

To answer these and similar questions, it is necessary to measure the productive lexicon of the subjects. The most popular measures used in the description of the productive lexicon are lexical variation, lexical originality, lexical density, lexical sophistication and the Giraud (1960) index. Other less frequently employed measures are semantic variation, lexical quality, t-unit length and error free t-unit length. Yet all these measures of lexical richness are seriously flawed as research tools as they can be demonstrated to lack validity, reliability, or both. (For a detailed criticism of lexical richness measures, see Laufer and Nation 1993, 1995). These problems with measuring the productive lexicon may explain the dearth of studies of lexical development.

Lexical Frequency Profile–a measure of productive vocabulary

Because of the above limitations of the various measures of productive vocabulary size, a different measure of lexical richness was devised: the Lexical Frequency Profile, hence LFP. The LFP shows the percentage of words that learners use at different vocabulary frequency levels in their writing, or put differently, the proportion of words from different frequency levels vis-à-vis one another. Given a composition consisting of 200 word types, the LFP is calculated as follows: If, among the 200 word types, 150 belong to the first 1000 most frequent words, 20 to the second 1000, 20 to the University World List (Xue Guoyi and Nation 1984), and 10 are not in any list, then we convert these numbers (the number of words at each frequency level) into percentages out of the total of 200 word types. The LFP of the composition is therefore 75%–10%–10% –5%. The entire calculation is done by a computer programme which matches vocabulary frequency lists with a text that has been typed into the computer. The programme can identify each word form as a member of a word family. A word family includes the word's base form, its inflections and the derivational affixes *-able, -er, -ish, -less, -ly, -ness, -th, -y, non-*, and *un-*. (For further discussion of word families, see Bauer and Nation 1993). Having matched the text with the word lists, the programme calculates the profile as described at the beginning of this section. Two profiles are calculated: one in terms of word families, as illustrated in the example above, and the other in terms of word forms.[1] The validity and reliability of LFP as a research tool were shown by Laufer and Nation (1993, 1995).

Beyond 2000—a more convenient measure

The LFP described above is a detailed profile, showing four types of words used by the learner. We can also use a condensed profile which will distinguish between the basic 2000 words and the 'beyond 2000' words. Such a profile is attained by adding up the first two word lists (the first and the second 1000 most frequent words) and by adding the last two lists (the University World List category and the 'not in the lists' category). In Laufer and Nation (1993), it was found that, like the detailed profile, the condensed profile was also reliable and valid. It remained stable in different compositions of the same learners, and it varied significantly across groups of learners at different levels of language proficiency. To avoid the possibility of changes in the profile due to text length, comparisons were carried out on compositions of approximately the same length. (Some preliminary results of the relationship between LFP and text length suggest that the profile is stable if the lenght is between 200 and 400 words. Definitive conclusions about sensitivity of the profile to text length have, however, not been reached yet). The advantage of the condensed profile over the detailed one is in facilitating cross-linguistic and correlational studies. Detailed word frequency lists are not available for all languages. Yet for a number of languages there are 'minimal dictionaries' or lists of the most frequent words from which the 2000 basic words can be extracted, as in the cases of Finnish and Hebrew. In Russian, a list of the 2000 most frequent words is available in Vogt (1970). Therefore, the description of lexical profile in terms of basic and beyond-basic vocabulary makes it possible to compare profiles of the same subjects using different languages. In addition, if we have one measure rather than several, which numerically expresses the lexical richness of a composition, we can correlate it with other variables like passive vocabulary size, grades on a test, and so on. The single measure expressing the lexical richness in free production could be the percentage of the beyond-2000 words in the learner's sample.

Using the 'beyond 2000' measure

Several studies have been undertaken in which active vocabulary was measured by the condensed profile. I will briefly describe how this profile was used in these studies. (The profile referred to shows the relative percentages of word families at different frequency levels).

The effect of comprehension-based instruction on active vocabulary

The purpose of the study was to find out whether there would be an increase in active vocabulary as a result of comprehension-based instruction. Learners that were examined participated in a course of English for academic reading in which language input consisted of reading comprehension of academic texts. Vocabulary was explicitly taught, but for comprehension purposes only. There was hardly any active use of language during class time. The subjects were 37 adult learners of English as a foreign language from the Haifa Institute of Science and Technology. Their first language (L1) was Hebrew and their level of English was a rough equivalent of the Cambridge First Certificate of English. At the beginning of the experiment, all the learners were given the Levels Test of passive vocabulary size (Nation 1983) and were also asked to write a composition entitled 'How important is science to the modern world?' This topic was chosen as it was of interest to the students tested. A composition on a different topic would have produced a similar lexical profile as neither the LFP measure, nor the 'beyond 2000' measure are sensitive to the subject matter of the learner's writing.[2] The compositions were analysed by condensed profiles, that is, in terms of the basic 2000 words and beyond 2000 words. The same tests were repeated at the end of the semester.

Table 1 shows the group means of the passive vocabulary and the mean lexical profiles of compositions at the two testing points. The conclusion of the study was that teaching vocabulary for comprehension will result in an increase in the passive vocabulary, but this increase will not affect the growth of the productive lexicon.[3]

Lexical attrition in immigrants' mother tongue

The study attempted to determine whether different sociolinguistic factors pertaining to the use of English and Russian in Israel would result in different lexi-

Table 1: Passive and active vocabulary change (n=37)

	vocabulary size (passive) mean	sd	percent beyond 2000 words (active) mean	sd
pretest	3000	637	11.6	3.9
post-test	3300	752	11.1	4.2
difference	t=2.30, p=.03		not significant	

cal change patterns in these languages as spoken by old immigrants to Israel. Two groups of immigrants were compared. One group consisted of native speakers of Russian, the other of native speakers of English. Both groups left their country of origin in their mid twenties or early thirties and have been living in Israel for about 20-25 years. All subjects completed at least secondary education in their countries of origin and are now middle class professionals. The two groups wrote a composition in their L1. The Russian group wrote about the problems facing the new immigrants to Israel, the English group had to argue for or against the government's right to control family size. For purposes of comparison, two groups of young *new* immigrants, speakers of Russian (age 20-25) and speakers of English (age 18), were given the same compositions, respectively. All of the compositions were analysed in terms of basic and beyond 2000 vocabulary. Even though Russian and English morphologies differ from each other (Russian words are heavily inflected), the beyond 2000 measure is not likely to produce very different profiles for the two languages. This is so because it describes the vocabulary in terms of percentages of word families, not word forms. Therefore, *girl* and *girls* are counted as one 'word' for English, and the 10 forms of the Russian equivalent *djevochka* (5 different case forms in singular and 5 in plural) are also counted as one 'word'.

Table 2 presents the comparison of the new and the old immigrants in the two L1 groups. The results showed that the two languages, English and Russian exhibited different patterns of lexical change, probably due to the differences in the opportunities of the two immigrant groups to use their respective mother tongue, the degree of readiness to maintain it and the different status each language has in Israel.[4]

Table 2: New and old immigrants' lexis by percentage of beyond 2000 words

	Russian			English		
	n	mean	sd	n	mean	sd
new immigrants	10	21	3.57	10	19	6.05
old immigrants (20 years in Israel)	11	13	5.17	26	21	12
difference	t=5.82, p=.01			not significant		

Progress in the lexical richness of advanced learners

The first stage of the study attempted to determine whether there would be a significant increase in the productive lexicon of advanced second language learners' writing over a period of one academic year. The subjects in the study were 48 first-year university students in the Department of English Language and Literature, speakers of Hebrew or Arabic as L1. During the first year of study, the learners take twelve to sixteen hours of language courses in English language and literature per week with a variety of teachers, most of whom are native speakers of English. New vocabulary input is received through listening to lectures and through the reading material assigned by teachers. All of the learners took an entrance exam to the department in which they wrote a composition. In this composition, they were asked to argue for or against one of the following statements. (Their choice was kept on record in the department).

a. A person cannot be poor and happy, because money is always needed to gain something that is important to that person.
b. It is always what you do not have as a child that is important to you as an adult.
c. In a free country, industry has the right to develop any product that will sell, and sell it to anyone who can pay for it.

At the end of the first semester (14 weeks of intensive study), 23 students were asked to write the same composition again; at the end of two semesters (28 weeks), the remaining 25 students were given the composition of the entrance exam.

Table 3 shows the changes in the lexical richness in the compositions of the two groups. As the table shows, the percentage of beyond 2000 words has increased significantly in the two groups. This increase may look like an indication of the learners' progress in productive vocabulary. The important question, however, is how the learners' lexis compares with the lexis of the native speakers' argumentative writing. The attrition study described in the previous section (see

Table 3: Changes in lexical richness as percentage of beyond 2000 words

	entrance exam mean sd	post-test mean sd	difference
Group 1 *(n=23)*	9.96 6.2	13.17 5.85 (after one semester)	t=2.76, p=.01
Group 2 *(n=25)*	8.48 3.87	10.04 3.49 (after two semesters)	t=2.27, p=.03

Table 2) showed that 18 year old English native speakers, newcomers to Israel used, 19% of beyond 2000 words and old immigrants 21%. Furthermore, an LFP analysis of several texts in a standard reader for academic purposes (the texts were written by scholars, dealt with general subjects and had the style of argumentative prose) revealed that the percentage of beyond 2000 words in such writing was as high as 35%. When we compare these figures with our learners' performance, we can see that the progress in lexical size which was found in our study, though statistically significant, does not look very impressive from the perspective of vocabulary learning. If the ultimate goal of L2 learning is near-native competence, then our learners' journey is far from being over.

In the second stage of the study, we have been looking at the lexicon of more advanced learners in the English department, who are in their second and third years of study and also MA students, that is, in their fourth or fifth year in the department. The data, which is still being collected, should show if and when the active lexicon of L2 learners reaches a level similar to that of a native speaker.

Conclusion

In this paper, it was argued that vocabulary acquisition is reflected first and foremost in the increase in the learner's vocabulary size. Therefore, research in vocabulary acquisition has to resort to measures of vocabulary size, particularly the size of the active lexicon. It was suggested that a possible measure of the active lexicon could be the percentage of non-basic words used in a sample of the learner's language, namely, words that are not among the 2000 most frequent words in language, hence the name of the instrument, 'beyond 2000'. Examples of studies were given to show how the 'beyond 2000' measure was used to investigate some important issues in vocabulary: the extent of growth in active vocabulary over periods of time; the extent of lexical attrition; the relationship between particular input and lexical change; the lexical differences between different groups, speakers of the same language; differences between similar groups, speakers of different languages. It is hoped that use of the 'beyond 2000' measure will contribute to finding additional answers to much needed research in vocabulary development.

Acknowledgments

Some of the data discussed in this paper were collected by my students. I am grateful to Ms. Aliza Bar-Shlomo for collecting the data for the 'input study' and to Ms. Edna Collins for the English data in the 'attrition study'.

Notes

1. In the word families profile, the percentage of the most frequent words is lower than in the word tokens profile since all instances of the same word, i.e., its inflected forms and its derivations, are counted as one occurrence.

2. This is true for subjects of a general nature. A topic that requires a highly specialized vocabulary might yield a different profile. Such topics should be avoided in studies of general vocabulary knowledge and acquisition.

3. In the original study, the changes in the composition profiles were also checked for each student. Out of 37 learners, 9 progressed (i..e, received a higher percentage of beyond 2000 on the post-test), 3 showed no change in the profile and 25 deteriorated (i.e., a lower percentage of the beyond 2000 words at the end of the semester than at the beginning). These results corroborated the 'no progress' results reported in Table 1.

4. In the original study, there was an additional group of Russian immigrants who had lived in Isreal for 10 years. These did not exhibit patterns of attrition in lexical richness.

References

Bauer, L. & I. S. P. Nation. 1993. "Word Families". *International Journal of Lexicography* 6.253-279.

Giraud, P. 1960. *Principes et Mèthodes de la Statistique Linguistique*. Paris: P.U.F.

Laufer, B. & I. S. P. Nation. 1993. "Lexical Richness in L2 Written Production: Can it be measured?" Paper presented at the 10th Congresss of the International Association of Applied Linguistics. Amsterdam.

Laufer, B. & I. S. P Nation. 1995. "Vocabulary Size and Use: Lexical richness in L2 written production". *Applied Linguistics* 16(3).307-322.

Nation, P. 1983. "Testing and Teaching Vocabulary". *Guidelines* 5.12-24. (RELC supplement)

Nation, I. S. P. 1990. *Teaching and Learning Vocabulary*. Rowley, MA: Newbury House.

Xue Guoyi & I. S. P. Nation. 1984. "A University Word List". *Language Learning and Communication* 3/2.215-229.

Vogt, H. O. 1970. *Ryskans Centrala Ordförrad*. Lund: Språkförlaget.

A first crosslinguistic look at paths
The difference between end-legs and medial ones

Háj Ross
University of North Texas

Introduction: Basic features of paths

The present paper aims at a broad-brush characterization of some of the basic features of paths, those macro-constituents which specify the route through spaces of various sorts which is traversed by the Theme of a sentence, the fundamental notion introduced to theoretical linguistics through the work of Jeffrey Gruber (see Gruber 1976). Themes are the constituents which move, prototypically through three-dimensional space. Thus the Theme of (1) is the first-person pronoun *I* ; the path along which this Theme moves starts with the word *from*, and ends with the last word of the sentence.

(1)   Path

(Theme) V (Source)(Trajectory) (Direction) (Extent) (Speed) (Extent) (Goal) (Mode)
I traveled from LA along Rt. 1 northwards 450 miles at 60 all the way to SF on foot.

To give some idea of how large paths can turn out to be, I have presented here quite an elaborate one. In fact, paths are in principle unbounded, since a path can include any number of Trajectories: *along Route 1 past the church through the woods under the overpass* .... I have included in (1) two constituents of paths whose grammar will not concern us in this note; Speed and Mode do not occur in all types of path, and I will not discuss their idiosyncrasies further. Stripped down to its essentials, a path starts with at most one Source, and ends with at most one Goal, though either or both of these can also be elided in context, as we see in sentences like *They flew from NY to DC and we drove Ø Ø*. Trajectories, which specify the points through which the Theme passes en route from Source to Goal, are usually iterable and optional; I will not here go into cases in which all of these loose generalities about path structure fail to hold up (such as cases of individual lexical items which either require or exclude one or more types of subconstituents in their paths).

Furthermore, I will not be concerned with the many problems involved in determining the conditions under which it makes sense to talk of Themes in cases in which the concept of motion has been extended to predicates which transact in semantic fields that are far removed from three-space. I offer the examples in (2), in which I have italicized the Themes, as a starter kit for the interested reader to begin with; Dowty (1991) and Langacker (1987) provide an in-depth look at the subtleties surrounding this fascinating area.

(2) a. *Bonnie* went to the races.
 b. I threw *pieces of ham* to the barracudas.
 c. *Janet* turned green.
 d. We gave *our 30-30s* to Connie.
 e. Melchior learned *multivariate analysis* from Duane.
 f. Sharon revealed to Hunter *that she was his control*.

I note in passing that the most obvious extension of spatial paths is to the dimension of time. Thus in a sentence like (3) below, it is clear that we are dealing with a path through time; the most probable candidate for the Theme which undergoes the journey is the action of working itself, hence the italics.

(3)   Path
    ┌───┐
   Verb (Source)   (Trajectory)   (Extent) (Extent) (Direction?) (Goal)
   I worked from 9:00 through the morning 5 hours all the way up   to 2:00

It can be argued that paths can profitably be viewed as sequences of Legs, as specified by the rules in (4).

(4) a. Path   → (Leg)   +   Leg^n +   Leg,   n≥0
               [+initial]   [+medial]   [+final]

 b. Leg   → (Extent) (Speed) (Direction) (PP)

 c. Extent → *for* + NP$_{measure}$ (e.g., *for 2 miles / hours / degrees / yen*, etc.)

 c. Extent → *all the way / 5/16 of the way / partway / halfway*, etc.

 d. Speed → *at* + NP$_{measure}$ + *per* NP$_{time}$ (e.g., *miles / degrees / bankruptcies,*
                                        etc. *per hour / century / ice age*, etc.)

 e. Direction → *towards the farms / eastwards*, etc.

Further rules will specify that the prepositions in the PPs of initial and final Legs are *from* and *to*, respectively, and the the prepositions in the PPs of medial legs can be drawn from the (partial) set in (5).

A FIRST CROSSLINGUISTIC LOOK AT PATHS

(5) *Some spatial and temporal medial prepositions*
above, across, after, along, around, before, behind, below, beneath, beside, between, by, during, in, near, on, over, past, since, through, toward(s), under, underneath, upon ...

It is of course possible to reorder the Legs of (most) paths; thus reduced forms of (1) could appear as any of the sentences in (6).

(6) a. I traveled from LA to SF along Route 1.
 b. I traveled to SF from LA along Route 1.
 c. I traveled to SF along Route 1 from LA.
 d. I traveled along Route 1 from LA to SF .
 e. I traveled along Route 1 to SF from LA.

I will not go further into the phrase structure of paths, except to note that there is evidence to support my claim that paths are constituents. As we see in (7) below, they can be clefted, a process which can only apply to constituents. (In (7-10) below, I will contrast examples of simple paths with a sequence of two unrelated PPs, showing that only the path-examples pass muster as constituents.)

	Paths	*Non-paths*
(7)	It was from LA to SF that we drove.	*It was to Ed about grapes that we spoke.

Furthermore, paths can be the focus of *only* (see (8a)), of *even* (cf. 8b)), and of *also* (see (8c)), behaviors which Cooper and I argue to also be restricted to constituents (Ross and Cooper 1979).

		Paths	*Non-paths*
(8)	a.	Only from LA to SF will we drive.	*Only to Ed about grapes will we speak.
	b.	Even from LA to SF we drove.	*Even to Ed about grapes we spoke.
	c.	Also from LA to SF we drove.	*Also to Ed about grapes we spoke.

Similarly, in (9) below, I show that paths can appear as either *X* or *Y*, in expressions of the form *not X, but Y*, another environment which is indicative of constituency.

	Paths	*Non-paths*
(9) a.	Not from LA to SF but from NY to NH did we drive.	*Not to Ed about grapes but to Sal about about kiwis did we speak.

Finally, in (10), we see that paths can be conjoined by *both ... and ...*, a kind of conjoining which is also limited to constituents.

	Paths	*Non-paths*
(10)	We drove both from LA to SF and from NY to NH.	*We spoke both to Ed about grapes and to Sal about kiwis.

The utility of paths

Now that we have examined briefly the constituent structure of paths, let us proceed to see of what further utility it may be to postulate the existence of such nodes. What can be described with the help of the node path which could not be said without it, aside from the phenomena in (7-10) that we have just examined?

Here, There and *Everywhere; Now* and *Then* and *Sometime*

First, an obvious point: Spatial and temporal deictics (namely, *here / there* and *now / then*) can occur in any leg of a path, but not in non-paths–see (11).

(11) a. We are headed toward Moscow / toward there.
 b. We are friendly toward Moscow / *toward there.
 c. He retreated through the cornfield / through there.
 d. He succeeded through his inside knowledge of lard prices / *through there.
 e. Dr. Skritch put his patient under the awning / under there.
 f. Dr. Skritch put his patient under ether / *under there.
 g. They were completely sozzled by last Monday / by then.
 h. They will be horrified by last Monday / *by then.

In (12) below, I have indicated that a PP is a part of a path by underlining that PP; immediately after the example in question I indicate whether the PP is in an initial, a medial, or a final leg. The examples in (12) are all of spatial paths, while those of (13) are all of temporal ones.

(12) a. They drove *from Texarkana / from there*. [initial]
 b. We ran *past Baskin-Robbins / past there*. [medial]
 c. They retreated *to Mervyn's / to there* in disarray. [final]

(13) a. Mildred has lived in DC *since 1884 / since then*. [initial]
 b. We worked *past noon / past then*. [medial]
 c. We stayed drunk *till Monday / till then*. [final]

But now, an unexpected wrinkle: There is a systematic difference between 'end-legs'–that is, initial and final legs–and medial legs, with respect to the adverbial question-words *where* and *when*. Although spatial and temporal deictics can appear anywhere in a path, *where* and *when* can only occur in 'end-legs'–they are systematically excluded in medial legs, as we see in (14) and (15).

(14) a. Frieda hopped   from the conduit.
   from there.
   from it.
  b. Where did Frieda hop from?
  c. Who hopped from where?   *from* = P_{end}

  d. Frieda hopped   along the conduit.
   along there.
   along it.
  e. *Where did Frieda hop along?
  f. *Who hopped along where?   *along* = P_{medial}

  g. Frieda hopped   to the conduit.
   to there.
   to it.
  h. Where did Frieda hop to?
  i. Who hopped to where?   *to* = P_{end}

(15) a. Since when has Frieda been working?   *since* = P_{end}
  b. *Past when will Frieda work?   *past* = P_{medial}
  c. Until when will Frieda work?   *until* = P_{end}

It turns out that it is not only these two question words that are excluded from medial legs; more generally, what is excluded as the object of P_{medial} is not merely adverbial Wh-words, but all non-specific adverbial indefinites–spatial indefinites like *everywhere, nowhere, somewhere, anyplace, someplace,* and *places*; and temporal indefinites like *sometime*, etc., as we see in (16), where grammatical versions with end-prepositions are followed by ungrammatical ones with medial prepositions.

(16) a. Planes were flying from everywhere / *through everywhere.
  b. I fear that students may be escaping to / *past somewhere.
  c. I don't think that he will be sailing from /*along anyplace tonight.
  d. I don't like kids leaping (from places / *through places) in the dark.
  e Shipments will be arriving until sometime tonight / *past sometime tonight.

I will defer attempting an explanation of these asymmetries until later in the exposition. Even without an explanation for them, however, it is clear that such facts as those in (11-13) fall out naturally under an analysis which distinguishes prepositions in paths from those that are not in them.

On right, *and vice versa*

The phenomena presented in the previous section above may at first seem to be merely a reformulation of a distinction that is hoary with grammatical age–that between spatial/temporal PPs and homophonous PPs which have nothing to do with places or times. But I think that the end-preposition/medial-preposition asymmetry, with respect to non-specific adverbial indefinites, already shows that there is a deeper connection between spatial and temporal expressions than is generally held to obtain. The facts to be examined in the present section, which concern the adverb *right*, will strengthen this conclusion.

At the deepest level, the adverb *right* is a left adjunct of PPs–but only of PPs in paths, and most productively, of PPs in spatial paths. Thus observe what happens when *right* is inserted into the sentences from (11) above. I give the results below in (11').

(11') a. We are headed (right) toward Moscow / (right) toward there.
 b. We are friendly (*right) toward Moscow / *(*right) toward there.
 c. He retreated (right) through the cornfield / (right) through there.
 d. He succeeded (*right) through his inside knowledge of lard prices / *(*right) through there.
 e. Dr. Skritch put his patient (right) under the awning / (right) under there.
 f. Dr. Skritch put his patient (*right) under ether / * (*right) under there.
 g. They were completely sozzled (*right) by last Monday / (*right) by then.
 h. They will be horrified (*right) by last Monday / * (*right) by then.

A few words of explanation are in order. The fact that *there* can occur in (11a, c, e) argues that the *toward*-phrase, the *through*-phrase, and the *under*-phrase are parts of paths, that is, that they are spatial in nature. By contrast, the corresponding PPs in (11b, d, f) are not in paths, and thus cannot contain there. So far, so good, so far no surprises. But note that where *there* is possible, there *right* can be a premodifier of the PP which can contain *right*, and where *right* cannot be inserted, *there*ing is also impossible. '*Right*ability' parallels '*there*ability'.

However, when we examine the temporal path in (11g), we see that the parallel breaks down, because it is not all temporal prepositional phrases that can be modified by *right*. As far as I know, the only ones that can be are those headed by *after, at, before, past, till, until* and perhaps *from ... on*–see (17).

(17) a. The glove compartment melted (right) after / (right) at / (right) before 12:13.
 b. We worked (?right) past noon / (?*right) past then.
 c. Tila wants to work (?right) till 4:36 / (??right) till January.
 d. You can stay here (right) until then.
 e. Let's keep our checkbook balanced (??right) from 2AM on / (*right) from then on.

The adverb *right* can modify *there*'s (and *then*'s) which are the objects of P_{end}–but not those which are the objects of P_{medial}–see (18).

(18) a. Frieda hopped [from (right) there].
  b. Frieda hopped [along (*right) there].
  b'. [Along (*right) there] hopped Frieda.
  c. Jason may be able to sneak up [to (right) here].
  d. Jason may be able to sneak up [past (*right) here].
  e. I can work here [from (right) then] to suppertime.
  f. I won't work [after / before / past (*right) then].
  g. OK – I'll work [until [(right) then] after all.

These facts would be accounted for if it could be argued that there are different sources for the *there*'s which follow medial prepositions, and the *there*'s which follow end-prepositions. I believe that this is exactly the right approach, as will emerge from the following discussion of superficial sequences of prepositions.

Note that while we find surface sequences of prepositions which start with end-prepositions (as in *leap from under the bed* and *retreat to behind the tree*), such sequences are impossible when they start with medial prepositions–see (19).

(19) a. (*Through) under the fence dashed the terrified mouse.
  b. (*Past) behind the tree scooted the canny janitor.

When we add to these observations that fact that *right* can modify the PPs which can follow end-prepositions, as in (20),

(20) a. Midge leapt from (right) under the bed.
  b. The canny janitor ran over to (right) behind the tree.

we are led to investigate the possibility that the *there* that follows end-prepositions might somehow be derived from a PP, while the *there*'s that follow medial prepositions would not be so derived.

In particular, the preposition that I posit as preceding words like *there* in the deep structure of end-legs is *at*. However, since such sequences as those in (21) are ungrammatical,

(21) *at there, *at here, *at now, *at then, *at everywhere, *at when, etc.

it appears that we must formulate some rule to delete this *at*, in an environment which I will not attempt to formalize for the present. That will thus mean that the deep structure of *from there* will be [*from* [*at there*]$_{PP}$]$_{PP}$. Then the fact that *from right there* is possible will be traceable back to the fact that a *there* after an end-preposition like *from* was originally a PP–the prototypical modifiee of *right*. By contrast, the *there* in a sentence like (22) will derive from a plain NP, one which is in a spatial context, and which therefore can be pronominalized with the adverbial proform *there*, though this proform cannot be modified by *right*.

(22) If you want me to drop you off at the bank, I can, because I'll be driving past (*right) there.

Let me summarize here by presenting a schematic outline of what I have proposed thus far.

(23) a. *Anaphoric processes*: These produce (or license, depending on your theoretical frame of mind) definite proforms like *she, he, it, they* in NPs which are not part of paths, and also adverbial proforms like *there* and *then* in paths, after all prepositions, end-prepositions, medial prepositions, *at*–anything spatial or temporal. Thus such forms as the following will be produced/licensed: *from at there, until at then, through there, past then*

b. *At* Zap–the offending body (*at*) will be gotten rid of.

But what then of the contrast between the sentences in (24)?

(24) a. Myron moved the thundermug from under the bed to the closet.
b. Myron moved the thundermug from the bed to the closet.

Are we going to say that *from* sometimes has PP objects, and other times NPs? The answer here is no: *from* will always have a PP following it–in the case of (24b), the missing preposition is *at*, which we can see the need for from such sentences as those in (25).

(25) a. Myron moved the thundermug from right under the bed to the closet.
b. Myron moved the thundermug from *(right) at the bed to the closet.

In other words, *from* will always be followed by a PP, never by an NP, while medial prepositions, like *past, along*, and *through*, will always be followed by plain, non-prepositional NPs. But then what will be necessary to block *(25b'), in which there is no *right*?

(25) b'. *Myron moved the thundermug from at the bed to the closet.

What we need here is another rule which deletes *at*, but this time in a different environment–when *at* immediately follows an end-preposition, with nothing like *right* or *down* or any other adverb to keep the prepositions *from* and *to* separate from the *at* which heads the PP that I posit as the deep object of end-prepositions.[1]

In the above section, I have sketched some of the processes in which elements of paths are involved, processes which differentiate them from plain NPs, NPs which have nothing to do with either space or time. A fundamental observation in the discussion was the fact that not all prepositions in paths are equal–some are more equal than others. Things can happen at the beginnings and ends of paths that cannot happen in their middles.

Differences between P_{end} and P_{medial} in Portuguese and German

My understanding of paths is highly tentative, and I have only begun to compare how paths behave in English with the way that they behave in other languages. Nonetheless, I think that the distinction between end-prepositions and medial prepositions that we have seen for English may well be widespread. Let us briefly examine some facts from Brasilian Portuguese and German.

First, in (26) and (27) below, we see a distinction between the end-preposition *de* 'from' and the Brasilian medial preposition *por*, whose basic meaning is 'through'. A simple sentence is shown in (26a); note that there, the *da* represents a contraction of the preposition *de* and the feminine definite singular article, *a*. A Brasilian adverbial proform, *lá*, which corresponds roughly to *there*, can stand for *a casa* 'the house', as we see in (26b). In (26c), we see that the object of *de* can be the phrase headed by *dentro*, which translates roughly as '(the) inside (of)'. Since *dentro* is a spatial word, if it is modified by a spatial phrase like *da casa* 'of the house' as in (26c), the adverbial proform *lá* can replace *a casa*, as we see in (26d).

What happens now is opaque to me; I do not yet know whether it is correct to maintain that (26d) can be converted into (26e) by fronting the *lá* and obliterating the stranded *de* after *dentro* (which would yield the desired result), nor whether it is correct to postulate another rule that will front the whole PP *de lá*, thus converting (26d) to (26f). What is fairly certain is that with an end-preposition like *de* 'from' [and exactly parallel facts could be adduced for *para* 'to'], there are two 'permuted' versions–(26e) and (26f).

(26) a. Yara saiu da casa. Yara left from the house
    b.   de lá.   Yara left from there
    c.   de dentro da casa.   Yara left from inside of-the house
    d.   de dentro de lá.   Yara left from inside of there
    e.   lá de dentro.   Yara left from inside of there
    f.   de lá de dentro.   Yara left from inside of there

By contrast, when we make the nearly minimal change of substituting the medial preposition *por* 'through', for *de*, we find that there is only one permuted version possible, as we see in (27), immediately below. I have no good account of the syntactic mechanisms which would produce these observed differences, but it does seem significant that we seem to find the same contrast between end-preposition and medial preposition, again, with the end-preposition having more freedom than the medial one does.

(27) a. Yara foi pela [= *por* + *a*] casa.　　Yara went through-the house
　　b.　　　 por lá.　　　　　　　　　　Yara went through there
　　c.　　　 por dentro da casa.　　　　　Yara went through inside of-the house
　　d.　　　 por dentro de lá.　　　　　　Yara went through inside of there
　　e.　　　 lá por dentro.　　　　　　　Yara went through inside of there
　　f.　　　 (*por) lá por dentro.　　　　Yara went through inside of there

Moreover, we find a contrast between *de* and *por* that is cognate to the one pointed out for end-prepositions and medial ones in English: Only the former type can have non-specific indefinite adverbial objects, as we saw in (14) and (15) above, which should be compared with the sentences in (28) below.

(28) a. Yara saiu de algum lugar.　　　　Yara left from someplace.
　　b. Yara foi por algum lugar.　　　　Yara went someplace.
　　　　　　　　　　　　　　　　　　　　[Impossible with the expected meaning of 'Yara went through someplace']

In (28a), we see that *de* can have non-specific indefinite adverbial objects. By contrast, (28b) shows us a sentence which is grammatical, but only with *por* in a different sense, that of 'to'. Since it would be an end-preposition on that sense, it does not surprise us that (28b) is grammatical–it is irrelevantly grammatical. What is important about (28b), however, is the fact that in it, *por* cannot be heard as a medial preposition. Thus again, we find the end/medial contrast within Brasilian Portuguese.

In German, we find that the two end-prepositions, *von* 'from' and *bis* 'to', can be followed by two adverbial pronouns, *dort* and *da*, both of which mean 'there'. The German process which converts a locative PP like *unter der Brücke* 'under the bridge' if the object has been pronominalized (which would yield an expected **unter ihr* 'under it') into *darunter* 'thereunder' will not work at all with *bis*, and there are restrictions with *von* which I have no understanding of. If the rule which forms *darunter* worked unrestrictedly for *von*, we would get sentences like those in (30), but they are worse than merely odd.

(29) a. Klaus ging von dort / von da.　　Klaus went from there.
　　b. Klaus ging bis dort / bis da.　　 Klaus went to there.
　　c. *Klaus ging dabis.　　　　　　　Klaus went thereto [= (to) there].
　　d. ?Klaus ging davon.　　　　　　　Klaus went therefrom [= from there].

(30) a. Anna fiel　 vom　　Bett, und Hannes fiel　 vom　 Bett / *davon auch.
　　　 Ann fell from-the　bed,　 &　 Jack　 fell from-the bed / ?* therefrom too.

　　b. Von Berlin /　**Davon bis Potzhaufen liefen wir 6 Stunden.
　　　 From Berlin / there-from to Potzhaufen we walked for 6 hours

By contrast, when we examine German medial prepositions like *durch* 'through' and *um* 'around', we find that neither *dort* nor *da* can follow them, and that they must undergo the inversion rule that produces forms like *darunter*–see (31) and (32).

(31) a. *Klaus ging durch dort / da. Klaus went through there.
     b. Klaus ging dadurch.   Klaus went through there.

(32) a. Wir fuhren um   den Teich / **um da / **um dort.
        We drove around the pond /   around there.
     b. Wir fuhren darum.

Finally, the same impossibility of following medial prepositions in English and Brasilian with non-specific indefinite adverbial NPs manifests itself in German, as we can see in (33).

(33) a. Die 747s fliegen von nirgends.   The 747s are flying from nowhere.
                           irgendwo.   somewhere.
     b.*Die 747s fliegen durch nirgends.   *The 747s are flying through nowhere.
                           *irgendwo.   somewhere.
     c. Von wo fliegen die 747s?   From where are the 747s flying?
     d. *Durch wo fliegen die 747s?   *Through where are the 747s flying?

Conclusions

To sum up, I have tried to give a brief sketch of some salient properties of English paths, demonstrating that one of the interesting distinctions therefrom, namely, that between end-prepositions and medial ones, seems to crop up in Brasilian Portuguese and German. Importantly, in all three languages, the *direction of difference* is always the same: End-prepositions have more degrees of freedom than do medial prepositions.

Let me end by following a speculative train of thought. I will begin by asking why–*why* should end-legs have more syntactic fun? I believe that the answer must be that ends are unmarked *vis-à-vis* middles. There are many hints that there is a markedness differential here: Typically, in the languages I have looked at, at least, end-prepositions are phonetically shorter than most medial prepositions. Furthermore, they undergo reduction rules more than do medial prepositions: *from* [fəm] *Boston* vs. *past* [*pəst] *Boston*; *to* [tə] *Maine* vs. *through* [*θrə] *Maine*.

Moreover, while end-prepositions are rarely polymorphemic, medial prepositions often are: *a+cross, a+round, a+long, pas+t*; German *ent+lang* 'along'; Brasilian *ao longo de* [=to-the long of] 'along'. Furthermore, while there are contexts in which it is required to specify some end-leg, I know of no contexts in which it is required to specify a medial one–see (34).

(34) a. From LA (along the coast) to SF is 450 miles.
 b. ?To SF is 450 miles.
 c. *From LA is 450 miles.

There are verbs whose semantics seems to be able to include *from* [e.g., *leave (from) Arkansas, depart (from) Dallas-Fort Worth*] and *to* [e.g., *reach (to) the top of the cabinet*], but I believe it is rarer for verbs to include medial concepts. One is *pierce* [e.g., *pierce (through) the armor*]. Also, while there is a restriction to the effect that there can be at most one Source and at most one Goal in a path, there is no upper or lower bound on the number of Trajectories. Finally, I have been told that there are many languages in which the similarity in structure between end-legs and medial ones–that is, that both types of legs are expressed as PPs–simply does not obtain. In such languages, of which Korean is an example, while end-legs are expressed by postpositional phrases, medial legs are expressed as small clauses headed by verbs. Thus something like *drive from Texas through New Mexico to Arizona* would become something like *drive from Texas to Arizona, crossing New Mexico*. I might note that for end-legs to be unmarked with respect to medial legs is just what we would expect from Gestalt psychology, for peripheries are more salient perceptually than are middles.

What are the consequences, then, of the end-preposition/medial preposition asymmetry for reseach in language acquisition? In general, we expect that unmarked elements and constructions will be learned before marked ones, so I would definitely be very interested to know if there is any data in which medial prepositions are learned before end-prepositions. But let me go further out on a limb. I know of no language in which there is no way to express paths. However, while the few languages that I know all express Sources and Goals adpositionally, I see no necessity for this to be the case. It would not surprise me at all if languages should turn up in which Sources and Goals were expressed by non-finite verbs, something like the fictive example I give in (35).

(35) Max walked *leav(ing)* LA *reach(ing)* San Francisco. [= Max walked from LA to SF.]

Let us assume that such languages do exist. If they do, I would bet *reais* to *pães de queijo* that no such language would ever be able to express a medial concept prepositionally. That is, there should be no language without adpositional machinery for Source and Goal which could say something like (36).

(36) Max walked [*leav(ing)* LA] *along the beach* [*reach(ing)* San Francisco].

What I am suggesting is that the unmarked way of expressing legs may well be verbal; if so, then typologically, medial legs can only acquire an adpositional means of expression in a given language after end-legs have done so. I launch into such speculations only to pass a question on to my colleagues in second-language acquisition, one of whom, a gifted and inspiring one, we are gathered together in this volume to celebrate the thinking of: If verbal expression of legs is less marked than is adpositional expression of legs, then it should be easier for English speakers, whose medial legs are all done prepositionally, to learn a language like Korean, whose medial legs are, I understand, expressed verbally, than it will be for Koreans to learn this part of English.

Acknowledgements

I would like to thank audiences in Singapore, California, Canada, Michigan, Texas, Washington, and Chicago for helping me spiral ever deeper into this murk, and I would like to thank Rosália Dutra and Maria Beck for helping me to understand what is going on in Brasilian Portuguese and German. To Paul Postal, who has been patiently wading through a lot of e-rubbish for many years, sifting out the infrequent gleanings, la Legion d'Honneur Syntactique, with Asterisk Cluster.

Notes

1. There is not space to justify this here, but I believe that ultimately, it can be argued that the deep object of end-prepositions is also an NP, a spatial one, whose head is something like the noun *point*. Thus there would be no deep sequences of prepositions, and the difference between medial prepositions, which cannot be superficially followed by PPs, and end-prepositions, which can be so followed, would arise via a decapitation rule, which will delete the postulated head noun *point*, under certain conditions which I cannot take up now. A fuller treatment of these issues, and a statement of the rule–*Disappointment*–will appear in Ross (in preparation).

References

Dowty, D. 1991. "Thematic Protoroles and Argument Selection". *Language* 67.547-619.
Gruber, J. 1976. *Lexical Structures in Syntax and Semantics*. Amsterdam: North-Holland Publishing Company.
Langacker, R.W. 1987. *Foundations of Cognitive Grammar*. Volume One: *Theoretical Prerequisites*. Stanford, CA: Stanford University Press.
Ross, H. In preparation. "The Grammar of Paths".

Index

Abstract dimension (see Concrete vs. abstract dimension)
Adjemian, C. 18
Acceptability judgments (see Grammaticality judgments)
Adpositions (Prepositions, Postpositions) 274*ff.*
Adverb placement 36, 92*ff.*, 182*ff.*
Adverbial indefinite proforms (*here, there, everywhere, now, then, sometime*) 276*ff.*
Age of arrival 5, 224*f.*
Aglioti, S. 257, 258
Agreement (Spec-head) 199*ff.*
Albert, M. 256
Alderton, D. 93
Aphasia (see Bilingual aphasia)
Apperception 91
Arabic 33, 270
Archibald, J. 89, 90, 107
Ard, J. 31*ff.*
Asher, J. 116
Atelic dimension (see Telic vs. atelic dimension)
Atkinson, M. 180
Attainment 109, 116*ff.*
Attention to form 234
Attrition (see Lexical attrition)
Automaticity 52
Auxiliary selection 153*ff.*
Baayen, H. 160
Babbs, L. 241
Bach, K. 78
Bailey, N. 189
Baker, C. L. 178
Baker, M. 161, 200*f.*
Barriers 213*ff.*

Bauer, L. 266
Bazurgui, N. 219
Beck, M. 5, 189*f.*
Beebe, L. 242*f.*
Bell, A. 234
Bell, L. 38
Bennett, S. 32
Berent, J. 33
Berwick, R. 75
Bialystok, E. 58, 90, 220, 227*f.*
Biber, D. 235
Bilingual aphasia 257*f.*
Binding (theory) 37*ff.*, 65*ff.*, 147
Birdsong, D. 2, 49, 76
Blame assignment 84
Blanco-Iglesias, S. 6
Bley-Vroman, R. 32, 64, 90, 139, 220
Bohannon, J. 75
Boller, F. 258
Borod, J. 258
Bowen, J. 228
Broner, J. 6
Broselow, E. 32, 109
Brown, R. 229
Brinkmann, U. 160
Broner, J. 241
Bryant, P. 113
Burt, M. 190, 228
Burzio, L. 154, 156
Cantonese (see Chinese)
Carroll, J. 101
Carroll, S. 3
Carton, A. 90
Case 26*f.*, 199*ff.*
Centineo, G. 156
Chamot, A. 90

Chinese (Mandarin, Cantonese) 2, 11*ff.*, 17*ff.*, 58, 109, 208*f.*, 210*ff.*, 214*ff.*, 219, 226, 228
Chomsky, C. 213
Chomsky, N. 18, 55, 63, 64, 73, 74, 89, 91, 107, 148, 178*ff.*, 213
Clahsen, H. 4, 32, 90, 108, 124, 126, 133, 136, 140, 188, 189
Clark, H. 58
Classroom research 241
Code, C. 258
Code switching 6, 255*ff.*
Cohen, A. 90, 241
Cole, P. 66
Comment (see Topic-comment)
Compounds 132*ff.*
Comrie, B. 33
Concrete vs. abstract dimension 158*ff.*
Connell, P. 67*f.*
Constraint on extraction 213*ff.*
Control (see also Pronominals) 206*ff.*
Cook, V. 59
Cooper, R. 213
Cooperative principle 3, 80*f.*
Corder, S. P. 1, 4, 7, 9
Corrective intention 80*ff.*
Corrigan, K. 116
Court, J. 94
Crago, M. 188
Critical period 5, 219*ff.*
Crookes, G. 101
Culicover, P. 180
Cummings, J. 259
Damasio, A. 258
Damasio, H. 258
d'Anglejan, A 213
Data versus evidence 5, 177*ff.*
Dative shift (double object) 197*ff.*
Day, D. 219
de Bot, K. 233
Deixis, 236*f.*
Demetras, M. 75
Dewaele, J.-M. 6, 235*ff.*
Diaglossia 6, 241

Dissociation (morphology and syntax) 188*ff.*
Domain-specificity 3, 43, 50*f.*
Douglas, D. 260
Dowty, D. 157, 274
Dual mechamism model 123*ff.*
Dulay, H. 190, 228
duPlessis, J. 189
Dutch 109, 142, 160, 225*f.*, 235*ff.*
Dynamic vs. static dimensions 158*ff.*
Eckman, F. 38, 108, 115
Economy 64
El Tigi, M. 117
English 2, 11*ff.*, 17*ff.*, 33, 36, 58, 66*ff.*, 91, 111, 115, 123, 124, 148, 154, 160, 167, 178, 182*ff.*, 197*ff.*, 206*f.*, 210*ff.*, 214*ff.*, 225*f.*, 228, 235, 242*ff.*, 268, 269, 270, 284*f.*
E-language 18
Elsewhere condition 126, 135
Emonds, J. 183
Empty Category Principle 147, 213*ff.*
Eskimo 109
Eubank, L. 5, 31, 65, 188
Exceptional case marking 201
Expletive 15
Explicit data 178*ff.*, 185*ff.*
Fabbro, F. 257, 258
Feedback (see also Negative evidence, Postive evidence, Indirect evidence) 45*ff.*, 73*ff.*
Felix, S. 4, 32, 140
Finer, D. 32, 109
Finnish 267
Firth, S. 116
Fjerstad, L. 241
Flege, J. 118
Flynn, S. 5, 32, 59, 64, 140, 146, 211
Fodor, J. 76, 201
Foley, C. 211
Formal instruction (see also Therapy) 178*ff.*, 185*ff.*, 268
Formality 233
Fossilized variation 140

INDEX 289

Frazier, L. 145
French 33, 35, 36, 91*ff.*, 142, 148, 155, 160, 167*ff.*, 182*ff.*, 198*ff.*, 235*ff.*, 252
Fuller, J. 18
Gair, J. 214
Garcia, R. 118
Gardner-Chloros, P. 255
Gass, S. 2, 31*ff.*, 63, 75, 91, 101, 205, 219
Genesee, F. 59
German 83, 109, 111, 115, 123*ff.*, 148, 160, 198*ff.*, 281, 282*f.*
Gersh, F. 258
Giraud, P. 266
Gleitman, H. 114
Gleitman, L. 114
Gombert, J.-E. 77, 113
Goodglass, H. 258
Gopnik, M. 188
Gorosch, M. 112
Goswami, U. 113
Governing Category Parameter 65*ff.*
Government (see also Case) 199*f.*
Gradol, D. 234
Grammaticality judgments (Acceptability judgments) 220*ff.*
Graphemic input (see Orthographic exposure)
Green, D. 257
Green, E. 258
Gregg, K. 63
Grice, H. 76, 78, 237
Grimshaw, J. 153, 154, 157
Grosjean, F. 255
Gruber, J. 273
Gubala-Ryzak, M. 89, 182, 185*ff.*
Guernssel, M. 157
Gundel, J. 18
Haegeman, L. 156
Hakuta, K. 58, 220, 227*f.*
Hale, K. 157
Halliday, M. 235
Hared, M. 235

Harnish, R. 78
Hatch, E. 75
Hawkins, R. 219
Hebrew 267, 268, 270
Heitzman, S. 241
Hermon, G. 66
Hill, B. 220, 225
Hill, J. 117
Hilles, S. 34
Hirakawa, H. 32
Hirsch-Pasek, K. 75
Hoefnagel-Hohle, M 75, 109
Hoekstra, T. 155
Hornstein, N. 110, 178
Howerd, F. 220, 225
Huang, J. C.-T. 19, 22, 214
Hudson, R. 235
Huebner, T. 18
Hypothesis testing 43*ff.*
I-language 18*f.*
I-interlanguage 18ff
Immersion 241*ff.*
Implicit evicence (see Indirect evidence)
Implicitness vs. explicitness (style) 236*ff.*
Incorporation 200*f.*
Indirect evidence (data) 3, 50, 89*ff.*
Indonesian 214*ff.*
Inferencing 99*ff.*
Information processing 52
Intransitive verbs 153*ff.*
Inversion (see also Verb movement) 5, 198
Ioup, G. 117, 139
Irregular forms 123*ff.*
Italian 33, 127, 154*ff.*, 180, 237, 257
I°-to-C° movement (see Verb movement)
Jaeggli, O. 23
Japanese 11*ff.*, 17, 20, 23, 26, 33, 65*ff.*, 109, 142, 147, 207*f.*, 210*ff.*
Jin, H.-G. 18*f.*
Johnson, J. 5*f.*, 58, 219*ff.*
Jordens, P. 2

Karmiloff-Smith, A. 75
Kayne, R. 64, 202
Kean, M. 220
Keenan, E. 33, 143
Kellerman, E. 5, 49, 142, 220, 228
Kess, J. 90, 91
Keyser, J. 157
Kim, Y. 235
Kiparsky, P. 125, 126
Koff, E. 258
Koopman, H. 198*ff.*
Köpcke, K.-M. 124, 125
Korean 11*ff.*, 20, 58, 147, 219, 226, 228, 235, 284*f.*
Krashen, S. 189, 190
Kreiman, J. 259
Kummer, M. 126
L1=L2 hypothesis 8
Labov, Wm. 233*ff.*, 250
Lakshmanan, U. 33
Landau, B. 114
Landau, E. 114
Langacker, R. 274
Lardiere, D. 211
Larsen-Freeman, D. 189
Larson, G. 93
Lasnik, H. 89
Laufer, B. 6, 266, 267
Laughren, B. 157
Learnability 3, 43*ff.*, 161*f.*, 181*f.*
Learned linguistic knowledge 190*f.*
Lebeaux, D. 201
LeCompagnon, B. 197*f.*
Legendre, G. 155
Levelt, Wm. 233, 236*f.*
Levin, B. 154, 156, 157
Lexical attrition 268*f.*
Lexical frequency profile 266*ff.*
Lexical learning 265*ff.*
Lexical morphology 125
Lexical size 6, 265*ff.*
Li, C. 18, 20, 22
Lightbown, P. 63, 219
Lightfoot, D. 110, 178

Linguistic insensitivity 57*ff.*
Linking rules 160*ff.*
Literacy 112
Logical problem of language acquisition (see Poverty of the stimulus)
Long, M. 50, 189, 219
Lorch (Perlman Lorch), M. 6, 258, 259
Lust, B. 213
Madden, C. 189
Major, R. 115, 116
Mandarin (see Chinese)
Manzini, R. 65*ff.*
Marantz, A. 157
Marcus, G. 124, 136
Markedness 7, 48*f.*, 51, 197*ff.*, 284*f.*
Martin, J. 228
Martohardjono, G. 5, 214
Matthews, S. 2, 20
Mazurkewich, I. 49, 90
McClelland, J. 75, 123
Meara, P. 259
Meisel, J. 141, 188
Metalinguistic capacity 85
Meyer-Ingwersen, J. 126
Minimalist Program 64, 148
Moore, T. 90
Morphology 4, 123*ff.*, 266
Moselle, M. 117
Mugdan, J. 125
Mulder, R. 155
Muysken, P. 32, 90, 108, 140, 189
Napoli, D. 156
Nation, I. 265, 266, 267
ne-cliticization 153*ff.*
Negation 36
Negative evidence (data, see also Feedback, Positive evidence, Indirect evidence) 3, 4, 50, 74, 178*ff.*
Nelson, D. 38
Neufeld, G. 101, 109
Neumann, R. 126
Neurolinguistic evidence 255*ff.*
Neurological impairment 256*ff.*

Newport, E. 5*f*., 58, 219ff.
Nicholas, M. 258
Nishimura, M. 255
Notebook data 242*ff.*
NP-movement 147
Null subjects (*pro*-drop) 23, 27, 33*ff.*, 148, 180*ff.*
Nunan, D. 241
Obler, L. 256
Oller, J. 115
Olson L. 109, 116
Olshtain, E. 213
O'Malley, J. 90
Orthographic exposure (input, Graphemic input) 112*ff.*
Overgeneralization of findings 57*ff.*
Overregularization 129*ff.*
Oxford, R. 90
Oyama, S. 116
Paradis, M. 256, 257, 260
Parameter re-setting 64, 186*f.*
Parker, J. 241
Pater, J. 109
Paths 7, 273*ff.*
Patkowski, M. 116
Pedagogy 31
Penfield, W. 255*f.*, 257, 260
Perecman, E. 259
Percival, V. 220, 225
Perlmutter, D. 154, 157
Phonology 4, 107*ff.*, 134, 233
Pica, P. 66
Pica, T. 75
Pinker, S. 77, 84, 89, 121, 188, 190
Platt, J. 234
Plough, I. 3, 89
Plural formation 123*ff.*
Pollock, J.-Y. 182, 184, 187
Portuguese 127, 281*f.*, 283
Positive evidence (data; Primary linguistic data; see also Feedback) 4, 50, 110*ff.*, 178*ff.*
Post, K. 75
Postal, P. 157

Post-verbal subjects 180
Poverty of the stimulus (Logical problem of language acquisition) 73*ff.*, 76, 91, 178
Pre-emption 3, 43, 49
Prepositions (see Adpositions)
Presentative 14*f.*
Primary linguistic data (see Positive evidence)
Prince, A. 123, 188, 190
Principles and parameters theory 63, 180*ff.*
PRO (see Pronominals)
pro (see Pronominals, Null subjects)
Probabilistic evidence 50
Pro-drop (see Null subjects)
Progovac, L. 66*ff.*
Pronominals (lexical, null) 5, 197*ff.*, 206*ff.*
Proper Antecedent Parameter 66*ff.*
Pseudo-passive 27
Rampton, B. 234
Randall, J. 160
Rappaport, M. 154, 156, 157
Rappaport Hovav, M. 156
Raven, J. 93, 94
Reflexive binding (see Binding)
Regular morphological rules 123*ff.*, 188*ff.*
Relevance (principle of, maxim of) 3, 76, 78*ff.*
Resumptive pronouns 180
Richards, J. 234
Right 277*ff.*
Rizzi, L. 201
Rizzo, M. 258
Roberts, I. 197*ff.*
Rosen, C. 157
Ross, H. (J.) 6*f.*
Rothweiler, M. 124, 136
Rumelhart, D. 75, 123
Russian 65*ff.*, 148, 267, 269
Rutherford, Wm. 1*f.*, 11*ff.*, 17, 21, 23, 43, 48, 49, 59, 63, 181, 182

Saleemi, A. 89, 90
Samuels, S. 109, 116
Sato, C. 116
Schachter, J. 1, 4, 17, 21, 23, 32, 49, 64, 90, 139*ff.*, 227
Schmidt, R. 31
Schneiderman, M. 75
Schroten, J. 155
Schwartz, B. 5, 63, 76, 89, 90, 110, 182, 185*ff.*, 191, 198*ff.*
Scovel, T. 108, 116
Scrambling 148
Searle, J. 78
Seibert, A. 156, 160
Selinker, L. 7, 205, 219, 235, 255, 260
Sharwood Smith, M. 1, 43, 60, 90, 181, 182
Sherman, J. 213
Shi, D. 20
Skinner, B. F. 55, 60
Smith, M. 75
Snow, C. 75, 109
Sokolik, M. 75
Solin, D. 189
Somali, 235
Sorace, A. 4, 153, 157, 163, 167, 168
Spada, N. 219
Spanish 33, 34, 35, 127, 155, 209*ff.*, 216, 237, 242*ff.*
Specific language impairment 188*ff.*
Speech style 6, 323*ff.*
Sperber, D. 78*ff.*
Sportiche, D. 198*ff.*
Sprouse, R. 198*ff.*
Standard theory 179*f.*
Stanowica, L. 75
Static dimension (see Dynamic vs. static dimension)
Sternberg, R. 94
Stockwell, R. 228
Strategies 52
Strömquist, S. 219
Subjacency 145*ff.*, 213*ff.*
Sung, L.-M. 66

Suñer, M. 23
Suter, R. 116
Swain, M. 241, 251
Swann, J. 234
Switching (see Code switching)
Syllable structure 114*ff.*
Tarone, E. 6, 115, 234*f.*, 241, 251
Taylor, D. 112
Telic vs. atelic dimension 158*ff.*
That-trace 34*f.*, 180
Theme 158, 273*ff.*
Thematic role (Theta role) 26
Therapy (Instruction) 190*f.*
Thomas, M. 32, 68
Thompson, I. 116
Thompson, S. 18, 20, 22
Tomlin, R. 18, 27, 31
Topic-comment 12*ff.*, 17*ff.*
Topic prominence (see Topic-comment)
Torrego, E. 155
Towell, R. 219
Trahey, M. 89, 184
Transfer 5, 8, 107, 205*ff.*
Transfer of training 52
Travis, L. 189
Treiman, R. 75
Tropf, H. 116
Trusted, J. 90, 91
Tucker, R. 213
Turkish 126, 198, 200*f.*
Typological universals (see Typology)
Typology (Typological universals) 2, 5, 11*ff.*, 17*ff.*, 31*ff.*
Unergative-unaccusative verbs 4, 153*ff.*
Uniqueness (Uniqueness Principle) 49
Universal Grammar 2, 3, 8, 31*ff.*, 43, 63*ff.*, 75, 90, 107*ff.*, 139*ff.*, 177*ff.*, 197*ff.*, 205*ff.*
U-shaped behavior 49
Uziel, S. 32
Vainikka, A. 108
Valian, V. 89
van Hout, A. 157, 160
van Lancker, D. 259

van Valen, R. 156, 157, 160
van Wuijtswinkel 220*ff.*
Varney, N. 258
Varonis, E. 75
Vendler, Z. 157
Venetan 257
Verb movement (see Verb raising)
Verb raising (verb movement, I°-to-C° movement) 36*ff.*, 182*ff.*, 188*ff.*
Verb second (see also Inversion, Verb movement) 148
Verma, M. 116
Vernacular 250*ff.*
Villa, V. 31, 32
Vocabulary learning (see Lexical learning)
Vocabulary size (see Lexical size)
Vogt, H. 267
Wagner-Gough, J. 75
Wason, P. 50
Watanabe, A. 147
Waterbury, M. 213
Weber, H. 234
Weigl, W. 32

Weinberger, S. 115
Weissenborn, J. 160
Wexler, K. 65*ff.*, 180, 188
White, L. 3, 31, 32, 33, 36, 37*f.*, 48, 49, 59, 63, 64, 65, 68, 89, 90, 91, 107, 108, 139, 140, 146, 182*ff.*, 189
White Eagle, J. 157
Wh-movement 142*ff.*, 180, 213*ff.*
Wiese, R. 125
Wilson, D. 78*ff.*
Woest, A. 124, 136
Word order 64, 92*ff.*, 182*ff.*, 202
Wunderlich, D. 125
Xue Guoyi 266
Yip, V. 2, 20*ff.*
Young, R. 234
Young-Scholten, M. 4, 107, 108, 109, 111, 115
Zipf, G. 237
ZISA 126
Zobl, H. 18, 197
Zubizzarreta, M.-L. 156